Corpora and ICT in Language Studies

ŁÓDŹ
STUDIES IN LANGUAGE

Edited by
Barbara Lewandowska-Tomaszczyk

Vol. 13

PETER LANG
Frankfurt am Main · Berlin · Bern · Bruxelles · New York · Oxford · Wien

Jacek Waliński
Krzysztof Kredens
Stanisław Goźdź-Roszkowski
(eds.)

Corpora and ICT in Language Studies

PALC 2005

PETER LANG
Europäischer Verlag der Wissenschaften

Bibliographic Information published by the Deutsche Nationalbibliothek
The Deutsche Nationalbibliothek lists this publication in the Deutsche Nationalbibliografie; detailed bibliographic data is available in the internet at <http://www.d-nb.de>.

ISSN 1437-5201
ISBN-10: 3-631-56099-0
ISBN-13: 978-3-631-56099-0
US-ISBN 0-8204-8783-X

www.peterlang.de

TABLE OF CONTENTS

Part II. COGNITIVE LINGUISTICS

Part III. E-LEARNING

INTRODUCTION

PALC 2005 was the fifth in a series of corpus linguistics conferences organised biennially by the Department of English Language at Łódź University. The twenty-nine papers included in this volume are divided into three major parts. The first and largest part represents a fascinating variety of topics which are grouped under the necessarily general heading of **Corpora in Empirical Language Studies.** The recent surge of interest in cognitive linguistics is also amply evidenced by this volume. For the first time in the PALC book series we deemed it necessary to include a separate section on **Cognitive Linguistics**. **E-learning**, which was first incorporated among PALC themes in 2003, proved to be immensely popular and it seems it has now become a permanent fixture of PALC conferences. This is reflected in the large number of articles in Part III of the volume.

Part I opens with a plenary paper written by Randi Reppen (Northern Arizona University) in collaboration with Camilla Vásquez (University of South Florida). The authors take up the problem of using corpus linguistics to investigate the language of teacher training. Another plenary speaker, Renata Fox from the University of Rijeka deals in her paper with the ways in which corpus linguistics could be applied to study corporate identity. This theme of empirical LSP studies can be also found in a contribution by Sylvana Krausse of Fachhochschule Nordhausen, which offers findings from a corpus-informed study of environmental engineering English and in Stanisław Goźdź-Roszkowski's paper on pattern and meaning in judicial argumentation.

Part I also contains a number of papers devoted to the description of computational tools and methodologies for examining the richness of language data. Itziar Aldabe, Leire Amoros, Bertol Arrieta, Arantza Diaz de Ilarraza, Montse Maritxalar, Maite Oronoz and Larraitz Uria from the University of the Basque Country discuss computational systems based on learner and error corpora. Jakub Fast from the University of Warsaw and Collegium Invisibile and Adam Przepiórkowski discuss the problem of automatic extraction of Polish verb subcategorization.

There are three papers which attempt to demonstrate how the enormous potential of the Internet could be exploited. Jacek Waliński and Piotr Pęzik of

Łódź University show how the PELCRA corpus was enriched by implementing web access, while Daniel Janus from Warsaw University and Adam Przepiórkowski from the Institute of Computer Science, Polish Academy of Sciences, present some technical aspects of *Poliqarp*, a linguistic search engine for large corpora. Wiesław Babik of Jagiellonian University focuses on keywords in information retrieval system on the Internet.

The issue of methodology of data collection and analysis is addressed by Adam Bednarek (University of Łódź) in a paper devoted to Canadianisms in metropolitan Toronto and by Janusz Badio (University of Łódź and NKJO Kalisz), who shares his experience of designing a database for spoken discourse analysis. Piotr Pęzik employs corpus and computational methodologies in his comparative study of co-occurrence statistics, while Magali Paquot from the Centre for English Corpus Linguistics at the University of Louvain, discusses the possibilities of creating a productively-oriented academic word list. Finally, Anna Kaminski (Łódź University) takes us back in time to present the findings of her contrastive analysis of Old English and Old German grammar based on the examination of a fragment of the Battle of Maldon, Hildebrandslied and Ludwigslied.

Papers related to cognitive linguistics are included in Part II. Barbara Lewandowska-Tomaszczyk from the University of Łódź and Katarzyna Dziwirek from the University of Washington, Seattle, take up the issue of the syntax and semantics of Polish and English complex expressions. Cecilia Fróis, Belinda Maia and Arnaldo Videira from Universidade do Porto examine a case of meaning extension while Thomas Egan from Hedmark University College investigates the prototypical meaning of the *–ing* complement form. John Newman and Jingxia Lin from the University of Alberta examine the purposefulness of going. Steve Legrand from the University of Jyväskylä discusses the use of basic-level categories and their relation to idealized cognitive models in word-sense disambiguation. In the last paper in this section, Agnieszka Kaleta from Świętokrzyska Academy wonders what we gain in corpus-based research into metaphor.

The last part of the volume includes papers related to e-learning. Somsak Boonsathorn from the National Institute of Development Administration in Bangkok revisits C-tests by taking a closer look at a validation of semantic/ syntactic tests (s-test) for advanced students. Lexical issues are taken up in two papers. Mousa A. Btoosh from the University of Texas at Arlington investigates lexical complexity and frequency in L1 and L2 students' writing, while Kanyarat Getkham from the National Institute of Development Administration in Bangkok demonstrate the effects of using a multimedia computer programme on vocabulary acquisition and retention. Agnieszka Leńko-Szymańska of Warsaw

University discusses the role of L1 influence and L2 instruction in the choice of rhetorical strategies by EFL learners. John Osborne from the University of Savoy looks for evidence for error motivation in a learner corpus, while Richard Profozich (University of Łódź) and Tomasz Pludowski (Świętokrzyska Academy and Collegium Civitas) present strategies for successful online education at University of Maryland University College. F. G. F. Schulte from Open University, Nijmegen, shows the effectiveness of *Moodle* as an intrument to assist e-coaches and career switchers in mastering and refining their professional competencies as e-coaches and as teachers. Jacek Walińki concludes the volume by assessing the role of web logs in monitoring learners' progress.

We owe a great debt of gratitude to professor Barbara Lewandowska-Tomaszczyk for her support and encouragement in the preparation and execution of PALC 2005.

We also wish to acknowledge with gratitude the financial assistance of the British Council, the University of Łódź and Longman, which made it possible for us to invite a number of renowned scholars in corpus studies to the conference.

The efficient organization of the event would not have been possible without the involvement and support of all the colleagues from the Department of English Language at the University of Łódź, in particular Mr Piotr Pęzik and Ms Anna Kamińska.

Jacek Waliński
Krzysztof Kredens
Stanisław Goźdź-Roszkowski

Łódź, April 2006

Part I

CORPORA AND ICT IN EMPIRICAL LANGUAGE STUDIES

Randi Reppen

Northern Arizona University

Camilla Vásquez

University of South Florida

USING CORPUS LINGUISTICS TO INVESTIGATE THE LANGUAGE OF TEACHER TRAINING

1. Introduction

Recently, important advances have been made in using corpus-based research to inform course design and materials development as well as in using corpora in the classroom to enhance language learning. Increasingly, more and more resources continue to be available to teachers, and many of these resources are useful in identifying the types of language our students will encounter both in and outside the classroom. These corpus resources can help inform and shape the instruction provided to language learners in many different settings. In the area of using corpora and corpus-based information for language classes, good progress is being made, yet many needs remain, particularly in the areas of improving availability of corpus resources and tools. These changes will hopefully come about as a natural result of the increasing use of corpora by teachers and students.

Examining the language used to train teachers, particularly graduate students in TESL (Teachers of English as a Second Language) programs, is one area in which, little work has been done in using the tools of corpus linguistics. Two recent works have begun to address this. *Language in Teacher Education*, edited by Trappes-Lomax and Ferguson (2002), contains chapters that investigate the language used in the classroom as well as in teacher preparation. In the 2003 *TESOL Quarterly* issue dedicated to corpus linguistics, Farr and O'Keefe describe how corpus linguistics has been incorporated into their teacher training program. In particular, Farr and O'Keefe explore the potential of using corpus linguistics to inform teacher training by analyzing corpora of two settings that are common in teacher training programs – teacher meetings and post observation meetings between a novice teacher and the mentor who has observed that teacher's classroom practice. Furthering this line of investigation, this paper examines the language of teacher training using a corpus approach. In addition, we also explore how different analytical techniques and tools can provide different insights on the data.

2. The setting

Our data were collected in the Program in Intensive English (PIE) at Northern Arizona University, Flagstaff, Arizona, USA. PIE is a small intensive English program, with an average enrollment of about 30 students who come from countries all over the world. The curriculum has two major components: theme-based instruction with all language skills integrated (i.e., Core, Intercultural Communication, Multi-experience) and skill-focused classes (Pronunciation, Writing, Reading, TOEFL). In addition to providing English instruction, a major goal of the PIE is to provide a mentoring environment for training ESL/EFL teachers (Reppen and Stoller 2002).

All of the instructors in the PIE are graduate students in the MA TESL program, typically in their second and final year of coursework. Usually, the graduate students teach in the PIE for one academic year. This paper uses data from two years, and in this respect, the data represent two 'cohorts' of teachers. However, there is some overlap in teacher participants, with one teacher who taught in the program for one extra semester (i.e., three semesters).

The authors regularly work with the teachers as mentors. In addition to a pre-program teacher orientation and regular individual meetings, we also hold weekly group meetings, and at least one observation per class, per semester, which is followed by a one-on-one post observation meeting.

3. The corpus

For this paper, we consider four weekly meetings from one semester and all of the post observation meetings from four semesters. Although more weekly meetings have been recorded, as with any collection of recorded multi-participant spoken language, transcription of these data is a slow and challenging process. Therefore, for this paper, we include only one semester of weekly meetings. Table 1 shows the word totals for the weekly meetings used in this study.

Table 1. Words per meeting in Fall 2002 semester weekly meetings

	Sept 19	Oct 3	Oct 31	Nov 21	TOTAL
Words	6,739	5,409	7,042	4,987	24,177

In contrast, all four semesters of post observation meetings are included, and these consist of 19 meetings among nine teachers and the two mentors. Table 2 shows the word totals for each speaker: the two mentors (Camilla and Randi) and the nine teachers. Six of the teachers are native English speakers (NES) and three are non-native English speakers (NNES). (All of the names are pseudonyms except for the two mentors, the authors of this paper.)

Table 2. Words by speaker by semester in post observation meetings for four semesters (Total words = 73,858)

	Fall 2002	Spring 2003	Fall 2003	Spring 2004
Camilla	7,788	8,520	12,375	1,140
Randi	4,692	2,964	–	5,363
Maya*	600	1,094	–	–
Michelle	1,464	–	–	–
Anne	1,358	1,954	–	–
Sara	251	1,753	1,000	–
Chris	–	4,417	4,178	–
Karina*	–	–	1,766	–
Kaitlin	–	–	-	3,532
Elisabeth*	–	–	4,280	–
Lauren	–	–	467	2,902

* = NNES (L1 for NNES: Maya = Russian; Karina = German; Elisabeth = Polish).

4. Setting and context descriptions

A variety of analytical techniques ranging from simple counts to multivariate statistics are used to explore the language of the weekly group meetings and the post observation meetings. In order to begin the analysis, we describe the context and goals of the two settings for these meetings, because these situational factors can directly impact the language used. Below is an outline of the context and goals of the two settings for the interaction analyzed in this paper:

Weekly group meetings:
Structure:
Participants: All of the teachers and one or both of the mentors
Setting: Teacher office or classroom – informal gathering

Goals:
Discuss procedural aspects of program
(e.g., field trips, schedules, supplies, etc.)
Communicate and coordinate classes in the program
(e.g., test dates, student issues)
Share ideas and resources
Build community

Post Observation meetings:
Structure:
Participants: Mentor and teacher
Setting: Mentor's office

Goals:
Discuss the lesson that was observed
Provide feedback on what was effective
Provide suggestions on areas in which the teacher and/or mentor has concerns
Discuss future ideas and directions for the course

As a result of these different structures and goals, we expect to see differences in the language associated with these two types of events, the weekly group meetings and the post observation meetings. The weekly group meetings are much less face threatening and also less focused on a specific event than the post observation meetings. For example, many different topics are typically discussed in the weekly group meetings. In contrast, because the post observation meetings consist of a one-on-one interaction in which a particular lesson is discussed, the language is more constrained and focused.

Word type/token ratios allow us to capture some of the differences between the two types of meetings. The difference between the two settings is reflected in a lower average type/token ratio for the post observation meetings than for the group meetings. The type/token ratios were computed using the first 400 words of each text to control for the effect of using texts of different lengths. The average type/token ratios for the two settings were 46.57 for the weekly group meetings and 40.21 for the post observation meetings. These ratios serve as indices which reflect the greater diversity of topics discussed in the weekly group meetings in comparison with the more topically focused post observation meetings.

5. Lexical bundles in post observations and group meetings

In the next analysis, we explore the language used in these two settings by examining lexical bundles. In this portion of the study several techniques were used. First, the recurring lexical bundles were identified. Next, after counting the occurrences, the bundles were categorizes by function. Finally, our analysis focuses on a more detailed look at a particular frame (i.e., … *I think*…) to see how it is distributed across speakers.

Lexical bundles are chunks of language that repeatedly co-occur; they are a type of extended collocation (Biber *et al.* 1999). Lexical bundles do not need to be structurally complete units, and, in fact, they typically are **not** structurally complete. The words in the bundles presented here were not pre-determined, or pre-selected by us, but rather they were identified by a computer program that scans the texts and keeps track of the patterns of co-occurrence.

Because most of the research on lexical bundles to date has concentrated on four-word lexical bundles (rather than on other possible multi-word units such as two-word bundles, five-word bundles, etc.), we selected a bundle length of four words for our analysis. The program that we used to identify the lexical bundles was developed by Douglas Biber (see Biber, Conrad and Cortes 2004 and Biber *et al.* 1999 for a fuller description). In addition to identifying the four-word lexical bundles, the program also identifies the number of texts in which each lexical bundle occurs, thus allowing us to rule out idiosyncratic use of a particular expression by an individual speaker. Table 3 shows the list of the most frequent lexical bundles in both types of meetings. (Note: the bundles displayed in Table 3 reflect the natural break in the rate of occurrence for each of the two settings, and therefore, this table does not provide a comprehensive list all of the four-word bundles that occurred in the data.)

Table 3. Lexical bundles from post observation meetings and weekly group meetings (Normed per 10,000 words)

Post observations	Raw cnt	Normed cnt	Text cnt
and I think that	42	5.72	15
I don't know if	41	5.59	14
I thought that was	29	3.95	13
I thought it was	28	3.81	12
but I think that	24	3.27	12
and I think that's	21	2.86	11
so I think that's	21	2.86	11
I think it was	20	2.72	13
I think that you	20	2.72	12
I think it's good	19	2.59	12
I think that's good	17	2.32	11
so I think that	17	2.32	11
I mean I think	16	2.18	9
and I think it's	15	2.04	10
you know I think	15	2.04	8
and I don't know	14	1.91	8
end of the semester	14	1.91	5
the end of the	14	1.91	6
what do you think	14	1.91	9
and I thought that	13	1.77	9
I think that's really	13	1.77	9
at the beginning of	12	1.63	7
I think you know	12	1.63	7
and I was like	11	1.50	7
I don't know what	11	1.50	5
it was kind of	11	1.50	10
on the board and	11	1.50	9
the rest of the	11	1.50	5
a lot of the	10	1.36	8
at the end of	10	1.36	7
do you think that	10	1.36	7
I think that that	10	1.36	8
so I don't know	10	1.36	5
so I thought that	10	1.36	6
you know what I	10	1.36	8

Weekly meetings	Raw cnt	Normed cnt	Text cnt
I don't know what	8	3.31	3
I don't know if	7	2.89	4
I think it would	5	2.07	2
think it would be	5	2.07	2
and then you know	4	1.65	3
at the end of	4	1.65	3
but I don't know	4	1.65	3
I mean I think	4	1.65	3
that's a good idea	4	1.65	3
the end of the	4	1.65	2
are you gonna do	3	1.24	3
a little bit more	3	1.24	2
and I don't know	3	1.24	2
have to talk to	3	1.24	2
I don't know I	3	1.24	2
I think that there	3	1.24	2
I thought it was	3	1.24	2
it would be a	3	1.24	2
it's kind of a	3	1.24	2
put it on the	3	1.24	2
to get them to	3	1.24	2
was supposed to be	3	1.24	2
we don't have to	3	1.24	2
you need to do	3	1.24	2

In addition to the raw counts of the bundles and the counts for the number of texts where each bundle occurred, Table 3 also includes the normed counts for each bundle. Although the sizes of the two subcorpora are not equal (i.e., 73,391 words versus 24,177 words), the normed counts enable us to compare the bundles from the post observation meetings with those from the weekly group meetings.

Looking at the two sets of lexical bundles in Table 3, we can immediately see that the bundles from the weekly meetings are much more procedural, with bundles like: *are you gonna do... you need to do... the end of the... at the end of... have to talk to...*; whereas those from the post observation meetings appear to be more reflective: *and I think that... I think it's good... so I think that's... you know I think...* Furthermore, because the post observation meetings are more focused on a past event, the post-observation meetings tend to contain more past-oriented bundles (such as *it was kind of... so I thought that... and I was like...*) than the weekly meetings.

After examining the types of bundles, our analysis now shifts to explore the functional roles served by these bundles in these two settings. To conduct this portion of the analysis, a concordance program was used to look at the bundles function in context. Then, after reading the concordances of the various bundles in each of the settings the lexical bundles were categorized into various functional roles (e.g., expressing the unknown, evaluating, eliciting). Table 4, below, shows the numbers of different bundles performing each function and gives some examples of some the bundles. By grouping the lexical bundles according to function strong differences between the two settings are revealed. For instance, the post observation meetings have much more evaluative language than do the weekly group meetings. However, the post observation meetings have elicitation bundles, which do not occur at all in the weekly meetings.

Now our analysis will shift to focus to a particular re-occurring frame. By examining the complete set of lexical bundles from both types of meetings, it is evident that the many of the same words or phrases occur frequently in several different bundles. For example, one of the very common frames in the post observations bundles is *...I think...* Table 3 shows that 20 of the 35 bundles (57%) in the post observation meetings include some form of *think* in the expression, and 15 of those 20 occur as *...I think...* In contrast, only 5 of the 24 bundles (21%) from the weekly meetings include a form of *think*. This difference seemed worth further exploration to answer the question of which participants are doing all of the *think*ing in the meetings. Is it only the mentors using *...I think...* as a frame for providing feedback to the teacher? Or is it the teachers, offering their own reflective commentary? Table 5 shows that both mentors and teachers used the …*I think*… frame regularly.

Table 4. Lexical bundles by function

Function	Post observation meetings	Weekly meetings
Expressing unknown: *I don't know what* *and I don't know*	2	2
Expressing uncertainty: *was supposed to be* *I don't know if* *but I don't know*	2	4
Evaluating: *I think it was* *that's a good idea* *and I think/thought that* *it would be a* *so I think that* *I think you know*	17	3
Advice/suggestions: *I think it would* *think it would be* *you know I think*	1	3
Procedural: *at the end of* *the end of the* *at the beginning of* *have to talk to* *put it on the*	5	8
Hedging/vagueness: *it's kind of a* *it was kind of* *and then you know*	3	3
Measure: *a little bit more* *a lot of the* *the rest of the*	2	1
Elicitation: *what do you think* *do you think that*	3	0

Table 5. Use of ...*I think*... by speaker (Normed to per 1,000 words)

	...*I think*...
Camilla	12.10
Randi	10.68
Maya*	9.44
Michelle	16.39
Anne	5.74
Sara	14.31
Chris	6.51
Karina*	3.11
Kaitlin	3.96
Elisabeth*	5.61
Lauren	6.53

* = NNS of English.

The analyses described above offer a preliminary look at the distribution of the lexical bundles through several different types of analyses; clearly, more work needs to be done to tease apart other aspects of their distribution. However, at this point, the goal was to identify differences between the two settings that warrant further exploration, and to demonstrate how different corpus techniques can be used to explore a corpus of teacher training language.

6. A closer look at post observation interactions

This portion of the paper focuses on the post observation meetings, because it is primarily in these interactions that the majority of teacher mentoring takes place. It is important to point out that in this study we performed multiple roles simultaneously, as a) mentors participating in these interactions, b) researchers analyzing these interactions, and c) program administrators, who could make adjustments to these interactions, based on our findings. Therefore, in this action research situation, we were able to notice aspects of our language use that we otherwise may not have been able to observe. One of the first features that struck us, when looking at the transcripts from first semester of post observation meetings was our 'dominance'. As the mentors, we were responsible for well over 70% of the talk during the meetings and, in many cases, for as much as 80 to 90% of the talk produced!

Because it was not our intention to dominate the meetings, we made a conscious effort to shift to a more teacher-centered style in the post observation meetings for the next semesters. Table 6 shows the amount of interaction between teachers and mentors, using simple percentages. The shift from the Fall 2002 semester – during which the mentors completely dominated the amount of talk in the meetings – to a more even distribution of the talk between the mentors and teachers in subsequent semesters is apparent in the table below. (Teacher names have been underlined for easier identification.)

Table 6. Proportion of talk by mentors and teachers in post observation meetings*

FALL 2002	SPRING 2003	FALL 2003	SPRING 2004
Anne 22% Camilla 78%	Anne 38% Camilla 62%	Elisabeth 61% Camilla 39%	Kaitlin 47% Randi 38% Camilla 15%
Maya 10% Camilla 90%	Maya 34% Camilla 66%	Lauren 26% Elisabeth 17% Camilla 57%	Lauren 54% Randi 46%
Sara 10% Camilla 90%	Sara 45% Camilla 55%	Sara 29% Camilla 71%	
Maya 20% Randi 80%	Maya 23% Randi 77%	Karina 35% Camilla 65%	
Anne 18% Randi 82%	Chris 51% Camilla 49%	Chris 58% Camilla 42%	
Michelle 52% Randi 48%	Chris 63% Randi 37%		

* Table adapted from Vásquez (2005).

This shift reflects not only of the number of words spoken by the mentors, but also in what they said that resulted in the teachers engaging more in the meetings and thus, producing more language. An example of this can be seen by looking at the 'matched sets' of Maya, Anne and Sara in Table 2. The contributions of these teachers in the post observation meetings greatly increased from Fall 2002 to Spring 2003: Maya from 600 words to 1,094 words; Anne from 1,358 to 1,954 words; and Sara from 251 words to 1,753 words.

Our efforts to shift to a more teacher-centered meeting were successful. Thus, even using a technique as simple as basic percentages can provide valuable information about language use in particular contexts. Did this shift make our interactions more effective? We don't know. This is a question that requires additional investigation, and different data in addition to the corpus (e.g., survey and interview data). However, it is clear from these data that we were effective in changing our interaction style. The shift in the percentage of talk from the mentors is greatly reduced after the first semester – in many cases changing from over 80% of the talk to around 50% or less.

7. A multi-dimensional look at the language of post observations

The final question explored in this paper involves the linguistic features associated with the language of the teachers and mentors in the post observation meetings. The previous techniques and tools used thus far have allowed us to investigate questions related to pieces of language, such as the number of words and percentages, and particular 'bundles' of language. Now we step back and take a more macro perspective and explore how many features of language work together. Multi-Dimensional analysis is a tool that examines the co-occurrence of multiple linguistic features. This paper uses the 1988 Multi-Dimensional model (Biber 1988). This model has been successfully used to explore variation across and within registers and texts. This section begins with a brief overview of the methodology used in Multi-Dimensional analysis (for a more detailed description, see Biber 1988; Biber, Conrad and Reppen 1998; Conrad and Biber 2001).

To create the 1988 Multi-Dimensional model, the texts in a corpus were 'tagged' (i.e., grammatically annotated) for 67 linguistic features and interactively edited for accuracy. A factor analysis was then used to identify linguistic features that had strong co-occurrence patterns. In a Multi-Dimensional analysis, features that are identified as having a statistically significant co-occurrence are said to 'load' onto particular factors. In the 1988 analysis, five factors were identified. The five factors or 'groupings' of linguistic features have a complementary distribution pattern. (That is, if there are a high number of features on the positive end, there will be a low number of features on the negative end of a particular factor.) After the five factors were identified, they were assigned descriptive labels through a process of looking at the linguistic features that co-occurred on that factor and the distribution of the texts in that factor. Once labeled, the factors were referred to as Dimensions. These 5 dimensions reflect ways in which texts vary. For example, texts can be more or less interactive, more or less narrative, more or less argumentative, etc. This type of analysis characterizes texts by co-occurrences of linguistic features along different dimensions, hence the name, Multi-Dimensional analysis. The 1988 model provides a basis for comparing, or plotting, texts along these five dimensions. The linguistic features in each text are counted to arrive at a 'score' for each text. These scores can then be used to plot the texts and examine the relationships across different texts.

Of the five dimensions identified in Biber's 1988 study, this paper uses only one of those dimensions – Dimension 1: 'Involved vs. Informational production'. Each text in the subcorpus of post observation meetings has a count for each of the linguistic features associated with Dimension 1. The counts for the features are then added together. Because the features of these dimensions occur in complementary distribution, there are positive and negative features associated with Dimension 1. Positive and negative are not evaluative terms; rather, they represent values used in computing the dimension scores for the texts. The negative features are subtracted from the positive features to compute a score for that text along a particular dimension. Then, using the text scores, mean scores for various registers, or groups of texts, can be computed.

All of the individual linguistic features associated with Dimension 1 are listed below in Table 7. Each of these linguistic features were counted in each text. Then a mean score for each group of texts was computed (i.e., the mean of the mentor texts; and the mean of the teacher texts). The mean scores for each group of texts were then used to plot the groups of texts along Dimension 1. The linguistic features associated with Dimension 1 are presented below in Table 7.

Multi-Dimensional analysis was used to examine how the language of teachers and mentors vary according to Dimension 1. The mean scores and ranges for the three groups are plotted on Figure 1 – the three groups consist of 1) mentors 2) NES teachers and 3) NNES teachers. (In Figure 1, the range is denoted by the symbol --- and the means are indicated by a *). Figure 1 shows that there is a difference in the ranges between the mentors and the teachers; this difference is most likely a result of the number of speakers in the teacher group versus the mentor group.

Table 7. The linguistic features of Dimension 1: Involved vs. Informational production (Biber 1988)

Dimension 1: Involved vs. Informational production
Positive features - Involved production
private verbs
that-deletion
contractions
present tense verbs
second person pronouns
do as pro-verb
analytic negation
demonstrative pronouns
general emphatics
first person pronouns
pronoun *it*
be as main verb
causative subordination
discourse particles
indefinite pronouns
general hedges
amplifiers
sentence relatives
wh- clauses
final prepositions

Negative features – Informational production
nouns
word length
prepositions
type/token ratio
attributive adjectives

The most surprising finding from examining the data in this manner is the difference that emerges between the native English speaking teachers and the non-native English speaking teachers. As can be seen from Figure 1, the mean score of the Native English speaking teachers and the mentors is basically the same (i.e., Mentors = 36.62; NES Teachers = 36.06), only the ranges differ. However, there is a large difference between the two groups of teachers with respect to first languages. The non-native English speaking teachers have a much more interactive profile on Dimension 1 when compared with their native English speaking counterparts. The difference between the two groups of teachers was not apparent in the other analyses that focused on individual features (e.g., amount of talk, use of *...I think...*), yet this difference between the groups emerges here, when exploring the interaction of multiple linguistic features.

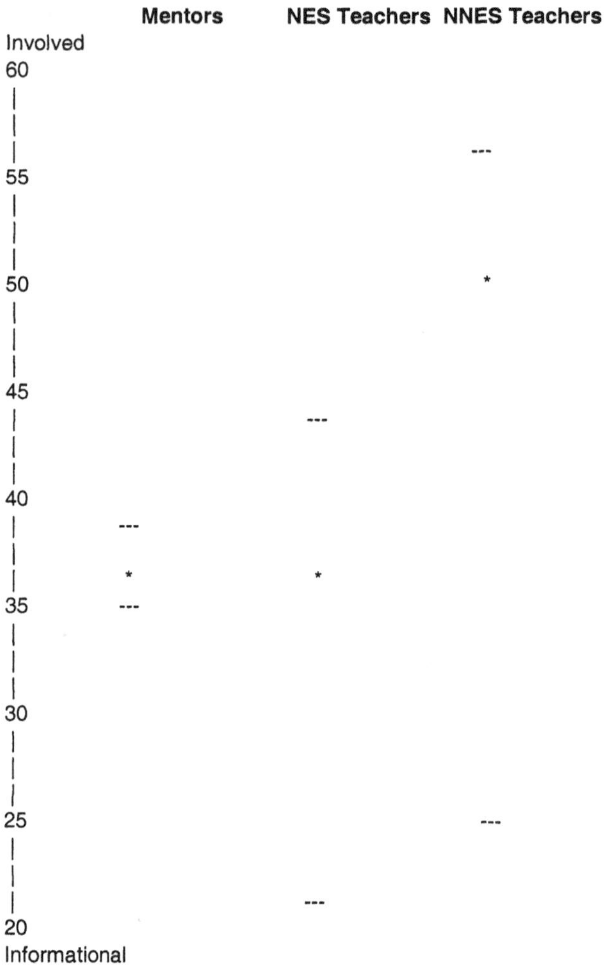

Fig. 1. Mean and ranges for Dimension 1 for Mentors, NES Teachers and NNES Teachers (Ranges: Mentors 35.02–38.22; NES Teachers 23.77–44.49; NNES Teachers 46.08–55.94. Mean scores: Mentors = 36.62; NES Teachers = 36.06; NNES Teachers = 51.19.)

The two text excerpts below highlight some of the differences between the L1 English teachers and the non L1 English teachers. In the excerpts, the positive features of Dimension 1 are indicated in bold and the negative features are underlined. At the end of each excerpt, a summary of the number of positive and negative features used by the speakers is given, both as a raw count for the excerpt and as a percentage, to allow for a comparison between the speakers in the excerpt.

<u>Text sample 1</u>: Camilla (C), Lauren (L), and Elisabeth (E) post observation meeting (Elisabeth's L1 = Polish; Lauren's L1 = English)

E: **This is** scary <u>for</u> **me**. **This is** a <u>language</u> <u>class</u>, **you know, it's not** like real <u>life</u>, right? **Really you** will have all **this** <u>food</u> here
L: yeah, maybe **you** will [unclear]
E: {[unclear]
C: {[laugh]
L: They had an <u>argument</u> <u>about</u> **that** <u>vocabulary</u> <u>game</u>
E: {yeah
L: the <u>week</u> <u>before</u>.
C: mhm
L: Like **we** almost [unclear] playing, **cuz they were** just **so** nasty <u>about</u> **it** all <u>of</u> a sudden. Like "**They're** cheating and rrrrr"

L: 37 words 9 **positive Dimension 1 features** → 22%
8 <u>negative Dimension 1 features</u> → 22%
E: 28 words 12 **positive Dimension 1 features** → 43%
5 <u>negative Dimension 1 features</u> → 18%
C: 1 word 0 features of Dimension 1

In the excerpt above, Lauren (L1 English) used about the same number of both positive and negative features (22% of each) – which results in a score very close to 0. Elizabeth (L1 Polish) on the other hand, used many more positive features than negative features (43% versus 18%) resulting in a much more involved style of interacting. In the excerpt below between Maya (L1 Russian) and Randi (L1 English), the same interaction pattern emerges.

<u>Text sample 2</u>: Maya (M) and Randi (R) post observation meeting (Maya L1 = Russian)

M: **I** just **kind_of** wanna see the <u>progress</u> and
R: {yeah
M: {[unclear] **I** mean if **it's** bad **this** will probably upset **me**
R: {[laughing] noooo
M: but **I don't know**
R: {oh **you** mean **do you** mean taking actually taking one <u>of</u> the <u>sections</u> <u>of</u> the <u>TOEFL</u>?
M: um

R: or doing the answer sheet **I** mean **not** the yeah filling in the answer sheet
M: {mhm

M: 26 words 9 positive Dimension 1 features → 35%
1 negative Dimension 1 features → 4%

R: 33 words 5 positive Dimension 1 features → 15%
8 negative Dimension 1 features → 24%

In both of the excerpts, the non-native English speakers have many more features associated with the positive end of Dimension 1 and fewer features associated with the negative end of Dimension 1; this combination results in very high scores on Dimension 1 when compared to their L1 English speaking colleagues. These very high Dimension 1 scores were surprising and contrary to our initial impressions. (That is, we felt that many of the non-native English teachers tended to be more reserved in their interactions than their native English speaking peers). This may be another area where corpus linguistics can provide insight to information that 'passes beneath our radar,' just as corpus findings have provided information about the use of linguistic features (e.g., the use of progressive vs. simple aspect in conversation) much more accurately than native speaker intuitions (Biber and Reppen 2002). Certainly there is more work to be done in this area. The next step in our investigations is to examine language used in the group meetings, in order to see if similar patterns to those found in the post observation meetings emerge. A further step to expand the study would involve including the actual classroom discourse of the teachers to see if there are additional differences between the two groups of teachers, or if perhaps these differences only exist in the particular setting of post observation meetings.

8. Conclusion

In this paper, we have used a variety of techniques and tools to begin to construct a picture of the language used in teacher mentoring. The picture is far from complete, but it is a beginning, and provides useful information about a little-known and little-explored area that is central to much of the work that is done by teacher trainers. This paper has demonstrated how techniques as simple as counting words can provide useful insights that may run counter to our perceptions, such as the amount of talk contributed by the various members in a meeting. We have also shown how each different technique, or tool, has provided different insights, which contribute to understanding the language used to mentor and train teachers. Future research in this area could certainly include other aspects of teacher training. Furthermore, other techniques and approaches are needed to create a complete picture of the complex process of teacher mentoring. However, at this stage, we hope that the findings presented here provide useful information for mentors to consider when exploring the language used in training teachers.

REFERENCES

Biber, D. (1988). *Variation across Speech and Writing*. Cambridge: Cambridge University Press.

Biber, D., Conrad, S. and R. Reppen (1998). *Corpus Linguistics: Exploring Language Structure and Use*. Cambridge: Cambridge University Press.

Biber, D., Johansson, S., Leech, G., Conrad, S. and E. Finegan (1999). *The Longman Grammar of Spoken and Written English*. Harlow, Essex: Pearson Education.

Biber, D. and R. Reppen (2002). "What does frequency have to do with grammar teaching?". *Studies in Second Language Acquisition*, 24: 99–208.

Conrad, S. and D. Biber (eds) (2001). *Variation in English: Multi-dimensional Studies*. Harlow, UK: Longman.

O'Keeffe, A. and F. Farr (2003). "Using language corpora in initial teacher education: Pedagogical issues and practical applications". *TESOL Quarterly*, 37: 389–418.

Reppen, R. and F. Stoller (2002). "IEP and MATESL Program Linkages: Creating a Symbiotic Relationship". In: Dimmitt, N. and M. Dantas-Whitney (eds). *Intensive English programs in postsecondary settings*. Alexandria VA: TESOL: 51–63.

Trappes-Lomax, H. and G. Ferguson (eds) (2002). *Language in Teacher Education*. Amsterdam: Benjamins.

Vásquez, C. (2005). Unpublished Ph.D. dissertation. *Teacher Positioning in Post-Observation Discourse*. Northern Arizona University. Flagstaff, AZ.

Vásquez, C. (2004). "'Very carefully managed': Advice and suggestions in post-observation meetings". *Linguistics and Education*, 15: 32–58.

Itziar Aldabe, Leire Amoros, Bertol Arrieta
Arantza Díaz de Ilarraza, Montse Maritxalar
Maite Oronoz and **Larraitz Uria**

University of the Basque Country

LEARNER AND ERROR CORPORA BASED COMPUTATIONAL SYSTEMS

1. Introduction

This paper presents learner and error corpora based computational systems designed for Computer-aided Error Analysis (CEA). The aim of these systems is twofold: on the one hand, to store learner corpora (in our case, Basque learner corpora) for further systematic studies in the field of Intelligent Computer Assisted Language Learning (ICALL); and, on the other hand, to collect error instances for the development of new Natural Language Processing (NLP) tools for automatic error treatment. Actually, computer-aided learner corpus research is an interesting field which offers many possibilities for error collection and analysis (counting errors, retrieving lists of specific error types, viewing errors in context, etc.), and, consequently, for studies in different fields such as Intelligent Computer-Assisted Language Learning, Second/Foreign Language Learning, Learner Corpora and Automatic Error Treatment.

Error Analysis (EA) has often been the basis of some of the mentioned research fields. Till the seventies, it was very much criticized by researchers, who considered, among other things, that EA was based on heterogeneous learner data; that error categories were fuzzy; that it could not cater for phenomena such avoidance; that it was restricted to what the learner can not do; and that it gave a static picture of the second language (L2) learning. Bell (1974), for example, criticized EA for *its poor statistical inference, the subjectivity of the interpretations of errors and its lack of any predictive power*. And for Schachter (1974), the fundamental flaw in EA was that learners do not often commit the expected errors because they tend to avoid words or structures they are not sure about.

Nevertheless, there was a resurgence of interest in EA. Corder (1975) claimed that the study of errors is part of the investigation of the language learning process and that it provides us with a picture of the linguistic development of learners. Indeed, *errors should not be viewed as problems to be overcome, but rather as normal and inevitable features indicating the strategies that learners use* (Richards and Sampson 1974).

At present, and thanks to the important technological advances, EA has been computerized and we can now work on CEA, a new type of computer corpus annotation which overcomes some of the limitations and weaknesses attributed to EA. Indeed, CEA makes possible a faster, easier and a more accurate research in the mentioned fields.

Computer-aided Error Analysis is mainly based on Computer Learner Corpus (CLC), which has been defined as a *collection of machine-readable natural language data produced by L2 learners* (Dagneaux *et al.* 1998).

A wide-coverage learner corpus has been essential for us to develop the applications we present in this article. These computational systems have been developed in order to store Basque learner corpora for further research in the field of ICALL as well as to gather error instances for the development of new NLP tools such as a grammar and style checker for Basque.

2. Background of CEA for Basque: Irakazi and Erreus web applications

The IXA research group[1], from the University of the Basque Country, has been working on Natural Language Processing during the last twenty years. We have developed several NLP tools so far and some of the fields we are now working on are Computer-aided Error Analysis, Learner Corpora, Intelligent Computer-Assisted Language Learning and Automatic Error Treatment.

We started working on error detection some years ago with the aim of developing a robust spelling checker, called *Xuxen* (Agirre *et al.* 1992). Later on, a grammar checker approach was planned, for which the collection of error corpora was considered essential. This way, we started collecting learner corpora and we built an error classification in order to store the errors detected in texts. This error classification we will speak about in section 3.2 is part of the following web applications:

On the one hand, Irakazi is a web application, with a multilingual interface, designed for the study of the diagnosis of Basque learners' deviant instances and data. The users of Irakazi are language teachers and the application makes use of the DEVIATIONS database.

[1] http://ixa.si.ehu.es/Ixa

DEVIATIONS is a rich source of psycholinguistic information of learners' data about their learning process and specially about the diagnosis of their deviant structures. In fact, the study of language learners' deviations is nowadays considered really interesting to better understand the process of second/foreign language learning. By classifying and analysing language learners' deviations as well as the possible causes of those deviant instances, teachers can infer the strategies that language learners should adopt to repair the deviations they make. And this way, teachers can also provide learners with a more individual help and more appropriate tools depending on their specific needs and difficulties. As Richards and Sampson (1974) recommended, we should provide *feedback of the knowledge and understanding acquired from error analyses to language teaching practice and to general linguistic theory*. DEVIATIONS is a database where we collect:

– information about the deviant structures, the reason(s) why they have been made and the way they can be repaired;

– information related to the texts where deviations have been detected, specifying the number of words and the type of text;

– information concerning the student (his/her name, age, language school, language knowledge level, mother tongue, learning history, etc.).

On the other hand, Erreus (Arrieta *et al.* 2003) is a web application created to store the linguistic and technical information about ungrammatical instances. The errors stored in this application, which is used by anyone interested in error collection (linguists, writers, editors, etc.), are made by native speakers as well as by any user of the language. Actually, we considered native speakers' error instances necessary for the development of new NLP applications. The main goal of Erreus is automatic error treatment and, more specifically, to be a repository of error corpora for the development of a robust grammar and style checker for Basque. This application makes use of the ERRORS database.

ERRORS stores error instances, their possible corrections, the text's reference, information about the NLP tools which can automatically detect/correct that error and its corresponding linguistic category (figure 1 shows the information stored in each database).

Despite their different purposes, the two databases are focused on computer-aided error analysis and treatment, and they share some information concerning the deviation/error[2], its linguistic category and its corresponding correction(s).

[2] We make a distinction between errors and deviations. We consider errors the ungrammatical structures produced by native speakers; and deviations, for us, are errors or inappropriate structures used by language learners during their learning process. However, since our goal is not to go deep into this matter, from now on we will use the term 'error' in all cases.

As a consequence, we thought that DEVIATIONS and ERRORS databases could be complementarily linked to each other; firstly, because they have some data in common; secondly, because both viewpoints have, in the end, an underlying equivalence which is compatible; thirdly, because this way we avoid duplicated information; and, finally, because if we decided to have two independent databases, we would need two copies of the same classification and it would have been hard to maintain an equivalence table that should have been updated every time one of the copies were changed.

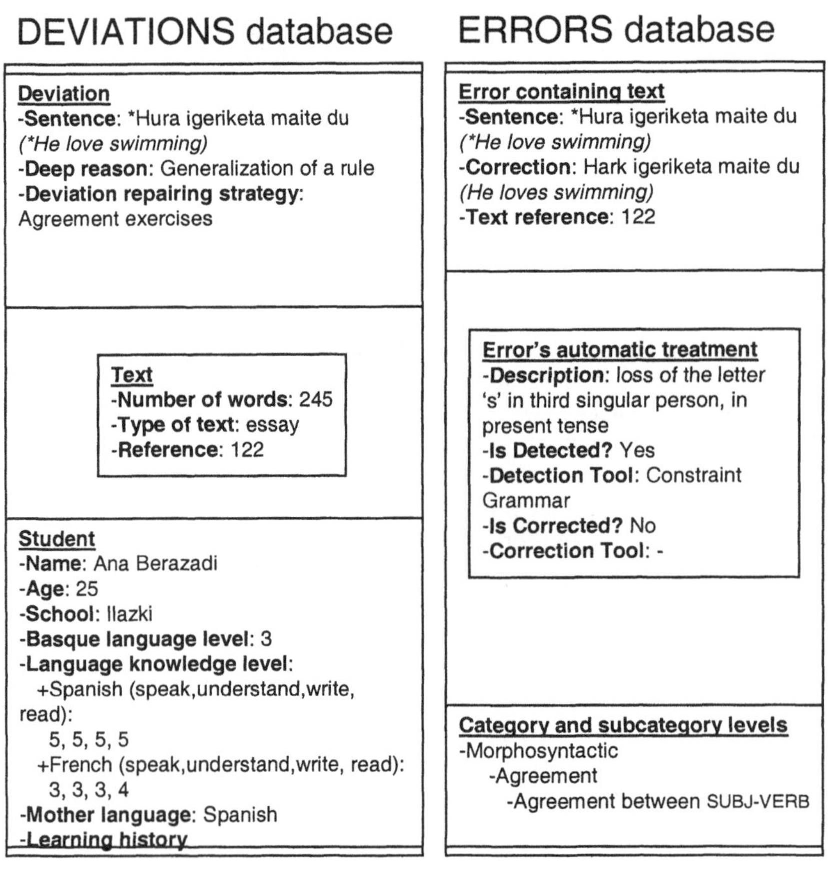

Fig. 1. DEVIATIONS and ERRORS databases

Therefore, thanks to the union of the two databases, they both share the same error classification and, consequently, for each error-containing-text, we have its technical and linguistic information in the ERRORS database as well as its corresponding psycholinguistic information in the DEVIATIONS database (see figure 2). Actually, we consider the union of the two databases very interesting because, this way, we get a double perspective: the psycholinguistic and computational approaches of each error instance.

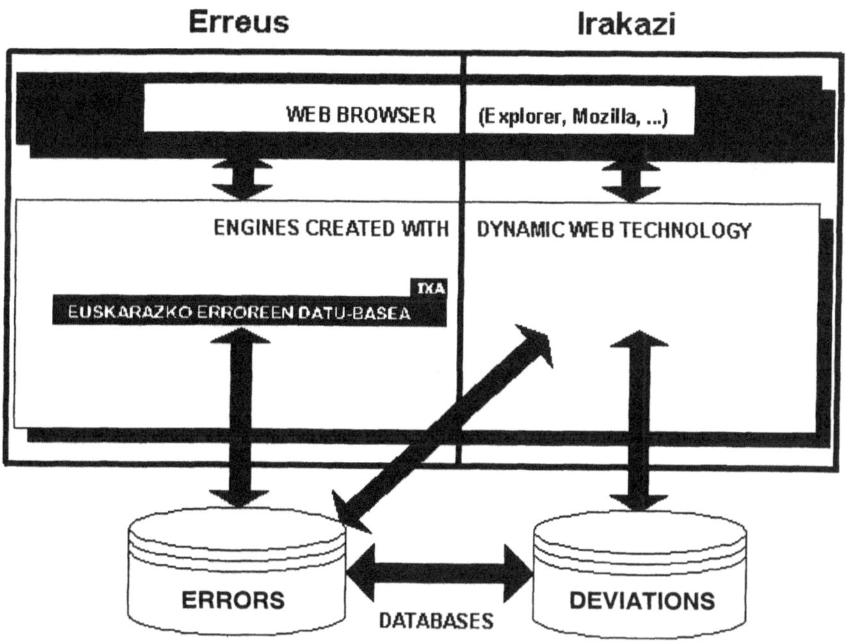

Fig. 2. Union of both databases

Since Erreus and Irakazi are thought to be used by a considerable amount of users – each one with a different viewpoint, knowledge and experience in this field –, we considered important to have both a public and a private use of each web application. In both cases, the public one contains two sites: non-registered and registered. The former is available for those users who just want to consult the stored examples. And the second site, where users need to be registered, is available to add examples and enrich the databases with new data. As regards the private sites, they are controlled by a computational linguist in Erreus and by a computational psycholinguist in Irakazi. In Erreus, the computational linguist verifies that the data introduced via the public site are right, corrects the examples if necessary and completes the specific information related to the techniques for automatic error treatment. The computational psycholinguist in Irakazi checks the data introduced by language teachers. The error classification can be modified or updated only from the private sites.

3. Computer-aided Error Analysis

For the diagnosis and analysis of errors, we first select the texts to be analysed from our learner corpora; then, we identify the error instances and classify them by means of Irakazi and Erreus applications. Depending on which application we use for categorization, different type of information is required. As we have already said, using Irakazi, we introduce Basque learners' errors and their psycholinguistic information. On the contrary, by means of Erreus we collect error instances as well as technical and linguistic information for automatic error treatment.

3.1. Basque Learner Corpus

Learner corpora are necessary to carry out descriptive and applied language studies in both fields, ICALL and NLP. Computer-aided analysis of learners' language pays a particular attention to error description and classification. In fact, these data provide information to carry out comparative studies about the stylistic and quantificational differences between native speakers and learners of a language, to obtain the most common error types at each language level, etc.

Several Basque Language Schools collaborate with us providing texts written by learners of different levels. The learner corpora we have collected so far consists of approximately 221.689 word forms. The collected texts are divided into different levels and students, who are identified in most of the cases.

3.2. The error classification for Basque

In order to collect, categorize and consult the errors detected in the corpora, we created an error classification. For the development of this classification, we basically based on the Basque Grammar *Euskal Gramatika Osoa* (Zubiri 1995).

Besides, our previous experience on automatic error treatment was important. In addition, in order to compare several Basque grammars as well as to see grammar classifications specified for other languages, we consulted further bibliography: Norrish (1983), C. James (1998), Becker *et al.* (1999), S. Fernández (1997), J. Ortiz de Urbina (2001), etc. And we also considered the language programs followed in the *Euskaltegis* (Basque Language Schools), concretely the grammatical contents taught at each level.

Indeed, there are many possible error taxonomies. Errors can be classified according to their basic type: omission, addition, substitution, and word order. They can be classified by how apparent they are: overt and covert errors. And they may be also categorized according to the level of language: phonological errors, vocabulary or lexical errors, syntactic or grammatical errors, and so on. Granger (2003), on her part, claimed the great benefit of combining the two major descriptive error taxonomies:

– one based on linguistic categories (general ones such as morphology, lexis, grammar, and more specific ones such as auxiliaries, passives, and prepositions);

– the other one focused on the way surface structures have been altered by learners (omission, addition, misformation, and misordering).

In order to define the main taxonomy of our classification for Basque as well as to specify some criteria for error categorization, several meetings were arranged between linguists and computer engineers. As Granger, we considered very positive and appropriate the combination of the two mentioned approaches.

The error classification we have built for Basque is explained in the next section.

3.2.1. The structure of the classification

Spelling errors are classified according to the surface structures altered (omission, addition, misformation, and misordering). Non-spelling errors, on their part, consist of some general linguistic categories (lexis, morphology, syntax, etc.) and a series of more specific subcategories (verbs, pronouns, declensions, etc.). Each category/subcategory has a code (Maritxalar 1999), an explanation, and, at least, an example of that error type. This way, we have made up a tree-like hierarchy (see figure 3), which consists of seven main categories: 1 – Spelling errors, 2 – Lexical errors, 3 – Morphological, syntactic and morphosyntactic errors, 4 – Notion errors, 5 – Semantic errors, 6 – Errors in punctuation marks and 7 – Style errors.

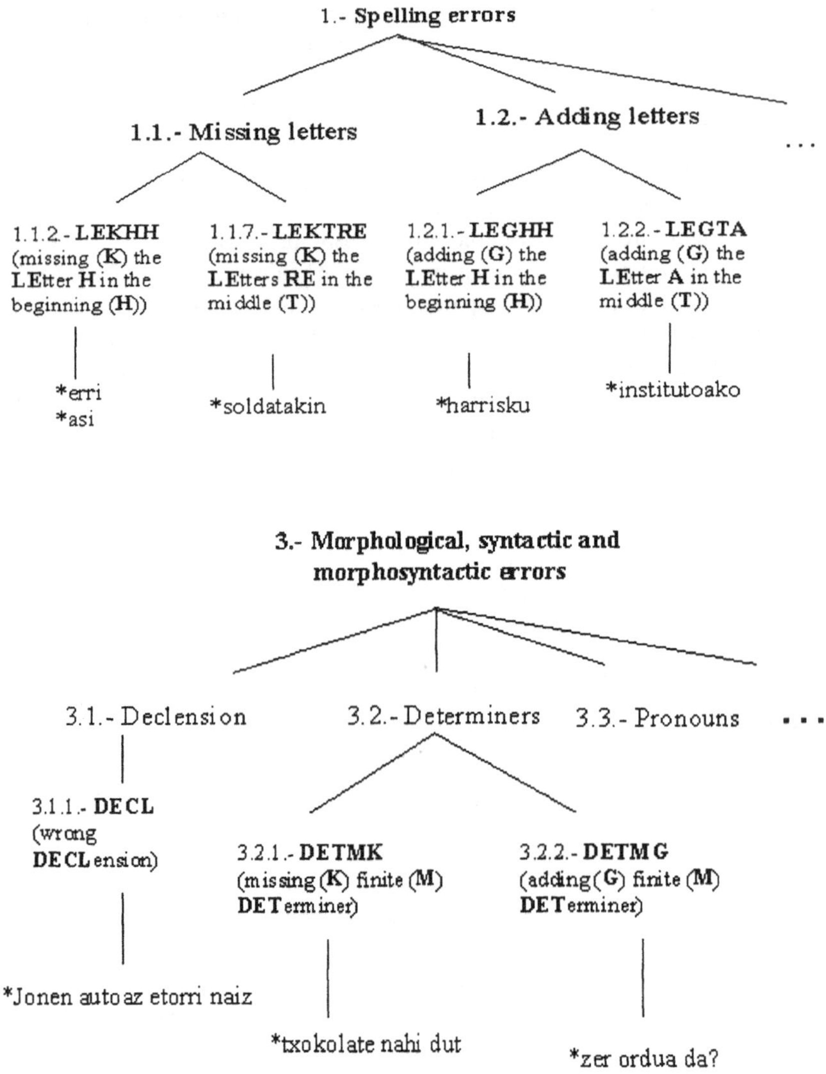

Fig. 3. Hierarchical structure of the classification

Besides, this is a dynamic error classification in the sense that it can be modified and updated depending on the data we collect. It means that computational linguists can prune the branches which are leafless. Or, on the contrary, they can also add new ones in case there are too many leaves, which could be grouped together, hanging from the same branch.

3.2.2.- Error correction

Indeed, error correction[3] also presents some questions and different viewpoints among us:

– when a sentence presents more than one error, should we correct the whole sentence or just the error we are treating?

– when we correct error(s), do we have to rewrite the whole sentence or just the erroneous part?

– when an error has more than a possible correction, should we give all the possible corrections or a single correction is enough?

The attitudes adopted by professionals in respect to error correction are really diverse; all teachers, computational linguists and computational psycholinguists correct errors depending on their particular criteria. As this fact affects the design of the databases, the correction boxes have been designed for the moment to consider the different possible types of corrections.

For example, we decided to treat spelling errors at a lexical level and the non spelling ones, on their part, at a syntactic or phrase level. In fact, context often turns out to be essential because, as in the following case, a word can be sometimes correctly written out of context but be an 'error' in a specific sentence:

****txoria daude***
bird there are

txoria (*bird*), as a lexical unit, is correct. However, in this sentence it is syntactically incorrect because the plural auxiliary ***daude*** (*there are*) requires the plural subject ***txoriak*** (*birds*), or the singular subject ***txoria*** (*bird*) needs the singular auxiliary ***dago*** (*there is*). Therefore, there would be two possibilities to correct this error.

3.3. Assessment of the classification

In addition to the problems commented on error correction, we realized that it is also difficult to define criteria for the assignment of linguistic categories. In fact, errors can sometimes be classified in more than one category of the classification, which makes the task of categorization even more difficult.

[3] We are speaking of manual error correction, not the automatic correction.

Guk geu
we ourself

For example, this instance can be classified in two subcategories: *Pronoun errors* or *Non-agreement in the Noun Phrase.* As both categories suit, we think taggers should feel free to decide the linguistic category to classify this kind of cases.

In order to corroborate the decisions we made and to study the criteria professionals adopt when classifying error instances, we decided to assess this error classification for Basque. For this, we prepared an exercise which consisted on 28 sentences with one or more error instances and we handed it out to eleven proofreaders, Basque language teachers and linguists. We wanted to assess how many errors they detected in each sentence and how they corrected them.

As we have already said, categorizing errors is not an easy task, but we obtained positive results. We here present a sample of the assessment. Out of the twenty-eight sentences, in seventeen sentences we foresaw only one error and below we show in how many of those seventeen sentences the assessors agreed with our prediction. In six sentences the eleven assessors (100%) detected a single error, in agreement with our prediction. In other six sentences, 90,9% of the assessors detected one error (as predicted) whereas 9,09% of them detected two. In two sentences, 63,63% of the assessors agreed with us detecting a single error and 36,36% of them detected two. Only in one sentence 81,81% of the assessors found one error, 9,09% of them detected two and 9,09% of the assessors detected 3 errors. Finally, in the last two sentences, 81,81% of the assessors detected one error and 18,18% of them detected two (see table 1).

Table 1. A sample of the assessment

Sentences (17)	Number of errors predicted	Assessors	Number of errors detected
In **6** sentences	1	**11** assessors (100%)	**1** error
In **6** sentences	1	**10** assessors (90,9%) **1** assessor (9,09%)	**1** error **2** errors
In **2** sentences	1	**7** assessors (63,63%) **4** assessors (36,36%)	**1** error **2** errors
In **1** sentence	1	**9** assessors (81,81%) **1** assessor (9,09%) **1** assessor (9,09%)	**1** error **2** errors **3** errors
In **2** sentences	1	**9** assessors (81,81%) **2** assessors (18,18%)	**1** error **2** errors

In addition to this sample, and considering all the results, we have also noticed that:

– 72,8% of the assessors have not considered deviations capital and small letters;

– it is very difficult to agree on semantic errors;

– agreement errors are easy to detect and to agree on;

– 61,74% of the assessors have agreed on the detection and classification of the errors.

As a general remark, all the collaborators have affirmed that the error classification we have developed is accurate and complete enough so as to classify the examples detected in real corpora.

Now, the classification is already accessible via Internet so that as many users as possible collaborate with us in storing errors.

4. The error editor tool

In addition to the error classification, and considering that manual error tagging is a time-consuming task, we have designed an error editor tool. This way, error detection, collection and categorization becomes easier and faster. This tool makes use of the described error classification and it will be connected to the above mentioned two databases.

Therefore, there are two possible ways to store and categorize error instances in our databases.

On the one hand, we can enrich DEVIATIONS and ERRORS databases by means of Erreus and Irakazi web applications[4] (see section two).

On the other hand, we can also store and classify error instances using the error editor tool, which requires the following steps (figure 4):

(1) The human tagger opens the texts to be tagged in the editor tool and marks the errors he/she finds.

(2) The detected instances have to be identified with their corresponding linguistic code in the error classification, which is exported from the databases.

(3) The coded error instances are then represented in four different XML documents:

– the first document specifies the location of the error in the text;

[4] **Irakazi**: http://ixa.si.ehu.es/ikasleDB/menua
Erreus: http://ixa.si.ehu.es/Erreus

– the second one represents which category of the error classification corresponds to each detected error instance;
– the third one links each error instance with its possible corrections; – and, finally, the last XML document represents which are the specified possible corrections per each error.

(4) By means of these four XML documents, the data will be automatically imported to the databases.

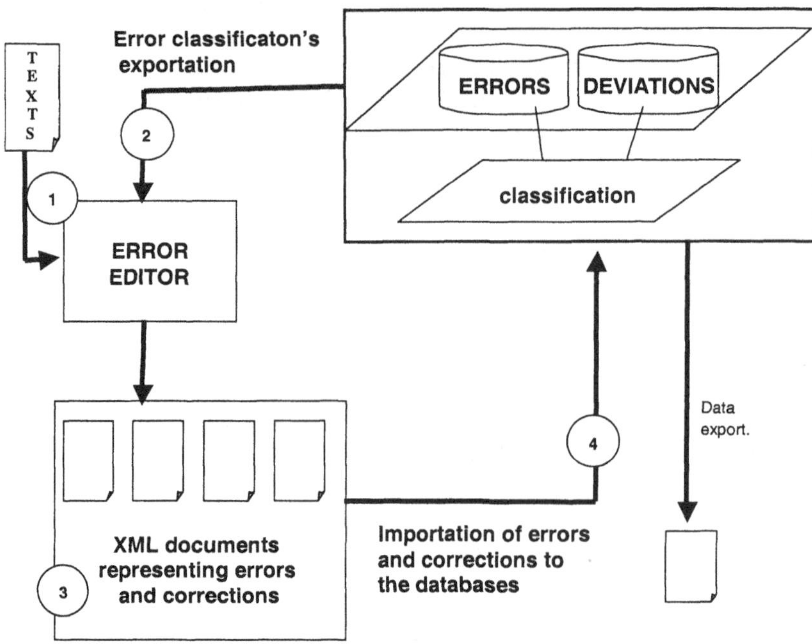

Fig. 4. Data collection process using the editor tool

5. Conclusions and future work

In this article, we have presented two web applications, Irakazi and Erreus, which have been developed in order to carry out research in the fields of Learner Corpora, ICALL and Automatic Error Treatment. These applications make use of different databases developed with the aim of collecting as much error instances as possible. The data stored will be an important source of information for two main research fields, ICALL and NLP. The psycholinguistic information stored in the DEVIATIONS database will be useful to adapt the teaching of some phenomena to each student, as well as to continue researching in the study of Basque learners' learning processes, strategies, materials, etc. As regards automatic linguistic analysis, the data collected in ERRORS is essential to continue searching, by means of different techniques, in the automatic detection and correction of some error types (agreement errors, errors in postpositions, wrong use of the comma, etc.), some of which have already been formulated and will be taken into account for the development of a grammar and style checker for Basque.

One of the most important features of Irakazi and Erreus web applications is the error classification they both share. In order to make easier the search of error instances, we built a thorough classification which consists of seven main categories and many subcategories. Then, we assessed the classification with the collaboration of some proofreaders, Basque language teacher and linguists. It is important to highlight that this classification is dynamic and that there is a team of computational linguists and psycholinguists who regularly check the information stored and modify it if necessary.

In addition, the information inserted in the databases will be used for different purposes. Since we have already tools which detect spelling errors, we will store and analyze them for the development of new pedagogical applications for learners to work on spelling. The errors of the rest of categories, on the contrary, constitute a source of relevant information, both for the development of a grammar and style checker as well as for the creation of new applications in the field of computer-aided language learning.

As concerns the error editor tool, we have not found any reference about the connection of two databases to this kind of editors. Therefore, we consider our work is novel in this matter and we think this is an interesting contribution to the CEA field.

Besides, we would like to claim that, despite we work in and for Basque, the systems for error categorization and error collection we present in this article may be transferable to other languages. In fact, Irakazi has been implemented with a multilingual interface.

To conclude, we foresee some PhDs to be carried out in the following years within the mentioned research fields.

REFERENCES

Aduriz, I., Aldezabal, I., Aranzabe, M., Arrieta, B., Arriola, J., Atutxa, A., Díaz de Ilarraza, A., Gojenola, K., Oronoz, M., Sarasola, K. and R. Urizar (2002). *The design of a digital resource to store the knowledge of linguistic errors*. DRH2002 (Digital Resources for the Humanities). Edimburgo.

Agirre, E., Alegria, I., Arregi, X., Artola, X., Díaz de Ilarraza, A., Maritxalar, M., Sarasola, K. and M. Urkia (1992). *Xuxen: A Spelling Checker/Corrector for Basque based in Two-Level Morphology*. Proceedings of ANLP'92. Povo, Trento: 119–125.

Arrieta, B., Díaz de Ilarraza, A., Gojenola, K., Maritxalar, M. and M. Oronoz (2003). *A database system for storing second language learner corpora*. Learner corpora workshop. Lancaster, UK.

Becker, M., Bredenkamp, A., Crysmann, B. and J. Klein (1999). *Annotation of Error Types for German News Corpus*. Paris: Proceedings of the ATALA workshop on Treebanks.

Bell, R. T. (1974). *Error analysis: a recent pseudoprocedure in applied linguistics*. International Review of Applied Linguistics. Vol. 25–26: 35–49.

Corder S. P. (1975). *Error analysis, Interlanguage and second language acquisition* (Survey article). Language Teaching and Linguistics Abstract. Vol. 8.

Corder, S. P. (1981) *Error Analysis and Interlanguage,* Oxford: Oxford University Press

Corder, S. P. (1967) *The significance of learners' errors*. Reprinted in J. C. Richards (ed.) (1974, 1984) *Error Analysis: Perspectives on Second Language Acquisition*. London: Longman: 19–27.

Díaz de Ilarraza, A., Maritxalar, A., Maritxalar, M. and M. Oronoz (1999). *IDAZKIDE: an intelligent CALL environment for second language acquisition*. Proceedings of a one-day conference "Natural Language Processing in Computer-Assisted Language Learning" organised by the Centre for Computational Linguistics, UMIST, in association with EUROCALL, a special ReCALL publication, UK: 12–19.

Ellis, R. (1985) *Undestanding second language acquisition*. Oxford: Oxford University Press.

Dagneaux, E., Denness, S. and S. Granger (1998). *Computer-Aided Error Analysis*. System. Vol. 26: 163–174.

Euskaltzaindia. (1993). *Euskal Gramatika Laburra*. Bilbo.

Fernández, S. (1997). *Interlengua y Análisis de Errores en el aprendizaje del español como lengua extranjera*. Ed. Edelsa.

Gojenola, K. (2000). *EUSKARAREN SINTAXI KONPUTAZIONALERANTZ. Oinarrizko baliabideak eta beren aplikazioa aditzen azpikategorizazio-informazioaren erauzketan eta erroreen tratamenduan*. Phd. Donostia.

Gojenola, K. and M. Oronoz (2000). *Corpus-Based Syntactic Error Detection Using Syntactic Patterns*. NAACL-ANLP00, Student Research Workshop. Seattle.

Granger, S. (2002). *A Bird's-eye view of learner corpus research*. Computer Learner Corpora, Second Language Acquisition and Foreign Language Teaching, Amsterdam and Philadelphia: Benjamins: 3–33.

HABE (1999). *Helduen Euskalduntzearen Oinarrizko Kurrikulua.* Donostia: 120–131.
James, C. (1998). *Errors in Language Learning and Use: Exploring Error Analysis.* Longman.
Laka, I. *A Brief Grammar of Euskera*, http://www.ehu.es/grammar/
Larsen-Freeman D. and H. Long M. (1994). *Estudio de la adquisición de segundas lenguas.* Gredos.
Maritxalar, M. (1999). *MUGARRI: A multisystem environment to acquire the linguistic knowledge of second language learners.* PhD, Donostia.
Norrish, J. (1983). *Language learners and their errors.* London: The Macmillan Press Ltd.
Ortiz de Urbina, J. (2001). *A Grammar of Basque.* University of Deusto.
Richards, J. C. (1974). *Error Analysis: Perspectives on Second Language Acquisition.* London: Longman.
Richards, J. C. (1974). *A non-contrastive approach to error analysis.* London: Longman.
Richards, J. C. and G. P. Sampson (1974). "The Study of Learner English". In: Richards, J. C. (ed.). *Error Analysis: Perspectives on Second Language Acquisition.* London: Longman: 3–18.
Sarrionandia, B. (1999). *Perfiles lingüísticos: modelo alternativo de evaluación de la competencia del euskera.* Phd. Bilbo.
Selinker, L. (1972). "Interlanguage". *International Review of Applied Linguistics*, 10 (3): 209–231.
Selinker, L. (1992). *Rediscovering Interlanguage.* London and New York: Longman.
Txillardegi (1978). *Euskal Gramatika.* Bilbo: Ediciones Vascas.
Zubiri, I. and E. Zubiri (1995). *Euskal Gramatika Osoa.* Bilbo: Didaktiker SA.

Renata Fox

University of Rijeka

PARTICIPATING IN THE TRANSDISCIPLINARY PROJECT: APPLYING CORPUS LINGUISTICS TO CORPORATE IDENTITY

1. Aim of address

The aim of this address is to bring to the attention of all involved in corpus linguistics the importance of the development and implementation of a *transdisciplinary approach*, an approach which supersedes the traditional use of corpus linguistics as an ancillary sub-discipline and emphasises its role as an equal participant in the production of new knowledge.

Corpus linguistics is a well established field of study, developing at an amazing speed and continually branching out in ever new directions. Initially disciplinary in nature, later multi- and interdisciplinary, today corpus linguistics is moving towards transdisciplinarity. Researchers in corpus linguistics are drawing from various non-linguistic fields of study, using concepts and methodologies from these fields to develop and enrich corpus linguistics. In recent years the study of a text corpus significantly surpasses (previously dominant) descriptive goals and helps generate theories founded on the link between language use and its cognitive and social aspects (cf. Aijmer and Altenberg 2004). More precisely, a researcher's relation towards the data obtained through analysis of a text corpus is moving from a "corpus-based" approach which, broadly speaking, uses data to test existing theories, to a "corpus-driven" approach in which the data constitute a departing point for creating new theories. Consequently, the role of the corpus data in understanding language processes (for example, language change and development, dialect and register patterns, style, etc.) is attracting the attention of a growing number of researchers. This, in turn, raises a question of methodologies, both in the sense of methods applied in corpus study and in the sense of corpus analysis as a method of language description. In result, the issue of data interpretation possibilities is continually questioned.

The theory of knowledge recognised long ago (cf. Gibbons *et al.* 1994; Nowotny *et al.* 2001) that intellectual production is increasingly market-oriented which makes it by definition transdisciplinary. In its nature knowledge is "transgressive", "seeping" in all directions: from science to society and from society to science. While science has always communicated to society, today society actively communicates to science. This is why transdisciplinarity – a combination of discipline-based and non-disciplinary informal, non-codified, tacit knowledge – is not just an exercise in style. It is the only means to address the increasingly intricate objects, problems and social contexts. Unlike all previous forms of knowledge treatment, transdisciplinarity enables an interaction of sciences with society involving all people (not only scientists) in the production of knowledge.

To demonstrate a transdisciplinary use of corpus linguistics, I apply it to corporate identity, a field of study calling for a holistic perspective, a perspective that can create new knowledge indispensable for researching corporate identity.

2. From compartmentalisation to unity

For at least the past two and a half millennia human knowledge in Western culture has been based on a linear, binary true/false syllogistic logic, first formalised by Aristotle. Things have been perceived as either true or false, without an in-between. Such logic has resulted in the perception of the existence of an "absolute good" and an "absolute evil" and has created the "win-lose" ideology of modern education, politics and business (cf. Henagulph 2000). In line with this linear logic and the need for progress it produced, human knowledge has for centuries been compartmentalised into separate disciplines, the number of which was continually growing, precisely due to this compartmentalisation. While the object of disciplinary thinking was understanding complex issues through simplification, the *understanding of the complexity* of the issue itself was, in fact, lacking (Ramadier 2004: 428). With time disciplines inevitably started overlapping, the need for their linking as well as communication and articulation among disciplines arose and the path towards transdisciplinarity was set.

What I wish to emphasise at this point is that the unity of knowledge, which is an imperative of transdisciplinary practice, is necessarily based on disciplinarity and disciplinary thinking. The fact that simplification and compartmentalisation of knowledge have been fought within the disciplines themselves, shows that it is not disciplinarity which is the problem, rather it is the attitude of researchers within single disciplines with respect to the transfer of knowledge to society (cf. Ramadier 2004: 428). A discipline typically inclined towards compartmentalisation is linguistics. Linguists, as argued by Fairclough (1999: 210), are not supplying the "models of language" that would enable researchers in non-linguistic disciplines to turn the "insights of linguists into comprehensible and usable forms". It seems that this rigid formalism of linguistics is the main reason for discouraging both linguists to transgress and researchers in non-linguistic disciplines to tap on areas of linguistics – sociolinguistics, critical discourse analysis, the ethnography of communication – thus failing to "develop appropriate models and theories" (Fox and Fox 2004: 22).

The first level of disciplinary interaction and the first step towards a unity of knowledge is multidisciplinarity: a process of juxtaposing of various theoretical models from various disciplines. In a multidisciplinary project methodology is essentially disciplinary. Investigating different aspects of a whole, different disciplines cooperate but remain self-contained producing little "cross-fertilisation" (Bruce *et al.* 2004: 459). Although different disciplines are often considered indispensable for the understanding of a certain phenomenon and therefore treated as complementary, the result of a multidisciplinary research is not a common model, but (separate) parts of different models which, however, due to a plurality of viewpoints, allows for a more informed insight.

A step further is interdisciplinarity[1]: a dialogue between various disciplines leads to the construction of a common model and synthesis. Typical for interdisciplinarity is the transfer of models and/or tools from one discipline to another: occasionally disciplines submit to the rule of one discipline, or, alternatively, the concepts of one discipline are used in other disciplines. Characteristic for interdisciplinarity, as too multidisciplinarity, is that it is essentially a form of disciplinary thinking: on both levels of interaction approaches are fragmented and paradoxes avoided. But unlike multidisciplinarity which fails to seek common solutions to the problem, an interdisciplinary project does plan such solutions. They, however, inevitably remain within the borders of purely theoretical, explicit knowledge. Nevertheless, the outcome of an interdisciplinary research, owing to disciplinary integration, is in many ways holistic.

A critical examination of projects referred to as "interdisciplinary" shows many of them to be, in fact, multidisciplinary: researchers from various disciplines contribute to a predefined topic from their individual disciplinary

[1] The term "interdisciplinary" has a long history: apparently it was first mentioned in the Sixth Annual Report 1920–1930 of the Social Science Research Council where the Council's intention to encourage "interdiscipline enquiries" was stated (Sills 1986: 17–18).

perspectives (cf. Balsiger 2004: 412). Because there is often no integration and no articulation, it entirely depends on the user of the project to deduce the impact of various disciplines upon the topic. Evidently, by referring to their projects as interdisciplinary, participants in the multidisciplinary projects assume that integration of various disciplines would be an automatic result of their contact.

The highest level of disciplinary interaction and the most recent among the major forms of disciplinary practice is transdisciplinarity: a process whereby two aspects of disciplinary thinking – knowledge compartmentalisation and existence of relationships between disciplines – are integrated for the purpose of articulation of different forms of knowledge. In other words, transdisciplinarity combines multidisciplinarity and interdisciplinarity. From multidisciplinarity transdisciplinarity has inherited the awareness of the existence of different realities, and from interdisciplinarity the endeavour to "reinterpret knowledge in order to readjust the different levels of reality" (Ramadier 2004: 434).

The idea of transdisciplinarity, however, is not new: it dates back to the Middle Ages and the creation of universities to provide a synthesis between different areas of knowledge. While the concept "transdisciplinarity" was first defined in written form in 1970, the debate on transdisciplinarity as a form of a supradisciplinary research practice did not start before the 1990s. A contemporary understanding of transdiciplinarity is rooted in the aims of the International Center for Transdisciplinary Research (CIRET), located in Paris and founded in 1987. According to CIRET, a transdisciplinary approach

- fights the compartmentalisation of knowledge
- narrows the gap between the research and decision making pertaining to social life
- studies similarities between different realms of knowledge.

In 1994, during a First international congress on transdisciplinarity held in Portugal, CIRET's ideas on transdisciplinarity were synthesised in a Transdisciplinarity Charter.

Further developing the notion of knowledge decompartmentalisation, Rosenfeld (1992) has defined transdisciplinarity as a process based on sharing theoretical models founded on concepts specific to individual disciplines. The core of Rosenfeld's thinking is essentially an interdependence among theoretical models underlying investigations into an object. A focus on interdependence among various theories is too fundamental to Nicolescu's *Transdisciplinary Manifesto* (1996) which defines transdisciplinarity as "that which is at once *between* the disciplines, *across* the different disciplines, and *beyond* all disciplines". According to Nicolescu, the goal of transdisciplinarity is to understand the present world through a unity of knowledge. Unlike other forms of knowledge treatment, transdisciplinary is marked by collaboration, not only among various disciplines but also among scientists and stakeholders. Therefore, solutions obtained by transdisciplinary research projects take into account experiences from affected persons (Balsiger 2004). Rather than aiming at consensus, which is typical for disciplinary thinking, a transdisciplinary research is based on a "controlled conflict generated by paradoxes" (Ramadier 2004: 434). To confront the paradox, methodologies originating in different disciplines are combined to create a single approach in which different knowledges are integrated.

Of course, by integrating different knowledges, transdisciplinarity creates a new quality which is more than just the arithmetical sum of the disciplines involved. Through integration, transdisciplinarity enables the application of insights, results and methodologies to provide more efficient solutions to problems in various fields of study. Integration leads to articulation (creating coherence) among two contradictory movements of disciplinary thinking: (1) compartmentalisation of knowledge, and (2) the existence of relationships among various disciplines rendering the potential to produce new and different forms of knowledge.

3. The Challenge to Corpus Linguistics

The growing complexity of tasks put before corpus linguistics has, not surprisingly, lead to its involvement with an ever greater number of other – mutually interacting, linguistic and non-linguistic – disciplines. The contacts, interactions and, inevitably, articulations of corpus linguistics with other disciplines have prompted the transformation of researchers' approach to corpus linguistics: from a disciplinary, through a multidisciplinary and interdisciplinary towards a transdisciplinary approach.

3.1. A disciplinary approach

By a disciplinary approach towards corpus linguistics I mean researchers' activities during the 1960s and 1970s the aim of which was mastering the use of language corpora to describe the lexico-grammatical patterning of text. The best known corpora of that time are the Survey of English Usage Corpus (a corpus of spoken and written British English) and Brown Corpus (a corpus of written American English). The disciplinary approach towards corpus linguistics was, typically, about a mono-discipline, about a specialisation in isolation (Fig. 1).

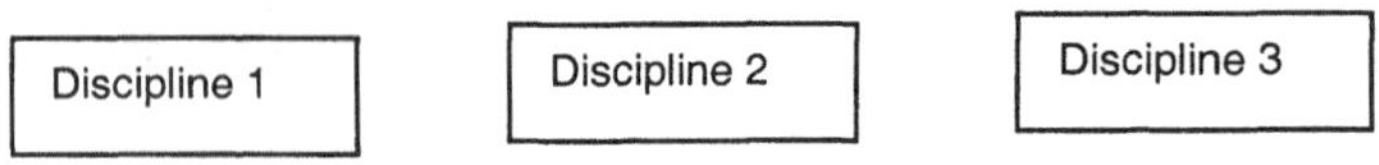

Fig. 1. A disciplinary approach

The narrow context in which the corpus linguistics-related concepts were applied limited the number of synthetic possibilities. Clearly, during the era of disciplinarity the teething of corpus linguistics as a field of study and establishing computational text analysis as a mainstream took place (cf. Leech 1991: 9).

3.2. A multidisciplinary approach

Wishing to overcome the obvious drawbacks of a disciplinary approach, researchers in corpus linguistics turned towards multidisciplinarity. By a multidisciplinary approach towards corpus linguistics I mean the efforts of researchers during the 1980s and 1990s to contrast theoretical models belonging to different disciplines and highlight different dimensions of the studied object (language). The multidisciplinary turn gave rise to special-purpose corpora, for example, the JDEST Corpus of Texts in English for Science and Technology and the Guangzhou Petroleum English Corpus. Researchers adopting a multidisciplinary approach towards corpus linguistics entered more areas of knowledge, yet did not establish a dialogue between these areas and corpus linguistics (Fig. 2).

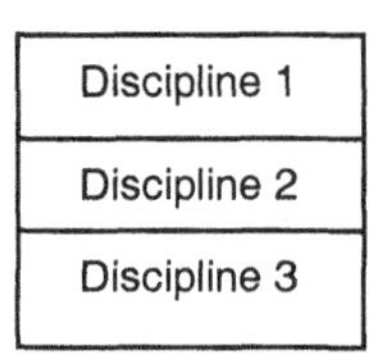

Fig. 2. A multidisciplinary approach

While various areas (in the Guangzhou research, these are science, technology, and oil industry) were considered complementary in the process of understanding a phenomenon (language), an attempt to take into account the entire theoretical implications underlying this research was not made.

3.3. An interdisciplinary approach

In the 2000s, aware of the need for syntheses between corpus linguistics and other fields of study, researchers in corpus linguistics are moving towards interdisciplinarity. By an interdisciplinary approach I mean the full solidarity between corpus linguistics and non-linguistic fields of study to solve problems and to provide "research methods that use systematic sets of procedures to develop inductively derived grounded theories about a phenomenon ... (in which) data collection analysis, and theory stand in reciprocal relationship with each other" (Strauss and Corbin 1990: 23–24). Rather than starting with a theory to be proven, Strauss and Corbin argue, a researcher should start with an area of study and allow whatever is relevant to that area to emerge.

Indeed, the interdisciplinary researcher in corpus linguistics adds construction to deconstruction, problem solving to problematising and prescription to reflexivity in both linguistic and non-linguistic areas of study. An interdiscplinary approach uses corpus linguistics to construct grounded theories in linguistic as well as non-linguistic fields of study. It, however, does not change boundaries and relations between different disciplines (Fig. 3).

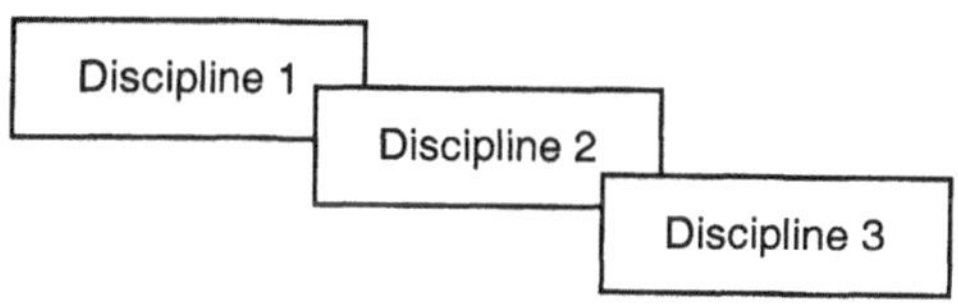

Fig. 3. An interdisciplinary approach

3.4. A transdisciplinary approach

As well known, research in corpus linguistics is not just about a researcher linking quantitative patterns found in a particular text and offering a functional interpretation of those patterns. It is primarily about a research methodology which allows researchers to identify statistical evidence of real choices of language vis-à-vis language as a virtual system. The underlying assumption being, of course, that language does not just describe action but is itself a form of social action, that language is not a reflection of the world but is world-constituting.

Therefore, looking to the future, the next step in the development of corpus linguistics, we may assume, will be transdisciplinarity, a move towards: eliminating boundaries between corpus linguistrics and other disciplines, narrowing the gap between the research and social effects of that research, studying similarities between corpus linguistics and other disciplines (Fig. 4).

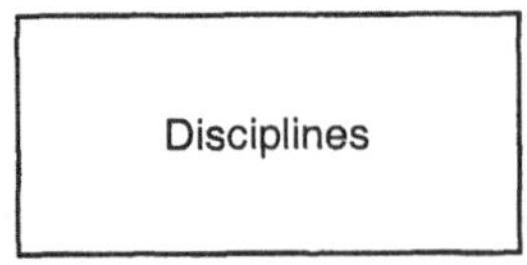

Fig. 4. A transdisciplinary approach

A transdisciplinary approach towards corpus linguistics would not only prompt the use of corpus linguistics to solve research problems in various non-linguistic fields of study, but also encourage the development and enrichment of both corpus linguistics and the non-linguistic scientific disciplines in which corpus linguistics is engaged. Corpus linguistics would articulate with other linguistic and non-linguistic fields of study to produce new knowledges. An assumption underlying a transdisciplinary approach is, of course, that researchers can distance themselves from the dominant perspectives of their disciplines.

4. Transdisciplinarity in Applied Research

To demonstrate a transdisciplinary use of corpus linguistics, I present analyses of two text corpora taken from the corporate public discourse (CPD) of two transnational corporations: Microsoft and ChevronTexaco. The salience of CPD lies in its being *the means* through which organisations institutionalise and legitimise their ideologies – sets of values, beliefs and ideas held as true, proper and correct (Fox and Fox 2004). Thought of as a shared social representation, corporate ideology equates with corporate identity which, I wish to stress, is not a personal identity governed by personal experiences and biography, but a group identity, governed more by identification processes related to group memberships. The role CPD plays in creating, legitimising and institutionalising a corporation's ideology, makes it the most obvious carrier of corporate identity and, as such, a key representation of the life of the corporation. The contribution of corpus linguistics to the exploration of CPD, and via that exploration, to a new understanding of corporate identity, as I will show, lies in the ability of corpus linguistics to, through the analysis of a text corpus, reveal the values, beliefs and ideas institutionalised and legitimised by a corporation and, through these values, beliefs and ideas, reveal the corporation. This means that, corpus linguistics can significantly contribute to both the production of new knowledge and the creation of a new attitude towards researching corporate identity.

Today, corporate identity is generally viewed as a strategic representation of the organisation, applied both internally and externally (Gioia *et al.* 2000), and offered to stakeholders through corporate communications which form a 'nexus' between an organisation's identity and its strategic objective (Balmer and Gray 2000:4). According to a total corporations communications approach, corporate identity is seen as everything a corporation says, makes and does, and is manifested through five forms of identity (actual, communicated, conceived, ideal, desired) present in any organisation (Balmer and Greyser 2004). The importance of corporate identities is best seen in the huge sums spent by corporations on creating those identities. For example, of Fortune 1,000 corporations 18.6 percent spend over $10m a year on corporate communication, 2.3 percent $7.5 – 10m, 5.8 percent $5 – 7.5m, and 43 percent $1 – 5m (*Practices and Trends* ... 2004).

In spite of some 50 years of thinking, debate and practice of corporate identity, researchers in corporate communication have made little progress in their understanding of this concept. The key problem of research into corporate identity is in it not having produced well-founded, data-rich empirical studies which would enable the objective description of corporate identity and prepare the ground for subsequent scientific moves, such as analysis, comparison, generalisation, interpretation, explanation, hypothesis-testing, experimentation, simulation, accreditation and application of corporations' identities.

Indeed, few theoretical descriptions, explanations and models of corporate identity have been put forward (cf. Balmer and Gray 2000). The scientific field corporate identity is characterised by a substantial confusion, so the concept corporate identity itself remains rather fuzzy. Almost a decade ago Balmer (1997), the most influential author in this field, suggested this to be a consequence of a lack of empirical research, lack of contact between different disciplines in this highly interdisciplinary area, and the inappropriateness of the positivistic research paradigm for explaining corporate identity. In their book "Revealing the Corporation" (2004) Balmer and Greyser expand these ideas by attributing the confusion to the "failure by scholars and practitioners to comprehend the multidisciplinarity and multifaceted characteristics of the domain" (p. 345). Although Balmer and Greyser do not explicitly refer to *transdisciplinarity*, it is quite obviously transdisciplinarity that the authors have in mind: they discuss the need for recognition of multifaceted nature of corporate identity (which means more than one perspective and more than one discipline), the importance of integrating academy and the world of practice

(p. 347), and the necessity of viewing the corporation holistically, as a "new gestalt" (p. 7).

Unquestionably, only a move by the scientific community (and the world of corporate practice) towards transdisciplinarity will help to alleviate the present problems of corporate identity as a field of study. Because transdisciplinarity takes into account experiences of all affected parties, transdisciplinary research into corporate identity will involve collaboration not only among a variety of disciplines but also among a variety of stakeholders (researchers, business schools, corporations). Put another way, transdisciplinary research into corporate identity will not only transgresses various scientific disciplines but also implement all stakeholders' practical and tacit knowledge to find solutions to various corporation-related problems. Therefore, it takes transdisciplinarity to create coherence among many different facets of corporate identity and different disciplines required for the understanding of these facets. Finally, only transdisciplinarity can help researchers into corporate identity to put a stop to knowledge fragmentation and thus contribute to understanding and solving paradoxes within a corporation.

The awareness of the need for corporation-related knowledge integration has existed for years. In the late 1980s and throughout 1990s leading organisational theorists (e.g., Drucker 1988; Argyris 1991; Garvin 1993; Davenport 1994; Leonard and Straus 1997) emphasised the importance of a learning and knowledge-creating company. While none of these authors explicitly refer to the idea of transdisciplinarity, all of them focus on the value of knowledge management for an organisation.

The salience of a holistic kind of knowledge for a corporation has been very much emphasised by Ikujiro Nonaka (1991), the leading Japanese organisational theorist. Objecting to the typically Western view of knowledge management which perceives an organisation as an "information processing machine" and accordingly considers only formal, systematic and quantifiable knowledge as useful, Nonaka mentions a number of highly successful Japanese organisations (e.g., Honda, Canon, Sharp) whose only secret is their unique approach to knowledge creation management. Nonaka explains the importance of integrating two types of knowledge: explicit knowledge which is formal and systematic, and tacit knowledge which, because it consists of taken-for-granted beliefs and perspectives, is hard to articulate. Integration of these two types of knowledge creates "spirals of knowledge" which stimulate continual knowledge articulation (conversion of tacit knowledge into explicit) and knowledge internalisation (using so gained explicit knowledge to extend one's tacit knowledge base).

5. Analysing CPD

The exploration of a corporation's CPD is possible through a "CPD nomenclature": a set of hierarchically positioned CPD units (Fox and Fox 2004: 31-39). The basic unit of CPD is defined as a communicative event which has two communicative purposes: general and specific. The general communicative purpose defines the goal of the event, while the specific communicative purpose defines its content. The general communicative purpose is common to all CPD communicative events, whereas the specific communicative purpose is particular to a CPD communicative event. The general communicative purpose of a CPD communicative event is to construct an ideology. A class of communicative events sharing the same specific communicative purpose constitutes a corporate genre. Corporate communicative events, corporate genres and CPD are brought together through a CPD continuum (Fig. 5) consisting of a matrix of combinations of corporate communicative events, corporate genres and CPD as a whole.

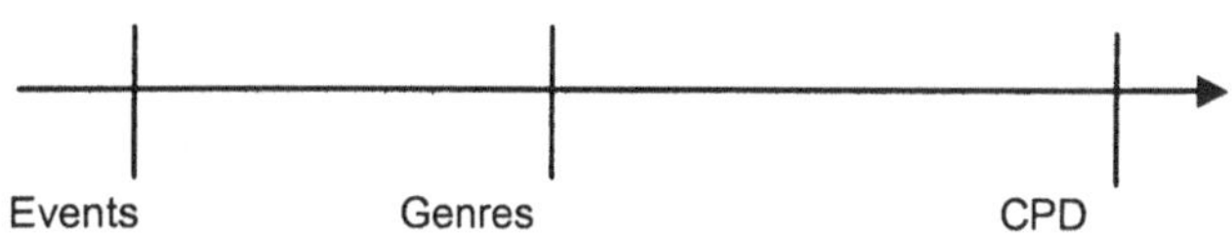

Fig. 5. A corporation's CPD continuum (Source: Fox and Fox 2004: 111)

Thus, a corporation's ideology may be thought of as a corporation's CPD continuum which may be analysed at different points: for example, at the point of an individual corporate communicative event, an individual genre, an assortment of corporate communicative events, an assortment of corporate genres, and so on. Each of these points can be represented by a text corpus which can be subject to linguistic analysis. The ideas upon which a corporation founds its ideology, it is *assumed*, are represented by highly frequent content lemmas (nouns, adjectives, adverbs, main verbs) which belong to two categories: thematic lemmas and key lemmas (Fox 1999). Thematic lemmas relate to a corporation's business activities, that is, the industry to which the corporation belongs, they are typical to a corporate genre and semantically specific. For example, in the case of an IT company, thematic lemmas related to a corporation's business activities would be "software", "windows", "integrated", "solutions", while thematic lemmas related to a corporate annual report, for example, would be "2004", "year", "financial", "annual" and "billion". Key lemmas, on the other hand, relate to the important beliefs and values of a particular era, culture, society, social groups and professions. Key lemmas are not typical to a corporation's business activities, nor are they typical to a corporate genre. They are semantically non-specific.

The classification of an item as either a thematic or a key lemma is objectified through reference to a CPD *relational data base* containing frequency lists for a large number of communicative events classified according to corporate genres for a large number of corporations classified according to industries. The following two tables containing top lemmas of the non-financial section of two corporate annual reports (CAR) were taken from that data base.

Table 1. Top fifty lemmas of the non-financial section of Microsoft's fiscal 2003 CAR

MICROSOFT			
Rank	**Lemma**	**Thematic (specific) lemmas**	**Key (non-specific) lemmas**
1	and		
2	the		
3	we/our/us		
4	more/much/most		more
5	to be		
6	of		
7	in		
8	a/an		
9	business(es)		businesses
10	customer(s)		customers
11	they/their		
12	products		products
13	Microsoft		a company's name (Microsoft)
14	new		new
15	help		help
16	on		
17	software	software	
18	technology	technology	
19	windows	windows	
20	innovation		innovation
21	provide		provide
22	people		people

23	services	services	
24	solutions	solutions	
25	integrated	integrated	
26	continue		continue
27	create		create
28	make/made		make/made
29	at		
30	it		
31	platform	platform	
32	have/had		
33	offers		offers
34	management		management
35	opportunities		opportunities
36	needs		needs
37	work		work
38	value		value
39	will		
40	organizations		organizations
41	support	support	
42	world		world
43	applications	applications	
44	partners		partners
45	server	server	
46	system	system	
47	important		important
48	tools	Tools	
49	great		great
50	power		power

A text sample taken from Microsoft's CAR:

At Microsoft focusing on the needs of customers fuels our passion for innovation. We believe innovative technology has the power to eliminate obstacles and create opportunities. Opportunities for people and businesses to realize their full potential. But there remains a great deal of work to make technology more affordable, easier to use, and less complex. Discovering new ways to help individuals be more productive and organizations more efficient is the inspiration for our investments in research and development.

Table 2. Top fifty lemmas of the non-financial section of ChevronTexaco's fiscal 2003 CAR

CHEVRONTEXACO			
Rank	**Lemma**	**Thematic (specific) lemmas**	**Key (non-specific) lemmas**
1	we/our/us		
2	The		
3	of		
4	to be		
5	in		
6	and		
7	to		
8	a/an		
9	date of year	date of year	
10	global/world		global/world
11	for		
12	have		
13	performance		performance
14	achieve		achieve
15	many/more		many/more
16	areas	areas	
17	natural gas	natural gas	
18	on		
19	total		
20	by		
21	capital	capital	
22	Chevrontexaco		Chevrontexaco
23	Nigeria		Nigeria
24	percent	percent	
25	projects		projects
26	return	return	
27	also		
28	annual	annual	
29	build		build
30	business		business
31	company		company
32	excellence		excellence
33	future		future
34	improve		improve

35	major		major
36	new		new
37	opportunities		opportunities
38	past		
39	production	production	
40	progress		progress
41	stockholder		stockholder
42	strategy		strategy
43	strong		strong
44	success		success
45	supply	supply	
46	will		
47	with		
48	America		America
49	upon		
50	financial	financial	

A text sample taken from ChevronTexaco's CAR:

Last year, I wrote of the challenge ChevronTexaco faced to improve its financial performance. I am pleased to report that we are succeeding. Not only was 2003 one of our best years ever, but we also built a solid foundation that should enable us to deliver sustained, strong performance into the future and continue to achieve our long-stated goal to be No. 1 in total stockholder return among our peer group.

As noted previously, integrating different fields of study, in our case corpus linguistics and corporate identity, creates a new quality – a synergy – which surpasses the arithmetic sum of individual disciplines. For example, an analysis of a corpus of CPD consisting of a large number of communicative events representing five corporate genres (the corporate mission statement, the CEO media interview, a corporation's business guidelines, the corporate media advertisement and the corporate annual report) for a large number of corporations has shown the key lemmas to be "company names", "people", "customers", "business", and "information" (Fox and Fox 2004). The high frequency of company names is definitely a consequence of a corporation's need to legitimise itself, and, to paraphrase Merleau-Ponty, "acquire its name in history". The remaining key lemmas together, however, offer various possibilities of interpretation. For example, they may be seen as showing contemporary corporations dominated by a humanistic belief system focusing on stakeholders and knowledge. Alternatively, they may be seen as corporations focusing on (the needs of) customers, that is, focusing on customers' self-actualisation, which, we know, is at the top of the hierarchy of all human needs. However, because people can never entirely satisfy their need for self-actualisation, customers will always want more and demand more from corporations.

6. Discussion

In this address I have presented a transdisciplinary approach towards corpus linguistics with the aim of demonstrating its role in the production of new (theoretical and practical) knowledge relevant to corpus linguistics, corporate identity, and society. The research was based on the analysis of two text corpora taken from the corporate public discourse of two transnational corporations. The quantitative analysis of the corpora produced lists of thematic and key lemmas. While thematic lemmas clearly reflect a corporation's business activities, key lemmas represent the beliefs and values, that is, the ideology/identity of a corporation. Considering the pivotal position of transnational corporations in contemporary society, it can be assumed that beliefs and values of corporations are too the beliefs and values of society.

In theoretical terms, the integration of corpus linguistics with organisational studies enables the creation of a metaparadigm which, integrating multiple paradigms and merging concepts characteristic to these paradigms, provides a new research potential for both sides involved. In this sense, I see transdisciplinarity as a research perspective which eliminates boundaries between disciplines – in this case corpus linguistics and corporate identity – with the aim of producing new forms of knowledge which can advance our understanding of society and have the potential to enhance the well-being of that society.

In practical terms, an integration of corpus linguistics with organisational studies enhances the legitimacy of both disciplines. The legitimacy of corpus linguistic will be enhanced through the adoption of its methodology by organisational studies. Vice versa, the legitimacy of organisational studies will be enhanced through the creation of new perspectives which have the potential to affect and change understandings of organisational studies.

In the long-term, the inclusion of corpus linguistics in transdisciplinary research will, I assume, take place through individual and collective efforts of researchers in corpus linguistics. At an individual level, transdisciplinarity will be the result of the personal interest of researchers and their published research.

At a collective level, transdisciplinarity will be the result of a deliberate effort of all of us involved in corpus linguistics to identify and systematise the gains of a transdisciplinary approach towards corpus linguistics.

ACKNOWLEDGEMENT

The author wishes to thank Microsoft and ChevronTexaco for their permission to use and reproduce their CPD.

REFERENCES

Aijmer, K. and B. Altenberg (eds) (2004). *Advances in Corpus Linguistics*. Amsterdam: Rodopi.

Argyris, C. (1991). "Teaching smart people how to learn". *Harvard Business Review*, May–June.

Balmer, J. M. T. (1997). "Corporate identity: past, present and future". *Working paper*, University of Strathclyde International Centre for Corporate Identity Studies, Glasgow.

Balmer, J. M. T. and E. R. Gray (2000). "Corporate identity and corporate communications: creating a competitive advantage". *Industrial and Commercial Training*, 32/7: 256–262.

Balmer, J. M. T. and S. A. Greyser (eds) (2004). *Revealing the Corporation*. London: Routledge.

Balsiger, P. W. (2004). "Supradisciplinary research practices: history, objectives and rationale". *Futures*, 36: 407–421.

Bruce, A., C. Lyall, J. Tait and R. Williams (2004). "Interdisciplinary integration in Europe: the case of the Fifth Framework programme". *Futures*, 36: 457–470.

Davenport, T. H. (1994). "Saving IT's soul: Human-centered information management". *Harvard Business Review*, March–April: 41–53.

Drucker, P. F. (1988). "The coming of the new organization". *Harvard Business Review*, January–February

Fairclough, N. (1999). *Critical Discourse Analysis*. London: Longman.

Fox, R. (1999). "The social identity of management ergolect". *English for Specific Purposes*, 18/3: 261–278.

Fox, R. and J. Fox (2004). *Organizational Discourse: A Language-Ideology-Power Perspective*. Westport, Conn: Praeger.

Garvin, D. A. (1993). "Building a learning organization. *Harvard Business Review*, July–August: 77–90.

Gibbons, M., C. Limoges, H. Nowotny, S. Schwartzman, P. Scott and M. Trow (eds) (1994). *The New Production of Knowledge: The Dynamics of Science and Research in Contemporary Societies*. London: Sage Publications.

Gioia, D. A., M. Schultz and K. Corley (2000). "Organizational identity, image and adaptive instability". *Academy of Management Review*, 25/1: 63–81.

Henagulph, S. (2000). "The three pillars of transdisciplinarity". Available at: http://www.goodshare.org/pillars.htm. Accessed June 16, 2005.

Leech, G. (1991). "The State of the Art in Corpus Linguistics". In: Aijmer, K. and B. Altenberg (eds). *English Corpus Linguistics*. London: Longman: 8–29.

Leonard, D. and S. Straus (1997). "Putting your company's whole brain to work". *Harvard Business Review,* July–August

Nicolescu, B. (1996). *Manifesto of Transdisciplinarity*. New York: State University of New York Press.

Nonaka, I. (1991). "The knowledge-creating company". *Harvard Business Review*, November–December.

Nowotny, H., P. Scott and M. Gibbons (2001). *Rethinking Science: Knowledge and the Public*. Cambridge: Polity Press.

Practices and Trends Study 2003 (2004). Corporate Communication Institute at Fairleigh Dickinson University, Madison, NJ. Available at: www.corporatecomm.org/. Accessed June 22, 2004.

Ramadier, T. (2004). "Transdisciplinarity and its challenges: the case of urban studies". *Futures*, 36: 423–439.

Rosenfeld, P. L. (1992). "The potential of transdisciplinary research for sustaining and extending linkages between the health and social sciences". *Social sciences and medicine*, 35: 1343–1357.

Sills, D. L. (1986). "A note on the origin of 'interdisciplinarity'". *Items*, 40 (1): 17–18.

Strauss, A. L. and J. Corbin (1990). *Basics of Qualitative Research: Grounded Theory Procedures and Techniques*. Newbury Park, CA: Sage.

Jacek Walinski and **Piotr Pezik**

University of Łódź

WEB ACCESS INTERFACE TO THE PELCRA REFERENTIAL CORPUS OF POLISH*

1. Introduction

The following article contains a presentation of the web interface to the PELCRA Corpus which is a large (over 100 million words) referential corpus of modern Polish, both spoken and written. It presents the design principles underlying the compilation of the corpus and summarizes the kinds of uses for which it is intended. Apart from information about the structure of texts contained in the corpus and the underlying relational database technology (RDB), the paper presents the wide range of features available in the WWW interface that was implemented for public access to its resources. Further information about the PELCRA Corpus with direct access to its resources and a variety of sophisticated processing tools is available at: **http://korpus.ia.uni.lodz.pl/**

2. Development of the PELCRA project

The acronym PELCRA stands for Polish and English Language Corpora for Research and Applications. The PELCRA is an ongoing joint project between the Department of English Language at the University of Lodz, Poland and the Department of Linguistics and Modern English Language at Lancaster University, Great Britain.

The motivation for the Polish-English collaboration was explained by the head of the Polish team – professor Barbara Lewandowska-Tomaszczyk (Lewandowska-Tomaszczyk 2004: 105) who remembers that: "The original idea behind a project which started in 1996 and was later called PELCRA (Polish and English Corpora for Research and Application) was connected with the fact that

* Polish State Committee for Scientific Research Grant No. 2H01D00825

we work at the interface of two languages. We are members of the Department of English Language and some of our studies involve a contrastive English-Polish perspective. Therefore, what we need in our research is access to large amounts of English and Polish data, representing different registers and styles, both in spoken and written form."

One of the goals set out at the very beginning of the project was to compile the "Polish National Corpus" which was intended to reflect the needs for a large referential corpus of Polish for linguistics applications. The main task of the PELCRA was thus to develop a fully professional corpus of modern Polish, including parts of speech tagging and TEI compliant annotation, mirroring the BNC in terms of genres and its coverage of written and spoken language. The cooperative work on building the corpus began formally in 1997 and is scheduled to complete at the end of April 2005.

Through the years the activities of PELCRA were not restricted to compilation of the referential corpus of modern Polish only, but included numerous activities geared towards collection of Polish Learner English Corpus (containing learner data from a range of learner styles at different proficiency levels), and the Polish-English & English-Polish Parallel and Comparable Corpora covering Polish materials translated from and to English as well as a range of authentic non-translated texts on comparable subject matters.

Recently, after the compilation of the referential corpus, the project has entered its final phase which focuses on developing a WWW interface for public access. This task was undertaken at the Department of the English Language at the University of Lodz with funding from the Polish State Committee for Scientific Research (Research Grant No. 2H01D00825).

The main goal at this stage of development is to import the corpus structure into a relational database serving as the underlying platform for corpus dissemination. One of prerequisites for this task involves correction of discrepancies in the headers marking the texts in the corpus by the implementation of XML markup. At the same time a set of applications has been developed to provide the end-user with a friendly interface for access to the corpus over the World Wide Web.

3. The PELCRA corpus

The purpose of a language corpus (see: Sinclair 1991, McEnery and Wilson 1996, Garside *et al.* 1997) is to provide professionals working with language (linguists, translators, lexicographers, teachers, etc.) with empiric evidence of how language is actually used in modern reality. This evidence is used to test hypotheses and theories about what particular entities of language mean. Traditional descriptive grammars and dictionaries based on human intuition usually provide information about what a word should mean, but sometimes only a careful observation in natural contexts shows what a particular word or expression is used to mean.

With the development of referential corpora it has become possible to base linguistic judgments about the language on evidence collected from a more varied range of sources than any one individual's personal experience or intuition. The PELCRA Corpus is a large referential corpus of modern Polish containing over 100 million words from both spoken and written domain. The corpus is intended to represent the widest possible range of modern Polish. The original idea of the corpus design is based on the British National Corpus. The following sections contain more details about the corpus design, contents, and structure.

Texts in the corpus are encoded in the XML format (eXtensible Markup Language) according to the Guidelines of the Text Encoding Initiative (TEI) to represent the grammatical tags identified in the texts and their structural properties (e.g. titles, paragraphs, authors, interlocutors, overlaps, etc.). Full classification, bibliographic, contextual, and demographic information is also included in the corpus database.

The strictly obeyed principle of representativeness coupled with the use of internationally agreed standards for corpus compilation and markup make us believe that the PELCRA Corpus is a comprehensive linguistic resource useful for a wide variety of applications in contrastive studies, language teaching, translation, lexicography and other varieties of practical and applied linguistic research based on natural language processing.

3.1. Applications of the PELCRA Corpus

The PELCRA Corpus was compiled to provide an opportunity to base linguistic judgments on empirical data to all language specialists who seek answers about language in their everyday activities. The main applications of the PELCRA Corpus were set out in a working document titled "Introduction to the PELCRA project", which was published on the project's website in 1999 (available at: pelcra.ia.uni.lodz.pl). This document identifies the following major areas of corpus applications which drove through the years the collection of different kinds of corpus materials in the project.

- *empirical base for publishing of linguistic reference materials.* Almost all modern language reference publications, e.g. dictionaries, thesauri, grammars, teaching courses, usage guides, etc. make use of corpus facilities.

- *academic linguistic research tool in synchronic linguistic studies.* This includes the fields of morphology, lexis, syntax, semantics, discourse analysis. When combined with the BNC the PELCRA Corpus is especially relevant for cross linguistic studies
- *base for development of language teaching aids for applied linguistics.* Corpus data lend extensive support to the lexical approach to language teaching, provided the lexicon is not conceived narrowly but is considered rather to be a linguistic space combining and networking an array of semantic, syntactic and phonological dimensions. It is evident that adequate and efficient theories of bilingual lexicon acquisition have to account for the acquisition of broadly conceived lexical patterns and structures occurring both in source and target language.
- *translation studies.* Multilingual corpus resources both parallel and comparable provide an effective aid to human translators making it possible to look up sentences in which a word or phrase occurs in one language and find its equivalents in the target language.
- *development and testing of natural language processing applications.* This embraces using natural language data for development and testing in the domain of all linguistic software programming from taggers, parsers, spell checkers to sophisticated natural language understanding and information retrieval systems.

3.2. Characteristics of the PELCRA corpus

The characteristic features of the PELCRA Corpus can be enumerated as follows:

- a **whole text** corpus: One of the basic rules followed in the compilation phase was to collect texts in their entirety. In some rare cases where the whole text was impossible to obtain for certain reasons and its incorporation in the corpus was crucial, only the available samples were included. In such cases a cohesive sample containing a continuous stretch of discourse from within the whole (e.g. a whole volume or several consecutive chapters) was chosen to avoid fragmentation of higher level discourse units. Wherever this necessity occurred the sample characteristics of a text was clearly identified in the corpus markup;
- a **synchronic** corpus: The PELCRA corpus includes texts published after 1970. Some texts were written earlier, but because of their importance to the

Polish literary heritage and continued popularity they can be treated as still functioning in the society. The corpus contains some texts from this category but their share in the corpus body is relatively very low;

- a **general** corpus: The collection of texts was not restricted to any specific sublanguage, register or genre. On the contrary, the compilation attempts to incorporate the widest possible range and variety of genres, topics, and registers;
- a **monolingual** Polish corpus: it comprises texts created by native speakers of Polish. In rare cases high quality translations of world-wide popular texts were also included;
- a **mixed** corpus containing both spoken and written language.

3.3. Design of the corpus

This section presents the design principles underlying the creation of the PELCRA corpus. The basic principle was to select texts according to a clearly stated methodology with specific target quantities of clearly defined types of language, which is similar to the approach taken for the creation of the British National Corpus. As explained by the BNC creators: "Such approach makes it possible for other researchers and corpus compilers to review, emulate or adapt concrete design goals" (Burnard 2000). On the other hand in many cases it was impractical or even impossible to follow the BNC structure to the letter.

3.3.1. Spoken vs. written representation

There is a general consensus among corpus linguists that any reference corpus of language should consist of a high proportion of spoken language in relation to written texts. However, in practice it is significantly more difficult (and expensive) to transcribe recording of natural speech than to collect written texts in a computer-readable form. The complexity of such an approach to the spoken vs. written language representation in a corpus is exhaustively explained in the Reference Guide for the British National Corpus (Burnard 2000) thus, similarly to the BNC, the spoken component of the PELCRA Corpus constitutes approximately 10 per cent of the total corpus. These quantity is assumed to be large enough to yield valuable empirical data about spoken Polish. The design principles for the spoken and written parts of the corpus are discussed respectively in the next two sections of the article.

3.3.2. Design of the written part

The written part of the corpus includes texts from imaginative and informative books, magazines and newspapers at both regional and national level of circulation, academic articles and journals, published commercial advertisements together with miscellaneous texts both published and unpublished like commercial leaflets and brochures, academic essays, letters, business documents, etc.

Collection of texts for the written part of the corpus was based on three major selection criteria: domain, time, and medium. The **domain** criterion indicates the type of writing a text contains. Therefore, a large number of texts was taken from published informative non-literary texts from domains of commerce, politics, social sciences, arts, natural science, current local and world affairs. The amount of texts in the corpus from this domain amounts roughly to 85 per cent. Another 15 per cent comes from imaginative and miscellaneous writing, mainly various literary works.

The criterion of **medium** indicates the medium of publication of a text. 28 per cent of written texts were published in books. 65 per cent comes from different periodicals, both magazines and newspapers with different circulation volumes. The remaining 7 per cent was taken from other kinds of miscellaneous published and unpublished material including for example academic thesis, essays, advertising brochures, legal regulations, business letters, official announcements, etc.

The **time** criterion refers to the date of publication of a text. As a modern synchronic corpus, the PELCRA contains texts published mostly between 1992–2002, which make almost 95 per cent of the corpus. The initial intention was to skip publications dating before 1989, which is the transformation date for the Polish political system, but for major literary works this condition was relaxed, because of their continued popularity and strong impact on the modern language.

Following the Reference Guide for the British National Corpus (Burnard 2000) it must be noted that "Text that is published in the form of books, magazines, etc., is not representative of the totality of written language that is produced, as writing for publication is a comparatively specialized activity in which few people engage. However, it is much more representative of written language that is received, and is also easier to obtain in useful quantities, and thus forms the greater part of the written component of the corpus."

Therefore, to provide a satisfactory basis for the sampling procedure various sources of information about the published written texts were taken into consideration. These sources for **books** include catalogues of books in print, which provide information books that not only were published but are also popular and available for purchase. This source can be supplemented by library lending statistics, where one can learn which books enjoy a wide reception and continue to be widely read. These are certainly good candidates for inclusion in the corpus. Although there is no direct arithmetical relation between the level of sales and the actual reception of a text, additional information about potential readership can also be inferred from bestseller lists.

As for **periodicals**, similar information can be obtained from the catalogues of magazines and periodicals, library lists of subscribed newspapers and magazines, and circulation figures showing which titles dominate the market. On the other hand, local newspapers with relatively low circulation also represent an important part of language reality. Because of that some specific local periodicals are included in the corpus to make this category include as broad as possible range of publication types.

The above statistics about books and periodicals that are published, bought or borrowed cannot be applied to **miscellaneous** texts, both 'published' and 'unpublished'. The distinction between these two categories is sometimes difficult to tell. The 'published miscellaneous text' usually refers to texts that were written for public dissemination, for example, commercial brochures, marketing and advertising materials, etc. The category of 'unpublished" includes personal and internal writing created for educational, commercial, and personal purposes. Because of the lack of statistics concerning the production or reception of such texts, the guidelines for text inclusion had to be based on common sense and intuition of project members.

The purpose of defining clear selection criteria for a referential corpus is to ensure that it contains a variety of different language samples for two reasons. The first is so that the corpus can be regarded as a representation of modern Polish in its different forms, without being biased for any particular type. Another reason is that by division of particular genres in sub-corpora one gains access to comparisons and contrastive studies about different types of text within a particular language.

3.3.3. Design of the spoken part

One part of the spoken component of the PELCRA corpus contains transcriptions of recorded informal conversations which were taped to acquire samples of natural spontaneous speech. This part is representatively balanced and includes speech of people from different age, sex and education level. Apart from the natural conversational data the spoken side of the corpus contains interviews, talks, debates and discussions collected from a variety of contexts, ranging from radio and TV broadcasts to minutes of court hearings and parliament proceedings.

Recording and transcribing natural speech for a computer-readable format is a complex and time consuming task. Until creation of the BNC in 1997 the difficulties of transcribing sufficiently large quantities of spoken text prevented the construction of a spoken corpus of over one million words (BNC FAQ online). Since the conversational dialogue is the dominant component of general language communication, the importance of inclusion of this particular type of language in the corpus cannot be underestimated. The PELCRA Project undertook to collect over 1 million words of orthographically transcribed natural speech, covering a wide range of spoken language variation. Over a half of it (600.000) is available together with full recordings of natural conversational Polish in the form of the Polish Spoken Conversational Multimedia Corpus.

As with the written part of the corpus, the most important considerations in constructing the spoken part were sampling and representativeness. The issue of speech representativeness in the case of conversational part was resolved by sampling a spread of language producers in terms of age, gender, and education level. On the other hand, spoken texts are also produced and received in more formal settings, hence the spoken part includes a substantial number of interviews, legal proceedings, parliament discussions, and formal speeches, etc. A spoken part composed solely with spontaneous conversations would omit other important spoken text types.

The methodology of collection of spontaneous natural conversations was another important issue. First of all, the volunteers recruited for the task were equipped with a pocket size personal recorder and specially trained how to record and transcribe conversations. In most cases the other interlocutors were informed about having been taped and asked to give permission for their speech to be included in the corpus only after the conversation. They were given the guarantee of absolute confidentiality and anonymity (all names and other personal details were removed in the digital processing of the recordings and replaced with fictitious names in the transcripts.) The recordings were then carefully transcribed and annotated with additional information about the respondents. Moreover, all the original recordings were digitized and compressed into the popular MP3 format to save storage space.

We decided to select some paralinguistic phenomena of interest to be included in transcripts, hence transcribers were instructed to mark the following elements:

- **voice quality**, for example, shouting, whispering, laughing, etc., which affects passages in a conversation;
- **important non-verbal events** influencing the conversation, for example, door opening, lighting a cigarette, someone passing by, etc.;
- **short significant pauses**, which were marked with a single full stop;
- **long significant pauses**, which were marked with a double full stop;
- **unclear passages** (with duration) that were either inaudible or incomprehensible for some reason;
- **overlaps** when more than one person was speaking simultaneously.

Other aspects of spoken texts are not explicitly marked in the encoding, but they are available for research, analysis, and further processing by referring to the digitized audio part, which enables carrying out further analyses of the spoken data.

4. Structure of the corpus

At the time of this writing (March 2005) the whole PELCRA Corpus is in the process of ultimate fine-tuning while being transferred to the relational database platform which is discussed later in the article. This process has embraced so far some 85 per cent of the corpus resources (85 million words have already been transferred to the target RDB format) and is scheduled to finish before April 26, 2005. Therefore, the details provided in this section may be slightly different in the final version of the corpus accessible over the Internet at: **http://korpus.ia.uni.lodz.pl**.

4.1. General information about the PELCRA Corpus

In the text format the corpus comprises 100,106,038 word units and occupies almost 1 gigabyte of disk space, which makes it fit on 2 CD-ROMs. Assuming that the average paperback book contains 400 words a page, it would take up about 250 000 pages to publish the whole corpus in print. At present the corpus comprises 84,876 texts. Each text is segmented into paragraph, sentence (utterance in spoken data), and token units, some of which have automatically assigned a part of speech label. There are 2,512,622 paragraphs and 5,305,347 sentence-like units in the whole corpus.

Table 1. Projected figures for the final version of the PELCRA Corpus

Number of	Quantity
Types:	Over 400,000
Tokens:	Over 100,000,000
Texts:	84,876
Authors:	14,234
S-units:	5,305,347
Paragraphs:	2,512,622

The table above shows the projected make-up of the final version of the PELCRA Corpus in terms of:

- **Types**: number of all distinct orthographic forms that were used to compose the texts.
- **Tokens**: number of all <w> elements identified by the annotation system, which is equivalent to words.
- **Texts**: number of distinct texts and text samples registered in the database.
- **S-units**: number of <s> elements identified by the annotation system which is roughly equivalent to the total number of sentences (written texts) and utterances (spoken texts) in the corpus.
- **Paragraphs**.

4.2. Structure of texts according to medium of publication

The following chart presents the structure of texts in the PELCRA corpus according to the medium of publication. Two different forms of periodical publication were distinguished (i.e. newspapers, and magazines). The 'magazines' category was distinguished, because magazine texts are usually longer, topic oriented and written with a specific target audience in mind. Apart from the literary and non-literary books, the corpus contains about 5 million words coming from sources classified as 'miscellaneous', which comprises both published ephemera, such as advertisements, intended for distribution to the general public and unpublished, such as internal business documents, essays and personal correspondence. The "spoken" share includes transcriptions of recorded natural spontaneous speech and materials taken from interviews, transcripts of public debates, public speeches, radio and television broadcasts.

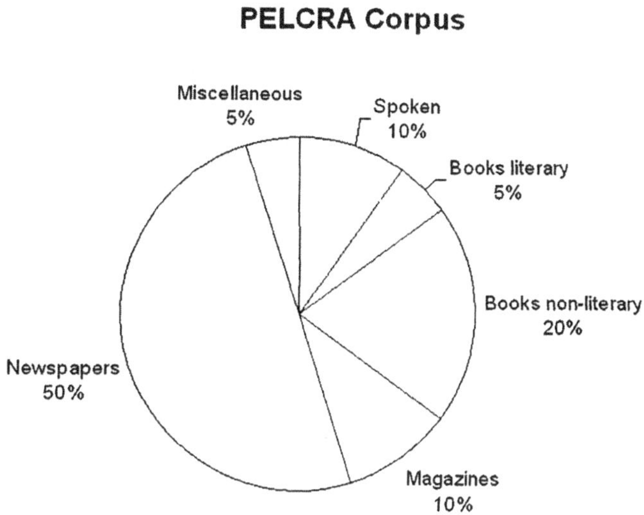

Fig. 1. Composition of the PELCRA Corpus according to medium

Standard bibliographic details such as author, title, publication details, etc. were registered for all the texts available in the corpus. Additional information about the written text structure according to different categories, such as domain, type of author (*sole, multiple, unknown*), sex of author (*male, female, mixed, unknown*), age band, target audience, and sample type are available in the PELCRA Corpus manual. The same applies to information concerning spoken text structure, which includes data about age, sex, education, interaction type, and topic of a given text.

5. Common language data storage formats

According to McEnery and Wilson annotated corpora can be defined as corpora which "have been enhanced with various types of linguistic information" whereas unannotated corpora "appear in their existing raw state of plain text". McEnery and Wilson further distinguish between a number of different types of linguistic annotation such as part-of-speech, discoursal, semantic or textual annotation (McEnery and Wilson 1996). The purpose of encoding additional information is to allow the linguist to search and process language corpora using metadata criteria which are not explicitly present in the original texts and transcriptions. The PELCRA project is an annotated web-based corpus in which special attention was paid to the efficient and scalable encoding of linguistic data.

Although various initiatives have been undertaken to standardize corpus data collection, a single format of storing linguistic resources has yet to emerge. In fact it is not even certain whether a universal solution to all annotation problems is a feasible idea in the first place. The exact requirements for an annotation scheme vary from one corpus project to another, which means that markup standards can only be verified empirically and are hardly ever predictable a priori (Leech 1993).

To understand the distinctive character of the annotation methodology used in the PELCRA Corpus, it is necessary to briefly outline the typology of existing schemes. Most corpus annotation methodologies utilize one of the following data storage formats:

- *Corpora stored in plain text files without additional annotation.* Such a basic format is very popular with corpus linguists and can be sufficient in many cases, but it has severe limitations. The only way of controlling untagged data stored in plain text files is through file naming conventions. Thus, many finer aspects of linguistic analysis such as morphological and syntactic markers may be impossible to encode in such corpora.
- *Corpora stored in plain text files with linear annotation schemes.* Ad hoc tagging can be used to represent selected aspects of linguistic analysis in the running text. Such formats, however, do not usually have an explicit documentation of the relationships and interdependencies between different tags used.
- *Corpora stored in plain text files with hierarchical annotation schemes.* Hierarchical systems of tags implemented in markup-languages such as XML or SGML may be verified against explicit document definition, which in turn facilitates the management of projects requiring large and complex tagsets.
- *Corpora stored in binary database files with a relational structure* (RDB). Although the process of compiling language corpora in such a format may be more demanding and time-consuming, there are a number of advantages of taking this approach to language data storage. The relational database approach is considered in more detail below as it is the main format used in the PELCRA project.

Custom binary formats. Depending on the project it may also be possible to use custom data structures implemented in a given programming language to store and process language data. However, such proprietary formats are usually less flexible than annotation schemes based on widely accepted standards.

The PELCRA corpus is one of the very few if not the only large-scale corpus stored entirely in a binary relational database. The main reasons for choosing this methodology of storing language data are discussed below.

5.1. Advantages of using relational databases for corpus and computational linguistics

The RDB methodology used to implement the core data storage tier in the PELCRA corpus has a number of advantages over most of the other formats discussed above. These advantages are especially evident when it becomes necessary to address the need to serve massive amounts of data to multiple concurrent users over the Internet. The advantages could be summarized as follows:

- **Scalability and fine-tuned indexing methods**. There is a long tradition of using relational databases for large-scale projects. Database engines provided by Oracle, Microsoft, Postgres or MySQL are widely applied in the IT industry whenever a need arises to store and manage data sets which can be scaled up to hundreds of millions of records. Thanks to the well-tested powerful caching and indexing algorithms as well as the possibility of supporting distributed computing such software has long been considered the solution of choice for the management of massive amounts of data. The speed of serving data from a central location was crucial to the PELCRA project where over 130,000,000 records have to be searched and served to multiple concurrent users. Therefore it seemed reasonable to implement an RDB engine as the project's core data server.
- **Programmatic compatibility**. All major RDB engines can be accessed from various programming languages by means of standardized programming interfaces. Thus, a Java or C++ desktop programmer can access the same database as a PHP web programmer without having to write access code, since such interfaces are provided by RDB vendors.
- **Flexibility of conversion to other formats**. Once the relational database is up and running, it is easy to export the data to almost any textual or binary format. This may facilitate the process of data exchange between different research groups.
- **RDB-based corpora conform to Leech's maxims** of creating corpus annotation (Leech 1997: 6), the most important of which require that corpus

annotation should be well documented and separable from the original texts or transcripts.

- **User management**. Some parts of the corpus may have to be protected from the general users. Most RDB systems have a powerful built-in system of granting access privileges which greatly facilitates the task of user management. The PELCRA corpus supports four levels of access to language data.
- **Versioning and update distribution**. In the PELCRA corpus changes and improvements are distributed instantly. Thanks to the centralized architecture corpus users always work with the most recent version of the corpus.
- **Accepted formalism of the RDB model**. The RDB model has its own widely accepted standards of modeling. This helps new project members or third-party programmers to overcome the problem of a "steep learning curve".
- The standard **Structured Query Language** (SQL) not only provides for the communication between the database and external client applications but it offers a standard way of maintaining the data within the storage. Although SQL comes in a number of varieties, they are all based on the same core sub-language. This allows programmers to join originally disparate projects under a single model.
- **Strong data typing**. Unlike most text file-based corpora, data stored in relational databases is strongly typed. This means that each segment of data is assigned an optimal amount of memory and disk space. Therefore relational databases tend to be more efficient than text files, where even numerical or Boolean values are stored as character strings.

5.2. Special requirements for the RDB approach

The above-mentioned advantages come with some basic requirements which are specific to centralized RDB systems. A number of such prerequisites are mentioned below:

- **A carefully designed data model** will ensure an increased speed of retrieval and faster development. An RDB system may thus be a rather inefficient solution in projects which only require ad hoc annotation.
- A centralized system means that data which is lost once is lost permanently for all users. This means that **a regular back-up procedure** must be implemented.

- **Ensuring maximum up-time** parameters of the system is another critical requirement for an RDB system, since problems with the central database are experienced by all of its users simultaneously.
- **Data security**. Data served over the Internet is naturally exposed to external attacks. Therefore RDB systems require a special level of security.

As shown above, the RDB methodology is a suitable solution for large-scale projects where fast, concurrent internet access to large language resources is of primary importance. The theoretical underpinnings of RDB language data modeling have been expounded in (Uzar, Pęzik, Levin 2004).

6. Access features as implemented in the Web interface

6.1. Logging in, user management and privileges

Web access to the PELCRA corpus is provided at 4 basic levels. Apart from *guest* users who can log in and use a public password to access the basic search functions, there are more advanced features of the corpus are available to the *student*, *linguist* and *administrator* groups. One obvious function of these distinctions is to ensure better control over the performance of the corpus. Another user group-based certain limitation had to be introduced for guest users who cannot view entire texts contained in the database due to copyright issues with the publishers who contributed their intellectual property to the PELCRA corpus.

6.2. General Concordancers

As the basic tools facilitating research in the field of corpus linguistics, concordancers are also the primary functionality provided by the PELCRA Corpus Web Interface. There are two main types of tools which allow the user to generate concordances of words, phrases and discourse events. The *Generic PNC Concordancers* can be used for all the data contained in the corpus and the *Conversational Data Concordancers* have been designed to search conversations transcripts based on a specific model. Both types of concordancers are briefly characterized below.

Word Concordancer

The *Word Concordancer* can be used to search the *word* table for strings matching the query pattern within the boundary of a single word. Because the table contains over 100,000,000 records a search limitation has been temporarily imposed for guest users, whose queries are run over 9000 out of 81000 texts in a single search. However, a maximum of 100 results per search are randomized for each query so as to ensure representative sampling form the entire corpus.

The search setup screen allows users to specify a number of bibliographic criteria and result set display options. The Word Concordancer is generally recommended for middle frequency word searches due to the fact that low frequency forms may be missing from random samples, and very frequent words may be underrepresented. Another potential limitation of this tool is the noticeably slower retrieval of strings containing wildcards.

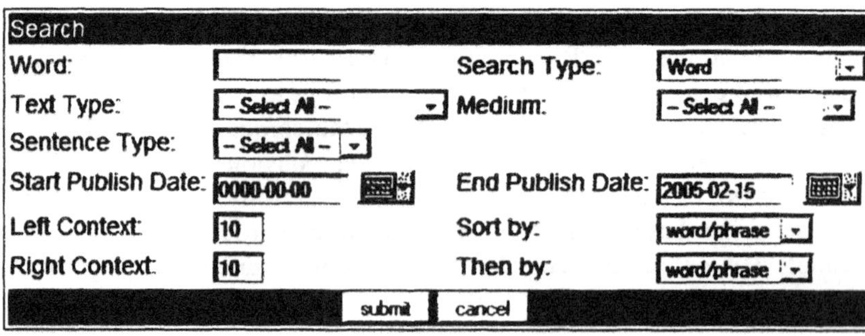

Fig. 2. Word Concordancer

Phrase Concordancer

The general usage of the Phrase Concordancer is to search of strings spanning one or more than one words within the same sentence. Searches are performed on the sentence table (currently some 4,000,000 records) and are generally faster than searches performed on the word table (100,000,000 records). A special version of this concordancer (*Phrase+*) also supports wildcard searches on multiword strings. There are two wildcards which can be used with this tool. The % character stands for any number of word characters, whereas the underscore symbol _ can be used to represent a single word character. The *Phrase Concordancer* is recommended for middle frequency and low single- and multi-word strings.

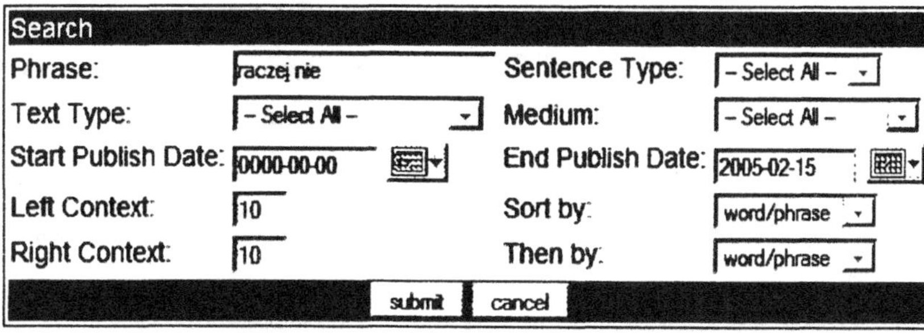

Fig. 3. Phrase Concordancer

The layout for the abovementioned concordancers follows the conventional *KeyWords-In-Context* alignment. Search phrases are centered on the screen with the immediate context aligned on both sides. The results are also linked to a wider context. Guest users can access a three-paragraph context by clicking on the + symbol next to each result. Clicking on the search word opens up a separate window which displays the entire text in which the result occurred. Due to copyright issues, the latter option is not available to guest users. To help users decide which occurrences are potentially relevant to the linguistic phenomenon under investigation, a metadata tooltip pops up when the mouse cursor is moved over the result. The tooltip contains basic bibliographic information about the text in which the search phrase occurred.

Boolean searches with the Sentence and Paragraph Concordancers

The Sentence and Paragraph Concordancers support boolean searches within the context of a single sentence and paragraph respectively. The basic condition in boolean searches is the absence or the presence of a given set of word forms within the same sentence regardless of the order in which these forms occur. The logic of query formulation is fairly intuitive and widely-applied in many non-linguistic search engines. The layout of the search screen does not require the user to know special conjunction or disjunction symbols as they are implemented as form elements:

Fig. 4. Boolean searches with the Sentence and Paragraph Concordancers

6.3. Conversational Data Concordancer

The Conversation Data Concordancer allows the users to run searches against the underlying spoken-conversational data model which is used to store transcribed recordings of natural spoken language. Apart from the basic functionality available for the generic concordancers, in the Conversational Concordancer it is also possible to specify certain socio-linguistic criteria such as the age, the education and the gender of the speaker. Another interesting feature of this tool makes it possible to search for extralinguistic events or intonation patterns annotated in the running text which may have influenced the flow of discourse.

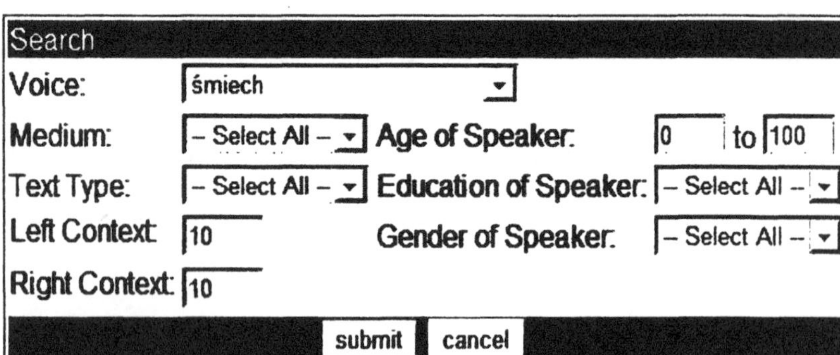

Fig. 5. Conversational Data Concordancer

6.4. Metadata browser

The metadata browser available in the PELCRA Corpus Web interface demonstrates how flexible language data becomes once it is moved to a relational database.

Apart from the standard options of searching for texts using author names or title strings as keywords, it also possible to dynamically transform the retrieved documents from the underlying relational format into XML documents. The following is a sample of an XML document representing an entire text which was instantly generated from the PELCRA relational database:

```
- <file>
  - <document>
    - <header>
        <content type="text" charset="ISO-8859-2"/>
        <type type="written" translation="n" medium="periodical" sample="n" topic="unknown"/>
      - <source>
          Gazeta Wyborcza nr 193, z dnia 1994/08/20-1994/08/21, str. 12
        </source>
        <pub_date>1994-01-01</pub_date>
      - <authors>
        - <author ed="" sex="">
            <first_name>wojciech</first_name>
            <last_name>tochman</last_name>
            <birth_date/>
          </author>
        </authors>
      </header>
    - <body>
      - <p>
          <s type="statement">GDZIE JESTEŚ, KAPITANIE</s>
        </p>
      - <p>
        - <s type="question">
            Kim naprawdę był Jan Żbik, oficer MO, superman epok Gomułki i Gierka, bohater masowej wyobraźni?
          </s>
        - <s type="statement">
```

Fig. 6. Example of an XML document representing an entire text which was dynamically generated from the database

The metadata browser also gives the user the option of compiling batch selections of XML-formatted documents and downloading them in a single file for the purposes of desktop processing.

6.5. Statistical analysis and further computational linguistics features

The core functionality of the PELCRA Web Interface briefly discussed above presents only a few of a whole array of possible computational linguistics applications that can be made available to the wide public through the relational database technology. Having designed a dependable database model the PELCRA team now concentrates on implementing more sophisticated features such as keyness-based text analysis or tools for detecting significant word collocations. Some of those features are already imbedded in the concordance result screens. The following is a comparison of a basic frequency word listing (left pane) and a list of Dunning's log-likelihood keywords (right pane) which can be dynamically generated for each text contained in the database. The keyness list gives the linguist a better insight into the terminology of a given text because it only contains words which are "unexpectedly" frequent in a given text (Oakes 1998):

#	Word Token	Frequency	#	Word Token	Keyness
1	w	61	1	Żydów	377.670282
2	Nie	55	2	listach	194.197670
3	się	52	3	ilu	109.712172
4	że	42	4	swoimi	103.210786
5	z	41	5	Żydzi	101.182256
6	o	40	6	je	72.893890
7	Żydów	40	7	Kilku	71.040959
8	i	28	8	posądzając	68.466320
9	DO	24	9	on	64.316056
10	on	18	10	tych	61.368557

Fig. 7. Keyness list in the PELCRA Web Interface

Such special database views are created dynamically from the generic tables and they illustrate the extensibility of the core relational model adopted for the online version of the PELCRA corpus.

7. Summary

The PELCRA Corpus presentation tier described above was written in the PHP scripting language. However, thanks to the great flexibility and programmatic accessibility of the RDB technology, it would be perfectly possible to ensure the same functionality in most other Web development technologies which provide MySQL interface modules.

The PELCRA Corpus is a referential corpus of Polish, mirroring in size and structure the BNC, which provides vast resources for academic and technological research as well as practical applications. As the next logical step in its development, a part of it is intended to be combined with a part of the BNC to create a Polish-English comparable corpus comprising texts from similar genres and registers in equal proportions. The corpus will be implemented using the RDB technology described above.

One of the major educational achievements of the PELCRA project is the development of a distance-learning MA program in co-operation with the Department of Linguistics and Modern English Language of the Lancaster University. The program called COBAL provides an MA level education in Computer-based English Language Studies with a strong emphasis on corpus tools and applications of corpora. Moreover, the PELCRA project has already resulted in five international conferences on Practical Applications in Language and Corpora/Computers (PALC) and numerous publications written using the PELCRA corpus resources (see PELCRA website for details).

BIBLIOGRAPHY

Burnard, Lou (2000). *Reference Guide for the British National Corpus (World Edition)*. Oxford University Computing Services.

Garside, R., G. Leech and T. McEnery (1997). *Corpus Annotation – Linguistic Information from Computer Text Corpora*. Longman, London & New York.

Leech, G. (1992) "Corpora and theories of linguistic performance". In: Svartvik, J. (ed.). *Directions in Corpus Linguistics. (Proceedings of Nobel Symposium 82, Stockholm, 4–8 August 1991)*. Berlin: Mouton de Gruyter.

Leech, G. (1993). *Corpus annotation schemes*. Literary and Linguistic Computing.

Leech, G. (1997). "Introducing corpus annotation". In: Garside, R., G. Leech and T. McEnery (eds). *Corpus Annotation – Linguistic Information from Computer Text Corpora*. Longman, London & New York.

Leech, G., P. Rayson and A. Wilson (2001). *Word Frequencies in Written and Spoken English: based on the British National Corpus*. London; New York: Longman.

Lewandowska-Tomaszczyk, B. (2004). "The PELCRA project – state of the art". In: Lewandowska-Tomaszczyk, B. (ed.). *Practical Applications in Language and Computers PALC 2003*. Frankfurt am Main–Berlin–Bern–Bruxelles–New York–Oxford–Wien: Peter Lang.

McEnery, T. and A. Wilson (1996). *Corpus Linguistics*. Edinburgh University Press.

Oakes, M. P. (1998). *Statistics for Corpus Linguistics*. Edinburgh University Press.

Sinclair, J. (1991). *Corpus Concordance Collocation*. Oxford University Press

Uzar, R., P. Pęzik, Levin (2004). "Developing relational databases for corpus linguistics". In: Lewandowska-Tomaszczyk, B. (ed.). *Practical Applications in Language and Computers PALC 2003*. Frankfurt am Main–Berlin–Bern–Bruxelles–New York–Oxford–Wien: Peter Lang.

WEBSITES

PELCRA Project website. Available on the Internet at: http://pelcra.ia.uni.lodz.pl/

PELCRA Corpus website. Available on the Internet at: http://korpus.ia.uni.lodz.pl/

British National Corpus website. Available on the Internet at: http://www.natcorp.ox.ac.uk/

BNC FAQ. Available on the Internet at: http://www.natcorp.ox.ac.uk/what/bncfaq.html

Daniel Janus

Warsaw University

Adam Przepiórkowski

Polish Academy of Sciences

POLIQARP 1.0: Some technical aspects of a linguistic search engine for large corpora

1. Introduction

The aim of this article is to present a new universal search engine for large corpora, Poliqarp,[1] whose first official version (1.0) was released in March 2006 under the terms of a free software licence (GNU GPL).[2] Although the tool was developed within a project aiming at creating the first large publicly available morphosyntactically annotated corpus of Polish, cf. http://korpus.pl/, it is universal in the sense that it uses an externally defined tagset and UTF-8 internal encoding, so it could be used for managing a corpus of any language.

The flexibility of Poliqarp and its rich query language has been discussed elsewhere (Przepiórkowski *et al.* 2004). In this article, we concentrate on some novel features of the current release, i.e., on various aspects of the client-server

---

[1] *Pol*yinterpretation *I*ndexing *Q*uery *a*nd *R*etrieval *P*rocessor.

[2] Poliqarp has been developed within two projects conducted at the Institute of Computer Science, Polish Academy of Sciences, led by by the second author (*The IPI PAN Corpus of Polish* – a national KBN grant, number 7T11C04320, 1 April 2001 – 31 March 2004, and *Automatic extraction of linguistic knowledge from a large corpus of Polish* – a national Ministry of Education and Science grant, number 3T11C00328, 9 March 2005 – 8 September 2007). Currently, the main developer of Poliqarp, responsible for the first official release of the tool, is the first author. The first functional version of Poliqarp, released as a binary executable program in mid-2004, was developed mainly by Zygmunt Krynicki, under the supervision of the second author, with the participation of the first author. Although the current release differs from that early version in many respects, including the general architecture and the user interface, it still contains crucial modules of the first functional version, including the corpus builder described below.

architecture of Poliqarp, as well as on the techniques used for greatly improving the efficiency of the tool.

2. Overview

2.1. From XML to the binary corpus format

The basic source format of the corpus assumed by Poliqarp is the XML Corpus Encoding Standard (XCES; cf. Ide *et al.* 2000). However, this representation needs plenty of disk space and is not efficient for the purposes of concordancing. Therefore, before one can search the corpus, it must be compiled to a space-efficient binary form. This is performed by a utility called *bp* (*b*uild *P*oliqarp representation), included in the distribution.

Of particular note about *bp* is the size of corpora produced by it: typically in the range of 10–12 bytes per text segment.[3] For example the 2nd edition of the IPI PAN Corpus, currently the largest corpus of Polish containing over 250 million morphosyntactically annotated segments, as well as structural information and metadata, corresponds to about 2.7 gigabytes of the binary Poliqarp representation, but as much as 7.3 gigabytes in the source format (with all texts compressed with the gzip utility).

Another feature worth mentioning is the ability of *bp* to retrieve metadata from XML header files. XCES requires that each document in the corpus contain a file named `header.xml` with, *inter alia*, bibliographical information about the source document. However, *bp* does not require this file to be fully XCES-compliant. Instead, it makes it possible to define templates of paths to XML elements for each kind of metadata defined for the corpus. If an element is found to match such a template, its value is retrieved and stored in the binary corpus. For example, the following three templates are among those used in the IPI PAN Corpus:

```
(multi  "styl" "/cesHeader/profileDesc/textClass/h.keywords/keyTerm")
(single "medium" "/cesHeader/profileDesc/textDesc/channel")
(multi  "autor"
```

[3] A *segment* is the basic textual token, defined as a unit of text which has a morphosyntactic tag assigned to it, i.e., roughly, a word, but smaller in some cases. Also punctuation marks are separate segments.

```
"/cesHeader/fileDesc/(sourceDesc/biblFull/)*sourceDesc/biblStruct
/analytic/h.author"
"/cesHeader/fileDesc/(sourceDesc/biblFull/)*sourceDesc/biblStruct
/monogr/h.author")
```

The first template defines the value of the 'styl' (genre) attribute as being the content of the XML element defined by the path '/cesHeader/.../keyTerm'. It is an attribute of type 'multi' because many such keyTerm elements may be present and the values of all of them should be collected into the value of the attribute 'styl'. The second template is similar, but it defines a 'single'-type attribute, i.e., if many XML elements defined by the given path are present, only the contents of the first one is copied to the value of the attribute 'medium'. Finally, the third template illustrates a more complex case, where the information about the author may be given by a number of different paths. In fact, each of the two path specifications in this template corresponds to an infinite number of paths, with any number of the (recursive) 'sourceDesc/biblFull/' subpath sequences.

Unfortunately, *bp* is currently only available for GNU/Linux, because of its heavy use of features that are specific to Linux and the GNU C library. This restriction will hopefully be lifted in future releases.

2.2. The corpus indexer

The *indexer* performs second (optional) stage of corpus building. Given a binary corpus constructed by *bp*, it generates sparse inverted indexes that are used to speed up execution of queries. For simple queries that yield few results (like searching for a word or a sequence of words), the speed boost achieved can amount to two orders of magnitude (from several minutes down to tenths of second). The details of the usage and the construction of indexes are discussed in section 4.2.

2.3. The user interfaces

Currently, there exist two user interfaces to the corpus presenting search results in the usual KWIC format. Both use the same corpus processing engine and support the same query language. One interface is a standalone cross-platform utility written in Java using the Swing toolkit. (Precompiled

Windows and Linux versions, as well as the source codes, can be downloaded from http://korpus.pl/ or http://poliqarp.sourceforge.net/.)

The other interface consists of a collection of PHP scripts designed to make corpora available for searching over the WWW; it is less feature-rich than the standalone GUI and currently not included in the source distribution, but available at the Web site of the IPI PAN Corpus (cf. http://korpus.pl/).

The GUI supports incremental displaying of search results as they are found, thus it is no longer necessary to wait for the end of searching to browse the results (as was the case with the preliminary version of Poliqarp). Besides being more efficient and stable, it also allows to browse metadata defined for documents containing the results, allows to impose default restrictions on the queries and has an on-line help facility.

3. The client-server architecture

The concordancer is split into two programs: the server (written in portable C) that performs the actual concordancing, and the client whose job is to present the results of searching to the user. Each of the interfaces introduced in the previous section is in fact a client, and they both communicate with the same server using a simple text-based protocol over TCP.

An obvious benefit of this approach is that it clearly draws the line between the logical and interface modules of the system, but it is not the only advantage of this architecture. First, the server supports multiple connections, so it is possible to connect two instances of a client, or even two different clients, to one server and use the clients concurrently, without the unnecessary duplication of system resources. Second, the protocol supports the notion of a session, which can span multiple connections. It is therefore possible to connect to the server only for a short period of time, to issue a query and/or see whether any new results of an already issued query have arrived. This is crucial in the case of Web-based clients, where the HTML-generating scripts must run quickly, or else the user will be distracted.

Furthermore, the entire functionality of corpus processing is contained in a C library with a well-defined interface. It is thus possible to create another library conforming to the same interface and use it with the rest of the system. The new library does not even have to support the same query language, or the same format of corpora.

In the rest of this chapter, we briefly describe the protocol used by the concordancing clients to communicate with the server. The idea is to demonstrate that Poliqarp may be viewed as a collection of reusable components: even if some of them are not feasible in a given application, others might be. For instance, one might imagine a simple J2ME-based client for mobile devices, or an altogether different corpus library that works on raw text instead of corpora in a dedicated format, etc. The protocol plays an important part in the interoperation between the components, and we hope that it will be more widely supported.

The protocol has been designed with simplicity and flexibility in mind. The client opens a two-way reliable communication channel (Poliqarp uses local TCP for this purpose) and sends requests to the server. Each request consists of exactly one line of text, terminated by a newline character.

The server replies to each request instantly, regardless of how long it might take to process it. The length of each message from the server varies depending on what type of request it replies to, but it always can be deduced from the first line the server sends. In addition, the server can also send asynchronous messages that are not instant replies to a request, but are used to notify clients that, for instance, execution of a query has just finished, or a new bunch of results has been found, and so on.

The client commands can be split into two groups: session manipulation commands and corpus manipulation commands. The first group is used to create sessions, remove them and bind or unbind connections to them. Each command in the second group is executed in the context of a session. At any time, a client can disconnect from the server, which does not result in removing its session or cancelling requests that might be executed in its context. In particular, it can reconnect later and access the session data as if it had not disconnected at all.

The corpus manipulation part of the protocol does not make any implicit assumptions about the query language. It is also independent of the internal structure of corpora, assuming only that a corpus consists of a number of documents that: (i) are mutually disjoint; (ii) sum up to the entire corpus (i.e. every segment belongs to exactly one document); and (iii) can have textual or date-type metadata assigned to them.

As of Poliqarp 1.0, the protocol consists of 25 commands, three of which are meta-commands (used to check whether the server is working, to retrieve its version and to terminate the server), three belong to the session manipulation group, and the remaining 19 are used for processing corpora. Due to space constraints, we will not attempt to describe each of these in full detail here,[4] but we will illustrate it with a transcript of the sample dialogue between a client and

[4] The M.Sc. thesis of the first author, currently in preparation (under the supervision of the second author) at the Institute of Informatics, Warsaw University, contains a detailed description.

a server ('-->' indicates messages sent by the client, '<--' marks messages sent by the server):

```
--> MAKE-SESSION user
<-- R OK 0
--> OPEN /usr/share/corpora/samplecorpus
<-- R OK
<-- M OPENED
--> MAKE-QUERY [pos=subst]{5}
<-- R OK
--> RUN-QUERY 100
<-- R OK
--> BUFFER-STATE
<-- R OK 1000 54
<-- M QUERY-DONE 100
--> SET wide-context-width 5
<-- R OK
--> GET-CONTEXT 0
<-- R OK
<-- R  Nie wiem, czy otrzymał
<-- R
<-- R  pan premier list szefów wydziałów
<-- R  w tej sprawie. Czujemy
--> CLOSE
<-- R OK
--> CLOSE-SESSION
<-- R OK
```

Some comments are in order. First of all, the first letter of each message from the server identifies the type of the message: `R` denotes a synchronous message (part of a reply to a request from the client), while `M` stands for an asynchronous message. Second, the `0` sent by the server in response to the `MAKE-QUERY` command is the session identifier which can later be used to reconnect. Third, after making a query, the client is expected to issue a command specifying how many results it wants to receive (cf. the '`RUN-QUERY 100`' above). Fourth, the client may at any point ask about the status of query execution, using the `BUFFER-STATE` command; the first number in the reply to the command denotes the overall capacity of the buffer, while the second indicates the number of results that are currently stored in the buffer (i.e., found so far). After finding the requested 100 results, the server issues an asynchronous message (cf. the 'QUERY-DONE 100' above). Before requesting the results, the client may specify the widths of left and right contexts, measured in segments (cf. 'SET wide-context-width 5'). Finally, the GET-CONTEXT command, followed by the number of the results (counting from 0), may be used to retrieve a query result (here, the five nouns in a row, 'pan premier list szefów wydziałów') together with its left and right context, preceding and following the match respectively.[5]

4. Efficiency

4.1. The binary corpus format

The binary corpus consists of several backends, i.e., collections of files that contain information related to the same aspect of the corpus. The backends use two main on-disk data structures to store data, namely vectors (sequences of fixed-size data, e.g., numbers, stored in a single file) and dictionaries (sequences of variable-size data, e.g., strings, stored in two files: the first contains the actual data, while the second contains a vector of offsets to particular elements, which provides constant-time lookup). These structures are mostly accessed using the underlying operating system facility of file to memory mapping (e.g., mmap() in Unix).

The main corpus backend is a vector of eight-byte long structures, representing segments and consisting of the following fields:

- a flag specifying whether there is a space before the segment;
- an offset into the dictionary of orthographic words;
- an offset into the dictionary of sets of disambiguated interpretations[6], i.e., those marked as correct in the given context;
- an offset into the dictionary of sets of ambiguous interpretations, i.e., those assigned by the morphological analyser, regardless of whether they were marked as correct in later stages of tagging.

---

[5] Actually, the match itself may be split into two parts: left match and right match (see Przepiórkowski 2004 for details). If no such split is requested, the match is returned by the server as the right match, with the left match empty. This explains the line in the sample session above which only contains the single R.

[6] An interpretation is defined as a tag with the base form of a given word.

Each of these dictionaries is kept in its own backend; moreover, there are backends that hold structural information about the documents comprising the corpus (offsets of each structural element's borders), document metadata, tagset, predefined aliases, etc. In total, there are nine or ten backends, depending on whether the *indexer* utility has been invoked on the corpus.

The description of the search algorithm is well outside of the scope of this paper, but it is worth mentioning that the queries are compiled to finite-state automata in which edges are labeled with expressions corresponding to specifications of a single segment. In its simplest form, a compiled expression is a vector of bits, with the meaning of the *n*th bit set being that the *n*th word (or set of interpretations) matches this expression. Thus, matching the segment against a simple expression requires only one bit test, without the need of accessing other backends.

4.2. The use of indexes

For typical corpora, the number of segments in a corpus greatly exceeds the number of *distinct* elements in each of the sequences described above (i.e., the sequence of orthographic words, and both sequences of sets of interpretations). Therefore, it is useful to have a data structure that, for each of those distinct elements, assigns to it a list of its occurrences in the corpus. Such structures are called *inverted indexes*, and are what the *indexer* utility produces.

Each of those three sequences has its own index. By default, *indexer* produces all three indexes, but it is possible to tell it to skip some of them, e.g., to produce only the index of orthographic forms. This is useful, for instance, in the case of a corpus devoid of morphological annotation (i.e., one that has a dummy tag assigned to each segment). In such a case, queries regarding morphological information will not be posed anyway, so the irrelevant indexes may be omitted.

The main problem with inverted indexes is that they can be very large when stored naïvely. Poliqarp overcomes this problem in two ways. First, not every occurrence of each word[7] is stored in the index. Instead, the corpus is artificially split into chunks (pseudo-documents) of equal size (by default, 1024 segments, but this is configurable). Then, for each item, only the numbers of the chunks in which it occurs are stored in the index, regardless of how many times it occurs in each chunk. This allows for compaction of those lists that contain a very large

[7] Or, more generally speaking, each item.

number of elements, while retaining most of the effectiveness gained through the use of indexes.

Second, a mechanism of index compression is employed. The compression schema used provides very fast decompression, while maintaining a reasonable compression ratio. The main idea is to store differences between elements of the lists with varying number of bits per element: thus, the lists corresponding to stop words, containing a very large number of elements, will be coded using few bits per element, while those corresponding to *hapax legomena* will contain many bits per element (but will not occupy much space anyway, thanks to their length).

This technique is known as Golomb encoding. The algorithms used to store and compress the indexes have been adapted (with minor changes to make them fit well with Poliqarp's method of storing corpora) from Witten *et al.* 1999.

Typically, the total size of indexes produced by the *indexer* utility is about 15% of the total binary corpus size, but it varies depending on the corpus structure and the indexes' granularity (i.e., size of the artificial chunks). For instance, in the case of the preliminary version of the IPI PAN corpus (over 70 million segments, 654 megabytes unindexed), the total size of indexes was 95 megabytes when indexed with granularity of 1024 segments, but only 67 megabytes when indexed with granularity of 4096 segments.

5. Concluding remarks

A question may arise as to why we decided to implement our own search engine and concordancer instead of either using the standard relational databases (the viability of such an approach has been demonstrated within the PELCRA Corpus of Polish project, http://korpus.ia.uni.lodz.pl/) or existing corpus management tools, such as the IMS Corpus Workbench (http://www.ims.uni-stuttgart.de/projekte/CorpusWorkbench/).

One reason for this decision is already alluded to in Przepiórkowski *et al.* 2004. Even though Poliqarp was designed as a universal corpus search tool, it also had to meet the specific requirements of the IPI PAN Corpus of Polish, esp., its handling of ambiguities and the fact that it contains much richer morphosyntactic information than other corpora that we were familiar with. In particular, we needed a tool that would make it possible to represent and query two layers of morphosyntactic information: all (possibly many-way ambiguous) information provided by the morphological analyser, or only the morphosyntactic information judged contextually correct by the tagger (but possibly still ambiguous, as some ambiguities cannot be resolved even on the basis of infinite context). To the best of our knowledge no tool offering such expressive power was available at the time, and an attempt at confining this complex hierarchical information into the straight-jacket of relational databases struck us as unmaintainable.

Even if such an attempt had succeeded, it would be still very hard to map Poliqarp's query language to the equivalent SQL queries. The high-level regular expression feature of Poliqarp's query language would make the corresponding SQL queries unnecessarily complex and hard for the optimizers to cope with. Apart from that, the standalone installation of a corpus on a user's workstation for local usage would be painful and very disk-consuming – Poliqarp makes it easy (to the best of our knowledge, this is a unique feature among programs that deal with corpora of this size).

Another reason for this approach was our need for a corpus search tool that would grow with the annotation layers of the IPI PAN Corpus. At the time no such open source tool that would make IPI PAN Corpus-specific modifications possible was available.[8] This need becomes important now, as the IPI PAN Corpus enters the syntactic annotation phase.

REFERENCES

Ide, N., Bonhomme, P. and L. Romary (2000). "XCES: An XML-based standard for linguistic corpora." *Proceedings of the Second International Conference on Language Resources and Evaluation, LREC 2000*. Athens: ELRA: 825–830.

Janus, D. (2006). *Metody przeszukiwania i obrazowania jego wyników w dużych korpusach tekstów*. M.Sc. thesis (in preparation). Warsaw: Faculty of Mathematics, Informatics and Mechanics, Warsaw University.

Przepiórkowski, A. (2004). *The IPI PAN Corpus: Preliminary version*. Warsaw: Instytut Podstaw Informatyki PAN.

Przepiórkowski, A., Krynicki, Z., Dębowski, Ł., Woliński, M., Janus, D. and P. Bański (2004). "A search tool for corpora with positional tagsets and ambiguities." *Proceedings of the Fourth International Conference on Language Resources and Evaluation, LREC 2004*. Lisbon: ELRA: 1235–1238.

Witten, I. H., Moffat, A. and T. C. Bell (1999). *Managing gigabytes: compressing and indexing documents and images*. San Francisco: Morgan Kaufmann Publishers Inc.

---

[8] In the meantime, the tool used by BNC, Xaira, has been released as open source (cf. http://xaira.sourceforge.net/), and we have been informed that there are also plans to make the sources of the IMS Corpus Workbench available.

Jakub Fast

University of Warsaw and Collegium Invisibile

Adam Przepiórkowski

Polish Academy of Sciences

AUTOMATIC EXTRACTION OF POLISH VERB SUBCATEGORIZATION
An Evaluation of Common Statistics

1. Introduction

Valence dictionaries are crucial resources in Natural Language Processing, and yet, for many languages, such resources are unavailable or they are available in paper form only. Early 1990s saw the advent of the use of corpora and statistical methods for the automatic learning of valence information, but it has been noted in the literature (cf., e.g., Korhonen 2002) that some of the commonly used statistics are less appropriate for the task at hand.

The aim of this paper is to evaluate such common statistics, as applied to very noisy data: in the experiments reported below, linguistic cues are identified by a simple and error-prone shallow grammar on the basis of a corpus automatically annotated with the help of a preliminary version of a morphological analyzer and a statistical disambiguator with a rather high 9.4% error rate (Dębowski 2004).

The rest of the paper is structured as follows. §2 briefly describes the linguistic input to the statistical module, while the next section, §3, introduces the statistics employed in the experiments. The following section, §4, describes the setup of the experiments. Finally, §5 discusses the results, while §6 compares them to the results of similar experiments reported in the literature.

2. Linguistic Data

The textual material for the experiments reported in this paper is the IPI PAN Corpus of Polish (Przepiórkowski 2004), the first and currently the only large, publicly available, morphosyntactically annotated corpus of Polish (cf. `www.korpus.pl`). Since the corpus is rather large (over 300 million segments), its 15-million segment (over 12 million orthographic words; punctuation marks and, in some special cases, clitic-like elements are treated as separate segments) subcorpus, `sample`, was used in the experiments. The corpus does not contain any constituent annotation apart from sentence boundary markers, but it employs a detailed positional tagset providing information about parts of speech, as well as values of inflectional and morphosyntactic categories (Przepiórkowski and Woliński 2003).

The process of collecting valence cues consists of four steps. First, a simple shallow grammar is applied to the XML corpus sources, resulting in the identification of some NPs, PPs and verbs. Second, each sentence is split into clauses, on the basis of those punctuation marks and conjunctions which are not constituents of NPs and PPs.

Third, for each clause containing exactly one verb, V, all NPs and PPs identified in this clause are collected into an observed frame F, and the pair $\langle V, F\rangle$ is added to the set of observations. Finally, all observations are collected into hypotheses represented by tuples $\langle\langle V, F\rangle, n, f, k\rangle$, where $\langle V, F\rangle$ is a verb/frame combination, n is the number of the verb's occurrences in the cue set, f is the total number of the occurrences of the frame, and k is the number of clauses in which they cooccur.

A simple cascade of regular grammars with some added unification-like functionality is used for the shallow parsing of the input and for handling NP- and PP-internal agreement. The whole grammar consists of 18 rules and, consequently, the range of phrases identified by the grammar is very limited: numeral phrases, adjectival phrases, adverbial phrases, clauses and infinitival verbal phrases are excluded from consideration here, i.e., the task at hand is constrained to the identification of possible NP and PP arguments. Two important simplifications in the grammar concern the treatment of nominative and genitive NPs: the former are ignored altogether, i.e., no attempt at distinguishing subject-taking verbs and subjectless verbs is made, while the latter are attached to the immediately preceding NPs and PPs whenever possible, rather than always being treated as potential arguments of verbs.

3. Statistics

Once all the hypotheses are collected, they are rated depending on the dependability of the evidence they provide for inferring that a given frame is valid for a given verb. Two classes of statistics were used for evaluating the strength of the hypotheses: the first class, discussed in §3.2, is composed of metrics which exclude certain hypotheses due to an insufficient verb/frame cooccurrence count given the number of verb's occurrences attested in the cue set; and the second class (§3.3) judges a given frame as likely to be valid for a given verb, if the verb's statistical association with the frame is higher than average for all other verbs in the cue set.

3.1. Probabilistic Model

The statistics presented below share a common probabilistic model. The probability of a frame F occurring given a verb V is taken to be Bernoulli-distributed, i.e., the event-space is defined as that of a single weighted coin toss, where success is defined as an occurrence of F, and failure as the occurrence of some other frame. This model is represented by a random variable $X_1 \sim \mathrm{Be}(\pi_1)$, where π_1 is the theoretical, conditional probability of F occurring in a clause that contains V. A complementary random variable $X_2 \sim \mathrm{Be}(\pi_2)$ will also be taken into consideration in the model, representing the probability of F occurring given some verb other than V.

On the basis of this model, and given a number C equal to the total number of clauses in the cue set, a hypothesis of the form $\langle\langle V, F\rangle, n_1, f, k_1\rangle$ is interpreted as describing two samples m_1 and m_2 taken from X_1 and X_2, respectively. m_1's size is taken to correspond to the number of V's occurrences, n_1, and the number of positive outcomes in m_1 is the number of F's occurrences with V, i.e., k_1. The size of m_2 is equal to the total number of clauses that do not contain V ($n_2 = C - n_1$), and the number of successes corresponds to the number of F's occurrences with verbs other than V ($k_2 = f - k_1$).

The elements of each sample are assumed to be independent. For i random variables $Y_1, Y_2, \ldots, Y_i$ with an identical distribution $\mathrm{Be}(\pi)$, the sum $Y = \sum_{j=1}^{i} Y_j$ (i.e., a random variable representing the total number of successes in a sample drawn from those i variables) has a binomial distribution $\mathrm{Bin}(i, \pi)$. Thus, the probability of F occurring k_1 times given n_1 occurrences of V is represented by the random variable $M_1 \sim \mathrm{Bin}(n_1, \pi_1)$, and the probability of F occurring k_2 times given n_2 occurrences of some other verb is represented by the random variable

$M_2 \sim \text{Bin}(n_2, \pi_2)$. Everywhere in this text, π_1 and π_2 are estimated on the basis of m_1 and m_2 as, respectively, $\hat{\pi}_1 = p_1 = \frac{k_1}{n_1}$ and $\hat{\pi}_2 = p_2 = \frac{k_2}{n_2}$.

3.2. Minimum Significant Count Statistics

Minimum Significant Count (MSC) statistics rate a given hypothesis on the basis of the numeric relation between k_1 and n_1, assigning every k_1, n_1 some measure of how likely it is for k_1 occurrences of F to have been observed in n_1 trials because of noise.

The general form of an MSC is $S = \phi\ (k_1, n_1)$ where ϕ is any function monotonically increasing with k_1 for a set n_1. A given F is considered a valid frame for V if S exceeds a certain critical value c, below which the evaluated cooccurrence count is deemed accidental.

3.2.1. Binomial Miscue Probability

For a certain independently established probability BF that a frame F occurs with a verb V even though it is not a valid frame for this verb, the Binomial Miscue Probability (BMP) is the probability of k_1 or more occurrences of F in n_1 trials being produced by a 'noise-generating' random variable $Z \sim \text{Bin}(n_1, BF)$. BMP was first introduced in (Brent, 1993).[1] The formula for BMP is the following:

$$\text{BMP}_{BF}(k_1, n_1) = 1 - \Phi_Z(k_1) \tag{1}$$

where Φ_Z is the distribution function for Z. Note that in the case of the formula above, the smaller the value of BMP, the more likely it is for F to be a valid frame for V.

3.2.2. Baseline: Relative Frame Frequency

The baseline MSC consists simply of taking the relative frame frequency for a given verb ($p_1 = k_1 / n_1$), and rejecting those verb/frame combinations, for which the resultant value is lower than some threshold.[2]

[1] BMP is also referred to as the Binomial Hypothesis Test.

[2] In the literature on valence extraction, this particular statistic is referred to as the Maximum Likelihood Estimate (of π_1).

3.3. Strength of Association Statistics

The Strength of Association (SOA) statistics are based, roughly, on comparing the conditional and unconditional distributions of a given frame by assessing the significance of the difference between p_1 and p_2. The expectation is that if p_1 is significantly lower than p_2, i.e., F occurs with V much less often than it does otherwise, F should be classified as an invalid frame for V.

3.3.1. Likelihood Ratio

The Likelihood Ratio LR statistic is based on comparing the probability that m_1 and m_2 were generated by the best among the models stipulating that $\pi_1 = \pi_2$ and the best one among those that do not need to satisfy this condition. Given that the best fit for the latter model is given by a joint distribution of M_1 and M_2, for $B_{n,p} \sim Bin(n, p)$, a value λ is calculated with the following formula:

$$\lambda = \frac{\max_p P(B_{n_1,p} = k_1, B_{n_{21},p} = k_2)}{P(M_1 = k_1, M_2 = k_2)} \quad (2)$$

where the maximal value of p equals $\frac{k_1 + k_2}{n_1 + n_2}$ and the relevant probabilities are calculated straightforwardly from the aproppriate probability density functions for the binomial distribution. Low values of lambda imply that the two models are distinct, i.e., the values of π_1 and π_2 differ significantly. An assymetrical LR statistic is given by

$$LR_{\pm} = -2 \log \lambda \times b \quad (3)$$

where $b = -1$ if $p_1 - p_2 < 0$ and 1 otherwise. The resultant statistic has a distribution related to $\chi^2_{df=1}$, and b is introduced in order to distinguish between V strongly favoring F and strongly disfavoring it. If the value of LR is lower than a certain critical value, F occurs with V significantly less than with other verbs, and should be classified as an invalid frame for V.

3.3.2. *t* Test

The *t* test measures the significance of the difference between the means of two independent samples. The formula for *t* is the following:

$$t = \frac{p_1 - p_2}{\sqrt{\frac{s_1^2}{n_1} + \frac{s_2^2}{n_2}}} \tag{4}$$

where s_i^2 is the estimate of the variance of X_i, calculated as $p_i(1 - p_i)$. Like with LR, low values of t mean that p_1 is significantly lower than p_2, and therefore F is not a valid frame for V. The distribution of t is $N(0, 1)$.

3.3.3. Baseline: Probability Ratio and Difference of Probabilty

The two statistics above were matched against two trivial measures of the difference between p_1 and p_2: p_1/p_2 and $p_1 - p_2$. In both these cases, the expectation was that the lower the value of such statistic, the less likely it is for F to be a valid frame for V.

4. Experiments

The performance of the statistics was evaluated in four experiments, the results of which are presented in Table 1. First, the shallow parsing mechanism described in §2 was applied to four distinct cue sets: one consisting of hypotheses containing all attested $\langle V, F\rangle$ combinations (ALL), and three cue sets containing only hypotheses concerning frames within a given frame frequency range: high (HF, with $f \approx 0.01 \times C$), average (MF, $0.001 \times C \leq f < 0.01 \times C$), and low (LF, $f < 0.001 \times C$). The values for all six statistics were then calculated for the four cue sets and matched against a baseline treatment consisting in considering all the frames seen with a given verb as valid.

The gold standard adopted for the purpose of evaluating the results of these experiments was Marek Świdziński's machine readable valence dictionary (Świdziński, 1998) containing 1492 entries.[3] This dictionary was processed by conflating multiple entries with the same lemma to single entries, which reduced the dictionary to 1369 entries, by translating the original sometimes complex notation, which allowed for optionality and disjunction, into sequences of atomic valence frames, and by removing all frames containing specifications different than NPs and PPs. From the resulting dictionary, 100 frequent verbs (each occurring at least 100 times in the cue set) evenly distributed across the scale of the number of

[3] The authors are grateful to Prof. Świdziński for making this dictionary available to them.

occurrences were blindly selected as the training set (see below), and other 100 verbs, not necessarily frequent, were selected the same way as the evaluation set. The evaluation set was then tailored to each specific cue set by removing frames which do not fall within the particular frame frequency category, therefore the recall values for HF, MF, and LF are calculated in relation to a standard containing only high, average, and low frequency frames, respectively.

The critical (cutoff) values for each statistic were established experimentally. For each cue set and each statistic, an exhaustive search was performed through all relevant critical values, and the one that resulted in the highest F-measure for the training set was chosen for the experiments.[4]

Table 1. Precision, recall, and F-measure for the four experiments. Boxes indicate the best-performing statistic in each of the cue sets

		ALL	HF	MF	LF
BMP	P	49.29	66.43	38.46	15.00
	R	47.76	59.01	39.22	17.65
	F	**48.52**	**62.50**	**38.83**	**16.22**
p_1	P	39.72	47.10	27.45	10.71
	R	50.52	75.78	41.18	17.65
	F	**44.48**	**58.10**	**32.94**	**13.33**
t	P	55.03	66.41	37.14	25.00
	R	31.96	52.80	38.24	35.29
	F	**40.43**	**58.82**	**37.68**	**29.27**
LR	P	50.71	47.11	41.67	30.00
	R	24.40	65.84	34.31	35.29
	F	**32.95**	**54.93**	**37.63**	**32.43**
$p_1 - p_2$	P	32.09	49.08	25.77	10.71
	R	47.42	66.46	41.18	17.65
	F	**38.28**	**56.46**	**31.70**	**13.33**
p_1 / p_2	P	4.86	36.93	24.39	1.88
	R	70.79	70.19	39.22	41.18
	F	**9.08**	**48.39**	**30.08**	**3.60**
BASELINE	P	4.89	20.30	9.47	1.80
	R	77.32	91.93	67.65	47.06
	F	**9.20**	**33.26**	**16.61**	**3.46**

[4] Note that the fact that critical values were trained for each category separately is the reason why for some statistics, the overall F-measure might be larger than that for some other statistic, while the F-values for the three cue subsets are all lower. This means that the statistic 'adapts' better to the smaller categories, while giving a worse fit for the complete dataset.

5. Discussion

Our initial theoretical prediction, in line with (Korhonen 2002), was that the SOA statistics should perform visibly worse than the MSC measures. The reason for this is that even though used considerably in the literature, they seem not to test for the right thing: deciding whether F is a valid frame for V should not, in principle, be based on how often it occurs with V in comparison to other verbs, as in this way, frames which are very rare for V, but otherwise common, would always be flagged as invalid. The principal source of error is the parsing procedure, when an actual frame observed in the corpus is classified as some other, possibly invalid frame. The rate of such misclassification should, however, be proportional to the number of classified clauses, and there seems to be no apparent relation between such error and the relation between frame frequencies in two conditional distributions. In this vein, the SOA statistics should be seen as operating on the level of some rough approximation of the actual error, most probably dependent, but definitely not directly conditioned by the true error variable.

These predictions were confirmed by BMP performing the best in three out of four categories, and p_1 performing surprisingly well in the mid- to high-frequency range despite its simplicity. The most serious discrepancy in this pattern, that is t and LR performing significantly better on the LF cue set, supports an unconfirmed suspicion expressed in (Korhonen *et al.* 2000) that these statistics should be particularly applicable to low-frequency data.

A surprising set of results is provided by the performance of the two baseline SOA statistics. p_1/p_2 performs worse than even the baseline, while $p_1 - p_2$ does astonishingly well. The probable reason for the former is that p_1/p_2 is extremely sensitive to low-frequency verbs – the less frequent frames occurring with such verbs yield very high values of p_1/p_2, thus significantly upsetting the desired ordering, where valid frames are ranked higher than invalid ones. The reason for $p_1 - p_2$ performing this well, on the other hand, is that the less frequent the frames it is applied to, the more it generally approximates p_1, and the conditional frequency comparison effect is diminished; the value of p_1 is usually much larger than that of p_2, and the difference is even more significant for rare (and in particular spurious) frames.

6. Comparison

Similar comparisons of common statistics for subcategorization acquisition can be found in the literature. (Lapata 1999) mentions in passing that BMP, with the BF (cf. §3.2.1) established separately for each frame on the basis of the information contained in the COMLEX subcategorization dictionary (Grishman *et al.* 1994), gives results comparable to, but slightly worse than, p_1[5] (Sarkar and Zeman 2000; Zeman and Sarkar 2000) compare BMP, t and LR and report identical results for t and LR, with BMP giving worse recall and better precision and F-measure, but it is not clear how reliable these results are, given various errors in the formulae for t and LR,[6] and given the unexplained discrepancy between the recall numbers reported in the two papers.

Finally, in a series of papers (see (Korhonen 2002) and references therein), Korhonen carefully compares BMP, LR and p_1, using an estimate of BF proposed by (Briscoe and Carroll 1997), i.e., an estimate based to some extent on the unconditional probabilities of frames. This means that her version of BMP is not a pure MSC statistic in the sense of §3.2, but should rather be classified as a SOA statistic, cf. §3.3. Korhonen notes that, of the three statistics that she compares, p_1 performs better than BMP and much better than LR, with the respective F-measures being 65.2, 53.3 and 45.1. In case of high frequency frames (above 0.01 relative frequency), p_1 results in a number of false positives similar to BMP and LR, but a much smaller number of false negatives, which implies a much higher recall. On the other hand, in case of lower frequency frames, BMP and LR show a much higher number of false positives than in the case of p_1. Similarly to the thesis of the current paper, (Korhonen *et al.* 2000) explain both differences by noticing that BMP and LR, but not p_1, refer not only to frame frequencies for a given verb, but also to estimates of unconditional frame probability.

REFERENCES

Brent, M. R. (1993). "From grammar to lexicon: Unsupervised learning of lexical syntax". *Computational Linguistics*, 19(2): 243–262.

Briscoe, T. and J. Carroll (1997). "Automatic extraction of subcategorization from corpora". *Proceedings of the 5th ACL Conference on Applied Natural Language Processing.*

---

[5] While BMP performs better than p_1 in the experiments reported here, with different sets of verbs for training and for the evaluation (cf. §4), the F-measure for p_1 is higher than that for BMP if the same set is used for both tasks.

[6] In both papers, their formula for LR mentions $L(p, k_1, n_2)$ instead of $L(p, k_1, n_1)$, while their formula for t assumes a wrong formula for variance and lacks normalization in the denominator. Interestingly, these errors are also present in (Maragoudakis *et al.* 2000) and – the former – in (Sarkar and Tripasai 2002). Moreover, the authors make no mention of distinguishing between likelihood ratios generated with positive and negative values of $p_1 - p_2$.

Dębowski, Ł. (2004). "Trigram morphosyntactic tagger for Polish". In: Kłopotek, M., Wierzchoń, S. T. and K. Trojanowski (eds). *Intelligent Information Processing and Web Mining, Advances in Soft Computing*. Berlin: Springer-Verlag: 409–413.

Grishman, R., Macleod, C. and A. Meyers (1994). "Comlex syntax: Building a computational lexicon". *Proceedings of COLING '94*.

Korhonen, A. (2002). *Subcategorization Acquisition*. Ph. D. dissertation, University of Cambridge.

Korhonen, A., Gorrell, G. and D. McCarthy (2000). "Statistical filtering and subcategorization frame acquisition". *Proceedings of SIGDAT 2000*.

Lapata, M. (1999). "Acquiring lexical generalizations from corpora: A case study for diathesis alternations". *Proceedings of the 37th Meeting of the North American Chapter of the Association of Computational Linguistics*.

Maragoudakis, M., Kermanidis, K. and G. Kokkinakis (2000). "Learning subcategorization frames from corpora: A case study for Modern Greek". *Proceedings of COMLEX 2000, Workshop on Computational Lexicography and Multimedia Dictionaries*.

Przepiórkowski, A. (2004). *The IPI PAN Corpus: Preliminary version*. Warsaw: Institute of Computer Science, Polish Academy of Sciences.

Przepiórkowski, A. and M. Woliński (2003). "The unbearable lightness of tagging: A case study in morphosyntactic tagging of Polish". *Proceedings LINC-03, EACL 2003*.

Sarkar, A. and W. Tripasai (2002). "Learning verb argument structure from minimally annotated corpora". *Proceedings of COLING 2002*.

Sarkar, A. and D. Zeman (2000). "Automatic extraction of subcategorization frames for Czech". *Proceedings of COLING 2000*.

Świdziński, M. (1998). *Syntactic dictionary of Polish verbs*. Ms., Version 3a, University of Warsaw.

Zeman, D. and A. Sarkar (2000). "Learning verb subcategorization from corpora: Counting frame subsets". *Proceedings of LREC 2000*.

Sylvana Krausse
University of Applied Sciences Nordhausen

FINDINGS FROM A CORPUS-INFORMED STUDY OF ENVIRONMENTAL ENGINEERING ENGLISH

1. Introduction

The research preceding this paper aims at describing and documenting the domain-specific language variety of Environmental Engineering English (EEE for short) in order to make reliable language data available for syllabus design of ESP courses at university level. This kind of research is necessary in the light of the situation in which ESP teachers repeatedly find themselves: their study provides them with a General English language competence and a pedagogical and methodological grounding – but once in the concrete teaching context – they face the problem of having to become all of a sudden a specialist in a particular ESP-variety (like in my case EEE). Usually a long process, the time to acquire this specialist language knowledge in a particular domain can be shortened by making intensive use of a suitable specialist corpus.

For the present paper, a small specialist corpus of texts concerning the branch of Environmental Engineering was used to analyse, describe and document a domain-specific language on the lexico-semantic and the morphological level. The currency of extended units of meaning as well as information on word-formation patterns were investigated in order to provide linguistic data as a basis for material and syllabus design to give language lecturers a firm grounding on which they can base their teaching. Furthermore, my research aims at providing a methodology language teachers of other ESP-varieties can replicate, as the findings and procedures will not be restricted to EEE. I claim that this is an important and necessary point as the long way of learning a new ESP-variety, namely by teaching it for a longer time, is – at least in the German context – the norm.

2. The context of study

Certainly, an initial obstacle to overcome is putting together a small specialist corpus. As a starting point the language lecturer needs to rely on expert information on what topics the particular branch of science deals with and which text types are usually encountered. Finding suitable texts on the internet should then be no problem.

As I have described the corpus design and analysis planning of my research elsewhere (Krausse 2005a), it will be suffice here to mention that the basis for research – the corpus (called ENGICOR) – consists of two million running words of EEE on topics like soil and wastewater remediation, mine reclamation and waste treatment and recycling in text types like reports, technology fact sheets, parts of a textbook and web journals.

The starting point was the determination of the objects of study by means of a keyword analysis of ENGICOR and the BNC from which the first 500 words were chosen for a detailed analysis of their collocational and WF patterns (word--formation). On the basis of concordancing the resulting 500 keywords, a usage profile of each word was established which displays all information brought to light by corpus analysis. These usage profiles in the form of simple tables include all information that can be extracted from the concordances like collocational and colligational information, information on semantic preference and semantic prosody as well as information on detected WF patterns but without the irrelevant information in the concordances usually included (for a more detailed illustration of the usage profiling see Krausse 2005b).

3. Usage Profiles

The work on the content of the usage profiles is based on Sinclair's tenet that phraseology and its textual realisations in the form of collocations are "due to become central in the description of English for Specific Purposes" (1996: 83). Conventional textbooks and dictionaries cannot fulfil the task of providing such specific teaching and reference material for the use in ESP courses that are to prepare students to be able to act in professional situations. Calls for the necessity to create "microgrammars and micro-glossaries of restricted languages with suitable texts" go as far back as Firth (in Palmer (ed.) 1968: 106). The usage profiles are the concrete realisations of these claims providing information on Sinclair's extended units of meaning (cf. 1996) where linguistic data on the level of lexical choices in the form of collocations is made visible, as well as the level of syntactic choices in the form of colligations. Moreover, there is the level of semantic choices which reveals what semantic fields the investigated language item prefers and the level of pragmatic choices, the semantic prosody, which indicates whether the item can functionally be interpreted as adding a positive, negative or neutral semantic prosody to it.

The following diagram shows the format of data collection and illustration in short. The head entry shows the investigated keyword, *exposure* in this case, together with its number of occurrences in the corpus, its part of speech and rank in the keyword list (comparing ENGICOR with the BNC). The columns N-1 and N+1 display the node word occurring in two-word collocations, the clusters section collects all longer structures. Here is also the place where – besides further collocational information – colligational information can be found (*exposure to a contaminant*). From the column N-1 we can furthermore infer information on semantic preference of the language item: *exposure* collocates with words in the Node-1 position which designate environmental factors like (*sun-)light*, *radiation* or a *contaminant*. These environmental factors mainly have a negative notion about them, a characteristic described by the phenomenon of semantic prosody. The co-occurrence of *exposure* together with the verb *prevent* further illustrates its negative semantic prosody.

The lower part of the usage profile is reserved to keep corpus-attested WF patterns for further use in the morphological investigations which will be described later on.

In this format the information can be used as an inventory of corpus-based data which can be relied on when choosing language items which should be included in the syllabus design. Language lecturers can concentrate on the relevant language items when designing teaching and learning material as well as setting communicative tasks and exercises in the actual courses. And last but not least, it can serve as reference material for lecturers and students. The usage profiles can for instance serve as a starting point of re-contextualisation exercises where students can go back to the corpus to locate typical sample sentences including structures from the usage profiles. Putting detached linguistic information into its context of situation again is a task which Heringer, who uses similar techniques, calls "putting flesh back on the bones" (1999: 140). It can further associative thinking and secures sustainable learning results. All efforts spent on the syllabus and the material design based on corpus information in the form of usage profiles aims at presenting the ESP students only with the most relevant language material and ensures a good balance between their learning efforts and learning outcomes with view to their future professions.

exposure (488x in corpus) noun rank 519 in keyword list	
N-1	N+1
contaminant ~(s) (8)	~ assessment (7)
inhalation ~ (8)	~ level(s) (5)
light ~ (6)	~ pathways (13)
radiation ~ (5)	~ period(s) (7)
sunlight ~ (6)	~ route(s) (7)
UV ~ (13)	~ time (14)
chemical ~(s) (6)	
chronic ~(s) (5)	
human ~(s) (19)	
prolonged ~ (7)	
prevent ~ (5)	
clusters	
risk of ~ (6)	
route(s) of ~ (7)	
permissible ~ limits (6) (PELs)	
potential ~ pathways (6)	
long(-)term ~ (5)	
UV ~ time (10)	
1/2/3/5/10/... minute(s) UV ~ time (12)	
~ to (145) (air and water/(airborne) contaminants/benzene/carcinogens/chemicals/dust/gamma radiation/high temperatures/humans/light/TCE/contaminated groundwater/microbes/the public/the weather/UV/...)	

corpus-attested WF patterns	
derivational	compounding
re-~ (1)	over~ (1)

Fig. 1

Whereas the above-mentioned previous papers on my research concentrated in more detail on the corpus and analysis design as well as on the lexical side as just briefly touched on in the description of the usage profiles; this paper will give more detailed information on some interesting findings in the field of WF patters.

4. Corpus-attested WF patterns

Looking at EEE specific WF patterns will verify whether Caso's claim that an "explosion of scientific knowledge is having a considerable linguistic effect as the need to communicate new concepts forces the devising of new terms"

(1980: 101) holds true for this specialist language as well. EEE as a relatively new and innovative field of knowledge expansion will be examined for WF patterns that reflect certain trends of language. In this paragraph I will summarize some noticeable findings from my PhD-research in progress.

While language learners have to deal with collocations unanalysed in the chunks they are, at least productive WF patterns should be the subject of reflection in the language learning process in order to be able to keep up with language change and facilitate the understanding of newly encountered words. Both again, collocations and all other WF products have in common that they gain easier access to the minds of students the more often they are encountered in language use.

Students might attribute the fact that they encounter new words to the fact that they are language learners but they need to be made aware of the notion that language is dynamic and new words are produced while old ones fall out of use. In addition to understanding the meaning of lexical items in their context, as discussed in the previous chapter, their understanding of morphological information is another vital key to making sense of learned language. Once they are familiar with certain base words, derived forms will be easier to grasp. They need to know which word-formation processes are active and how the resulting new language items differ from the bases in terms of a different lexical meaning and added syntactic information, as produced by the addition of affixes.

To this end, I investigated the products of the following WF processes with the corpus as foremost informant.

Every WF pattern found in the corpus was looked at in the light of the following basic questions:

1) What elements join or are involved in the WF process?
2) What are the results of the process in terms of form and meaning(s)?

The parameter which was used to put the categories in the order they are dealt with is the question of whether there has been a combination or an omission of word material. This is how I arrived at the order of the following categories whose most noticeable findings will be discussed in the following paragraphs:

+ Combination: compounding processes
combining processes
derivational processes

+ Omission:	abbreviations clippings backformation
+ Combination/ + Omission:	blends
– Combination/ – Omission:	conversion
Others:	word manufacture loan words

It has to be mentioned that only compounding, combining and derivational processes can be detected by the help of concordancing. But intensive work with the corpus over time yielded enough findings by chance to illustrate the remaining processes.

4.1. + Combination

4.1.1. Compounding processes

Compounds are complex lexical items "consisting of more than one base and functioning both grammatically and semantically as a single word" (Quirk 1985: 1567). They contribute a great deal to the extension of the lexicon in general English as well as to domain-specific language.

Discussing their function in a specialist language, Sager (1997: 30) remarks: "Functionally, (derivation and) compounding serve the purpose of closer determination of a concept – narrowing its intension – while at the same time showing the relation that exists between the new concept and its origin." Especially in such a very specialised branch of Engineering, it is of paramount importance to designate objects with highly specific meanings and characterise process parameters by a suitable name.

In order to elicit the existing WF patterns in EEE, the usage profiles of the first 500 keywords were searched. It was found that the elements used to form English compounds in this specialist language were nouns, adjective, verbs, particles and adverbs. Furthermore, it can be said that the patterns are not all used to the same extent. Nouns play an outstanding role in the formation of new words; noun + noun combinations are by far the most common type of compound (cf. Bauer and Huddleston 2002: 1647). As this statement gets confirmation from many researchers (Bauer 1983: 202; Plag 2003: 145), I did not aim at a frequency analysis of this fact. A look at the usage profiles' N+1 and N-1 sections is enough to get an idea how frequent they are as these sections consist of a huge amount of noun + noun compounds.

In the consulted reference works of WF, the compounds have often been subject to classifications according to their semantic features. All attempts at classifying are based on the fact that the elements of a compound have different relations to each other. Adams comments on her attempt at classification as follows: "like many others, (it) relies on rather loosely defined distinctions, and these groupings may not seem particularly homogeneous." (2001: 84). It follows that there has been no common denominator found for the semantic classification of compounds and that classification varies from author to author.

The motivation to nevertheless look at the semantics of the noun compounds in EEE did not come from investigations into General English but from an article on term formation by Sager (1997: 30): "According to the nature of the nucleus," (i.e. head) "it is possible to distinguish between types of compounds that designate objects, properties, processes, or operations". In order to find out whether this is true for compounds in ENGICOR, the usage profiles were searched again for evidence of these categories. Broadly speaking, Sager's categories were reflected in ENGICOR but according to the specificity of the language material in that specific corpus and also depending on the collected text types (reports, technology fact sheets, textbook, web journal), more specific categories could be established. Looking at the two-word compounds in EEE, the majority of items could be assigned to one of the following semantic categories:

category	**examples**
processes/operations:	dam construction DNAPL contamination VOC emission soil erosion membrane filtration
process indicators:	concentration level moisture conditions contaminant mobility data quality bulk density

process agents/products:	foundry waste exhaust gas carbon compounds demolition debris metal contaminant
process equipment/devices:	clay cyclone construction equipment collection sump distillation columns concrete paver
process locations:	combustion chamber collection point batch kiln aeration basin bottle depot

These five semantic categories mirror the immediate reality of Environmental Engineering. Processes happen under certain conditions (described by process indicators) by the help of certain equipment in specific locations. Agents are involved in these processes and they result in certain products. It is strongly assumed that these categories are topic-dependent as Sager's categories are much more general, and text-type-dependent too. It might be that with other text-types animate agents would play a bigger role or with more instructional text-types tools would more come into play. Still, language use reflects very well the restricted world of Environmental Engineering. I tried to illustrate this in Figure 2.

The processes forming complex adjectives in general are very productive, but the compounding of nouns and adjectives count as the most frequent. The nouns in first position correspond to the complements in prepositional phrases (*pollution-sensitive – sensitive to pollution, debris-free – free from debris, clay-rich – rich in clay*). One phenomenon occurs in the domain-specific language in particular, which is the propensity of some elements to "appear in series of forms" (Adams 2001: 96), like *-blind, conscious*, and *-mad*. EEE though has its own series-forming second elements like *-sensitive, -specific, -free, -dependent, -intensive, -rich, -prone, -resistant, -tolerant, -inhibitive*, and *-borne*. The task of the resulting complex adjectives is above all to describe properties and characteristics of materials, products and objects (*UV-sensitive chemical, corrosion-resistant alloys, lead-free solders, airborne particles, herbicide-tolerant plants*).

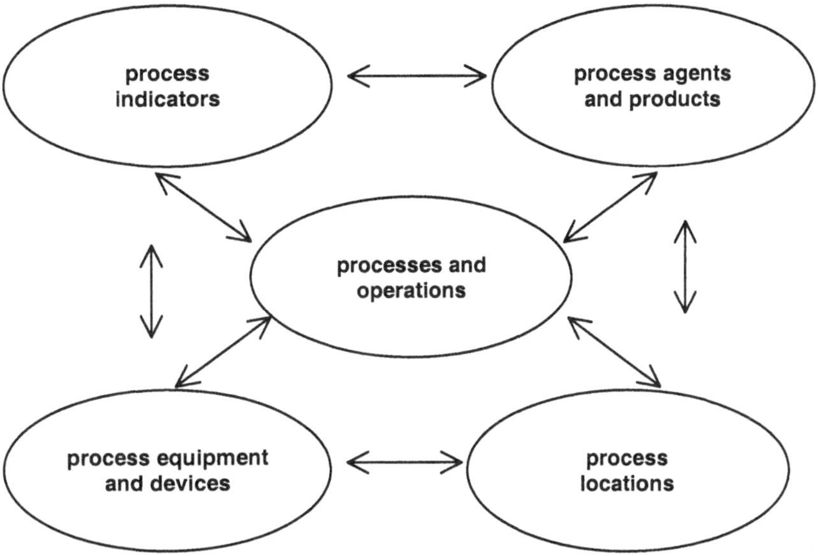

Fig. 2

A fascinating consequence of the fact that many of the second elements are series-forming is that the single elements show a clear affinity with a certain semantic preference and moreover semantic prosody, phenomenona that can be made visible by concordancing (see table 1).

In the next type of compounds, nouns appear in first position and present participial adjectives in second. If turned into a syntactic phrase, the noun corresponds to the object to the underlying verb. As this type of syntactic construction is quasi unlimited in language, so is the WF pattern producing compound adjectives of this kind. In the corpus though there are fewer and less varied examples than for the noun + adj. type.

With this type again, there are some second elements which are more frequently used and thus appear in a series. They are as well typical for EEE and will therefore be shown in the following table together with their semantic preference and semantic prosody.

Table 1

Second element	Attested collocations	Semantic preference	Semantic prosody
-free	debris-free product lead-free solders mercury-free equipment plastic-free organics	products, devices or substances that are free from a contaminant	positive
-rich	clay-rich tailings fuel-rich zones grass-rich yardwaste iron-rich barren solution	locations or substances that are rich in a certain element or substance	positive
-tolerant	drought-tolerant vegetation herbicide-tolerant plant metal-tolerant plants	plants that are tolerant towards certain contaminants or climatic conditions	positive
-sensitive	pollution-sensitive mayfly redox-sensitive contaminants UV-sensitive chemical	substances or animals that are sensitive to certain influences (contaminants, chemical reactions, climatic conditions)	positive or negative depending on whether the effect is wanted or not
-prone	erosion-prone silt erosion-prone soil strike-prone area	location that is prone to a negative influence	negative
-intensive	area-intensive construction capital-intensive system labor-intensive task	an endeavour that is intensive in input	negative
-resistant	abrasion-resistant materials corrosion-resistant alloys fire-resistant lubricants water-resistant surface	material that is resistant to chemical or mechanical influences	positive
-borne	air-borne concentrations fluid-borne species soil-borne plant diseases wastewater-borne nitrogen	harmful substances or diseases carried (borne) by a certain medium	negative
-friendly	user-friendly practices environment-friendly toothbrush PR-friendly name	an object, entity or practice which is either suitable or not harmful	positive

Table 2

Second element	Attested collocations	Semantic preference	Semantic prosody
-containing	asbestos-containing soils bromide-containing waters carbon-containing materials	substance or location holding a chemical or another kind of impurity	negative only if chemical is a contaminant
-bearing	dioxin-bearing wastes chromium-bearing wastewater copper-bearing rock fish-bearing streams groundwater-bearing unit	very close to –containing but there is an element of not just holding the chemical substance or the objects but of producing them as well	either neutral, positive or negative according to the wider context
-forming	acid-forming mine waste anion-forming elements chlorate-forming reactions glass-forming process	processes, substances or living agents that produce a chemical some other kind of result	either neutral, positive or negative according to the wider context
-generating	acid-generating waste rock electricity-generating stations metal-generating tailings	facilities or processes that produce an outcome	either neutral, positive or negative according to the wider context
-causing	disease-causing microorganisms erosion-causing events odor-causing compounds	living agents or activities that cause a negative effect	negative

Similar to the adjectives produced by the type noun + adjective, these compound adjectives mostly pertain to either processes and properties in environmental chemistry, here with an active meaning due to the involvement of present participial adjectives.

In the next type nouns combine again this time with past participial adjectives to form compound adjectives. If paraphrased by a syntactic construction, the nouns mostly correspond to the passive of a participial phrase (*site-related – related to the site, sewage-derived – derived from sewage*). Typical EEE-specific compound adjectives and their semantic preference and semantic prosody are illustrated in the table below.

Table 3

Second element	Attested collocations	Semantic preference	Semantic prosody
-related	combustion-related emissions composting-related program gas-related problems mining-related sites	two entities that have a certain relationship, relate carries less meaning load than the more specific words elements like –laden, is open for more constructions	neutral
-based	chlorine-based cleaners coconut-based GAC computer-based technology lead-based paint Jersey-based firm	either a product based on a certain substance, or a facility based in a certain location, or a technology, approach or similar based on certain facts	neutral
-contaminated	DNAPL-contaminated aquifer lead-contaminated soil metal-contaminated biomass	object or location contaminated by a contaminant	negative
-laden	bacteria-laden water BOD-laden wastewater cavity-laden surface copper-laden solution	substance full of contaminants or intrusives of some kind	neutral to negative
-treated	herbicide-treated pasture iron-treated zeolites pressure-treated wood UV-treated wastewater samples	objects treated by a chemical substance or physical phenomenon	neutral
-derived	sewage-derived contaminants landfill-derived methane gas plant-derived materials	product derived from a substance or a facility	either neutral, positive or negative according to the wider context
-generated	combustion-generated particles computer-generated light source contractor-generated incident	result caused by a process or an object	either neutral, positive or negative according to the wider context

4.1.2. Combining Processes

The objects focused on here are neoclassical combining elements like bio-, geo-, etc. that are added at the beginning of a base, or -phobic, -phyte etc. that are attached to the end of other bases. They differ from affixes in that they are able to combine with other neoclassical combining forms, which affixes cannot (i.e. hydrophilic). They occur "especially in the field of science and learning" (Quirk 1985: 1575) and are "extremely productive in English" (Bauer 1983: 216). These statements can definitely be confirmed by ENGICOR. Many neoclassical combining forms feature as well in the mother tongue of the students, and consequently, they should not create any learning problems. The following table shows the percentages of entries of language items with combining elements in the OED after 1900 and the number of items with no entry in the OED. This shows that items like photo- or multi- have been active during the last century and that items like phyto-, rhizo- and bio- are currently about to catch up in the language of EEE.

Table 4

Occurrences in OED after 1900		No entry in the OED		Tokens		Types	
photo	61.53%	phyto	100%	bio	3493	bio	114
multi	49.96%	rhizo	75%	hydro	2971	hydro	72
micro	40%	bio	73.68%	geo	1198	multi	66
thermo	39.13%	multi	43.93%	micro	714	micro	55
electro	35.48%	hydro	41.66%	phyto	614	photo	39
rhizo	25%	micro	38.18%	electro	475	geo	37
bio	18.42%	geo	37.83%	thermo	423	electro	31
hydro	18.05%	thermo	17.39%	multi	265	phyto	25
geo	5.4%	electro	16.12%	photo	180	thermo	23
phyto		photo	2.56%	rhizo	116	rhizo	8

Using dictionaries for determining the productivity of certain WF patterns has often been criticized (cf. Baayen and Renouf 1996) but during my work with the OED I found it (and particularly the Additions from 1993 and 1997) an excellent tool also for the specialist language investigated. In my view the oft-cited shortcoming – the fact that the choice of the lexicologist as to which words to include is arbitrary – is a systematic one and like that should have no impact on the statements made here. Determining the productivity in the narrow sense (cf. Plag 1999: 26) for such a small corpus did not yield reliable data, as it contradicted the reality of EEE, allocating a very low productivity in the narrow sense for instance to bio- (0.0103) whereas photo- ranked much higher (0.0944).

4.1.3. Derivational Processes

A process where either a prefix or a suffix is attached to a lexeme is called derivation. Prefixed items often retain the same word class as their bases, suffixed items often change word class. Students should be made familiar with the semantic load which prefixes add (i.e. negations through a-, de-, dis-, etc.) and the word class caused by adding a suffix (i.e. those specific for EEE: -ant(s), -ic(s), ive(s), etc.).

Instead of naming all sorts of affixes here in detail, I will only concentrate on the three noun-forming suffixes -ness, -ity, and -ion, -ity denotes qualities, states or properties, -ion events or results of processes (cf. Plag 2003: 90–91), and -ness states, conditions and qualities (cf. Marchand 1969: 334). Whereas -ity mostly attaches to adjectives in -able, and -al/-ar, -ion is added to verb bases in -ize, -ify, and -ate, and -ness can be used with any type of adjective and with some nouns as well. Looking at -ion, Plag states that "(t)hese forms are found primarily in scientific discourse with words denoting chemicals or other substances as bases" (2003: 90) (i.e. *epoxide-epoxidation*, *sediment-sedimenation*).

Interestingly, most authors agree that -ness is the most productive of the three (cf. Bauer 1983: 222; Plag 2003: 92). This statement is made for General English. The basis for this statement is the fact that the production of new words is put in relation to the number of existing items. As there exist much fewer words ending in -ness than in -ion, it yields comparatively more neologisms. Looking at the specialist language of EEE and at the absolute numbers (table 5) we get a totally different picture: 12.54% of ENGICOR's words ending in -ity have entered the OED after 1900 and 7.27% are not listed there and only 0.99% of ENGICOR's words ending in -ness entered the OED after 1900 and the same percentage is not listed in the OED. In my opinion that is a clear sign that the suffix -ity is more productive than the others in this special domain. *Flockability, wearability, settleability* and r*ecyclability* are only a few examples.

Table 5

Occurrences in OED after 1900		No entry in the OED		Tokens		Types	
ity	12.54%	ity	7.27%	ion	63672	ion	610
ion	5.57%	ion	1.31%	ity	19166	ity	271
ness	0.99%	ness	0.99%	ness	1860	ness	102

4.2. + Omission

4.2.1. Abbreviations

Abbreviations come in the form of initialisms, like *AMD*, *HDPE*, *LFG*, or *PRB* (*acid mine drainage*, *high-density polyethylene*, *landfill gas* or *permeable reactive barrier*) or acronyms, like *NAPL* (*non-aqueous phase liquids*) which are pronounced as a word. Sometimes the dividing line between the two forms disappears and we can find forms like *DNAPL* where the *D* is the pronounced letter followed by the acronym *NAPL* (*dense non-aqueous phase liquids*).

Some abbreviations are countable nouns and thus inflect for the plural like VOCs (volatile organic compounds) (D)NAPLs and PRBs.

4.2.2. Clippings

Clippings are products of processes "whereby a lexeme (simplex or complex) is shortened, while retaining the same meaning and still being a member of the same form class" (Bauer 1983: 233). According to Plag clippings like *lab* "are used to express familiarity" (2003: 116) with the object denoted by the clipped word. ENGICOR does not yield many products from clipping processes; besides of the above-mentioned example of *lab* there was just one more found: *moly* for *molybdenum*. The scarcity of clipped items might be due to the fact that the corpus only comprises written language whereas clipping is more a feature of spoken language when trying to achieve informality. *Moly* and *lab* are examples for back-clipping, i.e. the second part of the word got clipped. Apart from expressing familiarity with the object, language economy might be another reason for shortening words.

4.2.3. Backformation

Backformation is according to Bauer "the formation of new lexeme by the deletion of actual or supposed affixes in longer words" (1983: 232). Morphologically more complex words like the adjective *polymeric* existed before the noun was formed by deleting the -ic to arrive at *polymer* (cf. Bauer and Huddleston 2002: 1579). According to the OED corpus findings like *oxic* developed out of backformation from *anoxic*. *Sorbent* from *adsorbent* and *flocculant* from *deflocculant* might have gone the same way.

4.3. + Combination / + Omission

4.3.1. Blends

The process of producing blends is "the formation of a word of (at least) two bases with reduction of one or both at the boundary between them" (Bauer and Huddleston 2002: 1636, my insertion).

In *pervaporation* and *fertigation*, the first part of the first word and the second part of the second word form the new item (per(meation) + (e)vaporation, ferti(lization) + (irri)gation, in *evapotranspiration* only the first word is shortened whereas the second is retained (*evapo(ration) + transpiration*). In other examples blending occurs at the same time as derivational processes: *mafic* consists of *ma(gnesium) + f(errum)* + the adjectival suffix *-ic*, *surfactant* of *surf(ace) + act(ive)* + the nominal suffix *-ant* denoting agents (source: OED entries for mafic and surfactant).

4.4. -Combination/-Omission

4.4.1. Conversion

Conversion is a "non-affixational word-formation process" whereby new words get created "on the basis of already existing ones" (Plag 2003: 107).The major development in terms of conversion takes place from nouns to verbs, from verbs to nouns, from adjectives to nouns and adjectives to verbs (cf. Bauer 1983: 229) although it can happen to any word class.

From this vast variety of possibilities I chose the conversion from adjectives to nouns to illustrate the process. The starting point of reflection was an investigation into all nominal suffixes featuring in the corpus where, where amongst others, the following lexical items – all displaying the ending -ables- caught my eye:

Table 6

Lexical item	Corpus frequency	Lexical item	Corpus frequency
recyclables	129	extractables	1
floatables	106	imponderables	1
non(-)durables	12	moveables	1
deliverables	11	non-refillables	1
durables	11	nonusables	1
non-renewables	7	receivables	1
biodegradables	4	refillables	1
consumables	2	renewables	1
nonrecyclables	2	unrecyclables	1
expendables	1		

Surely a marginal phenomenon considering its frequency, yet its occurrence still triggered questions about its origin, and its extent of use in terms of restriction to a specific domain as well as about their semantic particularities.

The corpus was consulted in order to find out which nouns are modified by the corresponding -able-adjectives of the lexical items that were attested as -ables-nouns in Table 6. In this way, it was hoped to establish frequent adjective-noun collocations which might reveal more information on the process of conversion from adjective to noun.

It is noticeable that the adjectives which occur in the corpus show a clear preference to collocate with one particular noun or with a group of nouns that display the same semantic preference (i.e., semantic preference of nouns collocating with *biodegradable*: organic, mostly liquid substance that may be degraded). Furthermore, it can be stated that the collocating nouns are some kind of collective term, very often a material, product or good. These nouns are mostly generic nouns with little semantic weight whereas the actual meaning load rests on the adjective.

This meaning load was fully taken over by the resulting nominal elements like *recyclables* whereas the original noun was left out.

Table 7

Adjective	Frequency	Modified noun(s)	Frequency
recyclable	101	material(s)	44
floatable	38	material(s)/pollutants/solids	17/3/4
non(-)durable	47	goods/products	37/5
deliverable	/		
durable	110	goods/material(s)/products	37/3/6
non-renewable	21	resource(s)	21
biodegradable	135	(hydraulic) fluids/(organic) materials/ (organic) compounds/organic matter/ organics/product(s)/slurry/ies/ (organic) waste(s)	13/5/3/4/8/9/10/7
consumable	/		
nonrecyclable	8		
expendable	3		
extractable	8		
imponderable	7		
moveable	4		
non-refillable	17	((beer) and (soft drink))/(beverage) containers	17
non(-)usable	6	material	4

4.5. Others

4.5.1. Word Manufacture

According to Bauer and Huddleston (2002: 1632) word manufacture is an "extremely rare process" "creating a new word simply on the basis of the phonological resources of the language". Here the corpus is the source of anecdotal information on how such a process of arbitrary word creation can work. The following text is an extract from the corpus which describes how it came that two morphological elements were put together to form a new term *biosolids* to be able to avoid the name sludge which had – after a few scandals – acquired a bad reputation.

In June 1991 the task force selected the term 'biosolids' from more than 250 suggestions that included 'humanure', 'geoslime' and 'bioslurp'. (Reilly 2002)

4.5.2. Loan Words

Again, candidates for this category cannot be searched for systematically in the corpus but *schmutzdeck* and *trommel* were detected by chance to have found their way from the German to the English language probably following the transfer of a technology.

5. Summary

In this paper I tried to give an overview of the methodology of corpus investigations designed in order to retrieve information on the lexico-semantic and the morphological level of EEE and interspersed it with some interesting findings. This methodology aims at making Firth's demand of a micro-glossary (in Palmer 1968: 106) for each ESP-variety a reality. On the basis of the collected information, language lecturers should be able to make more informed decisions when designing the syllabus for ESP-courses, choosing learning material and have a vast and reliable source of reference material at hand.

On top of the above-mentioned concrete uses of lexical and morphological corpus data, I also want to point with this paper to the importance of making students aware of the specificity of collocational and morphological data in their language learning processes. They need to learn explicitly that also a specialist language is made of chunks and that they achieve more naturalness as well as the important exactness when they learn the words "in the company they keep". At the same time learning where language change is also expected for the future will prepare them as well for a life-long learning process when acting professionally in the foreign language. And finally, having some knowledge of the most important WF patterns and their characteristics will further vocabulary acquisition sustainably.

BIBLIOGRAPHY

Adams, V. (2001). *Complex Words in English.* Harlow: Pearson Education.
Bauer, L. (1983). *English Word-Formation.* Cambridge: Cambridge University Press.
Caso, A. L. (1980). "The Production of New Scientific Terms". *American Speech*, 55: 101–111.

Heringer, H. J. (1999). *Das höchste der Gefühle: Empirische Studien zur distributiven Semantik.* Tübingen: Stauffenburg Verlag.

Baayen, R. H. and A. Renouf (1996). "Chronicling the Times: Productive Lexical Innovations in an English Newspaper". *Language Volume*, 72(1): 69–97.

Bauer, L. and R. Huddleston (2002). "Lexical Word-Formation". In: Huddleston, R. and G. K. Pullum (eds). *The Cambridge Grammar of the English Language: 1623–1719.* Cambridge: Cambridge University Press.

Krausse, S. (2005a). *Testing the Validity of Small Corpus Information.* http://www.esp-world.info/ Articles_9/testing_the_validity.htm. accessed on 10 March 2005.

Krausse, S. (2005b). "Corpus-informed Groundword for Future Environmental Engineering English Syllabus Design". In: Dúill, M. Ò *et al.* (eds). *Zusammenarbeiten – Eine Festschrift für Bernd Voss.* Bochum: AKS-Verlag: 261–286.

Marchand, H. (1969). *The Categories and Types of Present-Day English Word-Formation.* München: C. H. Beck'sche Verlagsbuchhandlung.

Palmer, F. R. (1968). *Selected Papers of J. R. Firth 1952–59.* London Beccles: Longman

Plag, I. (2003). *Word-Formation in English.* Cambridge. Cambridge University Press.

Plag, I. (1999). *Morphological Productivity.* Berlin, New York: Mouton de Gruyter.

Quirk, R. *et al.* (1985). *A Comprehensive Grammar of the English Language.* London: Longman.

Reilly, M. (2002). *Toronto Sludge Fertilizer Ordered Removed from Farm.* http://list.web.net/archives/sludgewatch-l/2002-February.txt, accessed on 09 August 2005.

Sinclair, J. (1996). "The Search for Units of Meaning". *Textus*, IX: 75–106.

Sager, J. C. (1997). "Term Formation". In: Wright, S. E. and G. Budin (eds). *Handbook of Terminology Management.* Vol. 1: 25–41. Amsterdam: John Benjamins.

OED – *The Oxford English Dictionary* (Second Edition) on CD-ROM version 3.0

British National Corpus – information about the corpus can be found at http://www.natcorp.ox.ac.uk/. accessed on 12 August 2005.

Magali Paquot
University of Louvain

TOWARDS A PRODUCTIVELY-ORIENTED ACADEMIC WORD LIST

1. Introduction

Most studies of vocabulary in English for Academic Purposes (EAP) have emphasized the importance of a 'sub-technical' or 'academic' vocabulary alongside core words and technical terms in academic discourse (cf. Nation 2001: 187–216). A number of word lists have been compiled to meet the specific vocabulary needs of students in higher education settings. The *Academic Word List* (Coxhead 2000) is the most widely used today in language teaching, testing and materials development. It consists of the vocabulary required for academic reading comprehension, which can be broadly defined as a vocabulary common to a wide range of academic texts but not so common in non-academic texts. L2 learners, as well as EFL teachers and textbook developers, would greatly benefit from the elaboration of a productive counterpart to the *Academic Word List* as learners' needs and difficulties are clearly not the same in production as in reception. This should be reflected in the selection criteria of a productively-oriented academic word list. Although frequency remains an important criterion, it is only half of the story. A productively-oriented academic word list should also give L2 learners the lexical means necessary to do the things that academic writers do, e.g. stating a topic, hypothesizing, contrasting, exemplifying, explaining, evaluating, etc. Recent corpus-based studies of recurrent word combinations (Biber 2004; Biber *et al.* 1999), lexical phrases (Oakey 2002) and abstract nouns (Cowie 1997) in native academic writing have pointed to the existence of an EAP-specific phraseology. It is therefore particularly important that new words be introduced together with information on how to use them, especially their collocational and colligational environment. Descriptions of EAP words should then be refined on the basis of a careful analysis of learner corpus data that will highlight learners' attested 'difficulties' in using these words (cf. Flowerdew 1998; Granger 2004a). Learner corpora are the only type of data that can reveal learners' typical 'difficulties' in terms of underuse, overuse, misuse and idiosyncratic use of EAP words or multi-word sequences. These corpus findings will undoubtedly have pedagogical implications in the sense that teachers will, for example, be able to focus more on words that have been proved to be underused while at the same time warning their pupils against overusing certain words or multi-word sequences.

The aim of this paper is therefore twofold. First, it examines the major reasons why the *Academic Word List* is not ideally suited for productive purposes (section 2) and proposes a new extraction methodology for the design of a productively-oriented academic word list (section 3 and 4). Secondly, it illustrates how learner corpus data can be used to fine-tune the description of EAP words by providing valuable insights into learners' 'difficulties' in using them (section 5).

2. The *Academic Word List*

The *Academic Word List* (AWL) consists of 570 word families that are not in the first 2,000 most frequently occurring words of English as described in West's (1953) *General Service List* (GSL) but which have wide range and reasonable frequency of occurrence in a 3,500,000 word corpus of academic texts (e.g. *approximate, capacity, link, presume, summary, widespread*, etc.). Taken together, words of the GSL and the AWL plus discipline-specific items should approach the critical 95% coverage threshold necessary for reasonable reading comprehension (Nation 2001: 197). While the AWL is certainly a good supplement to the GSL for receptive purposes, it is not ideally suited to productive purposes for four main reasons. First, a classification into word families, without information on frequency, is not particularly helpful to learners as not all members of a word family are likely to be as frequent and useful in EAP. For example, under the headword *item*, which has a relative frequency of 36 occurrences per million words in the Micro-Concord academic corpus (see section 3.1), we find the noun *itemisation* and word forms of the verb *itemise*. However, the verb *itemise* has a relative frequency of 1 occurrence per million words and the noun *itemisation* does not appear at all in the same corpus. Secondly, as the AWL is based on word forms, meanings and parts of speech are not differentiated. For example, we do not know if the word form *issue* is a noun or a verb. Thirdly, like any other EAP word list, the AWL is based on single words. This goes against current trends in language acquisition and foreign language learning that stress the importance of prefabricated language over 'slot-and-filler' models of language (cf. Lewis 2002; Wray 2002; Schmitt 2004). Finally, Coxhead's criterion of non-appearance in the GSL is not really appropriate when it comes to productive purposes as lexical items may be included in the 2,000 most frequent words but used differently in EAP. Nouns such as *example, problem, reason, argument* and *result* appear with a particularly high range and frequency in academic corpora but are not considered as EAP vocabulary by Coxhead as these items are already in the GSL.

3. Data and methodology

3.1. Data

The corpus used for this study is the *Micro-Concord corpus collection B* (MC) (Scott and Johns 1993), a 1,000,000 word corpus of published academic prose which consists of 33 texts.[1] The corpus is divided into five subcorpora of about 200,000 words each: arts, belief and religion, applied science, science and social science. The classification of texts into five broad academic disciplines is particularly well suited for the purposes of this study as it seeks to extract words that are used by all members of the 'academic discourse community' (Swales 1990).

3.2. Methodology

Coxhead (2000) selected word families for the AWL on the basis of three criteria:

1. Non-occurrence in the GSL,
2. Range: a frequency of at least 10 occurrences in each section of the corpus,

[1] The relatively small size of the corpus and the limited number of texts may be considered two limitations of this study. However, the selection procedure described in section 3.2 has recently been replicated on a larger corpus which represents a wide range of academic sub-genres, i.e. published articles, samples of books, student essays, etc. in different disciplines and the results are quite consistent with those presented here.

3. Frequency: a minimum frequency of 100 in the whole academic corpus.

The method proposed in this study is primarily based on keyness (cf. Scott 2001), a criterion that has not been used by Coxhead (2000). A series of quantitative filters involving frequency, range and evenness of distribution is subsequently used to narrow down the resulting list of EAP words (cf. Figure 1).

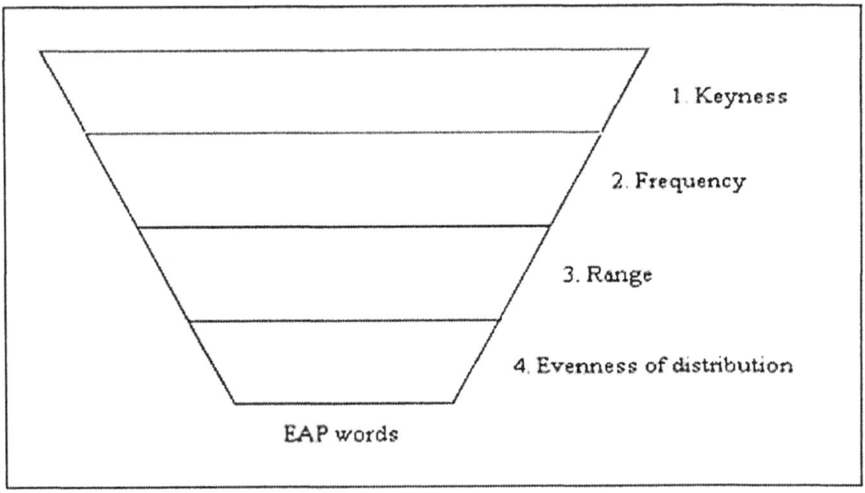

Fig. 1. A four-layered sieve to extract EAP words

3.2.1. Keyness

The keyness method has been used in a variety of fields to extract distinctive words, e.g. business English words (Nelson 2000). Keywords are words that appear significantly more often in the corpus under study than in a comparison corpus. For the purpose of this research, the MC corpus was compared with a large corpus of fiction writing on the basis of the hypothesis that typical EAP words would be particularly under-represented in fiction. The comparison was made using the compare list option of *WordSmith Tools* (Scott 1999) which produces a list of all the words that present statistically significant differences in frequency between the two corpora.[2] It is based on lemmas and

[2] The significance of the statistical test was set at 0.01, which means that there is less than 1% danger of mistakenly claiming a significant difference in frequency.

part-of-speech tags. Lemmas were chosen in preference to word forms as Granger and Paquot (2005) showed that, although the description of EAP words should be based on an analysis of key word forms, key lemmas give better results for the selection procedure. Part-of-speech tags made it possible to create lists of EAP nouns, verbs, adverbs, etc., and to distinguish between grammatical homographs, e.g. *use* as a noun or verb.

Used alone, keyness not only extracts highly frequent words in the academic corpus (e.g. *example, conclusion, view*) but also gives prominence to discipline or topic-related vocabulary, which is not necessarily frequent in the academic corpus but is typically under-represented in fiction writing (e.g. *bacterium, methane, DNA, penicillin, chromosome, enzyme, jurisdiction, rape, archbishop, martyr, rape*, etc.). The three criteria of frequency, range and evenness of distribution are subsequently used to refine the list of EAP keywords.

3.2.2. Frequency and range

Word families were selected for the AWL if they appeared at least 100 times in a 3,500,000 word corpus. The study presented here being based on lemmas in a 1,000,000 word corpus, for a keyword to be selected as an EAP word, its frequency should be equal to or higher than 30 occurrences. To distinguish frequent words that are liable to be found in most academic texts from others that are restricted to a specific discipline (e.g. *cell, gene, patient, treatment*, etc.), the criterion of range, i.e. frequency in terms of the number of texts, was also used. Range was calculated on the basis of the five subcorpora with the consistency analysis option of *WordSmith Tools*. Only words appearing in the five academic disciplines were retained as EAP words.

Used alone, range also has an important limitation: it gives no information on the frequency of a word in any text. Thus, the criterion of range dismisses the word *cell* as it only appears in two subcorpora but includes both the word *example*, which is intuitively regarded as an EAP word, and the lemma *law*, whose meaning is more discipline or topic-dependent (*the Canon Law, criminal law, the law of gravity*). Their sub-frequencies given in table 1 confirm this distinction. The frequency of the word *example* ranges from 20 to 125, while that of the word *law* ranges from 6 to 334. The wider frequency range of *law* can be explained by the highly frequent occurrence of *law* in the social science sub-corpus.

Table 1. Distribution of the words *example* and *law* in the 5 sub-corpora

	Normalized frequencies / 100,000 words				
	Arts	Belief and religion	Applied science	Science	Social science
example	20	77	111	125	56
law	6	129	71	16	334

Differences such as these can be highlighted by a measure of the evenness of distribution of words in a corpus, the last criterion applied to further restrict the list of EAP words.

3.2.3. Evenness of distribution

The evenness of distribution or dispersion of a word is "a statistical coefficient of how evenly distributed a word is across successive sectors of the corpus" (Rayson 2003: 93). One such measure is Juilland's D statistical coefficient. Its values range from 0 to 1 and the closer a Juilland's D value for a word is to 1, the more equal is the spread of occurrences of that word across the sectors of the corpus.[3] For a word to be selected as an EAP word, its Juilland's D value should be greater than 0.5.[4] Thus, the noun *example* is selected as an EAP word as its dispersion value equals 0.73 whereas the noun *law*, with a Juilland's D value of 0.4, is not. Dispersion values make it possible to avoid the wrong conclusion that these two words behave in the same way in academic writing and reveal that only *example* is of widespread and general occurrence in this particular genre, while the noun *law* is over-represented in the social science sub-corpus.

4. A productively-oriented academic word list

4.1. Results of the automatic extraction

The successive application of the four criteria described in section 3 – keyness, frequency, range and evenness of distribution – automatically restricts the number of EAP words to 838. Table 2 gives the first 100 EAP words sorted

[3] For more information on range and evenness of distribution, see Rayson (2003: 93–94).

[4] A Juilland's D value of 0.5 is arguably quite low; however, increasing this value would have resulted in a lower recall rate.

on their keyness value, i.e. the preposition *of* is the EAP word that has the highest keyness in the MC corpus.

Table 2. First 100 EAP words

of, the, which, in, be, by, may, this, or, these, such, example, also, case, that, however, social, effect, development, its, form, principle, system, theory, between, term, develop, problem, result, per, will, individual, not, different, general, particular, century, change, thus, therefore, government, process, subject, require, an, as, produce, group, occur, period, establish, include, element, common, history, view, study, structure, involve, condition, many, use, chapter, reason, important, argument, cent, other, according, environment, rule, nature, issue, evidence, consequence, their, describe, base, action, likely, most, natural, idea, response, consider, early, role, source, interpretation, method, value, relation, person, similar, provide, during, policy, cause, apply.

A high number of these words are typical of what would intuitively be regarded as EAP vocabulary, e.g. *example, principle, theory, develop, problem, result, view, study, reason, argument, issue, evidence, consequence, describe, source, interpretation, method, cause*, etc. Some words also stress the importance of considering multi-word sequences as well. For example, the lemma *term* almost always occurs in sequences such as *in general terms* or *in terms of* and *general* and *particular* often appear in the two-word sequences *in general* and *in particular.* Similarly, the two words *per* and *cent* are part of the lemma *per cent* and *according* does not stand alone but appears in the complex preposition *according to.*

4.2. EAP nouns

In this case study, we focus on EAP nouns as they have proved to be significantly underused in learner academic texts (cf. Granger and Rayson 1998; Hinkel 2002). Our list of EAP words initially contained 298 nouns, from which four categories of nouns were selected for their potential usefulness for productive purposes:

1. 'Shell nouns' are "abstract nouns that have, to varying degrees, the potential of being used as conceptual shells for complex, proposition-like pieces of information" (Schmid 2000: 4). Thus, in the following sentence, the noun *argument* is a shell noun which stands for the underlined proposition:

   Sir Norman's **argument** was that it should not be replaced but maintained (ibid: 132).

Examples of 'shell nouns' in the EAP list are *argument, consequence, favour, discussion, value, equivalent, example, suggestion, tendency, version, proposal, possibility*, etc. These nouns are particularly interesting as they constitute an important type of lexical cohesion (cf. Francis 1994) which has been shown to be pervasive in academic discourse and likely to be problematic for non-native, as well as native speakers, notably because they refer to abstract entities and introduce additional propositional density to a text (cf. Flowerdew 2003).

2. Quantifying collective nouns: *a **group** of, a **majority** of, a **set** of, a **series** of,* etc.
3. Species nouns: *a **kind** of, a **sort** of, a **type** of, a **form** of, a **class** of,* etc.
4. Metalinguistic text nouns (Francis 1994): *chapter, figure, article,* etc.

Examples of nouns that were not selected are *citizen, colleague, history, environment, education, work* and *welfare.*

A comparison of the final list of 237 EAP nouns with the *General Service List* and the *Academic Word List* shows that only one third of the nouns is shared with the AWL whereas two thirds are General Service words. Table 3 gives the distribution of EAP nouns in the GSL and the AWL together with examples.

Table 3. Distribution of EAP nouns in the GSL and the AWL

Lists	Number of EAP words	Examples
GSL	147 [62%]	act, addition, aim, argument, cause, change characteristic, choice, claim, comparison, difference, discussion, effect, example, exception, explanation, extent, fact, favour, group, idea, judgment, matter, measure, point, possibility, problem, question, reason, result, statement, study, subject, suggestion, term, variety, view.
AWL	83 [35%]	alternative, analysis, approach, aspect, assumption, chapter, conclusion, consequence, contrast, criterion, debate, definition, evidence, factor; implication, instance, interpretation, issue, method, proportion, research, summary, theme, theory, version
Off-list	7 [3%]	appeal, criticism, opposition, reference

These results highlight the important role played by General Service words in academic prose and justify their inclusion in a productively-oriented academic word list.

5. Fine-tuning the list: the contribution of learner corpus data

The value of a productively-oriented academic word list or of any other EAP pedagogical tool is greatly increased if findings from learner corpus data are also used to select the words that should be given special attention in EAP courses. By way of illustration, the frequencies of the EAP nouns described in section 4.2 are compared in a subpart of the *Louvain Corpus of Native Speaker Essays* (LOCNESS) which consists of 150,000 words of argumentative essays written by American university students and a comparable corpus of essays written by higher-intermediate to advanced French-speaking university students. The learner corpus, henceforth referred to as ICLE-FR, is a sub-part of the *International Corpus of Learner English*, a large corpus of English as a foreign language produced by learners from eleven different mother tongue backgrounds (Granger et al 2002). The comparison shows that while a restricted set of EAP nouns are massively overused by French learners (e.g. *action, difficulty, conclusion, development, example, importance, instance, possibility, problem, question*, etc.[5]), the majority of them are typically underused by this learner population (e.g. *argument, issue, claim, evidence, support, effect, type, research, debate, case, method, value, reason, approach, emphasis, consequence, alternative*, etc.). A very high number of overused and underused EAP nouns belong to West's GSL, which provides further justification for their inclusion in a productively-oriented academic word list.

Learner corpus data can also be used to fine-tune the description of the phraseology of EAP words by providing useful information on learners' difficulties in terms of underuse, overuse and misuse of multi-word sequences and use of nonnative-like sequences. French learners' use of the noun *example* is a case in point. A comparison of the use of the EAP noun *example* in native and French learner writing first shows that learners significantly overuse the conjunct *for example* and sometimes even use it to introduce what is definitely not an example:

a) *As far as the European culture is concerned, I could say that to a certain extent the unification of Europe is leading to a loss of identity.* ***For example****, the question of the language that will be spoken in the community arises, and many problems are still not solved.* (ICLE-FR)

[5] It should be noted that the nouns *conclusion, example* and *instance* are not overused alone but in the multi-word sequences *for example, for instance* and *in conclusion*.

b) *As soon as you practice or simply like music, novels, poetry, theatre, etc., you give a place for dreaming and imagination. Some people might then infer that* ***for example*** *children's imagination is threatened precisely because they sit most of the time passively in front of the television.* (ICLE-FR)

By comparison, French learners typically underuse the two productive frames with the verb *to be* commonly found in native academic writing, i.e. 'X *is a(n)* (adj.) *example of* Y' and '*a(n)* (adj.) *example of* Y *is* X', as illustrated in the following two sentences:

c) *However, the microwave uses radiation to excite water particles in food, thus creating friction, which creates heat. This* ***is a prime example of*** *thinking that does not follow in old footsteps but breaks away from convention and forges new routes.* (LOCNESS)

d) *Because the case against teaching New Ages ideas reaches more people, the argument is more powerful.* ***An example of this is*** *the magazine Christianity Today.* (LOCNESS)

Non-native tendencies to overuse the fixed formula *for example* (even when another phrase would be more appropriate) and underuse productive frames are clearly in line with Granger's (1998:156) conclusion that "learners' repertoires for introducing arguments and points of view are very restricted and they therefore 'cling on' to certain fixed phrases and expressions which they feel confident in using." An analysis of adjective and verb collocates also reveals learners' lack of feeling for what are native speakers' preferred ways of saying things. Learners use fewer typical collocations such as *set an example, cite an example, prime example* or *classic example* but tend to favour less typical or clearly erroneous combinations such as *a little example, an opposite example, state an example,* etc.

French learners repeatedly use the sequence *let's take the example of*, a frame that is not found in native formal writing. Academic writing is a genre characterized by high degrees of formality and detachment and the speech-like nature of this frame leads to an overall impression of stylistic inadequacy:

e) *One form of this is nationalism. To show what I mean,* ***let's take the example of*** *an Englishman in Belgium.* (ICLE-FR)

f) *One of them is the loss of contacts in families. (..)* ***Let us take an example:*** *many people eat while watching TV. I personally think that this is a pity.* (ICLE-FR)

Whereas the conjunct *for example* is significantly overused in most ICLE subcorpora (from 44% to 66% vs. 35% in LOCNESS), the frame *let's take the example of* is quite rare in other interlanguages and seems to be characteristic of French learners. This over-representation may well be L1-induced as the frame has a congruent counterpart in French, i.e. *Prenons l'exemple de* ..., which is found in student and professional formal writing.[6] Similarly, Nesselhauf (2004) suggested that German learners' erroneous combination *X is an example **for*** was most probably modelled on German *ein Beispiel für*. For more examples of the potential influence of the mother tongue on phraseological patterns in EFL academic writing, see Paquot (forthcoming).

Descriptions of EAP vocabulary in native corpora are becoming available (cf. Verdaguer and González 2004) but information derived from learner corpora analysis, and more crucially, L1-specific information, is currently sorely lacking (cf. Granger 2004b). Although L1-specific findings may be more difficult to incorporate into generic EAP textbooks, patterns shared by all learner populations could be used to increase the pedagogical value of these materials: lexical means found to be typically underused by all learner populations could be presented as useful alternatives to learners' preferred patterns. Thus, instead of presenting *for example*, 'X *is a* (adj.) *example of* Y' and '*a* (adj.) *example of* Y *is* X' as interchangeable means to introduce an example, EAP textbooks could draw learners' attention to the fact that EFL students generally tend to overuse *for example* and advise them to use the productive frames as well.

6. Conclusion

This study highlights the importance of a rigorous and empirically based selection of vocabulary and presents a new methodology for the identification of lexical items that should be part and parcel of a productively-oriented academic word list. The results suggest that while a distinction between General Service words and Coxhead's academic words is valuable for receptive purposes, it is not totally adequate for productive purposes. Numerous General Service words have important discourse functions in EAP and their phraseological uses are not fully mastered by L2 learners, even at an advanced level. Learners need pedagogical tools to help them use these words to produce accurate and stylistically appropriate language. The trend towards more productive tools has already been

[6] First person plurals of the present imperative and indicative are much more frequent in French formal writing.

highlighted by Rundell (1998) in the field of pedagogical lexicography. The present paper shows that although foreign language teaching, and more especially EAP, has already started its own 'productive revolution', much remains to be done. It also brings out the high value of insights gained from learner corpus data in the design of productive tools for learners and supports Flowerdew's (1998) suggestion that EAP textbooks should pay more attention to aspects of overuse, underuse, misuse and learners' idiosyncratic use of lexico-grammatical means to fulfil rhetorical functions. Finally, a comparison of the phraseology of the noun *example* in several interlanguages reveals that if a number of features are shared by most learner populations and are therefore more likely to be developmental or teaching-induced, other aspects of learner phraseological use in academic writing are characteristic of one mother tongue background and therefore probably L1-dependent. These findings have important implications for EAP teaching as they suggest that the mother tongue deserves a place in the academic writing class.

Acknowledgements

I gratefully acknowledge the support of the Communauté française de Belgique, which funded this research within the framework of the 'Action de recherche concertée' project entitled 'Foreign Language Learning: Phraseology and Discourse' (No. 03/08-301). I would also like to express my deep gratitude to Sylviane Granger for her guidance and support.

REFERENCES

Biber, D. (2004). "Lexical bundles in academic speech and writing." In: Lewandowska-Tomaszczyk, B. (ed.). *Practical Applications in Language and Computers* (PALC 2003). Frankfurt am Main: Peter Lang: 165–178.

Biber D., Johansson, S., Leech, G., Conrad, S. and E. Finegan (1999). *Longman Grammar of Spoken and Written English.* Harlow: Longman.

Cowie, A. P. (1997). "Phraseology in formal academic prose." In: Aarts, J., de Mönnink, I. and H. Wekker (eds). *Studies in English Language and Teaching In Honour of Flor Aarts.* Amsterdam/Atlanta: Rodopi: 43–56.

Coxhead, A. (2000). "A new Academic Word List." *TESOL Quarterly* 34 (2): 213–238.

Flowerdew, J. (2003). "Signalling nouns in discourse." *English for Specific Purposes* 22: 329–346.

Flowerdew, L. (1998). "Integrating 'Expert' and 'Interlanguage' Computer Corpora Findings on Causality: Discoveries for Teachers and Students." *English for Specific Purposes* 17(4): 329–345.

Francis, G. (1994). "Labelling discourse: an aspect of nominal-group lexical cohesion." In: Coulthard, M. (ed.). *Advances in written text analysis*. London/New-York: Routledge: 82–101.

Granger, S. (1998). "Prefabricated Patterns in Advanced EFL Writing: Collocations and Formulae." In: Cowie, A. (ed.). *Phraseology: Theory, Analysis and Applications*. Oxford: Oxford University Press: 145–160.

Granger, S. (2004a). "Practical Applications of Learner Corpora." In: Lewandowska-Tomaszczyk, B. (ed.). *Practical Applications in Language and Computers (PALC 2003)*. Frankfurt: Peter Lang: 291–301.

Granger S. (2004b) "Computer learner corpus research: current status and future prospects." In: Connor, U. and T. Upton (eds). *Applied Corpus Linguistics: A Multidimensional Perspective*. Amsterdam/Atlanta: Rodopi: 123–145.

Granger S. and P. Rayson (1998). "Automatic profiling of learner texts." In: Granger, S. (ed.). *Learner English on Computer*. Harlow: Longman: 119–131.

Granger, S., Dagneaux, E. and F. Meunier (eds) (2002). The International Corpus of Learner English. CD-ROM and Handbook. Louvain-la-Neuve: Presses universitaires de Louvain. Available from http://www.i6doc.com

Granger, S. and M. Paquot (2005). "The phraseology of EFL academic writing: Methodological issues and research findings." Paper presented at ICAME 26 – AAAACL6 (International Computer Archive of Modern and Medieval English - American Association of Applied Corpus Linguistics), 12–15 May 2005, University of Michigan, USA.

Hinkel, E. (2002). *Second Language Writers' Text. Linguistic and Rhetorical Features*. London: Lawrence Erlbaum Associates.

Lewis, M. (2002). *Implementing the Lexical Approach. Putting Theory into Practice*. Heinle: Boston.

Nation, P. (2001). *Learning Vocabulary in Another Language*. Cambridge: Cambridge University Press.

Nelson, M. (2000). *A Corpus-Based Study of Business English and Business English Teaching Materials*. Unpublished PhD Thesis. Manchester: University of Manchester.

Nesselhauf, N. (2004). "Learner corpora and their potential for language teaching." In: Sinclair, J. (ed.). *How to use corpora in language teaching*. Amsterdam/ Philadelphia: Benjamins: 125–152.

Oakey, D. (2002). "Formulaic language in English academic writing: A corpus-based study of the formal and functional variation of a lexical phrase in different academic disciplines." In: Reppen, R., Fitzmaurice, S. M. and D. Biber (eds). *Using Corpora to Explore Linguistic Variation*. Amsterdam/Philadelphia: Longman: 111–129.

Paquot, M. (forthcoming). "Exemplification in learner writing: a cross-linguistic perspective." In: Granger, S. and F. Meunier (eds). *Phraseology in Language Learning and Teaching*. Amsterdam: Benjamins.

Rayson, P. (2003). *Matrix: A statistical method and software tool for linguistic analysis through corpus comparison*. Unpublished PhD dissertation, Lancaster University.

Rundell, M. (1998). "Recent trends in English pedagogical lexicography." *International Journal of Lexicography* 11(4): 315–342.

Scott, M. (1999). *WordSmith Tools version 3*. Oxford University Press.

Scott, M. (2001). "Comparing corpora and identifying key words, collocations, frequency distributions through the WordSmith Tools suite of computer programs." In: Ghadessy, M., Henry, A. and L. Roseberry (eds). *Small Corpus Studies and ELT*. Amsterdam: Benjamins: 47–67.

Scott, M. and T. Johns (1993). *MicroConcord*. Oxford: Oxford English Software.

Schmid, H. (2000). *English Abstract Nouns as Conceptual Shells: From Corpus to Cognition*. Berlin/New York: Mouton de Gruyter.

Schmitt, N. (ed.) (2004). *Formulaic Sequences: Acquisition, Processing and Use*. Amsterdam: Benjamins.

Swales, John M. (1990) *Genre analysis: English in academic and research settings*. Cambridge: Cambridge University Press.

Thurstun, J. and C. Candlin (1997). *Exploring Academic English: A workbook for student essay writing*. Sydney: Macquarie University Press.

Verdaguer, I. and E. González (2004). "A Lexical Database of Collocations in Scientific English: Preliminary Considerations." In: Williams, G. and S. Vesssier (eds). *Proceedings of the Eleventh EURALEX International Congress*. Lorient: Université de Bretagne-Sud: 929–934.

West, M. (1953). *A General Service List of English Words*. London: Longman.

Wray, A. (2002). *Formulaic Language and the Lexicon*. Cambridge: Cambridge University Press.

Piotr Pęzik

Univwerity of Łódź

LEXIS, THE LEXICON, TERMS, IDIOMS AND CO-OCCURRENCE STATISTICS – A CASE STUDY

Abstract

Co-occurrence statistics and linear algebraic (vector-space) models have been widely used in the field of computational and corpus linguistics. They are usually applied to tasks such as thesaurus construction, collocation and terminology extraction, word sense disambiguation and word meaning association. In this paper I present some results of experiments with co-occurrence statistics and algorithms used to detect ideologically motivated lexical differences between two samples of American political discourse. I emphasize an important distinction between the notions of *lexis* and *the lexicon* and I show how these concepts make it possible to distinguish between lexis-driven and lexicon-driven methodologies. I also attempt to show that lexical acquisition, especially if it is based on naturally occurring data has to strike a balance between the idiom and open-choice principles as described by (Sinclair 2004).

Some Theory

For a long time, the lexical dimension of linguistic analysis was clearly separated from the grammatical one. The lexicon was sometimes called "an appendix to grammar", and the behavior of lexical items was believed to be idiosyncratic and unpredictable (Bloomfield 1933 quoted in Zampolli 1994: 18). This sharp delineation between the lexical and the grammatical components of language began to be questioned in the second half of the 20th century, especially when corpus linguists started describing regular patterns in naturally-occurring lexis which escaped traditional syntactic and semantic explanations. Arguments against the "decoupling of lexis and grammar" were particularly well articulated within the 'Firthian tradition', whose representatives emphasized the importance of recognizing lexis as an independent linguistic level (Halliday 1966), (Sinclair 1966). At the same time, there was a great upsurge of interest in the compilation of comprehensive lexicons in computational linguistics. Research in the construction of abstract lexicons and data-driven lexical acquisition confirmed that lexical units are not simply place-holders for grammatical slots, and that they exhibit paradigmatic and syntagmatic lexical behavior.

Lexis and the Lexicon

For the sake of further discussion it seems useful to emphasize the difference between the notions of *lexis* and *the lexicon* as they are used in this paper, especially in view of the occasional interchangeable use of the two terms. Lexis can be understood as the totality of lexical units *as they are used* in a given language. The lexicon is the abstract system in which lexis is believed to be organized. The former is explicit and it can be studied directly (if sample-based analysis can be described as "direct"). The latter is implicit and can only be described indirectly. Furthermore, any formal model of a neatly structured hierarchy claimed to be an approximation of *the* lexicon is likely to be inconclusive and controversial. Even if by *the lexicon*, we simply mean the vocabulary of a language – the set of all distinct word forms – it is very difficult to agree on what exactly this set would contain, due to inconsistent orthographic conventions and idiomaticity issues. To date, no exhaustive description of such a structure has been provided for any language, although there have been numerous lexicons which have proved very useful for practical purposes. This distinction reflects to some extent de Saussure's classic concepts of *langue* and *parole* respectively, except that it only applies to the lexical dimension of language rather than to language in general.

The distinction between lexis and the lexicon may help clarify some of the important differences between the predominant methodological orientation of much lexicological and lexicographic research. As an example, the original model of the lexicon underlying Roget's thesaurus with its hierarchical nodes leading to terminal lexical forms was inspired by scientific taxonomies (Halliday 2004). We could describe Roget's methodology as lexicon-driven, since it focused on the construction of an abstract, underlying system determining the behavior of lexis. Obviously, at that time, there were no conceivable methods of analyzing massive evidence found in naturally occurring lexis, unless one was ready to do the amount of manual work that made the German linguist Kaeding a figure often quoted in introductory corpus-linguistics texts (e.g. MacEnery 2003). But even certain modern-day computational projects can be described as largely lexicon-driven, the most famous example of which is WordNet, at least in one of its early versions compiled from before it was enriched with empirical lexical data from the Brown Corpus (Miller 1998).

On the other hand, many lexical acquisition systems, where a more or less successful approximation of the lexicon is "acquired" from naturally-occurring lexis, can be categorized as lexis-driven. As an example, generally, in corpus-based lexical research ultimate conclusions about the structure of the hypothetical lexicon are not drawn, unless they are verified against lexis.

It has to be noted that many lexicon-driven descriptions tend to be conducive to committing the fallacy of treating single-words as the ideal units of lexical meaning, since they are easier to model out in an abstract lexicon. This in turn leads to a poor coverage of syntagmatic, contextual relations found in lexis in many such methodologies. Interestingly, this realization seems to have motivated the authors of WordNet (a largely lexicon-driven system by the criteria presented here) to enrich their lexicon with information that can only by found in representative samples of lexis:

"WordNet itself does not give any information about the context in which the word forms and senses occur. However as Miller and Charles (1991) have pointed out, speaker's knowledge of words must consist not only of the meaning of the words but also of the contexts in which they can occur. Knowing how a word interacts with other words in context is a requirement for knowing a word" (Fellbaum 1998: 13).

Admittedly, the distinction I have made above is very general. It is impossible to find a purely lexicon-driven methodology which would be completely detached from naturally-occurring lexis, just as it is hard to imagine a lexis-driven approach which does not make generalizations on the basis of observable lexis. In fact, the notions of lexis and the lexicon are two sides of the same coin. However, just as the quote above shows, deciding on one research methodology in favor of the other may seriously limit the range of lexico-semantic phenomena that a given study explains.

Terms and Idioms

Sinclair described two general tendencies which determine most lexical choices. One is the terminological tendency (a.k.a. the open-choice principle), which is:

the tendency for a word to have a fixed meaning in reference to the world, so that anyone wanting to name its referent would have little option, but to use it, especially if the relationship works in both directions (Sinclair 2004: 29).

Complementary to the open-choice principle is the phraseological tendency (a.k.a. the idiom principle):

Tending towards idiomaticity is the phraseological tendency, where words tend to go together and make meanings by their combinations. Here is collocation and other features of idomaticity (Sinclair 2004: 29).[1]

Sinclair thus extends the traditional notion of an idiom, by suggesting a graded phenomenon of idiomaticity which affects different lexical items to a different degree. Interestingly, lexicon-driven approaches tend to focus on the former phenomenon, while lexis-driven ones provide better descriptions of the latter. This can be explained by the simple fact that collocational and other idiomatic bonds between words are best inferred from results obtained from massive amounts of naturally occurring lexis. It is impossible to enumerate the set of possible collocates of a given word with their distributions and other subtle properties (such as the possible "semantic prosodies" involved) by way of deductive introspection. On the other hand, complex hierarchical lexicons can be built on an a priori basis. (To what degree such lexicons match lexical reality found in naturally-occurring lexis is another story.) The rest of this paper describes some results of a study in which the theoretical issues roughly sketched above had to be taken into consideration.

---

[1] The other day I noticed an interesting case of these two tendencies at work in the Polish edition of the internationally known *Family Feud* TV game show. "The original run of "Family Feud" featurs two teams composed of five members from the same family, who compete against each other to match answers to the results of a survey of one hundred people." Typical questions include: "Name an animal you might see at a zoo", or "Name an item of clothing worn by the 3 Musketeers." So generally the answers will reflect the terminological tendency, where the player is expected to come up with the correct term denoting a given referent. However, since the point of the game is to predict the typical, intuitive answers obtained in a survey, there are some questions which seem to confuse the players, because it is not sure whether those surveyed gave idioms or terms as answers matching questions like: "Name 5 things or people that can be harbored." It is in the instant answers given to such questions that one can observe the idiomatic tendency. The answers typically range from more (although certainly not purely) terminological, e.g. *criminals*, to very idiomatic ones (usually conventional metaphors found in fossilized collocations), e.g. *doubts*, *reservations*, *sentiment* (http://www.familyfeud.tv). The English examples given here were made up and perhaps they are not as good as the Polish ones I heard, but I found it impossible to translate the original Polish idioms.

A Case Study

The study discussed below is part of an ongoing PhD dissertation project in which I focus on two sample corpora of American discourse. The first corpus was compiled from texts published by the *Communist Party of the United States* and *People's Weekly World Newspaper* (found on *http://www.cpusa.org/* and *http://www.pww.org/* respectively). The other corpus is made up of texts published by the *Republican National Committee* on their website *http://www.gop.com/*. The current size of the samples is about 1,000,000 running words each. This size has been found to be fairly representative for the highly repetitive and controlled language it contains, since most of the results obtained from a sample of 700,000 were repeated in a 1 million word sample. In other words, exponentially diminishing returns where observed between these two benchmark figures.[2] The results given below were obtained from samples of the sizes specified. Both corpora represent ideology-loaded registers of political discourse, and needless to say, most of the time, the views expressed in the two samples of texts tend to lie on the opposite ends of the ideological continuum. American communists differ from American republicans on a wide range of political, economic and social issues, such as "the war on terror", the state of social security, male and female social roles, the role of corporate business in world economy, etc. By conducting this comparative study, I hoped to be able to focus on the acquisition of those items of the terminology of the two corpora which could illustrate the main ideological differences, but I ended up doing fairly extensive research in the phraseology of the registers in question due to the reasons explained below.

A False Start

Taking a methodological shortcut (by largely ignoring the idiom principle), I focused on the acquisition of terminology peculiarities of the two corpora. The potential terms were assumed to take the form of independent single-word units

[2] This phenomenon is well known in corpus linguistics as the decrease of the type/token ratio value with the increase of the corpus size (which is why this ratio is often standardized to compare the lexical variability of samples of different sizes). In Information Retrieval, the so-called Heaps' Law is sometimes used to describe this tendency. The law states that "the vocabulary of a text grows sublinearly with the text size, in a proportion close to its square root": $V = Kn^{\beta}$, where V – vocabulary size, n – text/corpus size, K and ß are corpus-dependent parameters which are found empirically (Baetza-Yates, Ribeiro-Neto 1999), (Heaps 1978).

which fulfilled the minimum frequency criterion of 5 occurrences. Then, by summarizing both the explicit and the more latent co-occurrence patterns of such terms, I hoped to discover their semantic associations with each other. Such association patterns would in turn reveal some ideological differences between the two samples of discourse at least at the lexical level.

The main two types of measures on which the identification of significant word-associations was based were:

a) Vector-space models with some advanced elements of linear algebra, such as the singular value decomposition of the term matrix. The association measures used within this approach included the traditional cosine of the angle of term vectors, different correlation coefficients and variations of Euclidean distance measures.
b) Statistics using (more or less explicitly) the concept of the ratio of the mathematically (naively) expected and the observed values of word-form co-occurrence. These included the well-known Mutual Information (e.g. Oakes 1998), and the Log-Likelihood (Dunning 1993) tests.

Because the correspondence between a linguistic form and its meaning is often an indirect one, the analysis was enriched with some measures of "latent" word associations.

Hence, in the case of the vector space model, the singular value decomposition of the term matrix (SVD) was carried out, so that the original term-sentence matrix of some 15,000 sentence-columns in width was reduced to 300 columns. Unfortunately, the transformation of the term-sentence matrix of the size 2600x15000 used up some 2GB of RAM[3]. This meant that the size of the two corpora had to be limited to roughly 300,000 words. Deerwester *et al.* (1990), and Berry (1993) suggest that an SVD-reduced term-document (in this case it was a term-sentence) matrix can be used to detect latent associations between documents, where two documents do not necessarily have to contain exactly the same words to be considered similar, as long as the words they contain tend to co-occur in other areas of the term-document space. By using the flipside of this Information Retrieval approach, we can focus on the association of terms obtained from their co-occurrence patterns in sentence units. The terms in both the republican and the communist term matrices were weighted using a sentence-term version of the standard tf-idf formula (Baetza-Yates 1999).

[3] I used the JAMA (http://math.nist.gov/javanumerics/jama/) linear algebra libraries, which can be accessed from any standard Java program. Even after reducing the precision level from doubles to floats, there arose the problem of limited addressing space on 32-bit processor machines. Solutions based on serialization (rather than in-memory processing) would require rewriting the linear algebra package, which was a task I did not feel worth the trouble.

As far as the statistics based on the ratios of Observed/Expected frequencies are concerned, a multi-link approach was used to detect latent word associations. This basically means that if word **A** co-occurs significantly with word **B**, and word **C** co-occurs significantly with word **B**, then **A** and **C** can be considered to be associated with each other, even if they do not directly co-occur in a significant way. As an example, this phenomenon can be observed with some complementary synonyms, which are used interchangeably in similar denotative, but different connotative contexts. The exact technique used for the extraction of such latent relations was similar to the one described in (Biemann, Bordag and Quasthoff 2001), who suggest using multiple iterations of co-occurrence test programs over a given corpus to detect indirect associations. In the first iteration, single sentence or n-word windows can be assumed to be the contexts of co-occurrence evaluated with the MI or the Log-Likelihood test. The first iteration produces a set of association clusters for each term found in the corpus whose frequency is greater then 5. In each subsequent iteration, the program uses those association-clusters as second-order "sentences" to compute association clusters on the basis of indirect co-occurrence.

The supposed advantage of both of the latent approaches used in this study lies in the stripping of the idiomatic associations between single-word forms on the syntagmatic axis. As it happens, this may be a mixed-blessing. Below are some results obtained using the multi-link approach for single-sentence context windows:

The results in Fig. 1 do seem to illustrate interesting ideologically motivated co-occurrence patterns of some nouns. In the corpus of communist texts, the noun *Iraq* is directly or indirectly associated with nouns such as *invasion*, *war* or *occupation*. This in turn reveals the negative attitude the communist authors have towards the U.S. operation in Iraq. The association cluster found in the republican texts tells us a very different story; *liberation* (from *saddam hussein*'s *regime* and his *weapons*) replaces *invasion*, while *occupation* gets replaced with *freedom*.

However, there are several problems with using such co-occurrence methods for identifying single-word association patterns. First of all, such tests fail to distinguish between those co-occurrences which are purely terminological choices, and those which reflect the idiomatic patterns of single words. Secondly, while generating association clusters for nouns is easy to justify since nouns are the ideal candidates for single-word terminological nodes, it is not so clear how to model the distribution of other parts of speech which are difficult to represent in hierarchical ontologies. Using multiple iterations of co-occurrence statistics does not really help to solve this problem, unless by solving the problem we mean sweeping it under the carpet by simply eliminating the idiomatic patterns altogether. As an example, in the result sets above, we can define only the most obvious and fossilized idiomatic associations, such as *united_nnp*, and *state_nnp*.

Communist Corpus		Double Link Log-Likelihood	Republican Corpus		Double Link Log-Likelihood
0	**iraq_nnp**	NaN	0	**iraq_nnp**	NaN
1	invasion_nn	199,43434	1	liberation_nn	101,3994
2	reconstruction_nn	101,1123	2	saddam_nnp	51,80101
3	war_nn	80,93884	3	weapon_nn	48,70969
4	troop_nn	57,18535	4	force_nn	47,2712
5	un_nnp	54,15685	5	troop_nn	46,81966
6	united_nnp	39,47069	6	coalition_nn	44,9636
7	occupation_nn	39,00013	7	regime_nn	42,42593
8	withdrawal_nn	36,69049	8	afghanistan_nnp	40,66312
9	afghanistan_nnp	34,92694	9	hussein_nnp	37,66223
10	policy_nn	33,35464	10	mass_nn	35,16874
11	world_nn	30,63683	11	freedom_nn	33,86563
12	weapon_nn	26,77682	12	ally_nn	32,32731
13	administration_nn	26,68725	13	democracy_nn	30,49217
14	preemption_nn	26,65348	14	terrorist_nn	30,02839
15	bush_nnp	23,73483	15	terror_nn	29,93175
16	state_nnp	23,43268	16	operation_nn	27,36298
17	doctrine_nn	23,37487	17	iraqi_nnp	27,13126
18	iran_nnp	19,91399	18	people_nn	25,74882

Fig. 1 Association test results for the lemma *iraq* (tagged as a noun) obtained using the double-link log-likelihood statistic from a 300K word corpus of communist and republican texts

Recognizing the idiom principle

To check how much denotative, connotative and ideological lexical meaning is lost when one ignores or misrepresents collocational relations, I decided to generate two dictionaries of collocations for the two corpora. Relational rather than positional collocation patterns were extracted from the samples (Evert 2005), which means that instead of using the traditional n-word windows, I used a set of part of speech automata. An automaton is basically a set of possible part of speech sequences within which a given seed word may collocate. A very basic automaton for collocations consisting of two words might look like this:

.*?_jj .*?_nn,

This means that in a given pass only sequences of adjectives followed immediately by nouns are taken into consideration. A similar approach used by Daille (1995) for terminology extraction is reported by Oakes (1998). A typical dictionary entry is included below[4]:

The top table gives some information about the data and parameters used to generate the list of collocates found in this entry. The entry in Fig. 2 was generated for the node *corporate*. The frequency of the node was 283 in the corpus of 694 630 words. The minimum frequency of co-occurrence for two words to be considered as potential collocates was 4. Then, there is some information about the automaton pattern used in this entry.

The bottom table contains the results sorted by their collocability values. Several well-know collocation tests are computed for each entry: **MI3** (Mutual Information 3), **F** (simple frequency of co-occurrence), $\mathbf{G^2}$ (Log-Likelihood), **T-Test**, **Loglog** (proposed by Kilgariff – as reported in BNCweb Manual), **Z-score**, and **Dice** (as reported by Matsumoto 2003). Additionally, there are two values which give the dictionary user some idea about how evenly a given collocation is distributed in the corpus. **R** stands for *range*: the number of segments (of the total 100 segments in which the corpus was divided) in which a given collocation was found. **JD** stands for Julliand's Dispersion (c.f. Aston, Burnard 1998). To avoid possible overgeneralizations resulting from POS-tagging and lemmatization the **Matching patterns** column shows the exact word sequences which were considered to belong to the same collocation pattern.

There is a wealth of meaning in the collocations of the adjective *corporate* which goes largely unnoticed in a strictly terminological approach like the one presented earlier. Particularly interesting are the "semantic prosodies" (Sinclair 1991, Stubbs 1995) exhibited by almost anything *corporate* in the communist texts. Apart from *corporate taxes*, and perhaps *corporate executives*, all the collocations of *corporate* seem to have either direct or indirect derogatory connotations. The sequence *corporate mass* may be part of a longer collocation (such as *corporate mass media*), and it can be tested in a different automaton. Obviously, these are just initial observations which would have to be verified against evidence from concordances. The only **jj + nn** collocations of the adjective *corporate* found in the corpus of republican texts were *corporate scandals*, and *corporate funds*. The latter has an extremely low dispersion value, which suggests that it was only used in one or two texts – most likely as an occasional technical term.

---

[4] Updated samples of the two dictionaries are available for viewing at: http://pelcra.ia.uni.lodz.pl/pezik/phd/

RESULT SET INFORMATION	
Corpus name	cpusa
Default sort by	MI3
Co-occurrence minimum	4
Search node:	**corporate_jj [corporate_jj]**
Search node frequency:	283 in the total of 694 630
Word order:	Automaton: jj_nn_gen2.ain
Automaton:	[.*?_jj, .*?_nn]
Total automaton patterns:	23 494
Segments for range and dispersion:	100
Collocate pos:	.*?_nn
Possible node positions:	[0]

#	Collocate	MI3	F	G^2	Ttest	Loglog	Zscore	Dice	R (%)	JD	Matching patterns
1	medium_nn	13.66	21	109.32	4.43	21.43	23.93	0.17	10	48.96	corporate media : 21
2	greed_nn	12.7	9	71.43	2.96	20.15	26.71	0.09	7	60.81	corporate greed : 9
3	polluters_nn	12.39	7	NaN	2.62	19.01	27.28	0.07	4	37.92	corporate polluters : 7
4	control_nn	11.38	10	49.34	3.04	15.73	15.65	0.08	7	53.71	corporate control : 10
5	profit_nn	11.31	8	46.81	2.76	15.94	17.31	0.07	6	53.84	corporate profit : 2 corporate profits : 6
6	interest_nn	10.79	9	40.47	2.86	14.11	13.33	0.07	8	64.16	corporate interests : 9
7	america_nn	10.06	7	31.41	2.52	12.49	11.75	0.06	7	63.17	corporate america : 7
8	corruption_nn	9.96	4	28.12	1.97	11.93	15.48	0.04	4	50.51	corporate corruption : 4
9	executive_nn	9.93	5	28.97	2.18	12.27	13.55	0.05	5	55.96	corporate executives : 5
10	tax_nn	9.26	7	23.43	2.43	10.24	8.59	0.05	6	57.9	corporate taxes : 1 corporate tax : 6
11	agenda_nn	8.88	6	20.59	2.26	9.6	8.16	0.05	5	53.46	corporate agenda : 6
12	domination_nn	8.45	4	17.9	1.91	8.9	8.88	0.04	3	38.97	corporate domination : 4
13	mass_nn	8.09	5	15.36	2.03	8.01	6.69	0.04	3	40.24	corporate mass : 5
14	power_nn	7.05	5	8.81	1.81	5.59	4.16	0.03	5	55.96	corporate power : 5
15	attack_nn	5.42	4	2.94	1.25	2.85	2.04	0.02	4	50.51	corporate attacks : 1 corporate attack : 3

Fig. 2. Noun collocates for the adjective corporate in the corpus of communist texts

Automata used for the extraction of collocations can be more complex than just two-word sequences. Below is an example of an automaton accepting 3 generic sequences of parts of speech – *noun-preposition-noun*, *noun-preposition-determiner-noun* and *noun-preposition-pronoun-noun*:

[.*?_nn, .*?_in, .*?_nn]
[.*?_nn, .*?_in, .*?_dt, .*?_nn]
[.*?_nn, .*?_in, .*?_prpd.*?, .*?_nn]

The automaton was used to generate collocations of the noun *war* featured on the first position in the automaton in both corpora:

WAR + PREP + NOUN – Communist Texts										
#	**MI3**	**F**	**G^2**	**T-test**	**Loglog**	**Z-score**	**Dice**	**R(%)**	**JD**	**Matching patterns**
1	18.57	120	651.67	10.55	32.82	54.76	0.55	48	83.95	war with iraq : 20 war against iraq : 21 wars in iraq : 1 war on iraq : 58 war in iraq : 20
2	15.19	38	191.73	5.93	24.65	30.06	0.21	19	67.92	war of terrorism : 1 war against terrorism : 11 war on terrorism : 26
3	11.77	12	57.6	3.32	16.47	16.23	0.07	8	61.82	wars in afghanistan : 1 war on afghanistan : 4 war in afghanistan : 7
4	10.33	4	?	1.98	12.66	17.62	0.03	4	50.51	war in yugoslavia : 1 war on yugoslavia : 2 war against yugoslavia : 1
5	9.56	6	26.8	2.33	11.36	10.63	0.04	5	53.46	war on terror : 6

Fig. 4. Collocations of *war +preposition + noun* in the communist corpus

WAR + PREP + NOUN – Republican Texts										
#	**MI3**	**F**	**G^2**	**T-test**	**Loglog**	**Z-score**	**Dice**	**R(%)**	**JD**	**Matching patterns**
1	20.28	133	1121.8	11.37	43.52	96.42	2.2	48	84.26	war against terror : 8 war on terror : 125
2	11.76	12	56.86	3.32	16.45	16.22	0.11	8	61.26	war against terrorism : 4 war on terrorism : 8
3	8.56	10	12.34	2.32	6.36	4.51	0.04	6	55.96	war with iraq : 1 war on iraq : 1 war in iraq : 8

Fig. 5. Collocations of *war +preposition + noun* in the republican corpus

There are a few interesting distributional tendencies in the results presented above, which can be explained in terms of the ideological bias involved. The communists seem to use the phrases *war on Iraq, war with Iraq* or *war against Iraq* to suggest the idea of *aggression*, *invasion* or *preemption* that cropped up in the results for the terminological test presented in Fig. 1. The collocations obtained from the republican sample show much a preference for the phrase *war on terror.* Also, when *Iraq* and *war* are used in the same phrase, then they typically take the more neutral form of *war in Iraq* instead of the ones potentially implying aggression. Here we can see how much connotative potential a single preposition may contain.

Conclusions

Even in a basic study in lexicon acquisition, the distinction between lexis and the lexicon has to be recognized. The objective of describing the lexicon cannot be achieved by ignoring the evidence found in naturally-occurring lexis. This may happen even in a seemingly lexis-driven approach, if one starts with a preconceived idea of the lexicon which determines the acquisition methods used. The results presented in this paper are a case in point since they show that it is easy to overlook idiomatic lexical meaning, by focusing only on the terminological axis. Lexicon acquisition should be sensitive to both the idiom and the open-choice principles.

REFERENCES

Aston, G. and L. Burnard (1998). *The BNC Handbook: Exploring the British National Corpus with SARA.*

Atkins, B. T. S., B. Levin and A. Zampolli (1994). *Computational Approaches to the Lexicon.* Oxford University Press

Baeza-Yates, R. and B. Ribeiro-Neto (1999). *Modern Information Retrieval.*

Berry, M. W., S. T. Dumais and G. W. O'Brien (1994). *Using Linear Algebra for Intelligent Information Retrieval.*

Biemann C., S. Bordag and U. Quasthoff (2001). *Automatic Acquisition of Paradigmatic Relations using Iterated Co-occurrences.*

BNCweb Manual http://homepage.mac.com/bncweb/manual/bncwebman-collocation.htm

Daille, B. (1995). *Combined Approach for Terminology Extraction: Lexical Statistics and Linguistic Filtering*. UCREL Technical Papers. Vol. 5. Department of Linguistics, University of Lancaster.

Deerwester S., S. Dumais, G. Furnas, K. Landauer and R. Harshman (1990). Indexing by Latent Semantic Analysis. *Journal of the American Society of Information Science.*

Dunning, T. (1993). *Accurate Methods for the Statistics of Surprise and Coincidence.*

Evert S. (2005). *The Statistics of Word Cooccurrences Word Pairs and Collocations.* Dissertationsschrift zur Erlangung der Würde eines Doktors der Philosophie (Dr. phil.), eingereicht bei der Philosophisch-Historischen Fakultät der Universität Stuttgart.

Fellbaum, Ch. (1998). *Introduction.* Wordnet – An Electronic Lexical Database, MIT Press, Cambridge, Massachusetts, London England.

Halliday, M. A. K. (1966). *Lexis as a Linguistic Level.* In memory of J R Firth. Longman's Linguistics Library. Longman's, Green & Co. Ltd.

Halliday, M. A. K. (2004). *Lexicology.* Halliday, M. A. K. *et al.* Lexicology and Corpus Linguistics. An Introduction. Continuum. London, New York.

Heaps, H. S. (1978). *Information Retrieval – Computational and Theoretical Aspects.* Academic Press.

Matsumoto, Y. (2003). "Lexical Knowledge Acquisition". In: Mitkov, R. (ed.). *Oxford Handbook of Computational Lingusitics.* Oxford University Press

McEnery, T. (2003). "Corpus Linguistics". In: Mitkov, R. (ed.). *Oxford Handbook of Computational Lingusitics.* Oxford University Press

Miller, G. (1998). In: Fellbaum, Ch. Wordnet – An Electronic Lexical Database, MIT Press, Cambridge, Massachusetts, London England.

Oakes, M. P. (1998). *Statistics for Corpus Linguistics, Edinburgh Textbooks.* Empirical Linguistics, series editors: McEnery, T. Wilson, A, Edinburgh University Press

Sinclair, J. MCH. (1966). *Beginning the study of lexis.* In memory of J R Firth. Longman's Linguistics Library. Longman's, Green & Co. Ltd.

Sinclair, J. (1991). *Corpus, Concordance, Collocation.* Oxford University Press.

Sinclair, J. (2004). *Trust the Text.* Ed. with Ronald Carter. Routledge.

Stubbs, M. (1995). *Collocations and Semantic Profiles*: On the Cause of the Trouble with Quantitative Studies. In Functions of Language. Benjamins Publishing Company.

Stanisław Goźdź-Roszkowski

University of Łódź

PATTERN AND MEANING IN JUDICIAL ARGUMENTATION
An Exploratory Study

1. Introduction

This study rests upon one important hypothesis according to which different written and spoken genres as well as different discourse communities opt for certain specific, perhaps idiosyncratic phraseologies (cf. Gledhill 2000; Groom 2005). The choices made may be motivated by different institutional purposes or constraints and by different "ideational interests and interpersonal practices" (Groom 2005: 258). It may be then hypothesised that for each genre or discourse there exists a unique 'always evolving phraseological profile' (Groom 2005: 258).

This paper aims to contribute to previous studies done in the area of EAP (e.g. Charles 2000, Hewings and Hewings 2002, Oakey 2002, Groom 2005) by extending the analysis to a different discipline (law) and a different genre (judgments). In this study, I will also attempt to answer the following questions: are there reasons to assume that 'introductory it' patterns are not only characteristic of academic language but they are also a common feature of the language used by judges in their opinions; what are the rhetorical purposes for which these patterns are used and are they different from other genres and disciplines?

In terms of methodology, this study basically follows the methods employed in Groom (2005) with some adaptations. The analysis focuses on 'introductory *it*' patterns defined as "phraseological units in which the dummy subject pronoun *it* is followed by a link verb such as BE, BECOME or SEEM, an adjective or noun group, and a finite or non-finite that-clause, to-clause, wh-clause or -ing clauses" (Groom 2005: 258). The focus of the analysis is narrowed down to that-clause and to-clause complementation since these were found to be a common feature of academic English (e.g. Biber, Conrad and Reppen 1998; Biber *et al.* 1999, Charles 2000, 2004; Hewings and Hewings 2002; Moore 2002; Oakey 2002; Thetela 1997). Additionally, for reasons of space, the discussion provided below will focus only on the three most frequent finite verb forms of 'is', 'seems' and 'would be'.

2. Data and Methodology

My analysis was based on data consisting of a 1,100,000 – word corpus of judgments given by the US Supreme Court and the UK's House of Lords between 2000–2005. For the purpose of this study, judgements are treated as one fairly uniform category of texts, although, clearly, it is possible to distinguish certain subgenres, for example appeal judgments, divorce judgments, default judgments etc. Individual texts may differ considerably in length. In my corpus, they run from 7 paragraphs and 3,000 words to 70 paragraphs and almost 24,000 words. The judgments are not the work of an individual judge but they contain the opinions of a bench of nine judges in the case of the Supreme Court of the United States and usually three or five (seldom more than five) in the case of the House of Lords.

In the case of US judgments, the opinion of the court is delivered, and then, if there is no unanimity among the justices, concurring and dissenting opinions follow. In the judgments given by the House of Lords, there are paragraphs numbered consecutively indicating the order in which the opinions were given. I shall not provide here an exhaustive description of the entire generic structure since such a description would fall outside the remit of this paper. Indeed, there is some variation depending on the type of court and jurisdiction. Basically, each judgment starts with an introduction where the parties are introduced, their legal relation is briefly indicated (e.g. 'Respondent', 'Appellant'), which is then followed by a section headed 'The Facts' in the case of many British judgements (Alcaraz and Hughes 2002: 113) or without any heading in the US Supreme Court's texts. This section contains the essential matters of the case which were assumed or proved. This part of a judgment is then followed by the descriptions and comments from the justices with regard to the relevant law and the parties' contentions. The highly argumentative nature of this text genre is best seen in the concurring and dissenting opinions. Interestingly, judgments tend to be classified as 'operative documents' (Tiersma 1999: 139 and then Gibbons 2003) just as legislation and private documents (contracts and wills) thus stressing its primary role as "official and authentic decision of a court of justice [...] resolving the dispute and determining the rights and obligations of the parties" (Black's Law Dictionary 1990). However, judgments also contain reasoning given by the court for its decisions, which is properly called 'an opinion'. The functions of opinions are both, to some extent, expository (explaining the law) and persuasive. As Solan notes "[...] judges usually care deeply about making the best decision they can, and about conveying their decision in a manner that makes the decision appear as fair as possible to the parties, and often to the public" (Solan 1993: 1). This might suggest that judgments as a text genre elude unequivocal categorisation.

The corpus material was studied with the aid of the *WordSmith Tools* (Scott 1999). The initial input for the analysis was gathered by extracting two-word, three-word and four-word clusters. For example, it turned out that 'it is' is the 11th most frequent lexical bundle with 2243 occurrences making up 0,21% of the whole corpus. Over 95% of all 'it is' sequences were used as introductory *it* patterns. Another sequence 'it would' ranks as 79th with 481 occurrences. By way of further example, consider the following three-word clusters:

It is clear appears 75 times
It is necessary appears 70 times
It is true appears 64
It would be appears 181 times

Apart from being relatively frequent (the frequencies are per one million word), all the clusters occur in at least five different texts, which might be indicative of a wide distribution of these patterns in the corpus data. The examination of four-word clusters helps to identify two types of clause complementation: 'that-clause' and 'to-clause':

It is clear that appears 60 times
It is true that appears 61
It is necessary to appears 53

It is now possible to notice an emerging pattern, which can be generalised as follows:

***it* v-link ADJ that** and ***it* v-link ADJ to-inf** (notation after Hunston and Francis 1999).

The scrutiny of five-word bundles led to the identification of phraseological sequences which were coded according to a system of classification based on Francis *et al.* (1998: 480–484, 494–498). The classification used in this study consists of six meaning groups: adequacy, desirability, ease or difficulty, neccessity or importance, validity and evaluating. The decision regarding assigning a particular sequence to a given category was made after an examination of relevant context.

3. Results and discussion

3.1. *It is* ADJ that/to inf

Let us now turn to the examination of the prevalent pattern/meaning associations for ***it is*** **ADJ that/to inf**. My data show that ***it v-link*** **ADJ that** tends to be essentially associated with VALIDITY and EVALUATION, while ***it v-link*** **ADJ to-inf** is more closely associated with ADEQUACY, DESIRABILITY, EASE or DIFFICULTY, NECESSITY/IMPORTANCE, and DIFFICULTY. This finding basically corroborates Biber's finding that the frequencies of these meaning groups vary across the two genres in terms of their distribution (Biber 1999: 721).

Table 1. Pattern/meaning association for *it is* ADJ that/to inf

<table>
<tr><td>ADEQUACY</td><td>in conformity with the required or expected standards</td><td>(5%) Sufficient, Proper, Reasonable, Unreasonable</td></tr>
<tr><td colspan="3">[1] It is not sufficient merely to articulate some connection between the group's expressive activities and its exclusionary activities.
[2] In answering that question, it is entirely proper to look to the common law</td></tr>
<tr><td>DESIRABILITY</td><td>appropriate to the circumstances</td><td>(5%) Desirable, Appropriate, Unfortunate</td></tr>
<tr><td colspan="3">[3] It is appropriate to begin by explaining why certain aspects of the case are not relevant to the narrow issue that we must resolve.</td></tr>
<tr><td>EASE or DIFFICULTY</td><td colspan="2">(15%) Difficult, Easy, Possible</td></tr>
<tr><td colspan="3">[4] It is difficult to see why in principle only those plaintiffs who negotiate guarantees may recover non-pecuniary damages for a breach of contract.</td></tr>
<tr><td>NECESSITY or IMPORTANCE</td><td colspan="2">(30%) Essential, Important, Necessary, Notable, Noteworthy, Significant, Remarkable, Relevant, Unnecessary</td></tr>
<tr><td colspan="3">[5] It is first necessary to decide, consistently with the Strasbourg jurisprudence, whether such a right does exist in domestic law.</td></tr>
<tr><td>VALIDITY</td><td colspan="2">(40%) Arguable, Apparent, Evident, Undisputed, Clear, Likely, Obvious, Plain, Possible, True, Understandable, Right;</td></tr>
<tr><td colspan="3">[6] It is abundantly clear that all of the land owned by the Tribe within the boundaries of its reservation qualifies as Indian country.</td></tr>
<tr><td>EVALUATION</td><td colspan="2">(5%) Useful, Surprising</td></tr>
<tr><td colspan="3">[7] It is not surprising that different Courts in cases before the present one should have taken different views as to the meaning of section (...)</td></tr>
</table>

As Table 1 shows VALIDITY is the dominant meaning group with ***it is* ADJ that pattern** prevalent in judgments. This tendency is similar to that observed by Groom (2005) in his study of research articles in history and biology. My data support the distinction made by Francis *et al.* (1998) between VALIDITY assessment based on *prima facie* evidence and thus relying on notions of *obviousness* and the other based on appeals to *plausibility.* The former could be exemplified by sentence [6] and the latter by the use of the pattern ***it is* LIKELY *that*.** However, in quantitative terms, the first type of VALIDITY assessment is by far the most frequent. ***It is* LIKELY *that*** and ***it is* POSSIBLE *that*** are in fact the only patterns expressing circumstantial evaluation found in the whole corpus with the total of 25 occurrences per million words. By contrast, there are ten patterns in the first type (note that ARGUABLE is used in the sense "as can be supported by argument" rather than "open to argument, dispute or question"). This discrepancy might be explained in extra-linguistic terms by referring to certain expectations on the part of litigants and perhaps the general public. As Solan notes "because judges wield such enormous power, there is pressure on them to speak decisively" (1993: 2).

The dominance of the VALIDITY meaning can be seen in a similar pattern ***It v-link* ADJ -ed that** (illustrated by Table 2).[1]

Table 2

***It v-link* ADJ -ed that**
Accepted, Agreed, Alleged, Argued, Averred, (well) Established, (well) Known, (well) Settled
It is accepted that if this case falls within Article 5 (1) it does not fall within Article 5 (3).

By way of digression, it is also worth noting the occurrence of other VALIDITY phrases such as: ***it is* COMMON GROUND that; *it is* NOT IN DISPUTE that; *it is* OUR JUDGEMENT that.**

The data used in this study also corroborate Hunston's claim that collocation is not confined only to individual words, but it works with larger phraseological units, which helps to achieve textual cohesion on a more global scale (2001). The sequence ***it is true that*** is frequently preceded by ***while*** thus forming a concessive clause which then pairs with a counterclaim:

---

[1] In fact, some authors do not make a distinction between ***It v-link* ADJ-ed that** and ***It v-link* ADJ that** (cf. Biber 1999).

[8] ***While it is true that*** *the language of section 7(5) of the 1963 Act was not materially different from that of section 14(3) of the 1980 Act, I think that the Court of Appeal in Forbes was right in saying that the introduction of the discretion under section 33 had altered the balance.*

[9] *In the first place* ***while it is true that*** *neither of the above quoted specifically excluded claims by the promisee for loss suffered by a third party,* ***it is equally true that*** *in neither case was the position of a third party under consideration.*

The emergence of larger phraseological units can be also observed in the pattern ***it is*** **DIFFICULT/EASY** ***to*** which in over 60% is followed by either *see* or *understand.* Even more interestingly, **SURPRISING** in the pattern ***it is*** **SURPRISING** ***to*** is invariably preceded by 'not', 'scarcely' or 'hardly' as in [7] above and:

[10] ***It is scarcely surprising*** *that this House, in Bellinger, held that these difficult questions of definition, demarcation and impact upon others were for Parliament rather for Parliament rather than the courts to decide.*

This would confirm Francis' observation made for general English that the phrase *it is not/hardly surprising that* is more frequent than *it is surprising that* (Francis 1995).

The **EASE or DIFFICULTY** group is the dominant phraseology for book reviews in history and literary criticism (Groom 2005: 266), while in judgments it is the third largest category. In all the disciplines, however, this phraseology is used to evaluate. In judgments, it is used to make negative assessments of reasoning or legal principles, for instance those espoused by a lower court as in [4] above or a majority opinion of fellow justices as in:

[11] ***It is difficult to understand****, and neither the Court, nor Justice Thomas explains, why the Constitution would require a state legislature to follow such a meaningless and formalistic difference in drafting its criminal statutes.*

Contrary to what Groom finds in his data, in judgments this pattern is very seldom used for praise. Below is the only exception found in my corpus:

[12] *This is a wider definition than is employed in our domestic law* [...], *but* ***it is easy to*** *apply and serves to give full effect to the policy of Section 3 without extending it further than is necessary to achieve its object.*

Groom notes that this phraseology is a fine example of a strategy employed by academic writers to construct 'an apppropriate academic persona' for themselves (Charles 2000 qtd. in Groom 2005).

Indeed, the ***it*** **v-link to-inf** appears to be useful in all those cases where writers want to be perceived as objective and rational and does not seem to be restricted to a particular discipline or genre.

3.2. *It would be* ADJ pattern

The three-word bundle ***it would be*** appears 181 times in the corpus with 150 instances conforming to the ***it would be*** **ADJ** pattern.

Table 3

it would be ADJ **pattern**
abnormal, absurd, anomalous, appropriate, difficult, equitable, extraordinary, fair, illogical, impossible, improper, inappropriate, incongruous, inconsistent, justifiable, necessary, odd, right, sensible, unconscionable, unfair, unrealistic, unusual, wrong, unwise

As examples 13–18 illustrate, the to-infinitive pattern dominates sequences beginning with ***it would be.*** It is EVALUATION rather than VALIDITY that appears to be the main meaning group. It is worth noting that most of the adjectives occurring in this patterns carry negative evaluations. Judges tend to use the pattern ***it would be*** **ADJ to-inf** to assess the consequences of deviating from some norm or standard except for the last sentence [18] which could be interpreted as a recommendation of what is perceived to be the proper course of action.

[13] ***It would be unfair to*** *take account of work to the extent to which it merely restored the property to its former state.*

[14] ***It would be objectively unreasonable to*** *require the respondent to employ the applicant as a police constable if in law and fact she could not carry out the full range of a police constable's duties.*

[15] ***It would be wrong to*** *adopt an excessively technical or formalistic approach to the case.*

[16] ***It would be anomalous to allow*** *relation back under Rule 15 (c) (2) based on a broader reading of the words 'conduct, transaction, or occurrence' in Federal habeas proceedings than in ordinary civil litigation.*

[17] ***It would be anomalous to allow*** *courts to sit in review of judgments entered by courts of equal or greater authority.*

[18] ***It would be equitable to allow*** *the claim to proceed having regard to the balance of prejudice.*

Sentences [16] and [17] illustrate an interesting observation that the pattern ***it would be*** **ANOMALOUS to** frequently co-occurs with *allow*. The concordances for **ANOMALOUS** show its restricted distribution. In more than half instances of its occurrence, **ANOMALOUS** is found in this pattern.

It would be patterns in judgments differ from those found in certain types of academic discourse (cf. Groom 2005). In both, they deal with anticipated objections to the unfolding argument presented in the text, but in academic texts, more emphasis is placed on persuading the reader to reject plausible alternative interpretations or even to persuade readers to accept interpretations "which might at first glance seem rather far-fetched" (Groom 2005: 271) as in the following example:

[19] *While* ***it would be naïve to identify*** *Utopia with any one of these geographical features, it is important to note there are plenty of islands in the Indo-Pacific Region that could have served as prototypes for Utopia* (Groom 2005: 271).

The tone adopted by judges and realised through this pattern is more 'categorical', decisive, almost succinct.

3.3. *It seems* ADJ

In quantitative terms, ***it seems*** **ADJ** pattern is the least frequent with only 112 occurrences although, admittedly, it is not considerably less frequent than the previous pattern. The comparatively low frequency of ***it would be*** **ADJ** and ***it seems*** **ADJ** patterns can be explained in terms of discipline-specific nature of judgments. Judges tend to adopt a way of conveying their decision in a decisive manner demonstrating their authority, which is supposed to make them appear fair to the parties. It is not surprising therefore that they would avoid indulging in a language that could give the impression that they might have their doubts as to the interpretation of the relevant law, even if this was actually the case (cf. Solan 1993: 2).

Table 4

it seems **ADJ** *pattern*
arguable, **clear** , difficult, impossible, indisputable, **likely**, nonsensical, obvious, odd, perverse, **plain**, proper, strange, unlikely,

The concordance analysis reveals a motivated association between the ***it v-link ADJ that*** pattern and the VALIDITY meaning group. This association suggests that ***it seems*** **ADJ that**, like ***it is*** **ADJ that** discussed above is first and foremost a resource for claim making (*clear, likely* and *plain* shown in bold in Table 4, account for over **90%** of all sequences appearing in this pattern!)

[20] ***It seems clear that*** *Parliament made no special provision for appeals because it considered that there was an appeal under the general jurisdiction of the Court of Appeal.*

[21] ***It seems likely that*** *in his students' handbook Mr Topham used the word 'liquidation', not as meaning 'winding up' but as meaning 'realisation'.*

[22] ***It seems indisputable that*** *an association that seeks to transmit such a system of values engages in expressive activity.*

In history, ***it seems*** **LIKELY/OBVIOUS that** dominates, while in literary studies, "the semantic focus shifts from VALIDITY to DESIRABILITY, and thus from the impersonal evaluation of autonomous written arguments to the highly personalised evaluation of individual scholarly acts" (Groom 2005: 271). In history, the patterns is used to assess the validity of the reviewed book's interpretation of the historical record. There appear to be discipline-specific differences in the rhetorical goals of this pattern. In judgments, the ***it seems*** patterns are employed primarily to assess the validity of claims, which is usually followed by some reference to the evidential basis.

Conclusion

The present study is too narrow in scope to support the claim that it is feasible to describe and differentiate between genres and disciplinary discourses in terms of their phraseological patterns. However, it has been clearly demonstrated that the two patterns ***it*** **v-link ADJ that** and ***it*** **v-link ADJ to-inf** are not phraseologies preferred only in academic genres but they appear to be popular with judges too. In addition, there is some evidence to suggest that the two patterns vary systematically across genres and disciplinary discourses depending on their different communicative goals and epistemological precepts. Clearly, more large-scale, corpus-based investigation is needed to ascertain whether it is feasible to identify a genre by building up its phraseological profile. This kind of analysis might be particularly useful to study phraseological variation within a particular disciplinary discourse. As a very brief and final observation, consider that in a different 1,000,000 corpus of contracts (compiled by the author of this study) the ***it v-link*** [is, would, seem] **ADJ** pattern does not appear at all. The ***it v-link*** **ADJ-ed** is realised in very few sequences such as, **it is agreed as follows, it is expected that, it is desired to, it is intended that**.

REFERENCES

Alcaraz, E. and B. Hughes (2002). *Legal Translation Explained.* Manchester, UK & Northampton, MA: St Jerome Publishing.

Biber, D., Conrad, S. and R. Reppen (1998). *Corpus linguistics: Investigating language structure and use.* Cambridge, MA: Cambridge University Press.

Biber, D., Johansson, S., Leech, G., Conrad, S. and E. Finegan (1999). *Longman Grammar of Spoken and Written English.* Harlow: Pearson Education.

Charles, M. (2000). "The Role of of an introductory it pattern in constructing an appropriate academic persona". In: Thompson, P. (ed.). *Patterns and perspectives: Insights into EAP writing practice*: 45–59. CALS: The University of Reading.

Francis, G. (1995). "Corpus-driven grammar and its relevance to the learning of English in a cross-cultural situation". In: Pakir, A. (ed.). *English in Education: Multicultural perspectives.* Singapore: Unipress.

Francis, G., Manning, E. and S. Hunston (1998). *Collins COBUILD grammar patterns 2: Nouns and adjectives.* London: HarperCollins.

Gibbons, J. (2003). *Forensic Linguistics. An Introduction to Language in the Justice System.* Blackwell Publishing.

Gledhill, C. (2000). "The discourse function of collocation in research article introductions". *English for Specific Purposes*, 19: 115–135.

Groom, N. (2005) "Pattern and meaning across genres and disciplines: An exploratory study". *Journal of English for Academic Purposes*, 4: 257–277.

Hewings, M. and A. Hewings (2002). "It interesting to note…: A comparative study of anticipatory 'it' in student and published writing". *English for Specific Purposes*, 21: 367–383.

Hunston, S. (2001). "Colligation, lexis, pattern and text". In: Thompson, G. and M. Scott (eds). *Patterns of text: In honour of Michael Hoey*: 13–33. Amsterdam: John Benjamins.

Hunston, S. and G. Francis (1999) *Pattern grammar: A corpus-driven approach to the lexical grammar of English.* Amsterdam: John Benjamins.

Moore, T. (2002). "Knowledge and agency: A study of metaphenomenal discourse in textbooks from three disciplines". *English for Specific Purposes*, 21: 347–366.

Oakey, D. (2002). "Lexical phrases for teaching academic writing in English: Corpus evidence". In: Nuccorini (ed.). *Phrases and phraseology – Data and descriptions*: 85–105. Bern: Peter Lang.

Scott, M. (1999). *WordSmith Tools (Version 3.0).* Oxford: Oxford University Press.

Solan, L. (1993). *The Language of Judges.* Chicago: Chicago University Press.

Thetela, P. (1997). "Evaluated entities and parameters of value in academic research articles". *English for Specific Purposes*, 16: 101–118.

Tiersma, P. (1999). *Legal Language*. Chicago: The University of Chicago Press.

Adam Bednarek

University of Łódź

METHODOLOGY OF DATA COLLECTION – CANADIANISMS IN METROPOLITAN TORONTO

1. Introduction

The purpose of this paper is to present the methodology behind collecting both spoken and written data concerning the occurrence of Canadian specific vocabulary in metropolitan Toronto – a study carried out in July 2004.

Toronto is a very cosmopolitan city and similar to Canadian culture it is a 'melting pot'. The purpose of the study was to ascertain the status of Canadian verbal culture, specifically Canadianisms, in such a multicultural environment. The author had prepared a series of questionnaires (based on entries from the "Canadian Oxford Dictionary") distributed among randomly chosen participants, who provided material referring to: the choice of an Americanism over a Canadianism; words and expressions concerning Canadian history and culture; elements of food and drink; finally, lexical items used in an 'everyday use' context. Furthermore, the author obtained a two years collection of articles from the Toronto Sun® consisting of over 600 000 text files, made references to the American National Corpus and the Aligned *Hansards* of the 36th Parliament of Canada (this release contains 1.3 million pairs of aligned texts from records of the 36th Canadian Parliament). This material constitutes, what the author refers to as LCCES (Lodz Corpus for Candaian English Study).

The first part focuses on presenting the questionnaires; the paper provides informational background concerning Canadian specific lexical items, presents the process of data collection and the obtained text files. The latter shows gives samples of collected material and obtained results. The author will focus on *Chesterfield* and *Fire Hall*.

2. Canadianisms

Howard B. Woods (1993) defines Canadian English as 'an off-shoot of American English", assuming that the essence of CE is the linguistic duality of Standard Southern British English being treated as 'correct and desirable', while North American English as 'honest and homey" (Woods 1993: 153). He assumes that Canadians will have to attempt defining national identity by other means than language, due to the fact that pronunciation, vocabulary and syntax appear to be becoming more American (Woods 1993: 174). Woods' study in Ottawa, showed that 'Canadians will more likely find a distinct identity in the way they carry out there daily activities" (Woods 1993: 174). However, many, as B. W. Powe (1987) argue that Canadian identity is inconclusive, suggesting that that 'Canada has a discontinuous character" (Powe 1987: 68–69) The question of whether Canadian verbal culture is giving way to American verbal culture, is of great interest to this study

'Canadianisms' should be considered as expressions of national identity, due to the need for socio-cultural background contextual knowledge in the interpretation of an utterance (Bednarek 2005: 481–482). Gumperz (1972) reminds that the choice of language is mostly subconscious and social information of a message is largely dependant on context (Gumperz 1972: 23–24). One talks of Canadianisms in pronunciation (Canadian-raising), grammar and in the case of this study – vocabulary.

Scargill (1955) initiated linguistic surveys in Canada as a way of describing Canadian English with reference to culture and identity. Scargill assumes that "where there is language, there must be a notion to have made it what it is" (Scargill 1955: 27). Canadian specific vocabulary is thus a representation of 'being Canadian'. These lexical items allow such a multicultural society to appear as one – to appear as Canadians (cf. Bednarek 2005: 482). And the interest in language variation and dialect topography of 'Canadianisms' continues with Chambers (1992) and Chambers and Heisler (1999) following Allan (1973: 76).

Canadian English pronunciation is frequently termed as General North American speech, therefore many of the differences between CE and GA can be seen through vocabulary. Canadianisms, thus express indigenous plant and animal life, politics and culture. The origins of these items vary. Many place names come from, or are derived from Indian languages (including the name of the country – from *kanata*, meaning *community*, *village*), appeared due to technological development, or became obscure and obsolete in England, with their meaning becoming unique to Canada (Chambers 2003: 18–19).

The study of Canadianisms shows that Canadian specific vocabulary acknowledges references to places (*beer parlour*, *beverage room*, *Parkade*, *Sportsplex*), actions (*tollgating*, *dream in color*), food (*backbacon*, *paska*, *smokie*, *clubhouse sandwich*), people (*hoser*, *import*, *homebrew*), objects (*enterphone*, *loonie*, *toonie*, *eavestrough*) and references to a particular historical or political Canadian context (*Big Blue Machine*, *Redcoat*, *Minister's Permit*, *Big Six*, *Revenge of the Cradle*, *Molson Muscle*).

3. The Study

In reference to assumptions as proposed by Woods (1993), the purpose of the study was to ascertain the status of Canadian specific lexical items in both the spoken and written medium in metropolitan Toronto. The initial assumptions involved studying 'Canadianisms' among a chosen ethnic group, with focus on 2nd and 3rd generation emigrants; in this case Polish emigrants. However, due to the lack of cooperation from the Polish community, the author had decided to focus on the multiethnic and multicultural background of Toronto, with no distinction made to a specific ethnic background. The idea was to treat Toronto's inhabitants in the Bibby (1990) tradition of a 'melting pot' or 'patchwork quilt of cultures', which contribute to the development of the 'official culture' and cultivate their own.

The author's interest lay in the following:

– Would Toronto inhabitants use a Canadian lexical item in a provided context,

– Would Toronto inhabitants recognize socio-cultural vocabulary,

– Would Toronto inhabitants chose a Canadianism over an item more preferably chosen by a speaker of General American (GA),

– Does Toronto media foster 'being Canadian' by using lexical items in the 'Canadian sense'.

The initial stage of the project involved preparing a list of chosen lexical items, defined as originating from, or having a meaning peculiar to Canada. The data came from the 1998 edition of the 'Canadian Oxford Dictionary'[1]. 969 items were chosen, with the next stage involving the exclusion of regionalisms. A group of randomly chosen 88 items was finally chosen for the study.

[1] The author makes use of the 1998 version: *The Canadian Oxford Dictionary*, ed. Katharine Barber; Oxford University Press, 1998.

The author had prepared a series of questionnaires, with the intention of distributing them among randomly chosen participants in downtown Toronto – an area between by Spadina Ave, Bloor St, Jarvis St and Gardiner Expwy. The questionnaires were divided into 4 thematic parts, each involving a different task. The study took place between the 1st and 30th of July 2004.

The 'American or Canadian' (1) questionnaire presented the participants with a text, in which a they had to choose between 2 items – one Canadian English (CE) element and a GA one. The respondent was not told of this distinction and was asked to circle the item, which he or she would most preferably use in everyday life.

The 'History and Culture' (2) questionnaire required the participants to explain in their own words a term presented, involving reference to Canadian history. The "Food and Drink' (3) questionnaire involved connecting a word with its definition from the 'Canadian Oxford Dictionary'. In order to avoid process of elimination, respondents where presented with only one item. There was no possibility of correction.

These three questionnaires were distributed in parks, shopping malls and fast food stands, between 10am and 4pm., Monday through Saturday. The researcher would switch the questionnaire every hour, that is (1) was distributed between 10am and 11am, and 1pm and 2 pm; (2) and (3) as above.

The 'Everyday Use' (4) questionnaire required filling in the gaps with an appropriate word in the given context. The sentences are extracts taken from articles appearing in the 2002 and 2003 editions of Canada's most popular daily – the Toronto Sun®. 10 items did not fit in with any of the contexts. Due to the length of the task, this questionnaire required the researcher to meet with a previously appointed group and provide them with 30 minutes to fulfill the task.

The distributed questionnaires are presented below:

(1)

PERSONAL DETAILS:
Age: (10–19) (20–29) (30–39) (40–49) (50–59) (60 and over)
Sex: Male/Female
Country of attended schools: (Poland, Canada, USA, Other)
Schools attended: (High School, College, University)
Instructions: **Choose out of those presented in bold the word that you would choose in everyday life**

John woke up early in the morning ready for a new day. He put the supper leftovers in the **garbage disposal/garbarator**.He wanted to clean the dishes but he realized that he was out of **dish soap/dishwashing liquid**. It was still early and the **milk store/convenience store** was probably still closed. He sat there for a minute watching the **Prime Minister/First minister** give a televised address when he realized that he was also out of **homo milk/whole milk**. He had no choice he so had to go out and buy what he needed.Since it was still early, he decided to visit his friend who worked at a **fire station/fire hall** neerby. Unfortunatly, he hadn't yet arrived for work. He stood there thinking what to do next, when suddenly an old friend passed him by. John hadn't seen Charlie since they were both kids. He thought of the great times they had – trips to the **ice rink/ice pad**, eating delicious **smokies/hot-dogs** at the mall and not to mention his mother's delicious **backbacon/Canadian bacon**. At school Charlie had the opinion of being a **keener/suck-up**. Many boys used to call him a **browner/brown noser**. But John didn't mind. He liked Charlie just the way he was. Charlie probably didn't notice his old friend and walked by. John followed him and a few minutes after he went into his apartment building, John called him up on the **intercom/enetrphone**. "Who is it?" – asked Charlie. "An old friend" – replied John. Once he got up the stairs, Charlie couldn't believe his eyes. They sat on the **Chesterfield/couch**. They had a lot of catching up to do. The apartment was rather big. The one thing that struck John's mind was a big poster on the wall representing the **Underground Railway/Underground railroad**, a time when the black slaves from the South fled North to salvation. John remembered his friend's obsession with this time in history. They sat there drinking a **Bloody Caesar/Bloody Mary** talking about their present lives. Charlie was working as a **beer slinger/bartender** at the pub. "I can tell" – stated John. "How?" – asked Charlie. "By your **Molson muscle/potbelly**" – John replied.

(2)

PERSONAL DETAILS:
Age: (10–19) (20–29) (30–39) (40–49) (50–59) (60 and over)
Sex: Male/Female
Country of attended schools: (Poland, Canada, USA, Other)
Schools attended: (High School, College, University)
Instructions: Please explain the following terms

1) Big Blue Machine
2) Big Six
3) Dirty Thirties
4) Great White North
5) Minister's Permit
6) Quiet Revolution
7) Redcoat
8) Revenge of the Cradle

(3)

PERSONAL DETAILS:
Age: (10–19) (20–29) (30–39) (40–49) (50–59) (60 and over)
Sex: Male/Female
Country of attended schools: (Poland, Canada, USA, Other)
Schools attended: (High School, College, University)
Instructions: Match the following terms to the definition

Javex, Stanfields, Forty-ouncer, Nanaimo bar, Varsol, Twenty-six, Two-four, Paska, Cottage roll, Brown Cow, Mickey, Butter tart

1) Mineral spirits (prop. name) –
2) A case of twenty-four bottles of beer -
3) A 26-ounce bottle of liquor –
4) Clorine bleach (prop. name) –
5) A desert consisting of a crust of chocolate –
6) Decorated egg bread -
7) Men's uderwaer esp. long underwear (prop. name) -
8) Pickeled, boneless ham from the pork butt
9) A forty-once bottle of liqour –
10) A coctail of coffee liqour and milk or cream –
11) A half bottle of liquor (375 ml.) –
12) A tart with a filling of butter, eggs, brown sugar and raisins –

(4)

PERSONAL DETAILS:
Age: (10–19) (20–29) (30–39) (40–49) (50–59) (60 and over)
Sex: Male/Female
Country of attended schools: (Poland, Canada, USA, Other)
Schools attended: (High School, College, University)
Instructions: Choose the word that best fits the context. Note that 10 items will not appear.

Loonie, Tollgating, Relief camp, Stickhandle, Booze Can, Ice pad, Steamie, Plug-in, Dipsy-doodle, Hang up one's skates, Garbarator, Francophonie, Joe job, Lob ball, Whiskey Jack, Dream in color, Tuck shop, Hydro, Pogey, Johnny Canuck, Rollie, Salter, Anglophone, Francophone, Health card, Impaired, Red eye, Clubhouse sandwich, Import, Texas mickey, Toonie, Jollie jumper, Suck, Parkade, Sportsplex, Pepsi, Eavestrough, Adavanced green, Cosmetic bag, Beer parlour,

1) How much did Enron charge for a kilowatt hour? Pennies. Enron's former CEO says. You wouldn't understand our workings. Heaven knows I didn't. Complex financial agreements. Partnership ________________. Foreward halfgainers with a backword twist.
2) The journalist liked the politician so he threw him a ________ __________. The politician thus turned out very competent.
3) She presented each birthday recepient with a card containing a sum of money which the residents appreciate as they can use the extra cash to purchase treats from the ________________.
4) The First Minister is going to ____________________ next month. Retirement finally caught up with him to.
5) That night the frost was sharp. "Thank God for the ___________. At least I will be able to drive to work once they go through the neighborhood", said John Knowls.
6) Put your cosmetics into the _________________
7) Keep on ____________________ Billy. You are never going to get that job.

8) Stephen Harper used his first major speech in Quebec to dismiss two ideals held dear by even the most moderate _______________ voters – protection of the French language and Quebec's status in the constitution.
9) The police cracked down on 3 _______________ this week. "There won't be any illegal bars operating at home in this city", said the mayor.
10) _________________ is illegal. You can't pay or extort a bribe for the right to do business
11) The 28th anual Athletes in Action Senior Bowl kicks off tonight at Minto Field at the Nepean ____________________
12) That man is _________________. You can tell that he is from Quebec.
13) Your child is such a ____________. Look he is making a face in front of the professor.
14) Can you make me a _________? I hate the cigarettes you buy in a pack.
15) Turning lanes at an _____________ lights in both directions would clear traffic and improve the intersection.
16) Last fall J. Wood, 26, switched from the University of Windsor to her current third-year B.A. courses at Universite du Quebec, where she is a rare ____________________ student.
17) Now, it was not my habit to make use of the popular ____________ aspect of the Albion, though it was interesting to hear that they that they had been "the longest bar in Western Canada" at one time.
18) Ontarians awoke to find competitive running through their ____________ sockets this morning under the new era of private companies generating and selling electricity.
19) Japanese embassy officials refused to waive Toguri's diplomatic immunity after he was charged with _______________ driving and failing to provide a breath sample.
20) Her duplex mate is lax with repairs to the building's exterior: the front __________________ is missing and resulting runoff is damaging the siding and causing water infiltration inside her home.
21) Canadian Matt Robichaud and ________________ Marcus Wiggins, the team's long snapper, are trying to land jobs.
22) A 70-year old _______________ must with draw a minimum of 5% from his RRIF and so can expect to live another 20 years. That's 7.4 years less than his U.S. Uncle Sam.
23) The _________________ closed at 64.07 US cents yesterday as the highest close since Oct. 15.
24) For those executives who wish to use or recharge any assortments of today's personal business tools, two 12-volt __________________ sockets are provided for the rear seated passengers.
25) Rick Savoie, 50, said he purchased a ticket at the CPA's Municipal Building ______________________. "I hate coming downtown because of the parking", he said.
26) In 1993, there were over 90,000 people in social assistance. Now, there are only 27,000 on _________________ .
27) "If I can't shoot or battle for the puck or _______________, obviously that's not good enough to return", Sundin said yesterday.

28) The birds are also astounding – hold your snack close or a brave _______________ will fly in to nab it.
29) You can't match last year's $10 donation. How about $5 or a _______________ or loonie.
30) Compiling the information together is a _______________. It is the most monotonous job I've ever done.

The author had collected 431 questionnaires, which included 158 for (1), 148 for (2), 107 for (3) and 18 for (4). The participants were of various social and educational backgrounds, both lower, middle and upper class and aged between 10 and 80.

Further study involved analysis of the written medium. Concordance results for each of the items were generated. The author had obtained 2 years worth of texts from the Toronto Sun® (daily issues 2002–2003). The 2003 editions contain 299 200 text files, while the 2003 editions contain 341 931 text files. The obtained texts include both articles and classifieds appearing in the newspaper.

The texts of each year are grouped into sub-files by the month. These are further grouped into 2 or 3 sub-files, depending on the amount of texts within that month. Treated as a whole, the corpus contains 24 monthly sub-files. These were grouped in such a way as to allow for the comparison of chosen months. The exact figures for each month are presented in Table 1 below:

Table 1. Number of text files by the month

Month	2002 number of files	2003 number of files
January	28 407	10 405
February	28 417	1 387
March	30 064	32 154
April	29 665	31 414
May	30 887	32 001
June	30 239	5 815
July	28 940	7 505
August	29 231	36 482
September	27 301	35 196
October	30 719	36 843
November	31 257	36 772
December	16 804	33 676

The discrepancies between the amounts of texts result from the fact that these were purchased from the Toronto Sun® archives and were the only ones available for the given month at the time of purchase.

Furthermore, the American National Corpus (ANC) and the Aligned *Hansards* of the 36th Parliament of Canada Release 2001-1a were used as reference material. The author made use of *Wordsmith Tools* version *3.0* in order to obtain concordance results. The ANC is used in order to ascertain the status of the studied elements in American English, while Hansards serves as comparison material.

Summing up, the LCCES contains 431 questionnaire based texts and approximately 640 000 text files of newspaper articles and classifieds from the Toronto Sun®, with the ANC and Hansards Corpus serving as reference material.

4. Chesterfield and Fire Hall

Allan (1973–1976) reports on the 1949–1953 LAUM[2] fieldwork, which identifies *Chesterfield* as 'uniquely' Canadian. Chambers (1979) acknowledges that "48.91% used *couch* compared to 34.58% for *Chesterfield*" (Chambers 1979: 176). This data was obtained in the 1970's. The 'Dialect Topography of the Golden Horseshoe Survey' (Chambers 1992) shows a further decline of the 'Canadianism' in favor of the GA term; The 2004 Toronto study showed further decrease in its use.

Fire Hall proved to far less popular within the city boundaries. What proves interesting, is that in surrounding cities, fire houses are called *fire halls (Brampton Fire Hall no. 5)*, while within Toronto they are *fire stations (Toronto Fire Station no. 1)*.

The following is a comparison of questionnaire and concordance results of the two presented lexical items. For the purpose of this paper, only the 2003 concordance results will be mentioned. Both appeared in the 'American or Canadian' questionnaire. The data is presented in the diagrams presented below. Diagram 1 compares the items on the basis of the number of respondents; Diagram 2 focuses on gender distinction; Diagram 3 looks at age groups, while Diagram 4 compares educational backgrounds of the respondents. Note the following:

[2] The Linguistic Atlas of the Upper Midwest

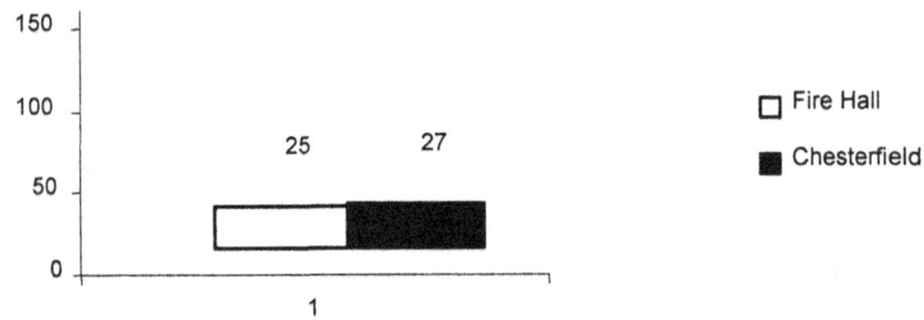

Diagram 1. Number of participants who chose the item

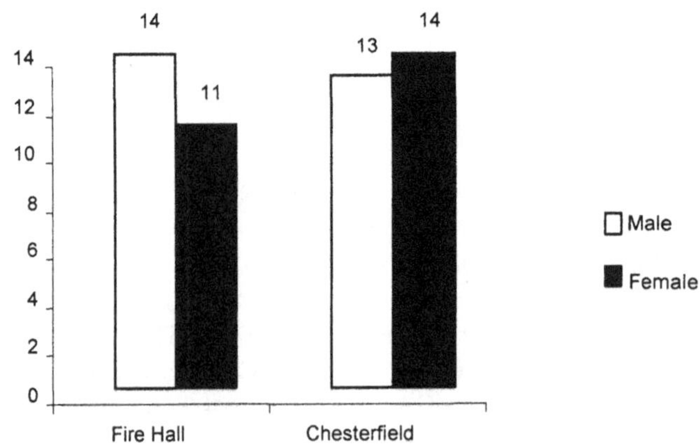

Diagram 2. Gender distinction

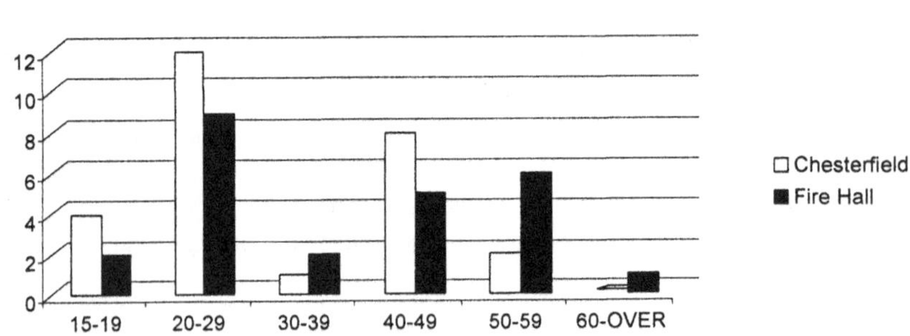

Diagram 3. Age group distinction

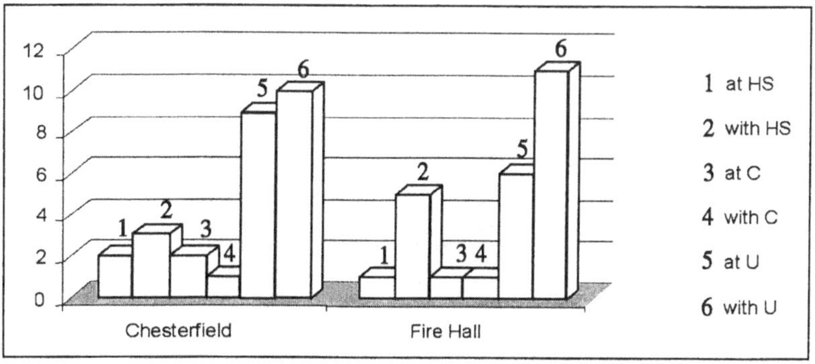

Diagram 4. Educational background

The study of the objects confirmed the decline in use of *Chesterfield* as the name for a piece of furniture one may sit or lay on as reported by Chambers (1992, 1995). The author's study showed that approximately 17.08% of the participants would favor this lexical item. Similarly, only 15.82% of the respondents would preferably use *Fire Hall.*

An analysis of concordance results, confirmed the decline of *Chesterfield.* The Canadianism accounts for 8 concordance results, in comparison with 818 for the GA item *couch.* On the other hand, *fire hall* accounts for 356 concordance results, compared with 127 for *fire station.* Please refer to Diagram 5 and 6 (cf Bednarek, forthcoming a):

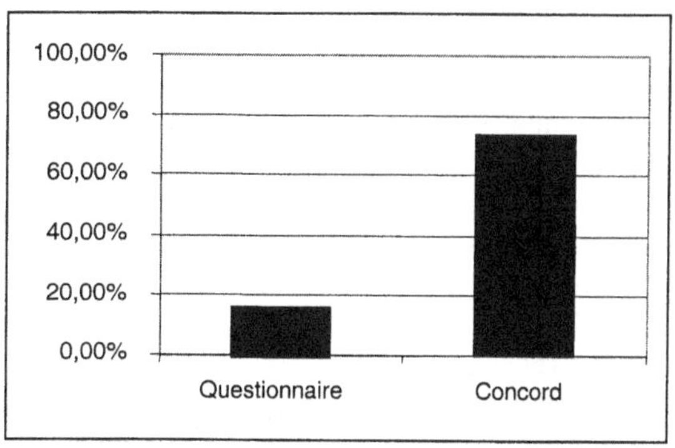

Diagram 5. *Fire Hall* questionnaire/concord comparison

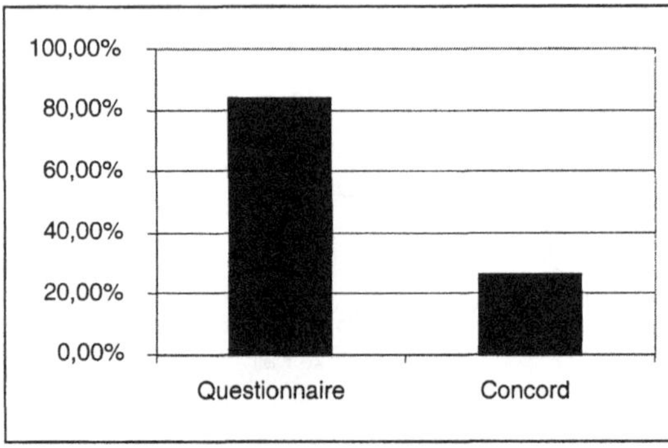

Diagram 6. *Fire Station* questionnaire/concord comparison

This clearly indicates that *Fire Hall* is much more preferably chosen in the written medium. One must also take into account, the fact that the Toronto Sun® also appears in areas outside the city; areas where, as mentioned before, *Fire Hall* is the preferable element. Observations concerning larger groups of items are found in Bednarek (cf Bednarek, forthcoming a, b).

5. Conclusion

Canadian domestic policy encourages the media to foster 'Canadian sense'. This includes both portraying symbols of Canada, as well as using CE. As presented in Bednarek (cf Bednarek, forthcoming a, b), many Canadianisms appear to be far more popular in questionnaire data, rather than in newspaper texts and vice versa. Many items considered 'textbook' examples appeared to be far less popular than their GA equivalent. Instances of this occur both in questionnaire and newspaper data.

The assumption put forward by Woods (1993) is supported by the fact that American media play a predominant role in Canada and Toronto "due to its geographical location has always maintained both economic and social relations with the United States" (Bednarek, in print – b). The influence of GA is visible both in everyday discourse, as well as in the media. What is more, the analysis of Hansards corpus showed poor results in the use of Canadianisms in political discourse. Toronto verbal culture, thus continues to be under great influence of General American.

BIBLIOGRAPHY

Allen, Harold B. (1973–1976). *The linguistic Atlas of the Upper Midwest.* Vol. 1–3. University of Minnesota Press.

Bednarek A. (2005). "Some observations on the context of culture in Canadian English Study". In: Cap, P. (ed.). *Pragmatics Today.* Frankfurt am Main: Peter Lang Verlag: 467–484.

Bednarek, A. (forthcoming a). "American or Canadian – a study of Canadianisms in Metropolitan Toronto". *PASE Conference Proceedings – Language Studies*, 2005.

Bednarek, A. (forthcoming b). "Some observations on Canadian Verbal Culture in Toronto". *Mediacom Conference Proceedings*, June 2005.

Bibby, R. W. (1990). *Mosaic madness: The poverty and potential of life in Canada.* Toronto: Stoddart.

Cap, P. (ed.) (2005). *Pragmatics Today.* Frankfurt am Main: Peter Lang Verlag.

Chambers J. K. (ed.) (1979). *English Around the World: Sociolinguistic Perspectives.* Montreal: Didier.

Chambers, J. K. (1992). "Dialect Topography: An Introduction". Presented at the *16th Annual meeting of the Atlantic Provinces Linguistic Association.* University of Moncton, New Brunswick.

Chambers, J. K. (1995). "The Canada-U.S. Border as a Vanishing Isogloss: The Evidence of Chesterfield". *Harold B. Allen Memorial Issue, Journal of English Linguistics*, 23: 155–166.

Chambers, J. K. and T. Heisler (1999). "Dialect Topography of Quebec City". *Canadian Journal of Linguistics*, 44 (1): 23–48.

Chambers, J. K. (2003) "English in Canada"; to appear in *Varieties of World English.* Ed. Tometro Hopkins. London: Continuum International.

Clarke, S. (1993). *Focus on Canada.* John Benjamins Publishing Company, Amsterdam/ Philadelphia.

Gumperz, J. J. (1972). "Introduction". In: Gumprez, J. J. and D. H. Hymes. *Directions in Sociolinguistics: The ethnography of communication.* Holt, Rinehart & Winston, New York.

Powe, B. W. (1996) *The Solitary Outlaw 1987.* Toronto: Somerville House.

Scargill, M. H. "Canadian English and Canadian Culture in Alberta". *The Canadian Journal of Linguistics*, 1 (1): 26–29.

Woods, H. B. (1993). "A Synchronic Study of English Spoken in Ottawa: is Canadian English becoming more American?" In: Clarke, S. (ed.). *Focus on Canada.* John Benjamins Publishing Company: Amsterdam/Philadelphia.

Anna Kamińska

University of Łódź

CONTRASTIVE STUDY OF OLD ENGLISH AND OLD HIGH GERMAN GRAMMAR: A corpus-based analysis of a fragment of *The Battle of Maldon*, *Hildebrandslied* and *Ludwigslied*

1. Introduction

This project aims to compare Old English and Old High German grammar, basing on two small corpora of authentic textual data. The assumption is that the two sub-branches of Proto-Germanic, after just 3–4 centuries of alienation, should still demonstrate substantial correspondences in syntax, phraseology and core vocabulary. In the course of the research, two corpora have been used. The first one is composed of the first 142 lines of *Battle of Maldon*, whereas the second one combines *Hildebrandslied* and *Ludwigslied*. The study is organised into three main parts. The first one focuses on the textual level, analysing the structure and stylistics of the above mentioned texts. The second part is devoted to syntactic analysis of sentences, focusing on clause-types, verb phrases and word-order patterns. Finally, the third one covers the level of phrases and words, examining core vocabulary (by means of frequency lists) and parts of speech distribution.

Since the whole project is a very detailed work, this article is only a shortened version of the analysis, with special attention paid to syntax, whose examination has proved most interesting. Full details can be found in the author's M.A. project (*A Contrastive Study of Old English and Old High German Grammar*, University of Łódź 2005).

2. Text Level

The main idea of the project has been to compare an Old English and an Old High German text, created at approximately the same time in a comparable form (either in verse or prose). The task of selecting the texts has been challenging, the reason being that there exist few Old High German texts to choose from. Finally, two comparable corpora have been created:

	OLD ENGLISH CORPUS	**OLD HIGH GERMAN CORPUS**
texts	142 lines of *The Battle of Maldon*	*Hildebrandslied* and *Ludwigslied*
words	940	938
form	verse	verse
topic	battle description	warriors, battle in the background
time	10th century	9th century

The analysis of structure and stylistics has revealed similar Germanic writing traditions still present in all the texts, with some differences related to the character of the text rather than to the language of its composition.

3. Sentence Level

This part of the analysis covers clause structure, verb phrases and word order.

3.1. Clause structure

One of the main differences between the Old English and Old High German samples is the number of clauses that appear in texts of approximately the same length. In fact, the average length of an Old English clause in the analysed text is 6,15 words, whereas for an Old High German clause that figure is only 5,6. These two numbers alone suggest a greater syntactic complexity of Old English at this stage of development. It is worth considering, however, that *The Battle of Maldon* is the latest text in the analysis, so syntactic developments of English may be more advanced simply because of its time advantage.

Another striking discrepancy is the dominance of non-dependent clauses in Old High German. This, again, indicates that Old English used more complicated sentence structures with a greater number of clauses in subordinating relations. Although Old High German texts contain more clauses in general, the difference is covered mostly by independent clauses, which is clearly visible in the chart. On the whole, Old English appears more paratactic, and Old High German – hypotactic.

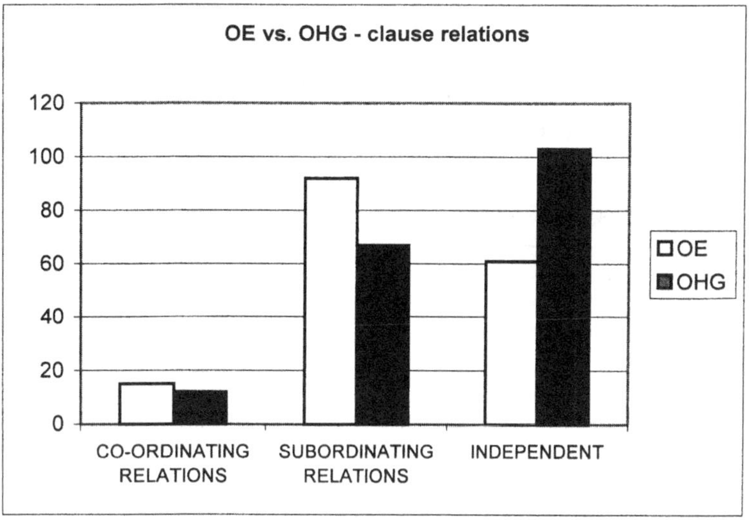

Fig. 1

The analysis of types of subordinate clauses reveals a more balanced distribution in the case of Old High German. By contrast, in the Old English sample noun clauses prevail over other types.

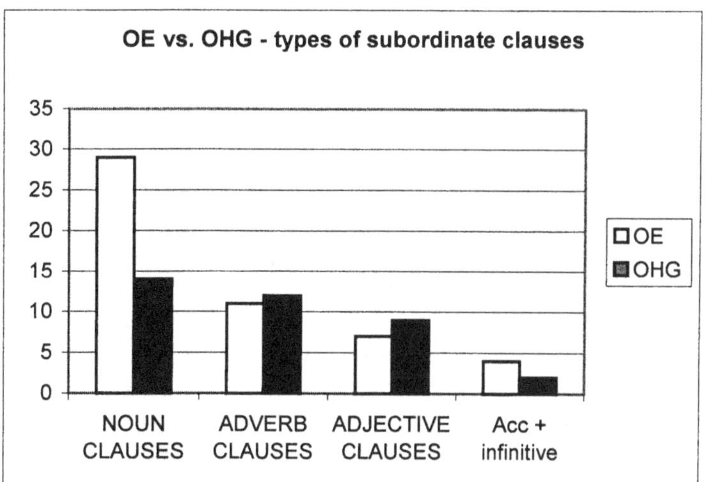

Fig. 2

Another point in which the samples bear little resemblance to each other is the distribution of various subordinate clause sub-types.

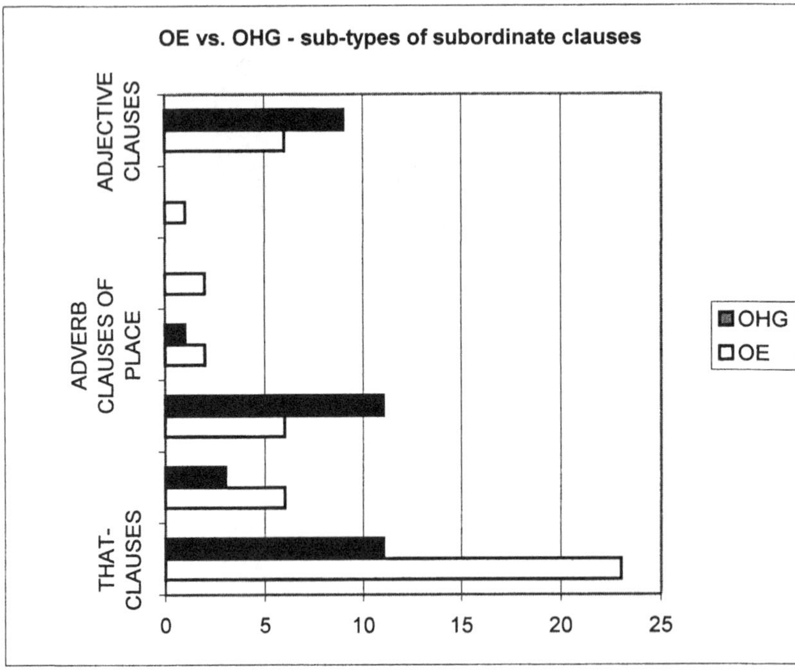

Fig. 3

Old English demonstrates more diversified patterns with 7 sub-types of subordinate clauses present in the sample. Old High German, on the other hand, leaves 2 of the categories empty with fewer sub-types of adverb clauses. In addition, Old English is strongly dominated by that-clauses, whose first position is unarguable. Yet, the reason for that phenomenon may lie in the stylistics of the texts. Old High German texts tend to use direct speech and dialogues written in a natural way. On the contrary, Old English prefers reported speech with fewer examples of real-life dialogues. Since that-clauses are usually used in such a linguistic situation, it is not surprising that they occur so often in the sample. Therefore, some differences may be beyond the scope of a syntactic analysis itself and should not be examined outside the stylistic context of the poems.

3.2. Verb phrases

Since verb phrase is believed to be the central part of any clause, it is interesting to analyse its structure in both languages. The analysis has been conducted with respect to verb types (auxiliary verbs and content verbs), voice (active or passive), mood (indicative, imperative, subjunctive) and negation techniques. In addition, clauses were divided into predicative and non-predicative ones.

➢ **Auxiliary verbs**

There are visible differences between the languages in question as far as auxiliary verbs are concerned.

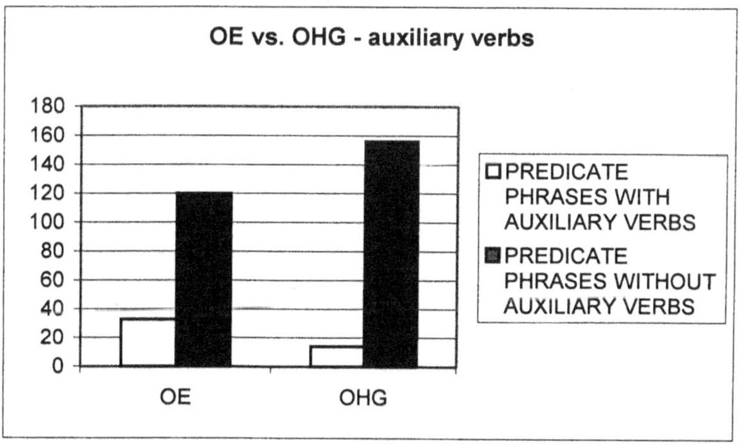

Fig. 4

Old English uses them quite often, and almost 25% of all its predicate phrases contain an auxiliary. By contrast, Old High German seems unwilling to use auxiliaries and chooses mostly content verbs. This may be a sign of today's relatively complex model verbs system of English that poses so many problems for its learners. The system of Modern German is simpler and it is reasonable to assume that the reasons for these differences are rooted in the history of the languages.

➢ **Predicative sentences**

Old English and Old High German differ in terms of predicative sentences frequency. Here, Old English avoids such structures, whereas Old High German uses them freely and regularly regardless of the text. They are as common in *Hildebrandslied* as in *Ludwigslied.*

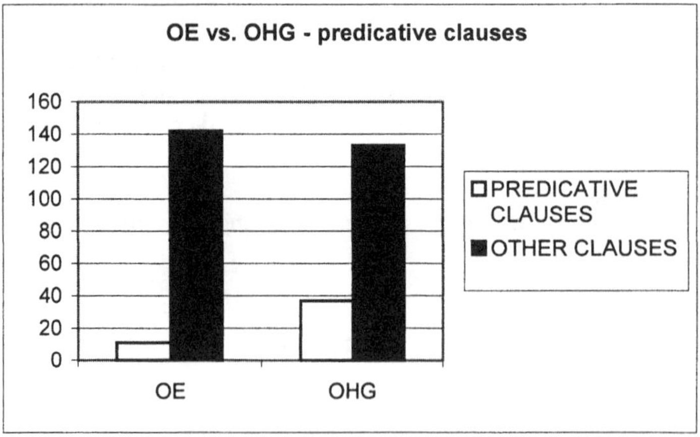

Fig. 5

Predicative sentences are the simplest possible structures of any language and their high incidence in the Old High German sample indicates lack of a varied verb system. Old English presents an impressive richness of verbal expressions, which are especially important for dynamic descriptions of armed conflicts. Thus, *Battle of Maldon* reads more smoothly and appeals to our imagination more than constantly repeated "to be" of Old High German. Yet, it must be said once again that Old High German texts are older, which is bound to affect their complexity and stylistic quality.

➢ **Mood**

Old English and Old High German display close resemblance with regard to mood. They both have three distinct moods: indicative, imperative and subjunctive. Distinction between them is possible thanks to conjugational endings. In both languages, subjunctive seems to be on the verge of extinction. The history of English and German proves that this is what happened to it in the course of the next centuries.

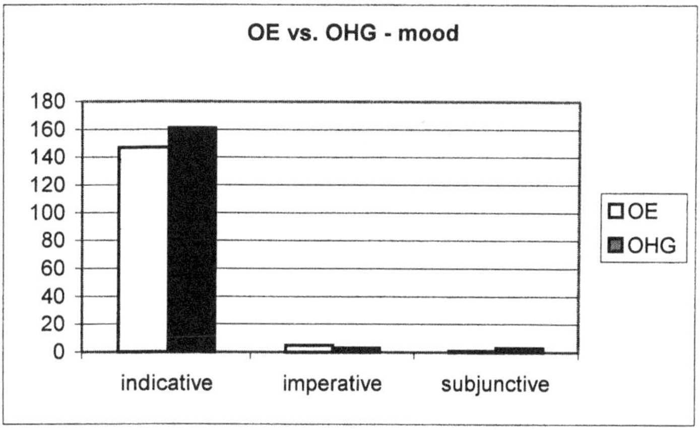

Fig. 6

➢ **Voice**

The analytic distinction between active and passive voice, visible in both Modern English and German, appears at its initial level in the samples.

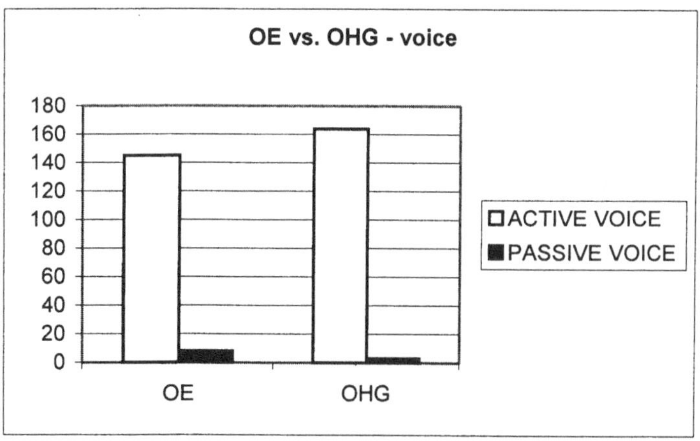

Fig. 7

There are few examples of passive voice in both languages, but there must have been some basis for the development of modern passive, as today English and German form it in similar ways. That correspondence does not seem coincidental so the traces of passive encountered in the samples must be the beginning of the modern systems.

➢ **Negation**

In terms of negation, English and German used to be very close to each other, unlike today. They both formed negative sentences by means of a negative particle (*ne* in Old English and *ni* in Old High German) put directly before a verb.

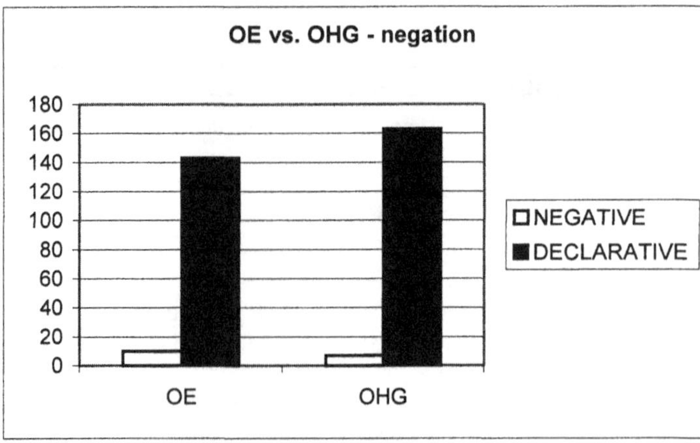

Fig. 8

Old English negated its sentences more often than Old High German, but this feature was influenced by the intention of the authors rather than any inner linguistic phenomenon.

3.3. Word order

This part of the analysis has required identifying functions of sentence elements and classifying them as S (subject), V / V1 (finite verb), V2 (non-finite verb), dO (direct object), iO (indirect object), cC (co-ordinating conjunction), sC (subordinating conjunction), Comp (complement) and A (adverbial). The classification has made it possible to describe word-order patterns and draw conclusions concerning word order in Old English and Old High German poetry.

There are some basic differences between the word-order patterns of Old English and Old High German.

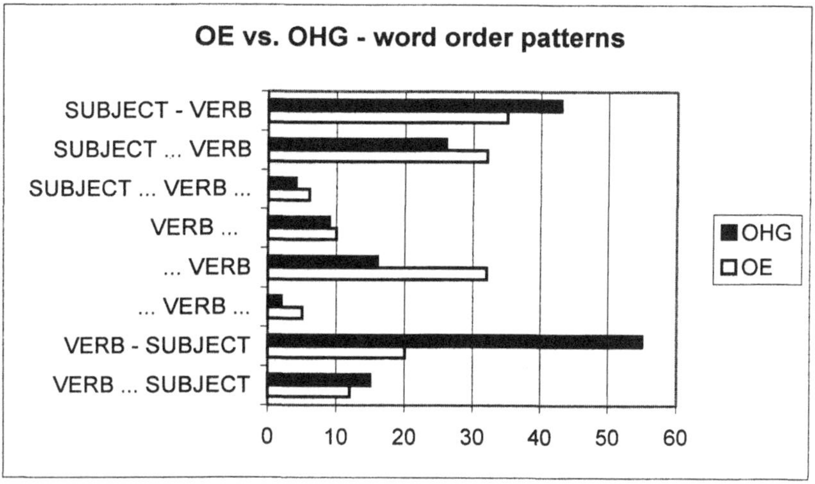

Fig. 9

Old English demonstrates a very balanced distribution of three basic word order patterns, namely Subject-Verb (35), Subject...Verb (32) and ...Verb (32). This indicates that the language tends to shift the verb to the final position of the clause and rather avoids moving it before the subject. By contrast, Old High German does the latter relatively often: the pattern Verb-Subject is undoubtedly the most frequent one (55).

According to Hopper's *The Syntax of the Simple Sentence in Proto-Germanic*, the most basic clause-type in Proto-Germanic is that in which the finite verb is placed at the end of the clause (Hopper 82). Old English seems to comply with that rule, whereas Old High German appears to have modified its word-order. Yet, all Germanic languages were affected by the change which made them shift the verb to the initial position. This word-order pattern, however, is said to be a later development (Hopper 1975: 86). This would suggest that Old High German was more innovative at the time of its formation than Old English, which mostly retained the original Proto-Germanic patterns.

4. Word Level

The aim of this section has been to examine the word level of the texts. The first part of the analysis focuses on the classification and distribution of different parts of speech. The second one consists in the semantic analysis of frequency lists. The frequency lists have been produced by WordSmith Tools (Mark Smith's programme, version 3.0). Since their analysis is very extensive, only the first part of the research is presented below:

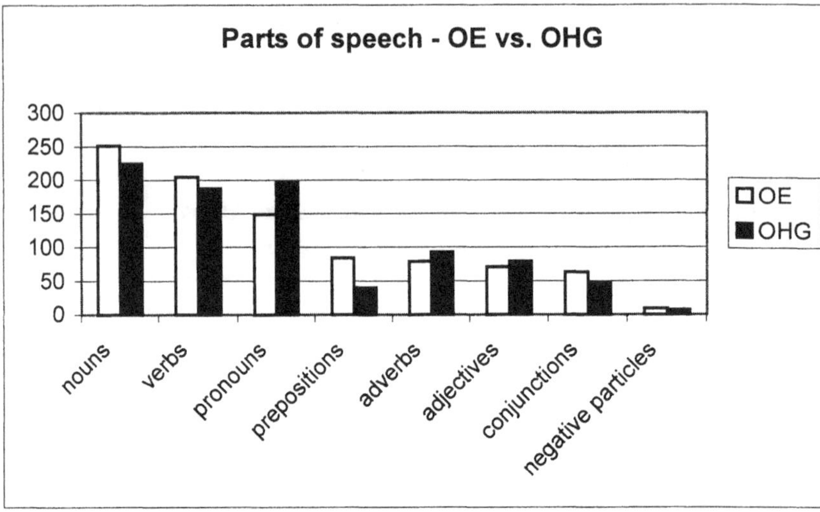

Fig. 10

Figure 10 clearly shows that there are some striking differences between the distribution of parts of speech in the Old English sample when compared to the Old High German one. While nouns, verbs, adverbs, adjectives, conjunctions and negative particles are represented by approximately the same numbers, two categories demonstrate a substantial discrepancy; that is: pronouns and prepositions.

The essential difference between the frequency of prepositions in Old English (84) and Old High German (40) makes it possible to draw the following conclusion: at that stage of development Old English had already begun to transform into an analytic language as it is today, whereas Old High German was still a highly inflected language that expressed the same meanings by means of endings. The history of English is a systematic transformation from an inflection-driven grammar to an almost inflectionless system. This observation proves that the changes which have led to the present state of affairs have their roots in the 10th century, or even earlier. By contrast, Old High German presents a more traditional – and more Germanic – way of expressing e.g. movement or verb complementation.

The other category in which the two languages differ is that of pronouns. In Old English (149) they are definitely less frequent than in Old High German (197). That phenomenon might stem from the fact that Old High German employed more dialogues. When people speak, the address each other by means of personal and possessive pronouns. Since *Hildebrandslied* makes an extensive use of that technique, it can be assumed that this striking discrepancy results from the differences on the textual level, which have been examined in the first part of the research.

5. Conclusions

The research shows areas of similarities and differences between Old English and Old High German, trying to establish possible reasons for the discrepancies and examining their correspondence to the present shape of both languages.

The textual analysis has revealed similar writing traditions employed by authors regardless of the language, with slight differences related to the topic of the text. The syntactic analysis makes it possible to assume that Old English was more syntactically developed, as it employed more diversified sentence structures, its verb phrases were more complex, and the average clause was longer than in the Old High German sample. However, Old English seems more faithful to the traditional Proto-Germanic word order, whereas Old High German was innovative in this respect. As for the word level, the languages come across as similar except for two phenomena: the shift from inflected to analytic undergone by Old English and the exceptionally high frequency of personal pronouns in the Old High German sample. The latter tendency may be caused by the fact that, in general, Old English omits subjects more often (30% of all its clauses have no expressed subject), whereas Old High German tries to fill in the subject position in any clause by means of pronouns (only 16% of all its clauses have unexpressed subjects).

On the whole, the results of the research have proved that after approximately 400 years of isolation, the languages spoken in Germany and Britain were already quite different from each other. The most of those discrepancies can be treated as traces of future changes, which have led to the present differentiation of English and German.

The next stage of the research would be a similar corpus-based study, analysing texts from Middle English and Middle High German in order to examine the ways in which the languages developed.

6. Acknowledgments

I would like to thank prof. Barbara Lewandowska-Tomaszczyk (The Chair of English Language, University of Lodz) for supervising the whole project, in particular the analysis of the Old English text, and prof. Ryszard Sadziński (The Chair of German Language, University of Lodz), who has supported the Old High German part of the research. Without their kind assistance, the project would have never been completed and I would like to express my gratitude for the advice they have given me during the time of its realisation.

REFERENCES

Baker, P. S. (2003). *Introduction to Old English.* Oxford: Blackwell.

Hopper, P. J. (1975). *The Syntax of the Simple Sentence in Proto-Germanic.* The Hague: Mouton.

Labirynth Library (2004). *The Battle of Maldon.* http://www.georgetown.edu/ labyrinth/library/oe/texts/a9.html.

Mitchell, B. (1995). *An Invitation to Old English and Anglo-Saxon England.* Oxford: Blackwell.

Quirk, R. and C. L. Wrenn (1959). *An Old English Grammar.* London: Methuen & Co.

Schmidt, W. (1984). *Geschichte der Deutschen Sprache.* Berlin: Volk und Wissen.

Bibliotheca Augustana, *Ludwigslied* (1996). http://www.fh-augsburg.de/~harsch/germanica/Chronologie/09Jh/ Ludwigslied/lud_intr.html.

Bibliotheca Augustana, *Hildebrandslied* (1996). http://www.fh-augsburg.de/~harsch/germanica/Chronologie/ 08Jh/Hildebrand/hil_intr.html.

Lexicon des Althochdeutschen (1998). http://www.cis.uni-muenchen.de/ahdeutsch/.

Middleton, A. (2005). *The Old High German Primer.* http://mysite.freeserve.com/Marmaria/ ohg/ohg_glossary.html.

Old English Made Easy (2004). *The Old English Dictionary.* http://home.comcast.net/~modean52/ oeme_dictionaries.htm.

Magdalena Turska
Natalia Kotsyba

Institute of Slavic Studies
Polish Academy of Sciences

PolUKR – POLISH-UKRAINIAN PARALLEL CORPUS (A PROJECT)

1. Introduction: available Polish and Ukrainian language resources

Nowadays there seems to be ever increasing need of digitalized and preprocessed language resources, especially for scholarly work but also for quotidian purposes of the wide audience. Such resources would be primarily on-line dictionaries and encyclopedias but also language corpora, either mono- or multilingual. For many users, especially language learners, bilingual parallel corpora prove very useful in their studies. These could also serve as learners' and translators' resources and provide basic material for linguistic research.

Although dictionaries and encyclopedias are quite common throughout the internet, corpora for less popular languages are still relatively rare and small, while parallel corpora based on them are still rarer, even to the point of non-existence.

Situation for Polish-Ukrainian language pair does not seem to look particularly optimistic in that field. Existing printed bilingual dictionaries tend to be either quite old, thus not reflecting the current state of the language and often difficult to reach or small in volume (up to 30 000 entries), not very useful in professional work. Another disadvantage is the common method of preparation of Polish-Ukrainian and Ukrainian-Polish dictionaries via Russian language that causes many inadequacies and errors in the resulting dictionary. As for on-line resources there are attempts to create bilingual dictionaries but for now no serious results were achieved (cf. www.slovnyk.org, and the magazine 'Ridna Mova', which covered up to now only letter 'A' of the Polish-Ukrainian dictionary). As for the explanatory dictionaries, there are digitalized versions of most popular Polish and Ukrainian dictionaries though these share the vices of printed editions.

Currently there exist two large electronic corpora of the Polish language: IPI PAN Corpus (www.korpus.pl) with 300 million segments and PELCRA Corpus (korpus.ia.uni.lodz.pl) with 85 million tokens. For Ukrainian language no corpus is yet available though the work is well advanced at Ukrainian Academy of Science.

At the moment there is no parallel corpus for Polish and Ukrainian languages, although it seems that with a reasonably sized parallel corpus one might achieve immediate goals, such as providing tools for students and translators (especially a parallel concordancer) and basis for linguistic work (with tools for corpora annotation and advanced search). Not only that, but starting from a parallel corpus it is possible to create high quality bilingual dictionaries that will reflect latest changes in the languages immediately, which is especially important considering the present speed of information growth.

2. Corpus representation

We have decided to base the structure of our parallel Polish-Ukrainian corpus on the existing IPI PAN corpus of Polish texts. The main tasks faced while creating such a parallel corpus are the necessity of extending the tagset to cover the Ukrainian language specific morphological information as well as adding information about the alignment of parallel documents.

The corpus consists of separate documents stored in CES file format. Every document consists of several files: the header part that includes all the metadata, the actual content (the body part) and additional part containing morphological annotation.

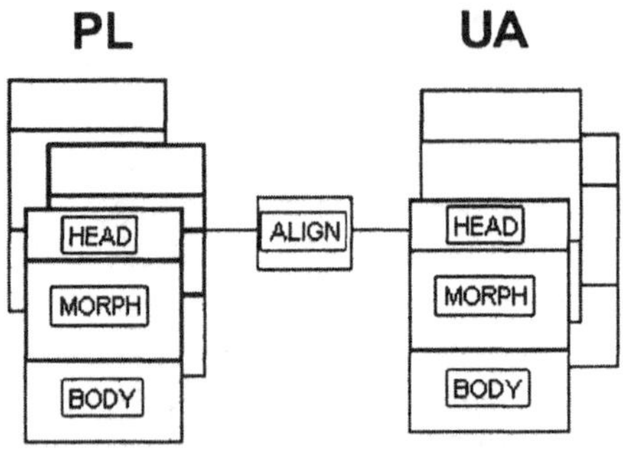

Fig. 1. Parallel corpus structure

For every document of the parallel corpus there exists a corresponding parallel document (co-text), containing either its translation or the original version itself. In addition, there is one file storing alignment information for every bi-text (a pair of texts).

3. Metainformation. The HEADER part

With every text in parallel corpus we associate metadata concerning author or translator, title, origin and publisher and many other. This information may be used to restrict the scope of the search e.g. choose only the texts created after a specific date or by a specific author. We believe this could prove very useful in various kinds of research, including dialectal studies, language interference, sociolinguistics etc., although in many cases some or even most of the metainformation is not available.

The information we strive to obtain is as follows:

Author & Translator	**Original Text & Translation**
– birth year – country and region of origin – mother tongue – other languages – education – location	– date of creation – date of first publication – author(s)/translator(s) – publishing medium – genre – first publisher – intended reader

4. Morphological annotation. The MORPH part

To transform a plain text into the morphologically annotated corpus bi-text additional tools are required, especially morphological analyzers for Polish and Ukrainian languages. We intend to use Morfeusz analyzer for the Polish part and the software created on the basis of the grammatical dictionary of Ukrainian at ULIF (Ukrainian Linguistic Informational Fund at Ukrainian Academy of Sciences) for the Ukrainian texts.

Morphological tags are stored as value lists containing morphological class and grammatical categories adequate for given class, e.g.: *jechać* (*to go*) it will be *fin:pl:sec:imperf.* If ambiguity occurs for a given segment, several tags are listed.

```
<chunk type="p" xlink:href="#p5">
<chunk type="s">
   <tok>
     <orth>dokąd</orth>
     <lex disamb="1">
      <base>dokąd</base>
      <ctag>qub</ctag>
     </lex>
   </tok>
   <tok>
     <orth>jedziecie</orth>
     <lex disamb="1">
       <base>jechać</base>
       <ctag>fin:pl:sec:imperf</ctag>
     </lex>
   </tok>
   <tok>
     <orth>?</orth>
     <lex disamb="1">
       <base>?</base>
       <ctag>interp</ctag>
     </lex>
   </tok>
</chunk>
</chunk>
```

Fig. 2. Morphological annotation

Our tagset for morphological information encoding is based on the IPI PAN corpus, yet it is still necessary to expand it to cover Ukrainian specific morphological classes. We tried to agree our extensions with the solutions developed at ULIF. The initial comparison of the available tagsets developed for Ukrainian and Polish allows at the moment only to make some preliminary generalizations: The approaches used to describe morphological systems in [Woliński 2003] and [Shyrokov *et al.* 2005] respectively differ considerably and it will take a great deal of effort to map the tagsets. One possible way seems to be to increase the common tagset by adding the categories that exist in one language description but not in the other. There will be an initially common group, of course, but *prima facie* it looks discouragingly small – only 6 categories coincide formally. As many as 21 of the categories from this formal union of the tagsets (counting 50 entries) are unique for the Ukrainian morphological system and 23 are unique for the Polish one.

Hence, the preliminary analysis shows that disregarding the intuitively assumed similarity of the two grammatical systems due to the kinship of the languages there are more differences in their formal descriptions than one could expect. The main reason, however, lies rather in different conceptualization of the grammatical categories. For instance, the ULIF scheme treats comparative and superlative adjectives as categories of the same order as positive adjectives (which is similar to some existing tagsets for other languages like the one used for the British National Corpus), while Woliński does that according to the traditional grammatical intuitions, namely, he introduces degree as the inflectional property of adjectives and adverbs. On the other hand, both tagsets include the category of "predicative", however, the scope of its grammatical meaning is different in the two cases. At the moment it would be too risky to make any claims about the common tagset, but it is clear that one cannot base it exclusively on the formal characteristics of the existing classifications. Some theoretical review is still necessary.

5. Alignment. The ALIGN part

The possibility of presenting parallel documents in the aligned form is indispensable for the parallel corpora resources to function properly.

AIESEC (międzynarodowe stowarzyszenie studentów ekonomii i zarządzania) to niepolityczna, naukowa i niekomercyjna organizacja, w całości zarządzana przez studentów.	AIESEC (міжнародна асоціація студентів, які займаються економією й управлінням) - неполітична, освітня і некомерційна організація, повністю керована студентами.
Działamy w ponad 950 szkołach wyższych. Do naszej organizacji należy 60.000 studentów z 84 krajów świata.	Діємо в понад 950 вищих учбових закладах і об'єднуємо 60 тис. студентів з 84 країн світу.
Naszym celem jest rozwój jednostek i krajów pod względem gospodarczym, kulturalnym i moralnym. Szczególną uwagę przywiązujemy przy tym do międzynarodowego wzajemnego zrozumienia, jedności i współpracy.	Наша мета - розвиток людей і країн в економічному, культурному і моральному аспектах. Зокрема, особливу увагу ми приділяємо міжнародному взаєморозумінню, єдності і співробітництву.

Fig. 3. Text alignment on paragraph level

Text alignment on the paragraph level is used comparatively rarely, mostly due to their size which tends to be unnecessary large for grasping the context of the searched item. More 'user friendly' attitude would be aligning the corpus on the sentence level. However, singular sentences of the original text may be sometimes translated as two or more ones and vice versa (see the second paragraph of the example below).


```
<cesAlign>
 <cesHeader>
...
...
  <translations xml:base="http://corpus.domeczek.pl/corpus">
    <translation trans.loc="exampleAna.ua.xml" lang="ua"
     xml:lang="ua" n="1" />
    <translation trans.loc="exampleAna.pl.xml" lang="pl"
     xml:lang="pl" n="2" />
  </translations>
</profileDesc>
 </cesHeader>

  <linkList>
    <linkGrp id="p1" targType="s">
      <link>
        <align xlink:href="#p1s1" />
        <align xlink:href="#p1s1" />
    </link>
      <link>
        <align xlink:href="#p1s2" />
        <align xlink:href="#p1s2" />
    </link>
  </linkGrp>
    <linkGrp id="p2" targType="s">
      <link>
        <align xlink:href="#xpointer(id('p2s1')/range-
     to(id('p2s2')))" />
        <align xlink:href="#p2s1" />
    </link>
      <link>
        <align xlink:href="#p2s3" />
        <align xlink:href="#p2s2" />
    </link>
  </linkGrp>
</linkList>
</cesAlign>
```


Fig. 5. Fragment of the alignment information file (sentences 1 i 2 of the second paragraph translated as one sentence)

AIESEC (międzynarodowe stowarzyszenie studentów ekonomii i zarządzania) to niepolityczna, naukowa i niekomercyjna organizacja, w całości zarządzana przez studentów.	AIESEC (міжнародна асоціація студентів, які займаються економією й управлінням) - неполітична, освітня і некомерційна організація, повністю керована студентами.
Działamy w ponad 950 szkołach wyższych.	Діємо в понад 950 вищих учбових закладах і об'єднуємо 60 тис. студентів з 84 країн світу.
Do naszej organizacji należy 60.000 studentów z 84 krajów świata.	
Naszym celem jest rozwój jednostek i krajów pod względem gospodarczym, kulturalnym i moralnym.	Наша мета - розвиток людей і країн в економічному, культурному і моральному аспектах.

Fig. 4. The same bi-text aligned on the sentence level

6. How to acquire bi-texts?

To acquire a substantial number of parallel texts in our case it is essential to organize the efficient cooperation of several institutions. The common sources are: publishing houses, translators, regulations and other legal documents, multilingual proceedings protocols, technical documentation and manuals, bilingual magazines and web sites. In our work we intend to gather data from all of these, trying to keep the corpus relatively 'balanced'.

As a means to gain translators' cooperation we propose to create a friendly, on-line working environment with the access to discussion forums and bulletin boards but above all to the growing digital language resources database with the possibility for the users to contribute to them. This, we hope, could be the meeting point for the scholars, translators and students community. As a desired side-effect the material database could steadily grow in size and cover many genres of modern texts.

7. Virtual lexicographical laboratory (VLL) – towards a high quality dictionary

With the available digital language resources it will be possible to create the Polish-Ukrainian bilingual dictionary using the following algorithm.

1. generating the entry list based on items found in corpora

2. distinguishing the senses that differ in translation after concordances analysis according to a coherent classification
3. joining the senses between languages

We are convinced that the outlined above corpus-based approach can help create a dictionary that will cover a wide range of lexicon, reflect the current state of both languages, clearly show the distinction between different word senses (especially when used on-line and linked with references to the parallel corpus) and have a relatively small number of errors.

An important step towards this goal is to create an environment for geographically distributed research teams in the field of linguistic. Such, as we call it, Virtual Lexicographical Laboratory should provide (besides above mentioned functionality) means to prepare mono- and multilingual dictionaries, freely annotate the corpus according to the users research goals and also work on semantic networks.

For this environment to work it is essential for it to be:

– on-line, to provide constant, simultaneous access for researchers everywhere

– user-friendly, to let even those not accustomed to computers cooperate and contribute to the research

– flexible, to change with changing users needs

– standardized, to allow information exchange with other databases and research teams.

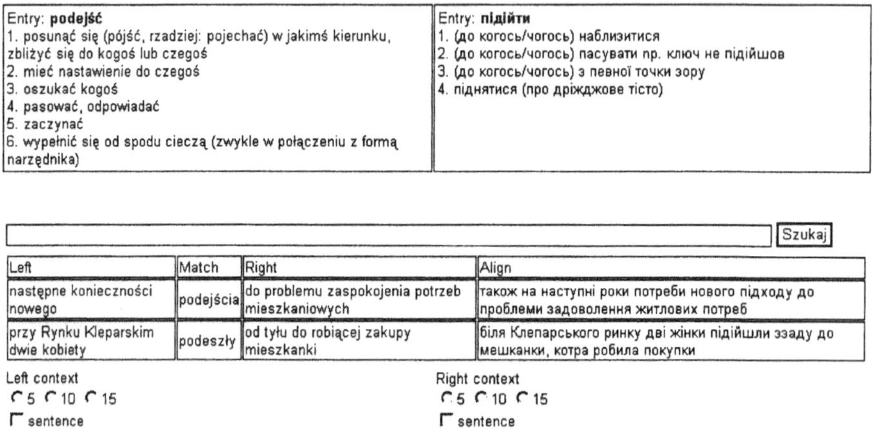

Fig. 6. VLL interface sketch

The latter two postulates are strictly intermingled, as only thorough standardization allows to replace and add some new modules, especially prepared by other parties, in the working system so that it does not disturb the other parts and the users. To meet this end we intend to comply with Unicode standard for language encoding, XML/CES for bi-texts representation and modular architecture allowing to use any specific tools (e.g. morphological analyzers) with the help of a wrapper translating input and output formats. This will guarantee the VLL to be suitable for use with other languages and prepared for further development.

8. Summary

At the moment, the preliminary version of PolUKR is freely accessible through the web site http://corpus.domeczek.pl. It contains ca 50 parallel documents in XCES format. New documents are added as they are obtained. It is possible to search the corpus in a simple method based on the regular expressions mechanism. The search engine is being developed and after the morphological annotation process is completed it will be possible to use much more powerful query language, similar to the IPI PAN solution. The search results are presented in the form of parallel concordances aligned on the paragraph level.

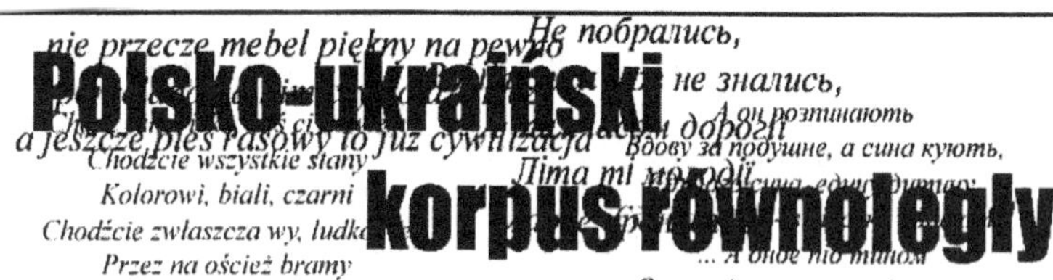

1	Szczególną uwagę przywiązujemy przy tym do międzynarodowego	**wzajemne**	go zrozumienia, jedności i współpracy. Podstawowe kierunki
	Наша мета - розвиток людей і країн в економічному, культурному і моральному аспектах. Зокрема, особливу увагу ми приділяємо міжнародному взаємозрозумінню, єдності і співробітництву.		
2	się wokół pięciu podstawowych kierunków działania: -	**wzajemne**	zrozumienie w dziedzinie kultury - wyższe
	- культурне взаємозрозуміння		
3	rozwiązywanie koniecznych problemów. Realnie działający system	**wzajemne**	j odpowiedzialności, przede wszystkim odpowiedzialności władzy

Fig. 7. Search results screen

Further work on our corpus may be divided in two main paths: organizational with its main goal to assure the cooperation of institutions and individuals in possession of translated Polish and Ukrainian texts and the technical one, that needs to provide means and tools to be used with the corpus. Priorities for the technical path are alignment on the sentence level and morphological annotation of the corpus together with the adequate search engine. The next stage will be the work on Virtual Laboratory software.

We believe that such a parallel corpus with an efficient search engine, a powerful yet easy to grasp query language and user friendly parallel concordancer could become one of most useful resources for all Polish and Ukrainian scholars, translators and students as well as be a contribution for future developments of parallel corpora for other languages.

REFERENCES

Corpus Encoding Standard: http://www.cs.vassar.edu/CES/CES1-0.html

Corpus Typology: http://webdeptos.uma.es/filifa/personal/amoreno/teaching/cl/corpus-typ.html

EAGLES Guidelines: http://www.ilc.pi.cnr.it/EAGLES96/browse.html

Korpus IPI PAN: http://korpus.pl

Korpus referencyjny języka polskiego PELCRA: http://korpus.ia.uni.lodz.pl/

Kotsyba, N. and M. Turska (2006). „Leksykografia polsko-ukraińska – stan obecny i perspektywy". *Semantyka i konfrontacja językowa*, t. III. Warszawa, SOW.

PolUKR – Polsko-Ukraiński Korpus Równoległy: http://corpus.domeczek.pl

Przepiórkowski, A. (2004). *Korpus IPI PAN. Wersja wstępna / The IPI PAN Corpus: Preliminary version*: http://dach.ipipan.waw.pl/~adamp/Papers/2004-corpus/

Przepiórkowski A. and M. Woliński (2003). *A Flexemic Tagset for Polish* http://nlp.ipipan.waw.pl/~adamp/Papers/2003-eacl-ws12/ws12.pdf

Turska, M. and N. Kotsyba (in print). „Polsko-Ukraiński korpus równoległy (PolUKR)". *Materiały LXIII Zjazdu Polskiego Towarzystwa Językoznawczego*. Warszawa.

TEI Guidelines for Electronic Text Encoding and Interchange: http://etext.virginia.edu/TEI.html

Ukrainian Linguistic Portal: www.ulif.org.ua

Woliński, M. (2003). „System znaczników morfosyntaktycznych w korpusie IPI PAN". *Polonica XXII–XXIII*: 39–55.

Широков, В. А. (1998). *Інформаційна теорія лексикографічних систем*. Київ: Довіра.

Широков, В. А, О. В. Бугаков, Т. О. Грязнухіна, О. М. Костишин, М. Ю. Кригін, Т. П. Любченко, О. Г. Рабулець, О. О. Сидоренко, Н. М. Сидорчук, І. В. Шевченко, О. О. Шипнівська, К. М. Якименко (2005). *Корпусна лінгвістика*. Київ: Довіра.

Wiesław Babik

Jagiellonian University

KEYWORDS IN INFORMATION RETRIEVAL SYSTEMS ON THE INTERNET

1. Introduction

This paper is devoted to the discussion of keywords as linguistic tools applied on the Internet to determine the main subject of web site content, as well as to specify the users' information needs at the meta-content level of the document (the object and its presentation). Keywords are also tools used by webmasters to give respective web sites a proper position or rank in cyberspace (positioning). The purpose of my presentation is to identify the functions of keywords that are used in the World Wide Web (WWW) system. It is my attempt at giving answers to basic questions of a selected scope of considerations concerning semantic interpretations of keywords, as well as their sources on the Internet, functions, types and selected pragmatic aspects.

2. Keywords and their Semantics

In the WWW system, a keyword is "a word or phrase placed in the Hypertext Markup Language (HTML) code of a web site intended to index a specific thematic category in the databases of search engines."[1] The information technology literature may give other meanings of "keywords"; for example in object programming "keywords" are used for defining classes in C++ and Visual Basic languages. Regardless of the field and scope of application, for the needs of this paper, we assume that keywords are results of a document content analysis, and they constitute specific essence of the document content, or a set of

---

[1] Cf. http://www.futuro.pl/pomoc_slowniczek.php/haslo/49

its labels, keys to this content. In practice, we may use several or several dozens of keywords to determine the subjects and selected aspects of document contents, which may be composed of several or hundreds of pages. Beyond doubt, the keywords used on the Internet are lexical units of an artificial language used for indexing (meta-information function) and information retrieval (retrieval function) in information retrieval systems (Babik 1999).

For a given word or phrase to become a keyword, it needs to be meaningful or significant from the information viewpoint. That condition is met by nouns and adjectives (in specific forms in the case of inflected languages: nominative singular or plural), but not by conjunctions, pronouns or prepositions. The issue of lexicographic preparation and standardization of the grammatical forms of keywords is also important in the case of inflected languages, including Polish (Babik 1996). However, it does not apply to those natural languages which do not have extensive inflections, e.g. English.

3. Sources of Keywords

Keywords are very important elements of the WWW system as a whole and of its components called web sites. In addition to keywords, sometimes key phrases are used. There are also systems in which each word, title or abstract of a text is treated as a keyword. The WWW system is composed of the documents developed with the HTML language. The sources of keywords are the following fields: <HEAD> <BODY>, <META NAME> <DESCRIPTION>, and <KEYWORDS>.

Search servers index web resources mostly on the basis of the content of the <KEYWORDS> field in the HTML document of a web site, or using free phrases derived from a natural language placed in the <BODY> portion.

All the search engines declare that they analyse the whole content of the <BODY> section of a web site, omitting only the STOP words, for which special lists are created. Those stop lists as they are called contain the words that occur most frequently in a given language, and thus they carry low information value.

To supply keywords to a search engine, those meta-codes are primarily used which, for various reasons, have not occurred in the document content. Examples can be here the application of meta-codes on *Splash* and *Frame* types of sites. *Splash* sites are entrance windows with a logo, often with the command *Enter*, which direct the user to a proper, often completely different address. *Frame* sites determine the form in which a site is presented in the search engine's window. The implementation of meta-markers often causes lifting of a given web site to the first position in search results. Meta-markers are very useful tools for searchers. The most important of them are *Description* and *Keywords*. The *Description*-code determines the site content for the search engine's needs, while the *Keywords*-code provides a searcher with additional keywords related to a given web site. It is very important when we use keywords from controlled vocabularies. The very appearance of a site after application of meta-codes is not changed. However, the site value is greatly increased for the needs of search engines. The *Description*-code allows us to control the description, which appears under the web site title as a result of our search (Lewandowski 2002). The operation of meta-codes is illustrated by the following application example:

```
<head>
<meta http-equiv="content-type"
content="text/html;charset=iso-8859-2">
<META HTTP-EQUIV="description" CONTENT="Instytut Informacji
Naukowej i Bibliotekoznawstwa - Pracownicy">
<META HTTP-EQUIV="keywords" CONTENT="jezyki systemy
lingwistyka metodologia technologia teoria ksiazka
bibliotekoznawstwo informacja naukowa edukacja studia
uniwersytet Babik">
<META HTTP-EQUIV="distribution" CONTENT="global">
<META HTTP-EQUIV="resource-type" CONTENT="document">
<META Name="Language" CONTENT="Polski">
<TITLE>Wieslaw Babik's Home Page</TITLE>
</HEAD>
<body background=/ibin/gify/ground.gif vlink=purple><center>
<IMG border=1 SRC="/ibin/kadra/babik.gif" align="left">
<BR><BR><BR><font size=+3 color=teal><b>Wiesław
Babik</b></font><br>
Associate Professor<BR>
Institute of Information and Library Science
JU</center><br><BR><BR>
<hr size=+3 noshade width=70% align=center>
<BR><BR><BR>
    Expert in information science and
linguistic foundations of information retrieval systems.<BR>
    From 1986 to 1994, research worker
at the Polish Academy of Sciences (OIN PAN in Kraków).
Certified Information Specialist (1991). Doctor of
Philosophy (Linguistics), majoring in the Theory of
Information Retrieval Languages (wrote his dissertation on
"The Use of the Facet Conception of the Organisation of the
Information Retrieval Language for the Construction of a
```

```
Classification System for Cartographic Materials," Faculty
of Neophilology of the University of Warsaw, 1991). Since
1994, a scholar at the Institute of the Library and
Information Science of the Jagiellonian University. From
1991 to 1994, member of the Scientific Council of OIN PAN in
Warsaw. Received the degree of Associate Professor in
Linguistics, majoring in Information Retrieval Languages and
Systems, published his second dissertation (habilitation) on
"Generating Information Retrieval Languages from
Terminological Dictionaries," Faculty of Neophilology of the
University of Warsaw, 1996.<BR>
[...]
</UL>
<hr size=+2 noshade width=30% align=center>
<center><a href=mailto:wbabik@inib.uj.edu.pl>
e-mail: wbabik@inib.uj.edu.pl</a></center>
<hr size=+2 noshade width=30% align=center></BODY>
</HTML>
</head>
```

4. Linguistic Description of the Keyword Language

Keywords are words or phrases originating from a natural language. They are of equal rank and mutually independent of each other. The keyword collection is called a vocabulary. In the majority of keyword languages, a vocabulary is open in nature, which facilitates addition of new lexical units.

The class of information-retrieval languages under discussion includes in its classical model very simple languages with respect to structure or application. Their vocabularies are alphabetically ordered. With time, however, certain drawbacks of classical keyword languages were revealed. It was found that lack of vocabulary control caused considerable information loss due to synonymy or information noise resulting from homonymy. To prevent such undesirable phenomena, people started to build keyword languages based on fully or partially controlled vocabularies. Such vocabularies developed a new form of word organization, as facet or category systems. The most recent form of vocabulary organization is represented by the keyword languages based on the authority files keyword index (Babik 2004).

Classical keyword languages are the languages with para-natural lexical units in vocabulary and non-positional grammar, basically equivalent to coordinate indexing consisting in the document description or information need description by integration of coordinates, which can be freely composed. The coordinates are elementary lexical units called keywords. A keyword language vocabulary is an alphabetically ordered keyword list. It is never closed, and basically no relationships between keywords are expressed in the vocabulary (Babik 2005).

A doubtless advantage of keyword languages is a possibility to develop a large number of information language sentences made of a fairly limited number of elementary lexical units. However, a disadvantage is a larger probability of false keyword coordination in comparison to other languages, which may cause information noise, i.e. issuance of documents or web sites that do not correspond to the information request formulated by the system user. Consequently, attempts are made at gradual limitation of the probability of false coordination owing to proper organization of vocabularies and suitable grammatical means, which create grounds for the development of keyword languages based on an overt vocabulary.

5. Keyword Language Varieties

Keyword languages occur in several varieties. A characteristic feature of a classical form of that language is occurrence of exclusively those keywords which have the status of auto-syntactic units or non-positional grammar in the overt language. Particular varieties or dialects of that language also admit the existence of syn-syntactic (dependent) units in the vocabulary and partly positional grammar.

Particular varieties differ as to the degree of word ordering and control. The keyword language variety which is the closest to a classical variety the keyword language based on a controlled list of terms, or the so-called authority file of keywords. However, the most frequent and almost generally applied keyword language variety is the free keyword language. It is the keyword language whose vocabulary is overt, and its elementary lexical units are the keywords which are words or phrases derived from the title, the document text, the document description or the system user's information need description that are selected by the indexer from his mental vocabulary (or active vocabulary resource) of a natural language in its respective vernacular version. In addition, there are keyword languages based on an overt but closed vocabulary, while the person who describes a document is limited by the existence or non-existence of a given word in a keyword list. There are also keyword languages based on a keyword vocabulary where the keyword list is not a closed vocabulary, but it only constitutes a collection of model keywords which can and should be regularly supplemented. In their developed variations, keyword languages contain exponents of paradigmatic relationships, modifiers and/or role indicators.

The characteristic features of keyword languages are the following:

– the identity of keyword forms with the forms of natural language expressions;

– lack of vocabulary control (or partial control only);

– mostly alphabetic control of the vocabulary that does not take into account any relationships that occur between vocabulary units;

– the grammar which refers to coordinate indexing rules; the keyword language grammar has the nature of non-positional grammar.

6. Selected Problems in the Pragmatic Aspects of Keywords

We will concentrate here on the issues which concern the use of keywords in information indexing or information retrieval on the Internet. During both indexing and retrieval with the use of a keyword language, usually the same problems occur as in the case of the difficulties in selection of suitable significant words, which is mostly a subjective process. The value of a keyword may be best appraised by a human indexer who analyses the title, the table of contents, the body of the text, or its fragments and selects keywords in particular form and rank, applying, at least partially, some vocabulary control. To make the process objective, specific software is developed to analyse specific texts and, based on the frequency of words and/or their forms or places of occurrence in sentences, select them to include automatically in an alphabetic vocabulary, together with document addresses (Vetulani 2004). That process may not always be visible to system users.

The problem with automatic selection of keywords and development of vocabularies may be inflection endings, or morphological changes of words, or spelling differences. To limit the number of forms referring to the same meaning, systems try to identify the main parts of words, or their roots. One of the methods to achieve that purpose is the so-called word truncation. Truncation side and word size depends on the word length. Specific collections of ANY files (synonymic forms) are created. That allows for limitation of the number of forms that correspond to the same meaning. Another method is to recognize meanings on the bases of consonants. In that case, all or some vowels are omitted. It was found that consonants are the meaning carriers in a language, while vowels perform the functions of links between consonants (similarly to Hebrew or semantic-code languages). Such an analysis is usually conducted by application of specific algorithms, or procedures which are programmable.

Under coordinate indexing, we understand the method of describing document contents or information needs using coordinates or independent, easily composed, elementary lexical units that have usually the forms of words or phrases derived from a natural language, called keywords in the case of keyword languages. In that way, the document contents are decomposed in the indexing process into a collection of keywords (an analytical process). The keywords which create the document search characteristics, or a search question instruction, are treated as mutually independent and equal components, or coordinates. Each such elementary lexical unit may fulfil the function of a search key, and therefore, it becomes an independent search element regardless of its position in the text. Such units may be located in any position in the text, and thus, they can be listed in any sequence.

7. Conclusion

The characteristic features of keywords on the Internet may be their connectivity and ambiguity, as well as the diversity of derivation criteria. Those features allow us to create many access points in the information indexing process, which is presently considered to be the source of search power of the Internet, despite the fact that it often leads to information noise or information silence (Pamuła 2004).

Despite often well-justified criticism of the existing methods of Internet or other system resource searching, using keywords, such languages seem to be the closest to the users' manners of thinking and the methods of searching for information by users (Chowdhury 1999).

Keyword languages are used for searching through the Internet resources, especially in the WWW (Keyword Search) system. For that purpose, the method of resource organization and search based on indexing and alphabetic ordering is used. Keyword search tools are provided by all search engines. They are effective programmes for identifying information sources in accordance with precisely specified names of objects or issues, although they also generate responses which contain a considerable number of irrelevant or insignificant value.

Keywords are lexical units of the simplest form of para-natural information and retrieval languages. In the expression plane, they are identical with the words or phrases of the natural language which constitutes the basis for keyword generation. In the content plane, it is assumed that the language user, having competence in his natural language, recognizes the meanings of keywords and discovers that the meanings correspond to the respective words or phrases of the natural language in the meta-information function.

Usually, the WWW system uses phrases which are keywords generated from a natural language based on association relationships. The keyword collection represents the so-called language of free keywords. That language constitutes part of the user's competence in a natural language, e.g. lexical competence[2] and semantic competence.[3]

Internet keywords constitute a lexical resource of the semi-natural language of the indexer and of the user of free keywords. The keywords are either derived from the contents of the documents subjected to indexing or they are selected by the indexer from his active mental vocabulary. The keywords explicitly present a language system, that is vocabulary and grammar, which allow to generate complex phrases (sentences and coherent texts), as well as semantic rules, which allow to assign language expressions to the elements of reproduced non-linguistic reality, and pragmatic rules, which determine the principles of correct language use, i.e. the rules of generating messages in a given language.

The intention is for the lexical and semantic keyword languages to have as natural character as possible. Such languages should be close to the highest degree to the methods of thinking and information search by people. An unrestricted access to the Internet causes that the natural aspect must be understood quite conventionally. In fact, there is no single "natural" image of the world of all the system users. Therefore, it is not the natural aspect or the correctness of the lexical-semantic system which create the search power of keyword languages, but rather the readiness of the system user who uses that specific type of language to accept proposed keywords which are at the same time a lexical tool of lexical categorization of information with which one may identify required information. The keywords, which create a verbal description of a document, also fulfil the function of information and retrieval languages, or the meta-informational and retrieval functions. Semantic relevance and power (or retrieval weight) of the keywords used for indexing are of decisive importance from the viewpoint of search effectiveness.

---

[2] Lexical competence is part of language competence which allows the language user to use efficiently the lexical system of a given language (author's lectures).

[3] Semantic competence is a type of language competence which allows the language user to code (create) or decode (recognize) information.

REFERENCES

Babik, W. (1996). "Inżynieria języka naturalnego na potrzeby języka dla systemów informacyjno-wyszukiwawczych". In: Vetulani, Z., Abramowicz, W. and G. Vetulani. *Język i technologia*. Warszawa: 66–69.

Babik, W. (1999). "Języki wyszukiwawcze stosowane do wyszukiwania informacji medycznej w systemie WWW". *Biuletyn Głównej Biblioteki Lekarskiej* 361: 9–14.

Babik, W. (2004). "Języki informacyjno-wyszukiwawcze kontrolowane kartoteką wzorcową". In: Pietruch-Reizes D. and W. Babik (eds.). *Usługi. Aplikacje. Treści w gospodarce opartej na wiedzy*. Warszawa: 187–193.

Babik, W. (2005). "Keyword Lists as Language Resources and Tools". *Human Language Technologies as a Challenge for Computer Science and Linguistics. 2nd Language & Technology Conference. April 21-23, 2005, Poznań, Poland. Proceedings*. Ed. Z. Vetulani. Poznań: 289–290.

Chowdhury, G. G. (1999). "The Internet and Information Retrieval Research: a Brief Review". *Journal of Documentation* 2: 209–225.

Lewandowski, R. (2002). "Metadane w dokumentach HTML". In: Krzemiński, W. and P. Nowak (eds.). *Przestrzenie informacji*. Poznań: 53–66.

Pamuła, N. (2004). "Efektywne wyszukiwanie w Internecie – przegląd problemów i rozwiązań". In: Głowacka, E. (ed.). *Biblioteki wobec nowych zadań*. Toruń: 62–75.

Vetualni, Z. (2004). *Komunikacja człowieka z maszyną. Komputerowe modelowanie komunikacji językowej*. Warszawa: Akademicka Oficyna Wydawnicza EXIT.

Janusz Badio

University of Łódź

DESIGNING A DATA-BASE FOR SPOKEN DISCOURSE ANALYSIS

1. Introduction

Corpus linguistics has become fashionable these days. Based on collections of language data, it has the potential of providing answers to research agendas stemming from structural, functional and cognitive orientations in language studies. Most importantly, however, the actual decisions concerning the format and design of a language corpus will depend on the goal one has in his/her analysis.

In this paper I present an approach for an analysis of speech, which I have found manageable and useful. Namely, I decided to store my corpus of speech in a relational dBase of the programme Microsoft Access, a part of the well-known suit of programmes Microsoft Office. In the next section I explain the rationale behind this choice and the mechanics of the process.

2. Why dBase

The decision to use a database programme was motivated by the nature of the basic unit of my analysis. The so-called *intonation unit* (IU) was defined as a cluster/beam of *conceptual* and *phonetic* parameters. Conceptually, it is a correlate of the *attention focus* that changes dynamically. Phonetically, it can be delimited with a set of perceptual criteria such as: pauses, key, tone or accents Chafe (1994: 64). The decisions to *chunk* a flow of speech recorded on a tape had to be motivated by considering both the conceptual and the phonetic. Additionally, since the categorisation into IU-s was fuzzy, which reflected the nature of speech and in fact the nature of various linguistic processes and categories, it seemed correct to define the unit operationally as well.

The segmentation of data had to be performed manually because there are no automatic tagging systems that would be able to consider both conceptual and phonetic aspects of speech in a tape-recording. The units I myself delimited reflected dynamic *chunking procedures* of speech.

The question to be answered at this preliminary stage of the project was whether to have one big table with all necessary information or many tables related in some ways. Although one can find numerous advice in the literature to try to keep different types of information in separate tables (cf. Roman 2000; Ray and Ray 2000), I do not think it is good to insist on having more tables than it is reasonable, given the goal one has in building the corpus and considering the need or no need to make later additions and changes. After all, the corpus that I was transforming from a word.doc format to a dBase format was later on to be displayed in ways adequate to my goal. I was not planning to introduce and reintroduce speakers, functions, topics and so on as it indeed happens in other everyday applications of dBases. The following three main objectives were guiding the work:

a) ease of conversion and input into the dBase,
b) multiple possibilities of display and grouping,
c) restricting redundancy.

In the section to follow I will concentrate on these three objectives and associated problems.

3 Ease of input/conversion

I decided to discuss this aspect of planning first because it is crucial for the successful completion of the task that consists of strenuous acts of deciding upon a number of parameters concerning every IU. In the case of my corpus of speech, nearly 3000 IU-s had to be described with the use of the following 17 parameters relevant to chunking procedures discussed above as well as to one of the major goals of building a model of language production based on the idea of chunking.

ID_INT UNIT	identification number of an IU
THE INT UNIT	the transcription of the IU
ID_SPEAKER	identification number of the speaker
NO. WORDS	number of words in an IU
THE WAVE	planned hyperlink to a recorded sample
ID_SAMPLE	identification number of a sample
TOPIC	name of a basic-level topic an IU belongs to

PAUSES	selecting the following possibilities:
	NO PAUSES, FILLED PAUSES, UNFILLED[1] PAUSES or
PAUSES BIS	BOTH
	selecting: BEFORE, WITHING or BEFORE AND
LANGUAGE	WITHIN
GR. CATEGORY	selecting English or Polish or other
TYPE	description of grammatical category in grammatical terms
SUB TYPE IF	selecting type of IU: substantive, regulative, fragmentary
REG	specifying sub-categorisation of type (see above)
LG FUNCTION	describing language function Carter and McCarthy (1997)
EPISODE	specifying episode (situation in which speech took place)
OTHER	some other observations concerning IU-s: anacrusis, repetition and the like

The above parameters were included into the basic form for input based on and related with six tables with the following names: INTONATION UNITS, LG FUNCTIONS, SAMPLES, SPEAKERS and TOPICS. I shall deal with them in turn now.

3.1. Intonation Units

The table called INTONATION UNITS is the main and the biggest table. It consists of 17 columns and 2958 records. The design of the table can be viewed in the design view accessible on the tool bar.

The ID_INT UNIT is a unique identifier of an intonation unit, which is an important provision one has to make in case of an error of omitting an IU. For example, revising original data, it is possible to insert 151.1 between intonation units 151 and 152. So the numbers that uniquely identify an IU also order them in the way in which they appear in the recording. In addition to this, this parameter is *indexed*, which excludes a possibility of applying the same number to different IU-s. Moreover, one could wonder why the value of this parameter is set to NOT REQUIRED if it identifies uniquely IU-s and orders them. The simple explanation is that sometimes wanting to put in a different number, setting the value to REQUIRED, one would be forbidden to do so.

[1] The definition of pausing that I assume here is that a pause is a moment appearing before an IU and that it is either silent or filled in the sense that a speaker hesitates before the actual, planned verbalisation commences (cf. Chafe 1994).

	Field Name.	Data Type
🔑	ID_INT UNIT	Number
▶	THE INT UNIT	Memo
	ID_SPEAKER	Number
	NO/WORDS	Number
	THE WAVE	Hyperlink
	ID_SAMPLE	Number
	TOPIC	Text
	PAUSES	Text
	PAUSES BIS	Text
	LANGUAGE	Text
	GR CATEGORY	Text
	TYPE	Text
	SUB TYPE IF REG	Text
	MODE	Text
	LG FUNCTIONS	Text
	EPISODE	Text
	OTHER	Memo

Fig. 1. Table Intonation Units – Design View with Parameters

The field THE INT UNIT contains the orthographic representation of an IU with marked accents and punctuation interpreted in agreement with Chafe (1994). The datasheet view of the table displays consecutive IU-s from the first to the last according to the order with which speech samples were converted from the word.doc format to the dBase.

The ID_SPEAKER is a field, which is a number and which uniquely identifies a speaker and is a pointer to a particular table called SPEAKERS. Appearing in the design of the table INTONATION UNITS and so also in its datasheet view, this parameter is repeated there as many times as there are units spoken by an individual speaker.

Every unit is also described by a number of words that it consists of. It was speculated that the complexity of an IU correlates positively with the number of words it consists of. Because this problem is outside the scope of this article, I will only say that though related to processing depth, planning, pausing and other suprasegmental phenomena, complexity was also shown to be dependent on the number of relations attended to at a time, parallely (Halford *et al.* 1998: 66). Although remaining unimplemented, I also predicted a possibility of including a field that would give one access to a cut out, recorded and saved in a separate file counterpart of the orthographic transcription of an IU. For example, given the number 1,

1 Our ^next song came ^out without a ^^guitar,

it is possible to provide a hyperlink in the field I called THE WAVE. This attractive option, however, presents certain problems, the biggest of which is having to decide upon the exact borderlines between the end of a previous IU and the beginning of a pause. This problem is especially acute if one agrees that many pauses in speech are not simply moments without phonation, but time during which speakers perform such cognitive operations as: planning, intending, configuring, categorising and so on. During this time, however, they do not abstain from producing such forms as:

2 . Ame .. ^^American ^style
. one .. ^one day we were up in ^^Prospect Road
. erm ... ^^ agreed with you

and this causes that attempts at automatising the process of dividing the recorded samples of speech into intonation units are even more complicated.

The next field, the ID_SAMPLE, is a combo-box, a non-indexed but required and duplicated reference to a particular sample, whose fuller description can be found in the description of the table SAMPLES. It is followed by the field TOPIC. The term encompasses what is more accurately called a *basic level topic* Chafe (1994: 121), that is intended discourse coherence of limited scope, having goal, focus and semi-active periphery. This is also a required, non-zero and indexed field that functions as a pointer to a specific basic level topic; the full list of topics is stored in another table with links to the main table INTONATION UNITS.

The next two fields are concerned with pausing. They are text fields, whose data type termed TEXT allows the use of up to 50 characters, fully satisfactory for describing pauses. The first of these fields, PAUSES, is a combo box with the following values to choose from: NO PAUSES, FILLED, UNFILLED, FILLED AND UNFILLED. In PAUSES BIS, also a combo field, one additionally chooses whether a pause has appeared: BEFORE, WITHIN or both BEFORE AND WITHIN an IU.

The next important characteristic that describes an IU is the text field GR CATEGORY. Very intricate if performed manually, it was still possible to confirm an observation that there is a strong tendency in speech to express momentary contents of intentional, verbal behaviour with a simple clause. An option, instead of the manual description of IU-s concerning their grammatical make-up, would be to use some grammatical tagger. However, as some researchers point out, not all problems suddenly disappear. For example, Altenberg (1990: 289–291) says that:

It is inevitable that the precision and reliability of the segmentation have suffered somewhat from the exclusion of clause functional categories. However, this complication of the segmentation rules must be balanced against the gain of a simplified and (presumably) more accurate parser.

Still another problem he notices is that a parser he uses treats some complex chunks or phrases as strings of unrelated grammatical constituents. Say,

3 from the day // he // started
PP NP VP

could be reanalysed as,

4 from // the day // he started
Prep NP CLAUSE

This rather simple observation shows that automatic tagging might not be more valuable except for the speed with which the task is performed. Anyway, the tags that will be inserted will inevitably depend on the kind of things that we want to see in the corpus and on the constituency superimposed by the speaker in an act of communication, his/her mastery of linguistic routines and so on.

The next three fields were quite crucial for the analysis rooted in the methodological tradition of Chafe (1994). The first of the fields, TYPE, is a combo box with values: SUBSTANTIVE, REGULATORY and FRAGMENTARY defined in the following way. *Substantive units* constitute the core of discourse; they transmit the actual intentions that speakers want to put across. *Fragmentary units* are never finished and the *regulatory* ones are further divided into: *interactional*, *cognitive* and *validational*. They are all also called discourse markers by Schiffrin (1987) and as the name suggests, they provide cohesion to discourse structure, regulate interpersonal aspects of speech and the like.

The field LG FUNCTIONS is a text box, required, non indexed, which serves the role of a pointer to the particular, unique record in the table FUNCTIONS. The key uniquely identifying a language function in that table is the name of a particular function. This field is followed by another one, called EPISODE differing from TOPIC in that the former can include many topics and is a synonym of a communicative encounter; the latter, TOPIC, is formed of a succession of IU-s (see above).

The last field, OTHER, was reserved for such phenomena as *anacrusis* or *repetition*.

3.2. The Table Language Function

The table LANGUAGE FUNCTION is related to the main table INTONATION UNITS in a one-to-many manner. That is, one function/record in the table FUNCTIONS relates to many unit-tokens in the main table. The design view of the table looks in the following way,

	Field Name	Data Type
	ID_LG FUNCTION	Number
	LG FUNCTION	Text

Fig. 2. The Table Functions – Design View with Parameters

		ID_LG FUNCTION	LG FUNCTION
▶	+	1	NARRATIVE
	+	2	IDENTIFYING
	+	3	LANGUAGE-IN-ACTION
	+	4	COMMENT-ELABORATION
	+	5	SERVICE-ENCOUNTERS
	+	6	DEBATE AND ARGUMENT
	+	8	LANGUAGE, LEARNING AND INTERACTION
	+	9	DECISION MAKING/NEGOTIATING OUTCOMES
	+	10	PRESENTATION

Fig. 3. Language Functions; Data Sheet View with expandable pluses to show IU-s

The field ID_LG FUNCTION is a key uniquely identifying records in the table and it is an integer, a general number. It is indexed (allowing no repetitions). The field LG_FUNCTION is a text field that is indexed, but not required. This last parameter allows the introduction of a function name not yet represented by any intonation unit. From the practical point of view, it causes that it is possible to list all the functions before starting the conversion procedure, as it was in the case of my work. In the data sheet view the table contains pluses, which means that all IU-s categorised as implementing this function can be viewed after clicking on the /+/ expand button. Most importantly, however, it is necessary to explain that any IU can perform numerous functions at the same time, which was not my intention to account for. Functions then must be here understood as a principle that organises a corpus, and that functionality was meant to refer to whole speech samples, rather than individual IU-s. The functions based on Carter and McCarthy (1997) are presented fig. 2.

The next table to be discussed is the table SAMPLES.

3.3. The Table SAMPLES

Like the table concerning language functions, it is also hooked to the main table by specifying an ID_SAMPLE parameter in the main table and linking it by a one-to-many relation with the unique ID of actual language samples in the SAMPLES table.

	Field Name	Data Type
	ID_SAMPLE	Number
	TITLE	Memo
	ID_LG FUNCTION	Text

Fig. 3. The Table SAMPLES; Design View

This translates to a similar (see above) possibility of clicking on the + button to expand and view intonation units belonging to a sample.

As the reader will notice, there are more names of language samples than functions, but of course, a larger corpus to study various phenomena across language functions would be needed.

The speakers are shown in still another table, the table SPEAKERS.

	ID_SA	TITLE	ID_LG FUNCTION
+	1	PHIL COLLIN'S MEMORIES OF LIFE AND SONG WRITING	IDENTIFYING
+	2	MICK HUCKNALL MEMORIES AND HIS MUSICIANS	IDENTIFYING
+	3	INTERVIEW ON INTERNET "P TO P" SERVICES	DEBATE AND ARGUMENT
+	4	THE COSTA BRAVA - HOLLIDAY DESTINATION OF THE BRIT	PRESENTATION
+	5	BRAZIL VERSUS AMERICAN PATENT LAW OF MEDICINE PRODUCTI(	DEBATE AND ARGUMENT
+	6	INTERVIEW WITH OLYMPIA DUKAKIS	IDENTIFYING
+	7	INTERVIEW WITH LAUREN LILLEY	IDENTIFYING
+	8	INTERVIEW WITH	IDENTIFYING
+	9	INTERVIEW WITH A DOCTOR ON A LIVER CLEANSING DIET	DEBATE AND ARGUMENT
+	10	INTERVIEW WITH FORMER U.S. PRESIDENT, JIMMY CARTER	DEBATE AND ARGUMENT
+	11	DANGEROUS CHILDHOOD PRANKS	NARRATIVE
+	12	AN ELDERLY LADY REMINISCES	IDENTIFYING
+	13	DOING A JOB	LANGUAGE-IN-ACTION
+	14	COOKING RICE	LANGUAGE-IN-ACTION
+	15	FAMILY AND RELATIVES	COMMENT-ELABORATION
+	16	AT THE POST OFFICE	SERVICE ENCOUNTERS
+	17	LOCAL RADIO PHONE-IN	DEBATE AND ARGUMENT
+	18	SCHOOL DISCUSSION	LANGUAGE, LEARNING AND INTERACTION
+	19	UNIVERSITY TUTORIAL	LANGUAGE, LEARNING AND INTERACTION
+	20	PLANNING A FAMILY HOLLIDAY	DECISION-MAKING/NEGOTIATING OUTCOMES

Fig. 4. Table SAMPLES; Datasheet View

3.4. The Table SPEAKERS

This table has eight fields,

Field Name	Data Type
ID_SPEAKER	Number
THE SPEAKER	Text
AGE	Text
OCCUPATION	Text
DISCOURSE ROLE	Text
EDUCATION	Text
LANGUAGE	Text
GENDER	Text

Fig. 5. Table SPEAKERS; Design View

The ID_SPEAKER uniquely identifies a speaker and it is a long integer required and indexed (allowing no repetitions). The next field, THE SPEAKER, provides a speaker's name. The remaining fields provide possibly relevant information on the speakers. As in the other tables, related to the main one, the datasheet view of the table SPEAKERS facilitates immediate access to intonation units uttered by an individual by clicking on the + (expand button). I will now present the discussion of the table TOPICS.

3.5. The Table TOPICS

This table has been designed to consist of only two fields, THE ID_TOPIC, which uniquely identifies a topic and various IU-s in the main table that realise the topic, so it is again a one-to-many relation. The datasheet view of the table makes it possible to expand and view the actual units that realise the topic by applying the already mentioned procedure of clicking on the + button.

	Field Name	Data Type
🔑	ID_TOPIC	Number
🔑	NAME OF TOPIC	Text

Fig. 6. The Table TOPICS; Datasheet View

3.6. The Table SOUNDS

The table could hold pieces of actual samples of speech cut out from the recorded material with the use of some such applications as: COOL2000 or Speech Analyser (the test version). The procedure is not straightforward. Although these programmes can look for moments of silence, pausing is much more than just becoming silent in speech. Hence, this procedure is now best performed manually. I would not insist that strict and clear boundaries between IU-s exist. On the contrary, the necessary imprecision with which chunking could be performed on the waveform such as the one below,

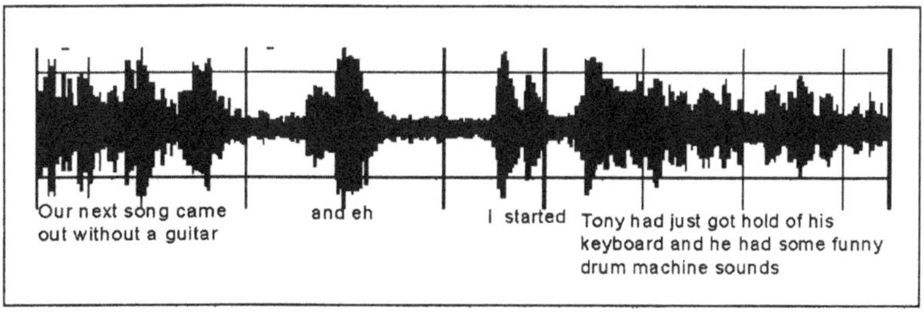

Fig. 7. A Wave Form of an IU

points to the inherent fuzziness of linguistic categories, which of course does not prevent us from perceiving chunking in general as an important conceptual and phonetic propensity characteristic of all intentional behaviour (Searle: 1984) with semantic implications.

3.7. Relations between tables

The design of the whole database and so also the relations can be traced back to considerations of all the three goals presented at the beginning of this paper: ease of conversion and input, display possibilities and restricting redundancy. The goals are of course interrelated and may even be seen as competing against one another.

For example, it was attractive to build only one big table with a lot of redundant data. Given the capacities of modern computers, one can hardly encounter technological barriers. Moreover, it is tempting to think that designing one huge table is also faster, so one can become absorbed in linguistics' tasks without having a feeling of wasting time on studying something that he/she only knows superficially. However, this becomes less obvious if you realise that building a relational database has at least the following advantages:

a. Wanting to change many descriptions in the main table, it is enough to change an appropriate and unique record in the related table.
b. Wanting to get rid of numerous descriptions in the main table, it is enough to delete an appropriate unique record in the related table.
c. During input the programme disables a possibility to introduce data not listed as type in the related tables.

The question of redundancy is a complex one. We expect as little redundancy as possible, especially if this speeds up the process of input into the dBase. That is, one hopes not to have to write down the same information in, say, three tables, instead of only once in a relational dBase. For example, designing a dBase for a library, the better solution is the one where a librarian notes the fact that a certain book has been borrowed in one place and due to built-in relations this fact becomes evidenced in the current list of books available, the book a reader has at home and so on. In the case of the dBase for the analysis of chunking procedures in speech, storing information about speakers in the separate table SPEAKERS, it was necessary to introduce every speaker with all relevant information only once in that table, and in the main table I had to select the ID for that speaker with every IU spoken by him/her. In practice, however, it is possible to select a default value of any field in order not to have to write the same word, number or phrase while introducing IU-s said by the same speaker belonging to the same sample or topic. This is illustrated below,

General	Lookup
Field Size	Double
Format	General Number
Decimal Places	2
Input Mask	
Caption	
Default Value	
Validation Rule	
Validation Text	
Required	No
Indexed	Yes (No Duplicates)

Fig. 8. A Possibility of Setting a Default Value of a Field

The figure below summarises the discussion of tables and relations that hold between them.

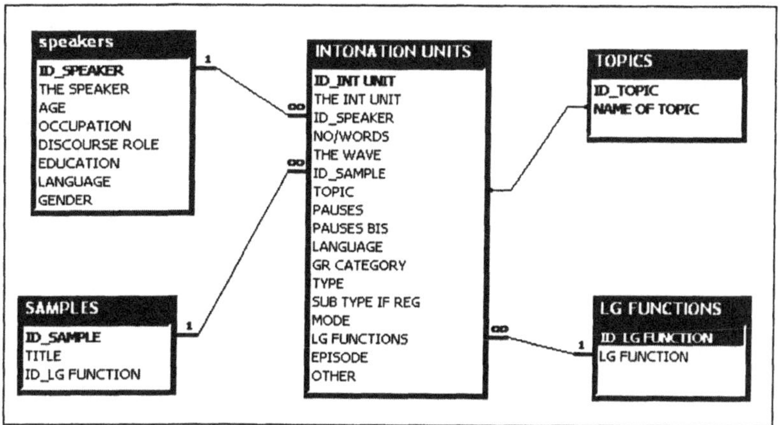

Fig. 9. Relations Between Parameters/field in the dBase

To construct the relations, one needs no expertise in SQL (Structured Query Language), even if this would clearly be an asset. The programme has a built-in wizard, and the role of the designer in simple cases is facilitated and limited to understanding that we can expect to have three types of relations:

a. one-to-one
b. one-to-many
c. many-to-many

In the case of my dBase the relation one-to-many was most useful. That is,

one speaker	many iu-s
one topic	many iu-s
one sample	many iu-s
one function	many iu-s

Some details concerning the formation of the relations are presented on the example of the relations between the main table INTONATION UNITS and the table SPEAKERS. It was necessary to enforce referential integrity between the field ID_SPEAKERS in the main table and ID_SPEAKERS in the table SPEAKERS, which helps make sure the relations are correctly defined and that the related record will not be deleted or changed by mistake. This option should only be selected if one wishes a change of the primary key in the primary table to update the values in all related records. By contrast, should one want to erase all related records in the related table, it is necessary to set the value CASCADE DELETE RELATED RECORDS. The conditions that must be met to set referential integrity are then as follows:

a. The matching field in the primary table is a primary key or has a unique value.

b. The related fields have the same data type.

Importantly, you cannot enter a value in the foreign key field of the related table that does not exist in the primary key of the primary table. Having discussed what I consider the most important aspects of the building block of the dBase, I will now go on to discuss the second guiding principle – the multiple possibilities of display, search and query.

3. Display, Search and Query

The importance of the aspects of dBase design highlighted in the heading of this part cannot be overestimated. In general, for the purpose of the analysis of language, it is the datasheet view of a table that is most useful. Since the primary unit of my analysis was the IU, I will concentrate on the table INTONATION UNITS solely. The button/function that is most useful for displaying filtered data according to a selected language form is the FILTER BY SELECTION button,

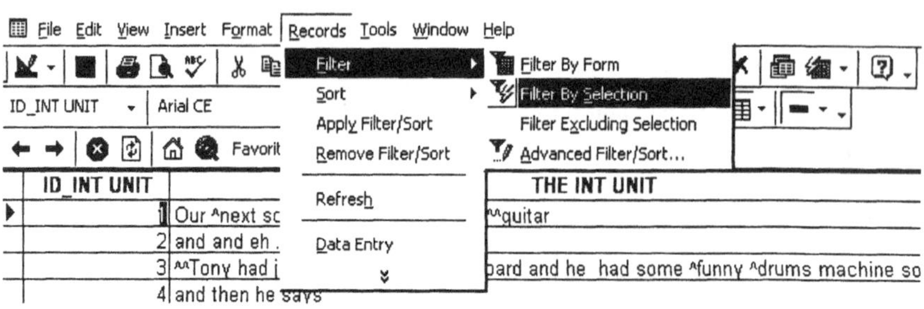

Fig. 10. Datasheet View and its Toolbar

If a cursor is positioned at any record, using this function/button will allow search for other identical units. Often, however, it is necessary to look for only a part of a field, in which case one has to manually select this part and then use the button . The program will render a list similar to a concordance. To view a context of the found examples, one has to click the unique ID of the unit and remove filter for the programme to be able to display the whole corpus. Alternatively, one can keep the table SAMPLES open for easy access to the desired part of the corpus. Another extremely functional alternative is using the

FILTER EXCLUDING SELECTION and the ADVANCED FILTER. As the name suggests, the first option allows filtering data to the exclusion of the selected form; it is fast and easy to perform. It is also possible to filter the already filtered results without saving them. Should one want to perform a more complex search, the ADVANCED FILTER has to be used. This filter does not have to be limited to one table. It can be based on many tables. For example, one might wish to filter the corpus in search of IU-s that form three word clusters, come from a narrative and include the word *the*. Of course, instead of building such a query in the ADVANCED FLITER view, it is sometimes more efficient to arrive at the same result via a serial application of FILTER BY SELECTION option in virtually as many steps as one can think of.

To build queries that one wants to save later on, it is recommended that one should use the QUERY design view or the wizard. Here I only discuss the first possibility and give an example of a query that I built for the purposes of my analysis. Let us look at the design view of the query.

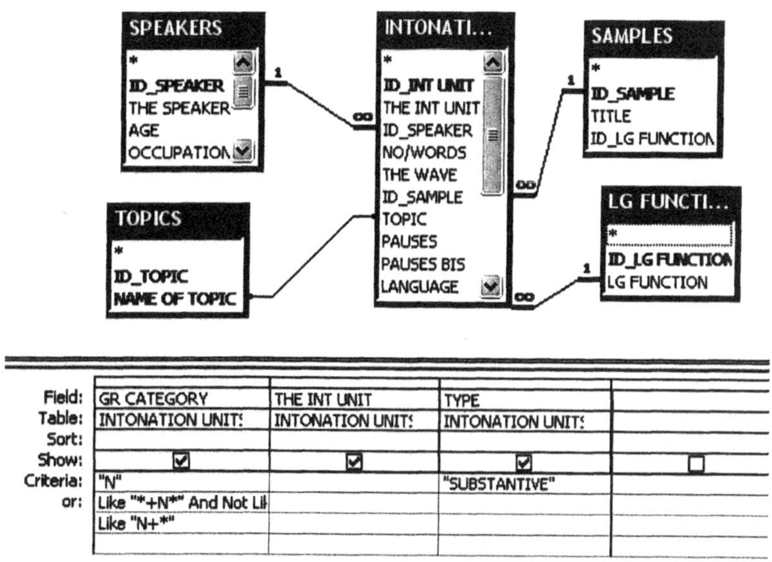

Fig. 11. The Design View of the Query

The view is divided into three sections: the tool bar, the section where the tables and relations are displayed and the one with the query table containing the desired parameters (see below).

Field:	GR CATEGORY	THE INT UNIT	TYPE
Table:	INTONATION UNITS	INTONATION UNIT!	INTONATION UNIT!
Sort:			
Show:	☑	☑	☑
Criteria:	"N"		"SUBSTANTIVE"
or:	Like "*+N*" And Not Like "*np*" And Not Like "*num*"		
	Like "N+*"		

Fig. 12. Parameters of the Query NOUN

The FIELD parameter is used to select a column from a table. One can as well decide if a given query column should or should not be displayed and the CRITERIA and OR serve the function of narrowing down the search to the aspects that we are interested in. The specifications displayed horizontally work conjunctively; the ones that are vertical form an alternative (OR). They form a mathematical product. So the query results in narrowing down the scope of the main table or tables in a programmed way. Some of the symbols used in building queries and a good introduction to relational algebra are provided in Roman (1999). Some of the useful expressions can also be found in the help file of the programme.

4. Conclusions

Without claiming expertise in dBase design and programming, my goal has been to suggest another attractive and competitive solution in the task of building a corpus of speech. My project was driven by the superordinate goal of providing additions to the already existing models of speech production on the basis of conceptual and phonetic chunking procedures, but I believe the actual solutions can be modified and improved. The task of building a corpus is best performed by a team of specialists. If a dBase design seems a laborious process, then the alternative use of taggers and parsers to mark texts is similarly, if not more complex. For many researchers with limited programming and computer skills, the Microsoft Access is a reasonable alternative.

I think that it is also important to speculate how such dBases could serve linguistics interests in general. First, it is possible to publish such projects on the Internet with fruitful implications for the so-called "e" learning. Second, considering the ease with which information is stored and found, the FL teacher can build corpora of texts, exercises, ideas, or topics. It is even possible to imagine a solution in which separately stored test items described with a number of parameters such as: level, topic, grammatical unit can be filtered and then reported with the use of REPORTS function. The function allows multiple varieties of layout for later printing, an ideal tool for designing EF/SL tests. In fact, only the imagination of prospective users is the limit to the number of possible linguistic and glottodidactic, practical applications.

REFERENCES

Chafe, W. (1994). *Discourse, Consciousness and Time.* Chicago: The University of Chicago Press.

Altenberg, B. (1990). "Automatic Text Segmentation into Tone Units". In: Svartvik, J. (ed.). *The London-Lund Corpus of Spoken English.* Lund: Lund University Press.

Halford, G. S., Wilson W. H. and S. Phillips (1998). "Processing capacity defined by relational complexity: Implications for comparative, developmental and cognitive psychology". *Behavioral and Brain Sciences.* Vol. 21: 803–831.

Ray, D. S. and E. S. Ray (2000). *Access 2000 Visual Quick-start Guide.* New York: Peachpit Press, a division of Addison Wesley Longman Press.

Roman, S. (2000). *Access Database Design and Programming.* Cambridge: O'Reilly™.

Searle, J. R. (1984). *Minds, brains, and science.* Cambridge, Mass.: Harvard University Press.

Svartvik, J. (1990). *The London-Lund Corpus.* Lund: Lund University Press.

Schiffrin, D. (1994). *Approaches and Discourse.* Malden, Mass.: Blackwell Publishers Inc.

Part II

COGNITIVE LINGUISTICS

Katarzyna Dziwirek

University of Washington, Seattle

Barbara Lewandowska-Tomaszczyk

University of Łódź

CORPUS-BASED ANALYSIS OF EMOTION PREDICATES *FEAR*, *WORRY*, AND *JOY* IN POLISH AND ENGLISH

1. Introduction

The paper presents analyses of several constructions expressing emotions in Polish and English. Our data comes from the British National Corpus and PELCRA (*Polish and English Language Corpora for Research and Applications* – Department of English Language, University of Łódź), which includes the Polish Reference Corpus. It is part of a larger Corpus-Based Contrastive Polish-English Grammar project, which is addressed to intermediate and advanced learners of Polish and English as foreign languages. Its main focus are complex syntactic constructions, a topic often underrepresented in textbooks and reference grammars. The corpora reveal a number of striking hitherto unnoticed patterns and generalizations. There are two main components to the paper:

1) Syntax: Here we focus on complex sentences with emotion verbs as main predicates. For intransitive verbs, only those in the domain of *fear* (e.g. *bać się*), *worry* (e.g. *martwić się*), *gladness* (e.g. *cieszyć się*) and, marginally, *anger* (e.g. *złościć się*) allow *że* 'that' clauses as complements. In English the range of such constructions is less limited. These fields are also the only ones where we find infinitival (subject control) complements in both languages, though much more frequently in English. English also allows *for-to* infinitive complements (*I hate for him to*), absent in Polish.

2) Semantics: Our study of Polish emotion nouns reveals a profound insight into how Polish speakers conceptualize emotions, which appear to be divided into two almost mutually exclusive sets. Some are seen as present inside individuals and thus part of human nature (albeit possibly in a dormant state),

while others are perceived as external. You can *awaken* (*wzbudzić/obudzić*) or *call forth* (*wywołać*) the former and *fall into* (*wpaść w*) the latter. We also discuss emotions "in need of nourishment": a person can *feed* certain emotions (*żywić*) in Polish, and foster similar ones in English.

2. Expression of emotions in Slavic languages and English

This paper has initially been inspired by Wierzbicka's (1995) observation that Slavic languages prefer to express "feeling emotions" with intransitive, often reflexive, verbs while English tends to use far more copular constructions with adjectives and participles. This, according to Wierzbicka reflects both a semantic and a cultural difference between Slavic and English. The semantic difference is that "adjectives ... designate passive states, not active emotions to which people "give themselves" more or less voluntarily" (Wierzbicka's 1995: 226), while emotions expressed by "reflexive verbs such as *bojat'sja* "to be afraid" ... are treated not as arising by themselves but by the speaker's conscious thoughts about the event". (Wierzbicka's 1995: 229). Thus, in a sense, by using reflexive verbs the Slavic speakers are manufacturing the emotion within themselves. The cultural difference is stated by Wierzbicka as follows: "I believe that this [use of adjectives in English] is not "accidental", but reflects an important feature of Anglo-Saxon culture – a culture which tends to view behavior described disapprovingly as "emotional" with suspicion and embarrassment.... Their culture encourages them to be *glad* rather than *rejoice*, to be *sad* rather than to *pine*, to be *angry* rather than to *fume* or *rage*, and so on." (Wierzbicka's 1995: 226–227) By contrast, Slavic speakers value emotional expression and "do it with verbs". We were intrigued by these observations and set out to see if they were true (cf. Lewandowska-Tomaszczyk and Dziwirek forthcoming) and along the way discovered a number of striking hitherto unnoticed patterns and generalizations, presented below.

3. Clausal complements of intransitive verbs

In this section we focus on complex sentences with emotion verbs as main predicates. For intransitive verbs, mostly those in the domain of fear (e.g. *bać się*), worry (e.g. *martwić się*), and gladness (e.g. *cieszyć się*) allow że "that" clauses as complements.

Let us take a brief look at some examples from these categories.

3.1. FEAR: bać się 'to be afraid'

There were 1421 occurrences of the verb *bać się* "to be afraid" in the 10 million PELCRA Sampler. Of those 580 (or roughly 40%) were complex sentences with *bać się* as the main clause predicate. Among the complex sentences 275 had *że* "that" complements, 234 infinitival complements, 55 *żeby* "lest" 16 *czy* "whether". Examples of the different types of clauses and their English counterparts are given below.

bać się + że:

(1) Zaniosłam kiedyś piłkę do klasy, a dzieciaki mi ją zabrały, bałam się, że ją zniszczą.
'I once brought my ball to class, but the kids took it away from me, I was afraid that they will wreck it'

(2) Ale koleżankom nic nie powiedziała. Bała się, że ją wyśmieją.
'But she didn't say anything to her friends. She was afraid that they would laugh at her.'

(3) Ale nie mogłam nic zrobić. Bałam się, że ona każe ciebie aresztować.
'I couldn't do anything. I was afraid that she will have you arrested.'

(4) Bałam się, że dalej nie pociągnę.
'I was afraid that I could not go on.'

(5) ale bałem się, że staruszek nie zniesie takiego ciosu.
'but I was afraid that the old man cannot stand such a blow'

(6) Bałem się, że zginiesz i nigdy cię już nie zobaczę.
'I was afraid that you will die and I will never see you again.'

afraid + that

(7) instead of being offended she was only afraid that he was not quite well.
(8) I'm afraid they won't be ready for you for at least another hour. [*that* – deleted]
(9) I'm afraid they weren't convinced. [*that* – deleted]
(10) I was afraid that if I simply pleaded ignorance, they would realise that I was lying

(11) and they're afraid if someone else gets a hold of it the Bureau'll look silly or they're hoarding it because they think it might make them a splashy case or two. [*that* – deleted]
(12) people really were afraid that the end of the world was imminent.

bać się + infinitive
(13) Zawodnicy boją się przyjeżdżać do centrum treningowego.
'The players are afraid to come to the training center'

(14) Rodzice boją się przestraszyć dzieci.
'The parents are afraid of frightening their children'

(15) Nawet w kościele boję się pokazać.
'I am even afraid to show up in church.'

(16) Bał się mieć dzieci.
'He was afraid to have children.'

afraid + infinitive
(17) is the price of having such a distinction doctors who are afraid to act and patients condemned to a lingering death?
(18) Mr Reynolds admitted that he had been afraid to eat or drink because of the possible effects on his bowel
(19) in my future profession – to make sure I dressed properly, and never be afraid to ask the question "Why?"
(20) where he falls in with thieves, but even at stealing he has no skill. He is afraid to climb walls or break into houses.
(21) mindlessly, do not eat unless you are properly hungry, and do not be afraid to leave food once you are full.

bać się + (że)by:
(22) Boję się, żeby nie dostał zgniłej gorączki.
'I am afraid lest he gets a rotten fever '

(23) Długo tak nie wytrzymają, a boję się, by nie padły.
'They won't be able to go on for long, I am afraid lest they die'

(24) Boję się, by nie skompromitowali mnie w oczach kibiców.
'I am afraid lest they make a fool of me in the eyes of the spectators.'

afraid + lest [hypothetical negative desire]

(25) she bathed her eye for a minute in cold water; but she was too dizzy. Afraid lest she should swoon, she returned to her rocking-chair, [*lest* Modal]

(26) Queen, the fight over the salmon in the Pleiades River He paused, afraid lest he say too much, but then he blurted out. [*lest* Subjunctive]

bać się + czy

(27) Boję się tylko, czy kłopotu nie będzie
'I was only afraid that there might be trouble'
lit. 'I was afraid if trouble will not be'

(28) Boję się tylko, czy pozytywne rezultaty odpowiadać będą tym obietnicom.
'I am afraid that these promises might not yield positive results.'
lit. 'I am afraid only if positive results will correspond to these promises'.

(29) Boją się jednak, czy zdążą.
'They are afraid lest they should be late.'
lit. 'I am afraid though if they will be in time'.

afraid + whether/if (Q) not found in 15 mln Longman corpus

3.2. Regularities revealed by the data

There are a number of regularities revealed in the data.

• **Complement correspondence**: There is no English counterpart of *czy* "whether/if" complement clauses. The closest English equivalent may be the *afraid that* construction with a range of modals, most notable *might*, as in:

(30) But she was worried about the spot on her forehead and afraid that Fleury might start seeing her as she really was [Pol. Bała się CZY FLEURY NIE ZACZNIE ... 'She was afraid if Fleury will not start...']

(31) He was afraid that I might not be able to bear the pain. [Pol. Bał się CZY BĘDĘ W STANIE... lit.'He was afraid if I will be able to...']

• **Time orientation of complement clauses**: future, present, or habitual/ generalized. By far the largest number of complements of *bać się* and of *afraid* refer to the future (or projected future): *że* complements of *bać się* have predominantly future meanings, even if the main predicate is in the past tense. Out of 275 examples only 5 refer to the past and 8 to generic present, the rest (95%) have future or projected future meaning. All *żeby* "lest" complements refer to the (hypothetical) future (see below). Sentences with infinitival complements, also, unsurprisingly, have a present, future, or generalized habitual orientation, which implies potential future (e.g. *Boję się latać* "I am afraid to fly"). The relatively rare *czy* complements tend to be future oriented as well (out of 16 examples in our data only 1 referred to the past).

In English, examples with *afraid* plus past tense *that* complements are more frequent. This is partly due to the sequence of tenses requirement (when the main clause verb is in the past, the verb in the subordinate clause must be in the past or past perfect), and to the conventionalized use of "I am afraid that" in the sense of "I am sorry to say that". Examples below do not convey the sense of "I feel fear", but rather represent a polite formula. Their complements, at least in British English, are often in present perfect and they may convey an understatement: "I think that something negative will happen, as a result of something that has happened already". Thus they may indirectly refer to projected future.

(32) I am afraid that he has been far from well for several months.
(33) I am afraid that the hon. Gentleman took a little too long in preparing this.

Polish does not use *bać się* so frequently in this type of construction, but rather a related verb *obawiać się*, which expresses a weaker emotion of fear:

(32a) Obawiam się, że nie będzie go tutaj przez parę miesięcy.
'I am afraid that he will be gone from here for a couple of months.'

• **Negation**: *żeby* complement clauses of *bać się* are always negated, they correspond to the inherently negative English *lest* complements. This was an unexpected finding for Polish: unlike *lest*, the clause introducer *żeby* does not have negation as part of its meaning. It is most commonly used as an introducer of purpose clauses and this use of it with negative emotion verbs is unique. *żeby* clauses all have a future orientation, that is, *boimy się ŻEBY coś się NIE stało w przyszłości*, "we are afraid LEST something happen in the future".[1]

[1] Neither English nor Polish actually use the future tense in these clauses, as it is not real but hypothetical or imagined future: Polish uses the subjunctive (or infinitive or modal), while English employs the present or, even more frequently, modal expressions (see Lewandowska-Tomaszczyk 2004), e.g.

He kept away from the classes lest he should meet Jill

'Unikał chodzenia na zajęcia, aby nie [musiał] spot(y)kać się z Jill. '

• **Subject orientation**:
infinitives – 100% same subject
że complements – 92% different subjects

Examples with *bać się* and infinitives are subject control sentences, and thus the subject of the infinitive and the subject of *bać się*, are identical. In sentences with ***bać się* and *że* "that" complements**: the subject of the *że* clause is different from the subject of the *bać się* clause in 92% of all examples. Yet, *że* complements with same subject as the subject of *bać się* are possible, as can be seen below.

(34) Ja w sądzie to sobie chyba klapki na oczy założę. Boję się, że odwołam. Mama i bracia odsunęli się ode mnie całkowicie.
'I think that in court I will have to put on a blindfold. I am worried that I will recant. My mom and my brothers have distanced themselves from me entirely.'

(35) Przedstawiciele niektórych organizacji boją się, że bez certyfikatu stracą uprawnienia.
'Representatives of some organizations are afraid that without the cerificate they will lose their licenses'

(36) Polacy ciągle boją się tu przyznawać do polskości. Boją się, że stracą pracę i Bóg wie co jeszcze.
'Poles are still afraid to admit to being Polish here. They are afraid that they will lose their jobs and God knows what else.'

A number of questions arises in connection with the analysis of the Polish data:
(i) Why should same subject *że* complements be possible with *bać się*?
(ii) What is the difference between *Boję się upaść*. "I am afraid to fall." and *Boję się że upadnę*. "I am afraid that I'll fall."
(iii) Why are both available to Polish speakers?

We would like to suggest that it is because *bać się* is polysemous in Polish, with at least three main senses that can be identified:
1. to feel fear in connection with (caused by) something [*prototypical* sense]
2. to feel fear in connection with something and have grounds to think that this can happen
3. to feel fear in connection with something and want this NOT to happen

The different senses are represented by different syntactic structures (caused by a different 'construal' of the whole scene cf. Langacker 1097, 1991). All three meanings refer to actions with either a temporal overlap (between 'being afraid' and 'its cause') or to a future/projected future. The extended implications present in sense 2. and sense 3. can also be implied (though not profiled) in sense 1.

Sense 1. requires the most reified construal (gerund)

(37) Boję się ciągania po sądach.
'I am afraid of being dragged through the courts.'

The verbal noun used here has a profile similar to that of a corresponding clause but does not posses full *temporal and person grounding*. It does possess the category of aspect,[2] understood as a bounded action for perfectives and unbounded for imperfective/duratives, so it is in fact partially grounded in Polish.[3] Sense 1. can also be used with the (perfective and imperfective) infinitive:

(38) Boję się być ciągana po sądach.
'I am afraid of being dragged through the courts.' [lit. to be dragged through the courts]

(39) Boję się patrzeć/spojrzeć na to.
'I am afraid to look at this.'

(40) Boję się upaść.
'I am afraid to fall.'

Sense 2. requires the *że* construction:

(41) Boję się, że będą mnie ciągać po sądach.
'I am afraid that I will be dragged through the courts' [lit. that they will drag me through the courts]

[2] Imperfective/durative in the case of *ciągać*, perfective in the case of *ciągnąć*.

[3] The difference between full clauses and their more radical nominalizations (e.g. deverbal nouns such as e.g. *budowa* (in the action sense) is, in Cognitive Linguistics terms, the presence of full so-called *sequential scanning*, expressing all the phases of the action performed in the sequential order in the former, and more abstract *summary scanning* expressing reification in the latter case (cf. Langacker 1987, 1991). In the case of gerundive form (*ciąganie*) the scanning is only partly phasal.

(42) Boję się, że upadnę.
'I am afraid that I will fall.'

The *że* construction, as noted in Lewandowska-Tomaszczyk and Dziwirek (2003), involves factual, frequently public, knowledge. It implies a higher probability that an event will take place than other types of complements. In Polish, the conceptualization of this construction activates grounding present in all referential elements of the subordinate *że* clause[4]. The difference between *Boję się upaść /Boję się że upadnę* refers precisely to the fact that it is the *że* S rather than INF that activates the whole grounded scenario as a projected 'fact'.

Sense 3. is quite characteristic too. The subordinate clause introduced with *aby/żeby* can be either infinitival or subjunctive, thus partly grounded. The identifying property of this sense is the fact that the subordinate construction is always negative (*nie* S).

(43) Boję się, żeby NIE być ciąganą po sądach.
'I am worried lest I am dragged through the courts.' lit. 'I am worried so that not be dragged through the courts'

(44) Boję się, żeby mnie NIE ciągali po sądach.
'I am worried lest they drag me through the courts.' lit. 'I am worried so that me not they would drag through the courts'.

Sense 3. is always less grounded than sense 2., as it is a hypothetical mental space (Fauconnier 1985, Lewandowska-Tomaszczyk 1996), that is activated here against a factual, verifiable space.

There is an intermediate 2–3. pattern of *bać się* complements involving (positive or negative) *czy* S (*whether* S) subordinate clauses in Polish only:

(45) A teraz – dodał – chodźmy; boję się, czyśmy wilka nie wywołali z lasu.
'I fear lit. whether we did not call out the wolf out of the forest' [idiomatic sense: 'cause an undesirable event to happen']

The embedded negated question in the above example clearly expresses a presupposition that the speakers are afraid that they might have caused an event to happen.

---

[4] Even though it seems less grounded than the equivalent English construction, where an additional grounding element pertaining to so-called sequence of tenses is present and implements an additional perspective of 'simultaneity' and 'anteriority'.

To summarize, it is in sense 1. that 'bać się' can be considered a full emotion verb. It expresses a simpler causal relation between a cause and the emotion. Sense 2. behaves more like mental or cognitive verbs [*I think that* S, *Myślę, że* S, *Boję się, że* S], while sense 3. is conceptually most similar to verbs of volition [*I wish that*, in Polish *Chcę żeby* plus subjunctive, *Boję się żeby NIE* plus subjunctive], where an additional – hypothetical negative – space is activated, which contains an *undesired* scenario.

Formally, too, each of the senses iconically expresses the degree of semantic complexity. Sense 1. is most direct and its form is the simplest, while sense 3. – conceptually most complex (hypothetical spaces, negation), is also structurally most complex. The first sense reflects a canonical FEAR scenario and is thus easiest to process, the third – most complex and most difficult to process. We can thus partly endorse Wierzbicka's claim that reflexive emotion verbs in Slavic reflect thinking about the emotion and manufacturing the emotion within oneself. However, all three basic senses discussed here, as well as their variants[5], reflect different degrees of the FEAR emotion's prototypicality.

To summarize, Polish and English speakers fear that which is to come, less so that which is here now or always, and rarely that which has happened already. They employ different types of syntactic complements to convey different perspectives on fear: gerunds and infinitives – when they fear something concrete, *że/that* clauses when they fear what can happen to them and which they think is quite likely to happen, *żeby/lest* clauses to express what they wish would not happen. *Czy* 'if/whether' clauses convey uncertainty as to the complement state of affairs [cognition] and, simultaneously, a desire [volition] that this state would (not) happen.

4. WORRY: (z)martwić się 'to worry'

Martwić się "to worry", displays a somewhat similar pattern, though allows different complement types. Over all, there are fewer occurrences of *martwić się* in the corpus (only about 338) out of which 89 (23%) contain complement clauses.

---

[5] The variants also employ the *o to* phrase:

Bać się o coś/kogoś 'to be afraid about/for someone/something'
Bać się (o to), że 'to be afraid (about it) that'
Bać się (o to), żeby NIE 'to be afraid (about it) that NOT'

The conceptualization of the *o to* variants relates to the semantics of the preposition *o* 'around/about', which refers to and profiles PATH around a LANDMARK (*ktoś/coś*) (Langacker 1987), where there is *no* direct (spatial, temporal) contact.

• **Complement types:**

As with *bać się*, *że* clauses constitute about half of all complements found with *martwić się* (46 out of 89):

(46) W 1993 roku martwiliśmy się, że postkomuniści przejęli parlament, a teraz że przejęli Belweder.
'In 1993 we worried that the post-communist took over the parliament, now we are worried they took over Belweder [presidency]'

(47) Nina martwiła się, że znowu zostanie sama.
'Nina worried that she will be left alone again.'

(48) Niektórzy ekonomiści martwią się, że problem polega nie tylko
'Some economists worry that the problem lies not only in...'

(49) Ja jestem sama i nie musiałam się chociaż martwić, że zaniedbuję męża – o tyle miałam łatwiej niż koleżanki
'I am alone, and at least I didn't have to worry that I neglect my husband – it was easier for me than for my friends.'

Next in frequency in our sample are *czy* complements (14 out of 89):

(50) Nigdy się nie martwił, czy mu starczy do pierwszego.
'He was never worried whether he had enough money till the first of the month.'

(51) Wciąż się martwią, czy kotki nie są głodne.
'They are still worried that the kittens are hungry.'

żeby complements are rare (4 out of 89). All are negated and future oriented:

(52) My się często przeprowadzałyśmy i mama zawsze bardzo się martwiła, żeby ta kartka nie zginęła.
'We often moved and mom always worried lest/that this piece of paper would go astray.'

Even though there are no bare infinitival complements of *martwić się*, there are clauses (both infinitival and finite) introduced by question words (10 out of 89):

(53) Inaczej Małgorzatę czekało więzienie. Cały czas martwiła się, co wtedy stanie się z jej dziećmi.

'Otherwise, prison awaited Margaret. The whole time she was worried what would then happen to her children.'

(54) Mukesh martwi się, co będzie, kiedy ktoś z rodziny zachoruje.
'Mukesh worries what will happen if one of the family should fall ill.'

(55) Dwa miesiące temu, podczas ostatniej naszej rozmowy, martwił się, kto obejmie redakcję, bo On nie miał siły na co dzień jej prowadzić.
'Two months ago, during our last conversation, he was worried who will take over the paper, because He was not able to carry on a daily basis.'

(56) skarb państwa nie musi potem martwić się, co począć z najgorszymi firmami.
'the treasury does not have to worry then, what to do with the worst companies.'

(57) W tej chwili jednak martwi się, jak sprzedać szybko za granicę 20 tys. ton wieprzowiny.
'At this moment, however, he is worried how to quickly sell 20 thousand ton of pork abroad'

• **Time orientation**: – **future, present, past**

Time orientation of complements of *martwić się* is more complex than in the case of *bać się*. Even though all clauses introduced by *żeby* and by question words refer to the future and most of the *czy* complements are future or present oriented (only 1 out of 14 refers to the past), *że* complements may refer to future, past, or present.

• **Complements with *to***

There are also examples with the pronoun *to* preceding the clause introducer (clauses of all kinds): infinitival, finite (że and wh-question). The use of *to* here is reminiscent of the English *it* in *I hate it when... I love it when...*, though much less predictable. We leave this issue for further research, though it is fair to say we are quite baffled as to how to account for the apparent randomness of its pattern of occurrence.[6]

---

[6] This apparent randomness is further illustrated by examples with the non-reflexive, transitive verb *martwić*:

martwić + że

(i) *Czy nie* ***martwi cię, że*** *Lewis waży aż 20 funtów więcej od ciebie?*
'Don't you worry that Lewis weights as much as 20 pounds more than you?'

(58) Nie rozumiem tylko, czemu się teraz martwisz tym, z czego niedawno radowałeś się tak głośno.
'I just don't understand why you now worry about what you were so happy about a little while ago.'

(59) Żołnierze i oficerowie martwią się zaś głównie o to, jak dostać wizę do Polski, by pojechać na zakupy do Gdańska.
'The soldiers and the officers mostly worry about how to get a Polish visa and go shopping in Gdańsk.'

(60) płoniesz z niecierpliwości, żeby poznać twego ojca i braci, martwisz się tylko o to, gdzie ich umieścić.
'you are burning with impatience to meet your father and brothers and you only worry about where to put them up.'

(61) Jest to bulwersujące wydarzenie, w rzeczywistości musimy się wszyscy martwić tym, że dochodzi do takich incydentów.
'It is a shocking event, in reality we must all worry that such incidents take place.'

5. JOY: cieszyć się "to be glad/to rejoice"

Cieszyć się "to be glad/rejoice" reveals yet another pattern. There are 1304 occurrences of *cieszyć się* in its various forms in the corpus. In that number there are 301 (23%) complex sentences. At 265 *że* complements predominate and constitute 88%.

(ii) **Martwi mnie, że** pani Krystyna Łukaszuk została wojewodą podlaskim.
'It worries me that Mrs. Krystyna Łukaszuk became the governor of the podlaski region.'

(iii) **Martwi mnie, że** zaraz po naszym wstąpieniu do NATO przypadł tak istotny kryzys międzynarodowy.
'It worries me that such an important international crisis arose immediately after our joining NATO'

martwić + to, że

(i) A czy **martwi cię to, że** nie jesteś faraonem i że twoim grobem nie będzie piramida?
'And does it worry you that you are not the pharaoh and that the pyramid will not be your grave?'

(ii) Dzień dobry panu. **Martwi mnie to, że** panu nie lepiej. Może posłać po lekarza?
'Helllo. I worry that you are not better. Perhaps I should send for the doctor?'

(iii) **Martwiło nas jednak to, że** zmusza ona czytelnika do pewnego wysiłku intelektualnego.
'We were worried, however that it requires of the reader a certain intellectual effort.'

cieszyć się + że

(62) sukienka, spięte włosy... Ekstra! Cieszyła się, że znalazła dobrego szewca
'dress, pinned up hair. Great! She was glad that she found a good shoemaker.'

(63) Lubiszewscy cieszą się, że budowa jest już za nimi.
'Lubiszewscy are glad that the construction is over.'

(64) – jak podają moje źródła – 30 m. Cieszę się, że zgadza się Pan ze mną, iż
'– as given by my sources. I am glad that you agree with me that'

(65) Dzień przed śmiercią dzwonił do domu ciesząc się, że wojna się kończy.
'He called home the day before he died, rejoicing that the war was coming to an end.'

(66) w stronę Agnieszki: – Boże, **jak się cieszę, że** panią widzę!
'towards Agnieszka: My God, I am so glad to see you!'

Other possible complements are *kiedy/gdy/jak* "when" and *bo/ponieważ* "because" clauses (26 out of 301):

(67) młodych aktorów, pomaga im zabłysnąć i cieszy się, kiedy ktoś odnosi sukcesy,
'young actors, helps them shine and is glad when someone is successful'

(68) Jest taki chłopina, cieszy się, bo wychodzi z więzienia.
'There is a guy, he is glad because he is getting out of prison.'

(69) i bardzo się cieszymy, ponieważ obiecywał, że przyjedzie
'and we are very glad because he promised that he would come'

And finally, there are also complements which begin with the pronoun *to*. There are 10 in our corpus and again the choice of *to* seems arbitrary, but one fact worth pointing out is that while non-clausal complements of *cieszyć się* are either instrumental (*cieszył się wiosną* "he enjoyed the spring") or *z* + genitive (*cieszył się z wiosny* "he was glad of the spring"), all examples with complex sentences and *to* involve *z* + genitive: *cieszyć się z tego, że*. There were no examples of *cieszyć się tym, że*.[7]

[7] The non-reflexive, "transitive" counterpart of *cieszyć się*, *cieszyć*, is much less frequently found with complement clauses. There were only 16 examples in the corpus, all with *że* clauses, 8 with *to* and 8 without:

(70) A ta Polka po prostu cieszyła się z tego, że wydała pieniądze
'And this Polish woman was simply glad that she spent her money'

(71) to fakt, że wielu Chorwatów bardziej cieszyło się z tego, że Serbowie odeszli
'It is true that many Croatians were more glad that the Serbs have left.'

(72) Czy pan sobie wyobraża, że ktoś się cieszy z tego, że lecą bomby?
'Can you imagine that someone is glad that the bombs are falling?'

(73) pobyt Twój w Norwegii dużo Tobie dał. Cieszę się z tego, że mogliśmy pomóc Ci
'Your stay in Norway was very useful. I am glad that we were able to help you.'

6. Summary

	bać się "to be afraid"	***martwić się*** "to worry"	***cieszyć się*** "to be glad"
Number of examples	1421	338	1304
Complex sentences (cs)	580 (40%)	89 (23%)	301 (23%)
że clauses	275 (47% of cs)	46 (52% of cs)	265 (88% of cs)
Infinitives	234		
żeby clauses	55	4	
czy clauses	16	14	
wh-questions		10	
to, że		15	10

The analysis of the Polish and English corpus data lead us to the following conclusions:

• *że*/that complements are allowed only in the three semantic fields exemplified above (FEAR, WORRY, and JOY) in Polish. In all three they are

(i) I szedł dalej bardzo już wolno. **Cieszyło go to, że** nie zbłądził, bo
'And he walked very slowly from then on. He was glad that he did not get lost, because '

(ii) Odpowiedź była enigmatyczna. – **Cieszy mnie, że** kibice pamiętają sukcesy
'T'he answer was enigmatic. I am glad that the fans remember our sucesses

the most frequent type of complex construction allowed. We were surprised that no *że* complements were found with anger verbs (e.g. *złościć się*, *wściekać się*) in the 10 million PELCRA Sampler, and only a few in the 150 million PELCRA Corpus, since such complements are frequent in English.

• We claim that the three verbs examined here and others like them are polysemous and can be construed as mental verbs as well as emotion verbs, possibly also as verbs expressing volition. Our analysis contradicts Wierzbicka's claim that all reflexive emotion verbs have a thinking component (that adjectives lack), since we associate the thinking component with the possibility of *że/żeby* complement clauses and e.g. *złościć się* "to be angry" does not occur with such clauses in our sample. Our findings would suggest that only *some* senses of *some* reflexive emotion verbs involve thinking.

• Another finding is that, unsurprisingly, most of our fears and worries concern the future, and the overwhelming majority of the complements of *bać się*/afraid and most of the complements ot *martwić się*/worry are future oriented. This is not the case with gladness/joy, as exemplified by *cieszyć się*. We can be glad because things are the way they are or because they have already happened.

• We also conclude that *żeby* complements are only found with verbs expressing "negative" emotions and are always negated. They correspond to the English *lest* complements and thus are incompatible with sunny, positive feelings such as joy and happiness. This makes perfect sense for *lest*, but is unexpected in the Polish context. Unlike *lest*, the clause introducer *żeby* does not have negation as part of its meaning and this use of it with negative emotion verbs is unique. This is a subject for further research.

• Yet another observation is that in Polish, in the three fields examined here, only fear as exemplified by *bać się* allows infinitival complements. This contrasts with English, where infinitives are frequent with *glad* and *happy*, the counterparts of *cieszyć się*. However, many cases of *glad/happy* with infinitives were found to be politeness routines, rather that true expressions of emotions. Thus saying *I would be glad/happy to help/do it/take that on.* does not necessarily imply gladness or happiness.

• And finally, relating to the previous point, we observe that English, much more than Polish, extends emotion expressions into politeness routines. Locutions like *I am afraid that… I fear that…*, *I'd be glad/happy to…*, and, from another project, *I hate to interrupt* and *I would like/love to help* don't convey the prototypical meaning of the emotion, whereas in Polish they tend not to be used in this type of function as much.

BIBLIOGRAPHY

Athanasiadou, A. and E. Tabakowska (eds) (1998). *Speaking of Emotions: Conceptualisation and Expression.* Mouton de Gruyter, Berlin, New York.

Harkins, J. and A. Wierzbicka (eds) (2001). *Emotions in Crosslinguistic Perspective.* Mouton de Gruyter, Berlin, New York.

Jędrzejko, E. (ed.) (1998). *Słownik polskich zwrotów werbo-nominalnych; zeszyt próbny.* Warszawa: Energeia.

Lakoff, G. (1987). *Women, Fire, and Dangerous Things: What Categories Reveal about the Mind.* Chicago/London: The University of Chicago Press.

Lakoff, G. and M. Johnson (1980). *Metaphors We Live by.* Chicago: University Press.

Lakoff, G. and Z. Kovecses (1987). "The cognitive model of anger inherent in American English". In: Holland, D. and N. Quinn (eds). *Cultural Models in Language and Thought*: 195–221. Chicago, IL: University of Chicago Press.

Lewandowska-Tomaszczyk, B. (2004). *Gramatyka angielska na autentycznym materiale językowym.* WSSM: Łódź.

Lewandowska-Tomaszczyk, B. and K. Dziwirek (2003). "A Class of Adverb/Adjective Controlled Infinitival constructions in Polish and English – A Corpus-Based Study". *Research in Language*, 1: 117–142

Lewandowska-Tomaszczyk, B., K. Dziwirek and A. McEnery (2004). „Polsko-angielska gramatyka kontrastywna konstrukcji złożonych oparta na językowym materiale korpusowym – projekt badawczy". In: Dąbrowska, A. (ed.). *Wrocławska dyskusja o języku polskim jako obcym.* Wrocław: Wrocławskie Towarzystwo Naukowe: 221–228.

Lewandowska-Tomaszczyk, B., K. Dziwirek (forthcoming). "A cognitive corpus study of FEAR expressions in Polish and English". Paper presented at CogSci06 conference, St. Petersburg, June 2006.

Mostovaja, A. D. (1998). "On emotions that one can "immerse into", "fall into", and "come to": the semantics of a few Russian prepositional constructions". In: Athanasiadou, A. and E. Tabakowska (eds). *Speaking of Emotions: Conceptualisation and Expression*: 295–330.

Peña Cervel, S. (2003). *Topology and Cognition: What Image-schemas Reveal about the Methaphorical Language of Emotions.* Muenchen: Lincom: Europa.

Radden, G. (1998). "The conceptualization of emotional causality by means of prepositional phrases": In: Athanasiadou, A. and E. Tabakowska (eds). *Speaking of Emotions: Conceptualisation and Expression*: 273–294.

Wierzbicka, A. (1999). *Emotions Across Languages and Cultures: Diversity and Universals.* Cambridge: Cambridge University Press.

Corpora:
BNC
Longman Corpus
PELCRA

Cecília Fróis

Belinda Maia and **Arnaldo Videira**

University of Porto

A CASE OF MEANING EXTENSION

Abstract

The focus of traditional Terminology was on the standardization of terminology in a specific domain at a certain stage of the evolution of that domain. Naturally, these standards had to be reconsidered over time, but the process aimed at univocity – or one concept = one term – and favoured the preservation of well-defined concepts and terms, even in domains where scientific progress advanced rapidly.

We have been studying the terminology of Genetics in a diachronic corpus of specialists' texts, in English using the research methods of cognitive semantics. Corpógrafo of Linguateca (http://www.linguateca.pt) was used to organize and analyse data.

Our studies have led us to the conclusion that terms and their meanings evolve. We are interested in illustrating the relationship between the diachronic study of terminology, and the understanding and evolution of knowledge. Terms in the area of Genetics cannot be separated from the history of the development of the domain. Since the discovery of the structure of DNA, Genetics has undergone considerable development. Research in this area has led to a boom of knowledge and many previous concepts have had to be reviewed.

We shall use the term *recombination* as an example of a term which extended its meaning due to the development of Genetics. We will analyse the use of the term in context, in several specialists' texts covering a span of seventy four years. The extension of the meaning of this term will become clear as we proceed and we hope to show why univocity between terms and concepts is not feasible. The human capacity for conceptualisation is dynamic and cannot be thus controlled.

1. Introduction

After a brief overview of the principles of "Traditional Terminology" and of "Modern Terminology", we shall discuss the extension of meaning of the term "recombination" using several specialists' texts written between 1919 and 2003.

2. Theoretical aspects of Traditional and Modern Terminology

In the traditional approach the emphasis was on the univocity principle – only one term should be assigned to a concept and vice versa. Wüster (1889–1977), the founder of the Vienna School of Terminology, considered the onomasiological perspective the only valid perspective. For him, terminological work should begin with the knowledge and organisation of the concepts in any area of knowledge, and then one designation should be assigned to each concept. The concept was the center of all terminological work, which was standardisation-oriented and essentially prescriptive.

Modern Terminology, by contrast, is communication-oriented, discourse centred and descriptive. Researchers look for terms in text corpora and use software for term extraction and for the creation of terminological databases. The analysis of data found in corpora has shown the existence of synonymy and polysemy among terminological units appearing in highly specialized texts. The analysis also stresses the role synonymy and polysemy play in the understanding process. Analysis of corpora leads us to the conclusion that special languages evolve over time, just as general language is constantly changing to adapt to new circumstances. In fact diachronic studies of corpora show the growth of the complexity of scientific knowledge over time. Empirical data also show that the evolution of knowledge about Genetics entails a proliferation of terms over time, and scientific advances have led to adjustments in the terminology used. New aspects of reality had to be named. What do data teach us about the practice of terminology by specialists?

3. Methodology

We have used several online publications on Genetics to build a diachronic corpus in English. The publications we have used are all articles by specialists and for specialists or specialists to be, and these online publications offer two advantages:

1. They store articles since the beginning of the XXth century.

2. The articles are available for free consultation and downloading, except for some recent articles.

We have collected articles since the beginning of the XXth century and our diachronic corpus consists of 14 articles written between 1919 and 2003. In order to process this work efficiently, we have used the Corpógrafo[1], an online suite of corpus construction, analysis and terminology tools intended for ordinary users.

The Corpógrafo allows the extraction and storage of text files, in several formats, into a personal area of the web server. It also enables the cleaning and segmentation of uploaded texts, and the semi-automatic extraction of term candidates using N-gram analysis and N-gram analysis with restrictions. It also allows for the semi-automatic extraction of possible definitions and semantic relations.

Using this web tool, we were able to find out quite quickly if the articles found online were really useful for our purpose and exclude those that were not. The useful articles provided the data to start the construction of a terminological database.

For this paper we focused on just one term – "recombination". We have done a diachronic analysis of this term using our corpus. Our aim was to test the hypothesis that the term "recombination" has undergone a meaning extension since 1919.

4. Terminology and Genetics

The History of Science shows that scientific knowledge is acquired progressively. The History of Genetics also shows how improvements in methods and techniques of observation made observable some events and thus helped us to understand certain phenomena better.

The date of the publication of Mendel's paper, 1865, signalled the birth of Genetics. However, nobody knew then what a "gene" was. The term gene was coined by Wilhelm Johannsen[2], in 1909, and it meant "mendelian unit". The identification of chromosomes as carriers of genes was already possible in 1902, as a result of cooperation between the area of cytology and the area of genetics.

---

[1] The Corpógrafo was developed at the Porto node of Linguateca by the team led by Eng.º Luís Sarmento. http://www.linguateca.pt/Corpografo

[2] Timeline of Genetics. Genetics. GlaxoSmithKline. http://genetics.gsk.com/history.htm

The discovery of the chemical nature of the gene came in 1952 with the works of Alfred Hershey and Martha Chase,[3] who established DNA as genetic material in viral infection.

Through the observation, formulation and testing of hypotheses, inductive and deductive reasoning, knowledge in the area of Genetics progressed, and geneticists introduced new terms to name recently discovered realities like "gene".

It was the need to respond to the phenomenon of designation in special languages that led Wüster, in 1930, to establish a theoretical framework to deal with this phenomenon in order to eliminate ambiguities in special language use and thus improve scientific and technical international communication.

According to Temmerman, in Traditional Terminology, concepts are considered as having an objective existence which can be named and defined.

In Traditional Terminology the concept and not the term or the word is taken as the starting point for meaning description. The concept is considered the meaning of the term (Temmerman 2000: 40)

On the other hand, Modern Terminology, in line with the cognitive sciences, considers,

...conceptualisation is a direct spin-off of experience and understanding. [...] Categorisation is part of human experience and human understanding of the world. (Temmerman 2000: 4)

So, for Modern Terminology, there are many concepts which may be reformulated when changes occur as a result of scientific progress. However, since Kuhn's "The Structure of Scientific Revolutions" (1962), scientific progress has been seen in a different light and Science's claims of achieving objective knowledge have been contested. Many philosophers of Science have attacked positivism, the theory which states that scientific knowledge is grounded in objective reality and, more recently, the cognitive sciences have contributed to the understanding of scientific activity. One of the major contributions to the understanding of scientific activity is given by Philosophy. As Rosenberg says,

... there is still much work to be done by philosophy if we are to understand fully the nature of science. Our project must include an understanding of categorisation and observation, both philosophically and psychologically. We must clarify the relations between meaning and reference... (Rosenberg 2000: 173, 174)

---

[3] Timeline of Genetics. Genetics. GlaxoSmithKline. http://genetics.gsk.com/history.htm

In our case study, we shall present the evolution of one concept over time and the corresponding evolution of its designation.

5. Example of a dynamic relationship between concept and term

We carried out a diachronic analysis of the term "recombination" and found that, in the oldest article of our corpus, the term was used alone or preceded by the adjective 'genetic'. In 1947, "gene" as an adjective, appears associated with "recombination". Different adjectives kept appearing associated with the term in the articles we have selected through time. The question we pose is if these adjectives refer to different realities.

We found that some of the terms are synonymous. For instance "genetic recombination", "homologous recombination" and "general recombination" form one group of synonyms and "illegitimate recombination" and "nonhomologous recombination" another.

We looked for sentences in our corpus which explained "recombination" through time. In the 1919 article, "genetic recombination" is recognized as the cause for differences in plants of the second generation.

If now we are dealing with an F_2 generation all of which originated from genetically equivalent F_1 plants, part of the differences in the F_2 would be due to environic effects and part to the effects of genetic recombination. (Freeman 1919: 12)

Bridges (1926: 42) describes how recombinations of characters are related with the mechanism of crossing over.

The individuals that come from the crossover chromosomes show recombinations of characters.

In 1947, Lederberg mentions recombination of genes in viruses.

Recombinations of genes controlling several growth factor requirements and resistance to a specific bacteriophage have been found.(Lederberg 1947: 682)

and in 1957, the same author relates genetic recombination with the redistribution of the information of more than one cell to the offspring, in bacteria.

For this analysis, exact replication tells us little more than its own bare fact, and most of our present understanding depends on treasured exceptions from the rule (mutation) and especially on those other modes of reproduction in which the information from more than one cell is redistributed to the progeny, that is to say, genetic recombination. (Lederberg 1957: 69, 70)

Meselson (1961: 865) gives an explanation of the recombination mechanism.

This suggests that recombination occurs by breakage of parental chromosomes followed by the reconstruction of genetically complete chromosomes from the fragments.

As these articles were written by specialists and addressed to specialists, the appearance of such an explanation in 1961 suggests that the phenomenon was not fully understood before that date. The sentence extracted from Holliday (1974: 273), confirms this suspicion.

It has now been demonstrated, particularly by the experiments of TAYLOR (1965), that recombination at meiosis does indeed involve breakage and reunion of chromatids.

The following sentence, extracted from an article published in 1974 shows that, for eukaryote, the process was not still fully understood then.

The initial steps in eukaryote recombination are still obscure. (H. L. K. Whitehouse 1974: 239)

In 1979, another type of recombination appears in an article extracted from Genetics online containing the term "site-specific recombination". This term does not appear before this date, in this publication, and the article has a sentence explaining the mechanism.

The site-specific recombination at the attachment site for prophage integration might proceed by two general mechanisms: (1) a concerted reaction without a free intermediate; (2) a sequential mechanism differing from typical general recombination only by an inability of the cross-strand intermediate structure to migrate into the region of nonhomology adjacent to the attachment site. (Echols and Green 1979: 297)

A search of the History of Genetics for data related to the evolution of the concept "recombination" revealed that it was only in 1909 that Jansens presented evidence of the pairing of homologous chromosomes during meiosis. In 1910 Morgan showed that recombination occurred between genes in the same pair of chromosomes. However, nobody knew, then, how the process of recombination did occur. It was only in 1931, as Sturtevant mentions (2001: 74), that the cytological proof of the process of recombination was obtained.

In 1931 two papers demonstrated independently, that genetic crossing-over is accompanied by an interchange of parts between homologous chromosomes.

The period from 1940 onwards brought great advances in the understanding of the mechanisms of gene recombination. Nevertheless, after 1953, the concept of gene evolved and so did the concept of gene recombination as a result of the discovery of DNA structure. Since then many other advances have occurred in Genetics and the way geneticists view reality has changed sometimes as a consequence of scientific progress.

6. Discussion

A search of the articles of our *corpus* for the term "recombination" showed that this term is associated with a variety of adjectives, as list 1 shows.

List 1

- Eukaryote recombination
- Gene recombination
- General recombination
- Genetic recombination
- Homologous recombination
- Illegitimate recombination
- Integrative recombination
- Interchromosomal recombination
- Nonhomologous recombination
- Normal recombination
- Prokaryote recombination
- Site-specific recombination
- Unequal homologous recombination

We have concluded that some of these compound terms were synonyms.

According to Sager, Dungworth and Mc Donald (1980: 268), in language for special purposes, the use of compounds has an objective.

> By the creation of compounds we can re-designate existing words to serve other functions.
> [...] Depending on the nature of the nucleus, the determinant can specify in greater detail, indicate a purpose, the means by which an operation is carried out, the object to which a process is applied, or the time, place or other circumstances, which in this way become an integral distinctive feature of the new concept.

So, this proliferation of compounds with the same nucleus "recombination" possibly reflects the need the geneticists felt to designate different conceptual features acquired by the concept "recombination" as the result of a deeper knowledge, progressively acquired.

As Sager (1990: 73) says:

Functionally, derivation and compounding serve the purpose of closer determination of a concept – narrowing its intension – while at the same time showing the relationship that exists between the new concept and its origin.

Meyer, Eck and Skuce (1997: 101) present this definition of intension and extension of concepts:

The sum of all the characteristics of a concept is traditionally called its intension, while the collection of objects to which a concept refers is called its extension. A concept having many characteristics is said to have a broad intension; consequently, its extension is narrow, as it can refer to only a limited number of objects. On the other hand, a concept having few characteristics is said to have a narrow intension, and a broad extension.

The glossary, included in Griffiths *et al.* (1999: 628), has the following definition of the concept "recombination":

(1) In general, any process in a diploid or partially diploid cell that generates new gene or chromosomal combinations not found in that cell or in its progenitors.
(2) At meiosis, the process that generates a haploid product of meiosis whose genotype is different from either of the two haploid genotypes that constituted the meiotic diploid.

In the same glossary, the definition of "site-specific recombination" is:

Recombination between two specific sequences that need not be homologous, mediated by a specific recombination system. (ibidem: 630)

Comparing the two definitions we realize that "site-specific recombination" is a type of recombination. In fact, Hardisson (2005, chapter 8) states:

At least four types of naturally occurring recombination have been identified in living organisms.

Nowadays "recombination" has become a generic concept with subordinate specific concepts. A generic-specific relation is now apparent, so we believe the extension of the term has become enlarged.

7. Conclusions

The data we have collected illustrate the evolution of both the designation, of a particular genetic phenomenon, and the evolution of the meaning of that designation. The understanding geneticists had of "recombination" has grown, through time, into a more complex notion. That complexity was expressed by a corresponding complexity of designation leading to a proliferation of compound terms.

We understand that a conference on cognitive linguistics is primarily interested in proving the psychological existence of language universals or categories of meaning. However, our work with special languages has heightened our awareness of the dynamic nature of both knowledge and the language used to construct and express this knowledge.

Our observations remind us of Putnam's position (1988: 120), when he argues that:

> ...the open texture of the notion of any object, the open texture of the notion of reference, the open texture of the notion of meaning, and the open texture of reason itself are all interconnected. It is from these interconnections that serious philosophical work on these notions must proceed.

When relating science and philosophy, we also need to heed Rosenberg (2000: 173–174) when he states that:

> ...in the attempt to restore the fortunes of an empiricist account of knowledge and metaphysics as well as an empiricist account of language, easy solutions will not avail

And he goes on to argue that an understanding of the nature of science:

> must include an understanding of categorization and observation, both philosophically and psychologically.

We hope that this short paper has contributed a little towards an understanding of the problems underlying any theoretical approach to classifying human knowledge and the language used in the process.

REFERENCES

Bridges, C. B. and T. M. Olbrycht (1926). "The Multiple Stock "XPLE" and its use". *Genetics*, 11 (1): 41. PDF version.

Dungsworth, D. and P. F. McDonald (1980). *English Special Languages. Principles and practice in science and technology*. Wiesbaden. Oscar Brandstetter Verlag KG.

Echols, H. and L. Green (1979). "Some properties of site-specific and general recombination inferred from int-initiated exchanges by bacteriophage lambda". *Genetics*, 93: 297–307. PDF version.

Griffiths, A., Gelbart, W. M., Miller, J. H. and R. C. Lewontin (1999). *Modern Genetics Analysis*. New York. W. H. Freeman and Company.

Hardisson, R. C. (2005). *Working with Molecular Genetics.* The PENNSYLVANIA State University, online edition.

Holliday, R. (1974). "Molecular Aspects of Genetic Exchange and Gene Conversion". *Genetics*, 78: 273–287. PDF version.

Kuhn, T. S. (1996). *The Structure of Scientific Revolutions.* 3rd edition. Chicago: The University of Chicago Press ISBN 0-226-45808-3.

Lederberg, J. (1957). Bacterial Reproduction. Harvey Lect. 1957–1959 (53): 69–82. PMID: 13640420 [PubMed – OLDMEDLINE for Pre 1966]

Maia, B. (2003). "The Pedagogical and Linguistic Research Implications of the GC to on-line parallel and comparable corpora", presented at Conference CP3A 2003 (Corpora Paralelos, Aplicações e Algoritmos Associados), 3 de Junho de 2003.

Meselson, M. and J. J. Weigle (1961). "Chromosome Breakage Accompanying Genetic Recombination in Bacteriophage". Proceedings of the National Academy of Sciences. PNAS 1961; 47 (6): 857–868. PDF version.

Meyer, I., Eck, K. and D. Skuce (1997). In *Handbook of Terminology Management.* Vol. 1. *Basic Aspects of Terminology Management* compiled by Wright, Sue-Ellen & Budin, Gerhard. Amsterdam/Philadelphia: John Benjamins Pub. Co. Sager, J.C.;

Putnam, H. (1988). *Representation and Reality.* Cambridge, Mass.: MIT Press.

Rosenberg, A. (2004). *Philosophy of Science. A contemporary introduction.* London and New York. Routledge.

Sager, J. C. (1990) *A Practical Course in Terminology Processing.* Amsterdam/ Philadelphia. John Benjamins Publishing Company.

Sarmento, L., Maia, B. and D. Santos (2004). "The Corpógrafo – a Web-based environment for corpora research". Proceedings of LREC 2004. Lisboa, Portugal, 25 May 2004.

Sturtevant, A. H. (2001). *A History of Genetics.* Published by Cold Spring Harbor Laboratory Press and Electronic Scholarly Publishing Project, online edition.

Tatum, E. L. and J. Lederberg (1947). „Gene recombination in the bacterium *Escherichia coli*". *Journal of Bacteriology*, 53 (6): 673–684. PDF version.

Temmerman, R. (2000). *Towards New Ways of Terminology Description. The socio-cognitive-approach.* Amsterdam/Philadelphia. John Benjamins Publishing Company.

Whitehouse, H. L. K. (1974). "Advances in Recombination Research". *Genetics*, 78: 237–245. PDF version.

Thomas Egan

Hedmark University College

THE PROTOTYPICAL MEANING OF THE *-ING* COMPLEMENT FORM

1. Introduction

The exact meaning of the modern English gerund has long been a matter of dispute. Cognitive linguists resemble linguists of other persuasions in differing among themselves in their interpretations of its basic characteristics. Table 1 contains a one-line summary of the views of a selection of linguists of various theoretical persuasions, including the cognitive linguists Wierzbicka, Dirven, Langacker, Verspoor and Smith and Escobedo. Obviously such a summary cannot do justice to the intricacies of the views expressed by these grammarians: it is merely intended to give a rough idea of the focus of their various approaches.

Table 1. Various opinions on the semantics of *-ing* clauses as complements

Authors	*-ing*
Wood (1956)	denotes something general (the infinitive something more specific)
Bolinger (1968)	encodes a situation as reified
Conrad (1982)	is used as a referring NP
Quirk *et al* (1985)	generally encodes events as performed, often progressive
Wierzbicka (1988)	vague simultaneity between the matrix verb and the complement
Dirven (1989)	encodes a phenomenon of unspecified, unbounded duration
Langacker (1990)	imposes a restricted immediate scope of predication
Dixon (1991)	encodes an activity or state as extended in time
Duffley (1995)	provides for a representation of the interiority of an event
Verspoor (1997)	denotes a bounded event with defocused boundaries
Smith & Escobedo (2001)	conceptual overlap between the matrix verb and the complement

This paper presents the results of a corpus-based study of *-ing* complement clauses. 133 matrix verbs in 178 constructions containing *-ing* complements were investigated, with the data being taken from the British National Corpus. Tokens were assigned to one of sixteen categories in a table containing four types of matrix verb and four types of complement predicate. The four types of matrix verb occur in the following construction types:

Same-time constructions, in which the complement predicate is realised simultaneously with the matrix verb

Forward-looking constructions, in which we can expect the complement predicate to be realised after the time of the matrix verb

Backward-looking constructions, in which the complement predicate has been realised prior to the time of the matrix verb

Contemplation constructions, in which the complement predicate is realised only in the mental domain.

The constructions in this study are listed in Table 2 according to the four categories. Only Same-subject (equi-subject) and Different-subject complement constructions were considered, constructions with unexpressed complement clause subjects (as in 'I heard shouting') being ignored.

Table 2. All the matrix verbs in the study according to construction type: verbs listed in two categories are in italics. 'SS' stands for Same-subject and 'DS' for Different-subject

Construction type	Verbs	Total
Same-time	abhor, abide, adore, ape, *bear*, begrudge, brook, catch, continue, deny, detest, discover, dislike, endure, enjoy, feel, feign, find, grudge, hate, have, hear, help, involve, justify, keep, lie, like, loathe, love, mean, mime, *mind*, *miss*, notice, observe, overhear, perceive, relish, remain, repeat, resent, *risk*, see, sit, smell, spot, spy, stand, stay, stomach, taste, tolerate, try, understand, value, watch	57 verbs in 75 constructions, 36 SS and 39 DS
Forward-looking	anticipate, arrange, attempt, avoid, *bear*, begin, bother, commence, defer, defy, delay, deserve, discuss, dread, envisage, escape, eschew, evade, face, fancy , fear, forbear, forbid, foresee, get, go, intend, invite, leave, *mind*, *miss*, need, neglect, postpone, preclude, prevent, propose, recommence, require, resist, resume, *risk*, save, set, shirk, shun, start, *stop*, undertake, want	50 verbs in 67 constructions, 41 SS and 26 DS
Backward-looking	acknowledge, admit, cease, complete, deny, describe, discontinue, finish, forget, mention, overlook, quit, recall, recollect, regret, remember, renounce, report, *stop*	19 verbs in 26 constructions, 19 SS and 7 DS
Contemplation	conceive, consider, contemplate, fancy, forget, imagine, try	7 verbs in 10 constructions, 6 SS and 4 DS

The four types of complement predicate considered were Vendler's (1967) categories of *avtivities*, *accomplishments*, *states* and *achievements*.

2. Comparison with the progressive

2.1. Introduction

Huddleston and Pullum (2002: 163) characterise the progressive in terms of six properties, *ongoingness*, *imperfectivity*, *interiority*, *duration*, *dynamism* and *limited duration*. Some of the scholars listed in Table 1 posit one of more of these properties as central to the meaning of the gerund-participial *-ing* form. Dixon, for instance, bases his characterisation on the notions of *duration* and *ongoingness*, Duffley his on the notion of *interiority*, and Langacker his on the notions of *imperfectivity* and *interiority*. There thus seems to be a degree of consensus that the *-ing* form as complement shares some meaning components with the progressive, although there is disagreement as to just which components these are. In the following I will consider to what extent each of the six properties which Huddleston and Pullum propose for the progressive may also be posited of the gerund-participial *-ing* form as represented in the corpus material.

The properties proposed by Huddleston and Pullum for the progressive are designed to account for its use with activities and accomplishments. They can also account for its use with achievements and states in marked contexts. The *-ing* complement form, however, can be used with stative predicates *without these thereby losing their stative meaning*. Moreover, the *-ing* form may be used in each of the four complement types with all of Vendler's (1967) four classes of predicate. Table 3 contains a truncated example from the BNC of each of the sixteen possible combinations. 'S-T' stands for Same-time, 'B-L' and 'F-L' for Backward- and Forward-looking, and 'Ctp' for Contemplation.

The next four sections contain a brief look at these sixteen combinations in turn and a consideration of the extent to which the sixteen construction types are compatible with Huddleston and Pullum's characterisation of the progressive.

Table 3. Vendler's four categories of activities, accomplishments, states, and achievements, as they are instantiated in Same-time, Backward-looking, Forward-looking and Contemplation *-ing* complement constructions

	A. Activities	B. Accomplishments	C. States	D. Achievements
1. S-T	... You can smell the barbecue sizzling away ...	... could hear doors opening and closing ...	I loved being pregnant...	I hadn't noticed him clocking the fact ...
2. F-L	... began picking at the bread ...	...and began screwing the inspection plate back into place ...	... had feared being out of the game ...	... have postponed making a decision...
3. B-L	I recall her pacing the sitting-room ...	I recollect one girl putting on dark glasses	I recall her being near one of the windows...	13 reported a condom coming off during intercourse ...
4. Ctp	... she had never imagined wearing clothes like this ...	... considered walking out on the Royal family ...	... ...so as to conceive them existing unperceived.	Greece contemplated extending its territorial waters...

2.2. Same-time constructions

Same-time activities such as 1A in Table 3, and examples (1)–(3), satisfy five of the six criteria posited by Huddleston and Pullum for the progressive.[1]

(1) It is not that teachers in our primary schools dislike *teaching bright children*. (CLY 1595)
(2) Guy's eyes were very brilliant when she risked *looking at him*. (JY3 2772)
(3) Also mares can be ticklish round the udder and resent the foal *nuzzling around that area*. (BPB 996)

They encode an activity *in progress* at the time referred to by the matrix verb, and this activity is profiled as *imperfective* in that the barbecue in 1A, for example, may be said to be *sizzling* at any point during its extension. It is also profiled as *mid-interval* – some sizzling has taken place and there is more to

[1] All examples are taken from the BNC. Apart from placing the complement predicates in italics, they have not been emended in any way and are cited exactly as they appear in the corpus.

come. It is *dynamic*, in that the sizzling consists of various heterogeneous components and it is *durative* in that it lasts for some time. The one point on which it does not conform to the progressive prototype is with respect to the latter's connotation of *limited duration*. There is no sense in which the *sizzling* in 1A, or the *teaching* in example (1), are to be construed as activities limited in time. (Of course, in the real world the sizzling properties of sausages, for example, are limited by the proportion of fat in them, but *sizzling* is not therefore construed as an accomplishment!) These properties are summed up in Table 4, which mirrors Table 3 in the composition of its rows and columns.

Accomplishments encode situations in progress which, unless interrupted, will come to an end of their own accord (under their own momentum, in force-dynamic terms). Same-time accomplishments, as in 1B in Table 3 and (4)–(6), resemble Same-time activities in that they share five of the six properties of the progressive, the exception being *limited duration*.

(4) And business executives have disliked *travelling to a special studio*. (B73 1029)

(5) He was breathless with the effort of clinging precariously to the limited footholds and it was time, he decided, to risk *climbing down to the ground*. (CKD 340)

(6) The insensitivity of the Benthamites, who promoted the Act, lay in their efusal to see how bitterly the poor would resent *becoming the designated victims of the Act*, as if their love for the dead were in some way inferior to that of 'their betters'. (ACA 1112)

These examples are all *ongoing*, *imperfective*, *durative* and *dynamic*. They are also *mid-interval*. In 1B, for instance, the *opening* and *closing* are *ongoing*. The process is *imperfective* in that at any point during their extension they may be said to be *opening* and *closing*. They are *durative* in that both processes take some time, and they are *dynamic* in that they consist of heterogeneous components. Finally, they are *mid-interval* since the doors have started to open and close but have not yet fully opened or closed at the time of their perception. Moreover, although we know from our experience that the processes of *opening* and *closing* doors only take a limited amount of time, these limits are not focused upon in this construction.

Same-time *-ing* constructions encoding states, such as 1C in Table 3 and (7)–(9) share three of the progressive's six properties. They are *imperfective*, *mid-interval* and *durative*.

(7) Though she had never admitted it to anyone, she disliked *being alone in the office* since Arabella had fallen to her death from the fire escape: and the feeling was always worse in the evening. (GUU 376)

(8) If she had the sense she'd been born with she'd get up from the table right now, wish him a polite good evening, and scuttle back to the safety of the dressing-room, there to make a pledge never to risk *being in his company* again. (JY5 329)

(9) Why had she never realised before now that Dana resented *looking like her sister*? (H8J 1990)

States are, by definition, *imperfective* and *durative*. They are neither *ongoing* nor *dynamic*. What about the property of *limited duration?* One effect of using the progressive with a stative verb is to impose a *limited duration* construal on the situation in question. This is not the case with the *-ing* complement construction. For instance, in the case of 1C, the natural boundaries inherent to the state of *being pregnant* are not in focus.

Achievements resemble states in that they do no occur freely with the progressive. They are not *durative*, but punctual. If used with the progressive, they acquire the property of *duration* and often resemble accomplishments, in that they may connote a period before an inherent right-hand boundary. The question now is how they are to be interpreted in Same-time *-ing* constructions, exemplified by 1D in Table 3 and (10)–(12).

(10) She disliked *losing her temper* against her will because it rarely achieved useful results and symbolised impotence rather than strength: always better to channel anger than display it, she thought. (G15 392)

(11) Any criteria for defining 'privileged information', or what the 'dangers' are in revealing such matters as dispositions (of manpower) are so vaguely incorporated as to ensure that few will risk *submitting an essay* without approval, which might later be assessed as an 'improper disclosure'. (A0K 428)

(12) Perhaps he'd always secretly resented *giving his name to another man's child*, she thought sadly. (H88 124)

What is the effect of adding *-ing* to an inherently perfective root such as 'clock' in 1D, 'lose' in (10), 'submit' in (11) and 'give his name' in (12)? In the progressive the total effect is the imposition of a (limited) durative construal. The *-ing* complement form also exhibits *imperfectivity* and *durativity*, although there is no implication that the latter is limited. Thus in (10) the *losing* which induces simultaneous dislike on the part of the subject is not presented as a single bounded event. It may occur again and again; and each time it occurs, it will prompt the same feelings of distaste. The potential for recurrence is obviously not present in a context such as that of 1D and (12). Nevertheless, it does seem to be the case that *giving his name* in (12) is also viewed imperfectively and as having a certain duration, just as it does in the progressive. It also seems to be the case that these constructions impose a *mid-interval* perspective on the situations in question. This is a function of the same-time nature of the construction. One dislikes or resents doing something as one is doing it. We may therefore conclude that Same-time achievements, like Same-time states, share four properties with Same-time activities and accomplishments. Like the latter they are *imperfective*, *mid-interval*, *durative* and of *unlimited duration*. Unlike them they are not *ongoing* and *dynamic*.

2.3. Forward-looking constructions

The next type of construction to be considered is the Forward-looking type, exemplified in row 2 of Table 3 and examples (13)–(24). Forward-looking activities, such as 2A in Table 3 and (13)–(15), share four of the five characteristics exhibited by Same-time activity *-ing* constructions.

(13) Lack of money prevents us *eating properly* when we are children, ruins our health, rots our teeth, makes our parents quarrel and take to drink, stops us having the clothes we want, the friends we like, the parties we long for, stops us having the tuition which would enable us to get an education (HGJ 277)

(14) On Harry's first day at play school, his mum was about to take him along to meet all the other kids when it started *snowing* outside. (CHR 907)

(15) First-class writers can defy this rule-of-thumb, but anyone else doing so risks *alienating readers* who have come to them for a particular sort of entertainment. (FF0 307)

These *-ing* complements all encode activities as *ongoing*, *imperfective*, *durative* and *dynamic*. They differ from Same-time activity constructions in that they do not normally adopt a *mid-interval* perspective on the unfolding activity. The subject in (13) does not anticipate *us* being in the middle of the *eating* process, as it were. Nor are we invited to view the *picking* in 2A or the *snowing* in (14) from a *mid-interval* perspective. This lack of a *mid-interval* perspective does not affect the imperfective nature of the activities concerned. They are profiled as ongoing unbounded activities that would be expected to unfold at some time after that of the matrix verb in the normal course of events. An inchoative matrix verb like *began* in 2A or *started* in (14) encodes the complement situation as having a left-hand temporal boundary, but this is a property of the matrix verb rather than the complement form.

The *mid-interval* property is not encoded in complement situations of the accomplishment type either. Consider in this respect 2B in Table 3 and (16)–(18).

(16) A construction company says it may sue a local authority which is trying to prevent its *demolishing a hotel.* (KRM 1518)
(17) At about nine o'clock I start *putting Mum to bed.* (HJC 177)
(18) The police risk *losing control of the streets* to lager louts, vandals and drug dealers, the Police Federation conference was warned. (ABG 1989)

In none of these examples is the accomplishment viewed from a particular point within its unfolding. And, although the complement situations, being accomplishments, may all be expected to run their natural course, their boundaries are not in focus, i.e. they are not profiled as being of *limited duration.* The other four properties of *ongoingness*, *imperfectivity*, *duration* and *dynamism* are exhibited by all four examples.

Forward-looking *-ing* constructions encoding states, such as 2C in Table 3 and (19)–(21) resemble Same-time statives in being *imperfective* and *durative.* They differ from them, however, with respect to the *mid-interval* property.

(19) The outcome is that national states, which exist to prevent life *being poor, nasty, short, brutal, and solitary,* are a match for the unreasonable person who commits conventional crimes, but 'are no match for the resources and size of ... great corporations: General Motors could buy Delaware ... if DuPont were willing to sell it' (Nader and Green 1973: 79). (CHL 1127)
(20) she started *being a cocky little bitch*, and she wears make- up, really plasters it on (KCX 6493)
(21) He mustn't be expected to make an effort when he doesn't feel like it, he mustn't risk *being hemmed in or bored*, but everyone has to be ever so careful of his feelings, poor sensitive soul, and when he wants a good fuck he comes to obliging loving little Ruth because he can relieve himself and have his morale boosted without having to do a damned thing about it but get himself into your bed.' (H9G 1635)

The states in these examples are viewed as extended wholes, without any particular time within their extension constituting a focal point. To put it simply, the subject in 2C fears the whole state of *being out of the game*, not just being in the middle of such a state of exclusion. This lack of a *mid-interval* perspective is not peculiar to Forward-looking -*ing* complements encoding states. As we have seen, the same point holds for activities and accomplishments.

Forward-looking achievements like 2D in Table 3 and (22)–(24) resemble Same-time achievements in being *imperfective*, *durative* and of *unlimited duration*. They differ from them in not adopting a *mid-interval* perspective.

(22) That admiration won't prevent Keegan *signing at least one more goal-scorer*, with QPR's Les Ferdinand the latest in his sights. (CBG 2690)
(23) The powerboats will start *arriving at Fort Perch Rock car park* on Friday, June 18. (K3X 996)
(24) She killed smiling, and there were few who, having seen her kill, wanted even to risk *dying at her hands*. (BN1 1132)

These utterances resemble achievements with the progressive in that they may focus on a process leading up to a point in time. Thus, whereas it only takes a moment for a boat to arrive, it is clear that (23) refers to a period up to and including the boats' docking. Similarly in (24) the focus is not restricted to the actual point of dying. With respect to the question of whether or not they imply a *mid-interval* perspective, however, these constructions resemble the other three sorts of Forward-looking constructions in not stipulating any particular point within the complement situation from which the remainder is viewed.

2.4. Backward-looking constructions

The next type of construction is the Backward-looking type, exemplified in row 3 of Table 3 and examples (25)–(36). Backward-looking activity -*ing* complements, like 3A in Table 3 and (25)–(27), are similar to both Same-time and Forward-looking constructions with respect to the four progressive characteristics shared by these two construction types.

(25) Well do I remember *walking up and down the hilly streets of San Francisco*, and also attending a performance of the San Francisco Symphony Orchestra, with that debonair veteran Frenchman Pierre Montreux conducting. (B11 820)
(26) He stopped *walking*, staring straight ahead of him into the forest. (JY5 3154)

(27) Three doctors deny *removing kidneys for cash*, as 'donor' insists he wouldn't sell one 'for the whole of Istanbul' Turk tells of transplant 'theft'. (A9F 240)

All these Backward-looking constructions encode activities profiled as *ongoing*, *imperfective*, *durative* and *dynamic*. The question is whether they imply a *mid-interval* perspective on the unfolding activity. In 3A the subject recalls to his or her mind an unfolding activity, and the subject appears to view this unfolding activity from the inside, remembering *her* being in the middle of *pacing*. Similarly in (25) the subject remembers being in the middle of *walking up and down*. It is not so obvious whether the perspective in (26) should be described as *mid-interval*. The ongoing activity of *walking* is construed from the point of its cessation, not a point prior to this. Note that the fact of its interruption does not imply that the activity itself is to be construed as having *limited duration*. We may conclude that activities in Backward-looking *-ing* constructions are *ongoing*, *imperfective*, *durative* and *dynamic*, and may or may not be *mid-interval*, depending on the semantics of the matrix verb in question.

Backward-looking accomplishment *-ing* complements, such as 3B in Table 3 and (28)–(30), differ from the nine types already discussed in one important respect, relating to the property of *limited duration*.

(28) I remember *recording 13 groups in one day*, and the only thing that kept me sane was knowing I was getting music together with Enya. (ED7 1806)

(29) 'If it had been anything else then a doctor would have been a sensible idea, but once somebody stops *strangling you*, you recover, don't you?' (GV2 751)

(30) He also denies *raping a 26-year-old woman* in her home earlier the same day. (K5D 13420)

These examples all encode complement situations profiled as *ongoing*, *imperfective*, *durative* and *dynamic*. This much they have in common with the activity types and the other accomplishment types. They also share with some of these the lack of a *mid-interval* perspective. However, they differ from them all in encoding events as having *limited duration*. This follows from the fact that an accomplishment, unlike an activity, is inherently bounded. One of the functions of the *-ing* form is to defocus such boundaries (see Langacker 2000: 230). However, in the case of Backward-looking accomplishments the boundaries are refocused.

Backward-looking *-ing* constructions encoding states, such as 3C in Table 3 and (31)–(33), are also *imperfective* and *durative*.

(31) I remember not *being able to stand outside a phone kiosk* any longer and dragging out a man who was obviously gossiping therein. (B2E 1350)
(32) How the hell did a man stop *being an agent* and suddenly become a civil servant? (CDA 397)
(33) Until then he'd denied *being the gunman*, but today pleaded guilty to the shootting. (KIU 2447)

The complements in these constructions are not *ongoing*, *dynamic* or of *limited duration*. This leaves the *mid-interval* property. Do 3C and (31)–(33) profile the states in question from a point within their extension? As was the case with Backward-looking activity-encoding *-ing* constructions, the answer to this question seems to depend on the semantics of the matrix verb. In Mental Process constructions like 3C and (31), the perspective appears to be *mid-interval*, in the sense that the subjects situate themselves mentally within the period during which the state pertained. Thus in 3C we view *her* as being in the middle of standing by the window. This does not seem to be the case with an Aspectual matrix verb such as *stop* in (32). It is the whole state that is stopped. In allowing for both perspectives Backward-looking constructions encoding states resemble Backward-looking constructions encoding activities rather than accomplishments. The latter are never construed from a *mid-interval* perspective.

Backward-looking *-ing* constructions with achievements are exemplified by 3D in Table 3 and by (34)–(36).

(34) The only other thing I remember *catching* was my right thumb. (AS7 1145)
(35) Give the board a good jolt and the l.e.d. should stop *flashing* for another minute. (C92 331)
(36) The couple, from north London, deny *murdering seven-month-old Christopher Palmer* last December. (A8K 750)

The first, and most basic, question to be addressed is whether the constructions in these examples encode the situation in question as perfective or imperfective. Does the *flashing* in (34) refer to a once-off or recurring process? Is the act of murder in (36) to be construed as lasting for a period of time? It is difficult to reach any firm conclusions on this question. For what it's worth, I am inclined to come down on the side of *imperfectivity* and to say that these predicates admit of an element of *duration*. As is the case with Backward-looking accomplishments, this element of duration is *limited*. This follows from the fact that the situations in question are telic and are located anterior to the time of the matrix verb.

2.5. Contemplation constructions

The fourth and last type of construction to be considered consists of Contemplation constructions. These are constructions which make no reference to the realisation in the real world of the complement situation. We begin with activities, exemplified by 4A in Table 3 and (37)–(39).

(37) You, I think you'll find she won't even contemplate *cooking by electricity*. (KBP 4500)
(38) And the thing is with my kids, if I was in the car on my own I could imagine *chatting away* (KB6 1929)
(39) When he invited farmers through the Darlington and Stockton Times to consider *growing mushrooms* as a way of diversifying he received well over 100 calls although he was only looking for ten. (K51 1384)

Again, as with the other types of constructions encoding activities, all of these examples encode activities as *ongoing*, *imperfective*, *durative* and *dynamic*. None of them are profiled as of *limited duration*. This leaves the *mid-interval* property. As was the case with the Backwards-looking construction, the Contemplation tokens seem to vary with respect to whether they encode a *mid-interval* perspective on the complement situation, with verbs like 'imagine', in 4A and (38), implying that the situation is viewed from a point within its unfolding. Verbs like 'consider' and 'contemplate', on the other hand, do not normally carry this implication. 'imagine' and 'fancy' are actually much more likely to occur with activities than are 'consider' and 'contemplate'. Over 40% of tokens of the 'imagine *-ing*' type in the BNC encode activities, as opposed to fewer than 10% of the 'contemplate *-ing*' type. We tend to *imagine* activities and states, to *consider* accomplishments and achievements. Be that as it may, with respect to the question of *mid-interval* perspective, we may conclude that Contemplation activity constructions resemble Backward-looking ones in that they may or may not encode such a perspective, depending on the semantics of the matrix verb.

Contemplation accomplishment *-ing* constructions such as 4B in Table 3 and (40)–(42) resemble Contemplation activities in most respects, the exception being the absence of a *mid-interval* perspective, occasionally present in the activity construction.

(40) Jane contemplated *designing a jumper* based on her favourite sport of canoeing, but found it too ambitious. (CA2 1084)
(41) Imagine *scanning an image* as a bitmap and then converting that to PostScript. (G00 231 338)
(42) Having just produced the film of Gore Vidal's political play The Best Man, Turman started to consider *making the movie* from Webb's book. (C9U 263)

While these tokens are undoubtedly *imperfective* and are profiled as unfolding before the mind's eye, there is no one privileged mid-position from which we are invited to view this unfolding process.

Stative *-ing* constructions of the Contemplation type are exemplified by 4C in Table 3 and (43)–(45).

(43) Unless action is taken only the rich will be able to contemplate *being solicitors* and only those firms doing commercial work are going to offer traineeships. (HAJ 1897)
(44) One poster to be displayed on Tube carriages will ask passengers to imagine *being trapped* in a carriage with 600 other people for 35 hours without food and water. (J2R 73)
(45) Can there be, Berkeley asks, 'a nicer strain of abstraction than to distinguish the existence of sensible objects from their being perceived, so as to conceive *them existing unperceived*'? (ABM 1466)

These stative complements resemble the other three stative types in that they are *imperfective* and *durative*. They resemble Contemplation *-ing* constructions with activity complements in that they imply a *mid-interval* perspective with certain matrix verbs. As with activities, verbs like 'imagine' and 'fancy' tend to invite such a perspective. In (44), for instance, the passengers are asked to picture themselves as being within the extended state of *being trapped*. This does not seem to be the case with a verb like 'contemplate'. In (43) the state of *being solicitors* is profiled as an extended whole. We may therefore conclude that the presence or absence of the *mid-interval* property depends on the semantics of the matrix verb.

The sixteenth and last class of *-ing* complement construction to be considered is the Contemplation achievement class, illustrated by 4D in Table 3 and by (46)–(48).

(46) If he had, how could he ever contemplate *marrying another woman*? (JY2 3477)

(47) Imagine *failing your examinations.* (CA5 2520)
(48) He has not said whether he will consider *taking a peerage.* (A5R 51)

In these four examples the inherently punctual actions of extension, marriage, failure and the acceptance of an honour are encoded as having a certain *duration.* That is, the whole predication is encoded as having a certain duration. It only takes a second to marry someone, but the idea of marriage evokes the notion of a protracted period of courtship and one can spend considerable amounts of time thinking about the prospect! The complement situations are *imperfective*, but they are not viewed from any particular point within their temporal extension. They resemble closely Contemplation accomplishments in both these respects.

3. Prototypical characteristics of the *-ing* complement

We have now looked at all four main types of *-ing* complement construction as they encode all four of Vendler's types of predication. The results of the discussions are shown in Table 4, which mirrors Table 3 in the composition of its rows and columns. We can see that as one moves from top to bottom and left to right in Table 4 the various construction types share fewer and fewer characteristics with the Same-time activity (and accomplishment) *-ing* complements. These two types may therefore be said to be prototypical for *-ing* complements as a whole. Same-time activities are also the most numerous type, as may be seen in Table 5 which contains projected totals for the BNC for all sixteen types of construction. These totals were projected on the basis of the downloaded random samples of 1,000 tokens of each matrix verb. We can see in Table 4 that Same-time activities and accomplishments share most characteristics with the other most frequent types. We can also see that Backward-looking achievements are the most peripheral members of the class of *-ing* complements. Only two of six features, *imperfectivity* and *durativity* are shared by all sixteen types of construction: these are schematic for *-ing* complements. Four other features – *ongoingness, mid-interval, dynamism* and *unlimited duration* – are shared by Same-time activities and accomplishments. The remaining thirteen types share three, four or five features with the prototype.

Table 4. Huddleston and Pullum's six characteristics of the progressive as exhibited by Vendler's four categories of Activities, Accomplishments, States, and Achievements, as these are instantiated in Same-time, Backward-looking, Forward-looking and Contemplation *-ing* complement constructions

		Activities	Accomplishments	States	Achievements
S-T	ongoing	+	+	-	-
	imperfective	+	+	+	+
	mid-interval	+	+	+	+
	durative	+	+	+	+
	dynamic	+	+	-	-
	limited duration	-	-	-	-
F-L	ongoing	+	+	-	-
	imperfective	+	+	+	+
	mid-interval	-	-	-	-
	durative	+	+	+	+
	dynamic	+	+	-	-
	limited duration	-	-	-	-
B-L	ongoing	+	+	-	-
	imperfective	+	+	+	+
	mid-interval	+/-	-	+/-	-
	durative	+	+	+	+
	dynamic	+	+	-	-
	limited duration	-	+	-	+
Ctp	ongoing	+	+	-	-
	imperfective	+	+	+	+
	mid-interval	+/-	-	+/-	-
	durative	+	+	+	+
	dynamic	+	+	-	-
	limited duration	-	-	-	-

Table 5. Projected totals, to the nearest 100, for the BNC as a whole, of the sixteen combinations of matrix verb and complement predicate

	Activities	Accomplishments	States	Achievements	Totals
S-T	28,000	6,000	3,000	1,900	38,900
F-L	17,500	6,100	900	1,000	25,500
B-L	6,700	2,100	1,500	700	11,000
Ctp	1,400	1,300	200	200	3,100
Totals	53,600	15,500	5,600	3,800	78,500

The totals in Table 5 are projected from samples of 1,000 tokens of each of the 133 matrix verbs in the study. (In the case of verbs the total number of tokens of which amount to fewer than 1,000, the numbers of complement clauses of the various types included in the table are real and not projected.) One can see in Table 5 that, with a few minor exceptions, one is likely to encounter fewer and fewer tokens of the various combinations as one moves from left to right and top to bottom. In other words, the further we get from the prototype, the fewer tokens we are likely to encounter.

4. Summary and Conclusion

In this paper I have compared various types of *-ing* complement constructions to one another and to the progressive. We have seen that the exact meaning of the complement form varies according to the type of matrix verb and the type of complement predicate involved in the complex predication. Moreover, we have seen that Same-time activity and accomplishment complements are prototypical for the class as a whole. They also share most features with the progressive. They occupy the central position in a network of related meanings. Same-time activities are also the most frequent of the sixteen types. Thus the cognitive analysis in this paper has been corroborated by frequency data.

REFERENCES

Bolinger, D. L. (1968). "Entailment and the meaning of structures". *Glossa*, 2.2: 119–127.

Conrad, B. (1982). *Referring and non-referring phrases.* Copenhagen: Akademisk Forlag.

Dirven, R. (1989). "A cognitive perspective on complementation". In: Jaspers, D., W. Wooster, Y. Putseys and P. Seuren (eds). *Sentential complementation and the lexicon, Studies in honour of Wim de Geest.* Dordrecht: Foris: 113–39.

Dixon, R. M. W. (1991). *A new approach to English grammar on semantic principles.* Oxford: Oxford University Press.

Duffley, P. J. (1995). "Defining the potential meaning of the *-ing* form in a psycho-mechanical approach". *Langues et linguistique*, 21: 1–11.

Huddleston, R. and G. K. Pullum (2002). *The Cambridge Grammar of the English Language.* Cambridge: Cambridge University Press.

Langacker, R. (1990). *Concept, image, and symbol: the cognitive basis of grammar.* Berlin: Mouton De Gruyter.

Langacker, Ronald (2000). *Grammar and conceptualisation*. Berlin: Mouton De Gruyter.

Quirk, R., S. Greenbaum, G. Leech and J. Svartvik (1985). *A comprehensive grammar of the English language*. London: Longman.

Smith, M. B. and J. Escobedo (2001). "The semantics of *to*-infinitival vs. *-ing* complement constructions in English". In: Andronis *et al.* (eds). *CLS 37: The Main Session*. Chicago: Chicago Linguistic Society.

Vendler, Z. (1967). *Linguistics in philosophy*. Ithaca: Cornell University Press.

Verspoor, M. (1997). "The story of *-ing*: a subjective perspective". In: Pütz, M. and R. Dirven (eds). *The Construal of Space in Language and Thought*. Berlin: Mouton de Gruyter: 417–454 .

Wierzbicka, A. (1988). *The semantics of grammar*. Amsterdam/Philadelphia: John Benjamins Publishing Company: 23–168.

Wood, Fredrick T. (1956). "Gerund versus infinitive". *English Language Teaching*, 11: 11–16.

Steve Legrand

University of Jyväskylä

THE USE OF BASIC-LEVEL CATEGORIES AND THEIR RELATION TO IDEALIZED COGNITIVE MODELS IN WORD SENSE DISAMBIGUATION

1. Introduction

If a word has only one sense, a non-native speaker can confirm its meaning by a quick look at a dictionary. Most of the words do have, however, more than one sense, and both the native and the non-native speaker need to use the word context in order to find its correct sense. For example, when we look at the sentence,

There was a large blister on the heel of his right palm.

it is obvious to us that the word *palm* refers to a body part rather than to a tree or a handheld computer. The words *blister*, *heel*, *his*, and *right* when combined in a certain way point us towards the correct meaning.

Most of the automated disambiguation techniques, one way or another, are context-based, making use not only of the words themselves, but also of the part-of-speech information, word order, document genre and so on. Generally, we can say that these techniques are justified by our observations that certain words do co-occur quite regularly with each other within certain contexts. This notion has been used somewhat heuristically in automated word sense disambiguation, and often there is no reference to any cognitive disambiguation mechanism that could have been involved. Nevertheless, it is not disputed that context plays a very important part in the word sense disambiguation by our cognitive faculties.

The question arises: what is this human disambiguation mechanism like if it exists, and would it be possible to mimic and exploit it in automated word sense disambiguation? Is it rooted in our biology, and consequently reflected in our cognitive abilities, including our ability to categorize? The classical view of categories is often interpreted as meaning that things belong to the same category only if they have certain properties in common. It might seem that car parts such as a wheel and an engine do not share any properties, therefore should one assume that they cannot belong to the same category? On the closer inspection one can, however, discover, that they have at least one common property, and that is that they are parts of a car. So partonomy can create categories of things that apparently do not have much to do with each other. In fact, we can divide and subdivide our universe in so many different ways that what we know as classical categorization may prove inadequate for many tasks, including word sense disambiguation. Using the Family Resemblance Theory (Wittengstein 1953), basic-level categories (Brown 1958) and experiments demonstrating these theories (Rosch *et al.* 1976), Lakoff (1987) challenges the classical view of categorization, proposing to correct it with a move to idealized cognitive models (ICMs) based, to a large extent, on prototype-level categories.

Here we will demonstrate that the type of categorization, "a human view of the world", that Rosch and Lakoff favour, may indeed be reflected in the language that we use to describe things, and, therefore, can benefit word sense disambiguation. The work is still at its preliminary stages, and the purpose of this paper is merely to explain the theoretical basis behind it and illustrate it with a simple example.

In what follows, we will go briefly through the concepts of basic-level categories (Chapter 2), idealized cognitive models (Chapter 3) and ontology structures (Chapter 4) before explaining how to use refined InfoMap (http://infomap.stanford.edu/) results for creating ontological categories that may be more suitable for word sense disambiguation (Chapter 5) than the conventional ones. Finally, to exemplify our suggested approach, the two major senses of the word *palm* are disambiguated (Chapter 6). A more extensive study is underway, the results of which will be published shortly.

2. Basic-level categories

Roger Brown (1958) explained his notion of a "first level" as a kind of category which allows children to learn object categories and name them, but which, as a category, falls somewhere between the most general and the most specific level. Later Rosch (Rosch *et al.* 1976; Rosch 1988) designed a series of experiments in which she demonstrated that the basic-level categories, as she started calling them, were somewhat inconsistent with the classical theory of categories, and she explained their specific properties:

From the point of view of human cognition, the categories seem to be divided roughly into three kinds: superordinate (*furniture*), basic-level (*chair, table, lamp*), and subordinate (*kitchen chair, living-room chair / kitchen table, night table / floor lamp, desk lamp*). The basic-level objects have most of the attributes that are common to all members of the category and they share the least number of attributes with other, contrasting categories. Category membership is also influenced by family resemblances (Wittengstein 1953) to prototypical members. Archambault *et al.* (2000) in their brief review of literature selected the following (most of it also investigated by Rosch or based on her research) as the most important issues to note about basic-level categories:

- Categories at the basic-level are verified fastest.
- Objects are named faster at the basic than at the subordinate level.
- Objects are preferentially named with their basic-level names.
- Basic-level names are learned before subordinate names.
- Basic-level names tend to be shorter.

Tversky and Hemenway (Tversky and Hemenway 1984; Tversky 1989) propose that parts may play a major role in the recognition of basic-level objects, which may have something to do with the so-called Gestalt peception (Koffka 1922) related to part-whole configuration. In their proposal there is a strong suggestion that our basic-level object perception may well be based around this part-whole division. Parts, in turn, are related to functions, shape and interactions of these basic-level objects. This gives rise to an interesting question: is the categorization around parts reflected in the language we use?

3. Idealized Cognitive Models

Lakoff (1987) believes that linguistics categories have the same character as other conceptual categories: they show prototype effects and can be demonstrated to have basic-level categories. But he makes it clear that neither he nor Rosch advocate the view that basic-level categories would explain any structural or procedural properties of cognition. Rather, they both regard basic-level categories as a mere surface phenomena related to cognition, and assume that below that surface there may be some other more interesting structures and processes to be found.

Lakoff's main thesis is that our knowledge is organized by means of structures to which he refers to as idealized cognitive models, or ICMs, and that category structures and prototype effects are their by-products. Each ICM is seen as a structured whole, a gestalt, with four structuring principles employed:

- propositional structure (Fillmore's (1982) frames)
- image-schematic structure (Langacker's (1986) cognitive grammar)
- metaphoric mappings
- metonymic mappings

These ICMs would then structure the mental space as described by Fauconnier (1985). As examples of ICMs, among others, Lakoff refers to a Balinese calendar system with three different "week" structures superimposed (Geertz 1973), the category defined by the English word bachelor (Fillmore) and other examples.

The importance of Lakoff's ICMs to this research is in that he shows how, by extending the basic-level categories to the linguistic domain, we can end up with novel categorical structures, which may have not been considered at all in the creation of ontologies that are widely used today. This, in turn, may be one of the reasons why these conventional ontologies may prove inadequate for linguistics tasks such as word sense disambiguation.

4. Example ontology – WordNet

WordNet 2 defines itself as "a machine-readable lexical database organized by meanings". It organizes English nouns, verbs and adverbs into synonym sets representing lexical concepts (Fellbaum 1998). The sets are linked by relations such as hypernym, meronym, synonym and antonym. WordNet has been critizised for not providing a useful organisational principle for information retrieval, reasoning, or knowledge management, being based on linguistic rather than encyclopaedic coherence (Brewster 2002). Concepts likely to occur together in a domain are often found widely separated from each other in the conceptual hierarchy (Stevenson 2002).

However, the linguistic principles employed in WordNet's construction have made it a useful tool for word sense disambiguation. WordNet has been used with many different WSD techniques, the resulting disambiguation accuracies ranging from 57% to 92% (Li *et al.* 1995; Mihalcea and Moldovan 2000; Nastase and Szpakowics 2001; Cañas *et al.* 2003). To make it even more useful for WSD, some important cognitive principles might need to be explicitly added to its organization. These could be implemented through pointers as ontological relations.

In fact, the authors of WordNet had this in mind when starting to construct it. As an example, Miller pointed out that the word canary should be associated with at least three types of distinguishing features: (1) attributes (small, yellow and other adjectives), (2) parts (beak, wings and other nouns), and (3) functions (sing, fly, and other verbs). The addition of the distinguishing features important to basic-level categories was contemplated, but was not implemented explicitly except for the pointers to the parts (Miller *et al.* 1993). Instead, glosses were added which contain some of these features. Many WSD implementations have used these glosses since for sense disambiguation.

In this research, feature sets incorporating these distinguishing features and also other associations and collocations are used. Most of these are not explicitly expressed in WordNet, and here we try roughly to gauge their relative importance to WSD.

5. Use of InfoMap as the first-stage disambiguator

To disambiguate with the help of context one needs a set of words that co-occur, more often than would be the case by chance, with the word to be disambiguated. One way to do this would be to collect co-occurrence statistics with whatever software were available for the purpose, but the drawback of this method is that the statistics do not discriminate between the senses. A better way is to use an application that is based on co-occurrences but which, nevertheless, can be made to discriminate, to some extent, between the senses when a judicious selection of the search terms is performed. One such application is InfoMap (http://infomap.stanford.edu), which is freely available from the Stanford University site and is explained in detail in (Takayma *et al.* 1998; Widdows 2004).

The principle behind InfoMap was developed by Schütze (1997) and implemented and modified principally by the InfoMap team at the Stanford University. The distribution of word co-occurrences between a word and sets of content-bearing words creates a profile of the words usage in a context, and thus a profile of the word meaning itself. A similarity between two words can be calculated by comparing the profiles of the words in question. It is possible to return related documents whose profiles are close to each other even though they may not include the query words themselves. The meaning can be narrowed down by the selection of search words and can thus be used to disambiguate the key search term to some extent at least.

To get a set of word clusters related to the word *palm* in the sense of a *hand* (Figure 1) we can simply enter the words *palm* and *hand* together as search terms together with any negative keywords. The web interface allows us to retrieve up to 200 words associated with the key search terms and divide them into 1–20 categories as desired. A prototypical example is given for each category. Other search strategies could also be used for the same end including contrasting pairs.

Prototypical Example	Cluster Members
hand	hand wrist elbow finger thumb forearm grasped glove holding squeezed grasping firmly coin ear torch cigarette lever grasp isambard pencil verbal button squeeze candle undone propped superiority mister tapped arm's
palm	palm tapping held knuckles squeezing aloft wrapped knotted cradle shield caf woven loom restraining cloth smacked clips begging salute raffle necklace delights twists cane embroidered
fingers	fingers cheek cupped clutched stroked grip touched stroking brushed gripped lightly kissed gently tenderly fingertips delicately hold flinched knife stretched touch rubbing rested touching blade lifted pins dagger limp slid knelt shake caress razor pressed gasping tip rope raised brush
shoulder	arm shoulder outstretched sleeve fist clasped clutching clamped thigh waved sword knee patted foot hip gripping rein gesture hips trouser knob leg reins swinging breast smoothing bend needle forward
pocket	pocket put picked wallet handed bag tore crumpled briefcase pen drawer pad cardboard paw pockets parchment suitcases handbag putting lend packet
left	left fork hemisphere edge side scars stile pictured
grabbed	grabbed gun pistol snatched fumbled wrenched grab
lips	tightly rubbed chin trembling clenched mouth handkerchief kiss boy's lips breath gasped brow twitched
jar	saucer basket teapot bottle plate crumbs biscuit jar tray
shoulders	forehead shaking bent resting waist arms jerked tugging tilting rolled curled chest palms slapped knees wrists shoulders

Fig. 1. Results of an InfoMap-query using palm and hand as keywords and tree as a negative keyword. 10 clusters were specified

6. Basic-level categories and ICM's in word sense disambiguation

The idea behind using InfoMap is to get a set of terms associated with the word to be disambiguated and occurring together in the same context. InfoMap is based on co-occurrence information and word vector relations and, therefore, seems suitable for the purpose. The public web interface for the application at the Stanford University site was included within the Java-based disambiguating application created for the purpose. The mode of the operation was, shortly, as follows:

The parameters posted to the site were the search term *palm* + other keywords., (hand), negative keywords (*tree*), corpus (British National Corpus), command (associate), and parameters specifying clustered results with 200 words divided in 10 clusters. The request to the site was sent separately for both of the major senses of the word to be disambiguated and the results received were combined to form a Disambiguation Feature Cluster set consisting of 20 clusters, the first 10 for the first major sense of the word to be disambiguated (keywords: *palm hand*, neg keyword: *tree*) the second 10 for the second major sense (keywords: *palm tree*, neg.keyword: *hand*). The returned information (Figure 1 showing half of the set) was then converted into an XML-format and indexed into a file database using Java Digester Libraries (http://jakarta.apache.org/commons/digester/). The context to be disambiguated was indexed to another data base using Digester and Porter Stemming Algorithm. In the process of disambiguation, the context sentences were iterated through and matched against the Disambiguation Feature Cluster set: each time a word in the context sentence matched the clusters 1–10 the first sense increased its score, and when 11–20 were matched the second sense increased its score. The maximum of these scores indicated the word sense. The matches were indicated either as correct, undecidable (no matches), even, or wrong. For the query matching, Java Lucene (Gospodnetik and Hatcher 2004; http://lucene.apache.org/java/docs/index.html) libraries were used.

First we tested our application with Rada Mihalcea's sense tagged data for six words with two-way ambiguities, previously used in word sense disambiguation research and extracted from BNC (TWA dataset in http://www.cs.unt.edu/~rada/downloads.html). We simply took her Meanings-labels as positive and negative keywords to create the feature-sets with the help of InfoMap and then used these feature-sets to disambiguate her examples. The results are shown in Table 1. As expected, the results were variable, ranging from 47.3 to 82.2% in accuracy, indicating that the selection of the keywords is significant. Changing *tank's* "vehicle"-keyword to "military", for example, increased the disambiguation accuracy to 64.7%. Increasing the number of the keywords also had a significant effect on the result.

Table 1. Disambiguation accuracies reached using the TWA dataset's Meanings-labels as keywords

Word	Meanings	Examples	Correct
bass	fish/music	107	82.2%
crane	bird/machine	95	68.4%
motion	movement/legal	201	49.8%
palm	hand/tree	201	72.0%
plant	living/factory	188	77.1%
tank	container/vehicle	201	47.3%

However, our purpose was not to find out the maximum disambiguating power of InfoMap, but to use it as a tool to help in our own experiments. We merely needed a rough set of context words to modify using basic-level category information to see how that information affected the disambiguation accuracy.

For our example, the word *palm* was selected, because it had an adequate number of hand-tagged contexts (201) and the disambiguation accuracy (75.1%) achieved was judged sufficient, but not too high, for our purpose. *Palm* is also a word that is associated with many basic-level concepts, unlike the word *motion*, for example. Moreover, we could extract an adequate number of contexts (1000) with the word *palm* from the BNC against which to test this set. As both sets come from the BNC, they may partially overlap, but, as said, the purpose of the experiment was to test the effect of the basic-level category words on the overall disambiguation against normal context words. More extensive n-way tests will follow based on this experiment. After pruning out some minor senses, 193 contexts remained. The remaining TWA contexts were processed using the unmodified InfoMap feature set for disambiguation. The results were as shown in Table 2.

Table 2. Results for the two major senses (part-of-hand, tree) of the word palm in 193 contexts when disambiguated with the unmodified disambiguation feature cluster set (UDFC)

Wide context (paragraph)			Narrow context (sentence)		
correct:	139	72.0%	correct:	130	67.4%
undecidable:	0	0.0%	undecidable:	0	0.0%
equal:	24	12.4%	equal:	22	11.4%
wrong:	30	15.5%	wrong:	41	21.2%
TOTAL:	193	~100.0%	TOTAL:	193	~100.0%

Even when disambiguating with the unmodified InfoMap results, the disambiguation achieved is significantly better than what could be expected by chance. Our purpose was to modify the feature set to see what the actual words were that played role in disambiguation and what was their number, in order to be able to roughly categorize the words participating in disambiguation. For this reason the words that had not played any part in disambiguation, were pruned from the Disambiguation Feature Cluster Set. Some words that were judged as missing were added, and to get a 100% disambiguation result for the TWA contexts (Table 3) further 4 collocations were added. The number of the words in the modified and unmodified set remained roughly the same. We call the original, unmodified set the Unmodified Disambiguation Feature Clusters (UDFC) set and the modified one the Modified Disambiguation Feature Clusters (MDFC) set. In the MDFC the feature categories were rearranged to create additionally a feature set for a) Parts, b) Objects Affected, and c) Functions in order to roughly isolate the features that might be related to basic-level information.

Table 3. Results for the two major senses (part-of-hand, tree) of the word palm in 193 contexts when disambiguated with the MDFC set

Wide context (paragraph)			Narrow context (sentence)		
correct:	193	100.0 %	correct:	193	100.0 %
undecidable:	0	0.0 %	undecidable:	0	0.0 %
equal:	0	0.0 %	equal:	0	0.0 %
wrong:	0	0.0 %	wrong:	0	0.0 %
TOTAL:	193	~100.0 %	TOTAL:	193	~100.0 %

1000 contexts containing the word *palm* were then extracted from the BNC out of which 749 contained either of the major senses (part-of-hand, tree) and these were then selected for disambiguation. First these contexts were disambiguated with the help of the UDFC set (Table 4) and then with the help of the MDFC set (Table 5).

Table 4. Results for the two major senses (part-of-hand, tree) of the word palm in 749 contexts when disambiguated with the UDFC set

Wide context (paragraph)			Narrow context (sentence)		
correct:	596	79.6 %	correct:	550	73.4 %
undecidable:	2	0.3 %	undecidable:	0	0.0 %
equal:	71	9.5 %	equal:	76	10.1 %
wrong:	80	10.7 %-	wrong:	123	16.4 %
TOTAL:	749	~100.0 %	TOTAL:	749	~100.0 %

Table 5. Results for the two major senses (part-of-hand, tree) of the word palm in 749 contexts when disambiguated with MDFC set

Wide context (paragraph)			Narrow context (sentence)		
correct:	702	93.7 %	correct:	692	92.4 %
undecidable:	11	1.5 %	undecidable:	32	4.3 %
equal:	13	1.7 %	equal:	12	1.6 %
wrong:	23	3.1 %	wrong:	13	1.7 %
TOTAL:	749	~100.0 %	TOTAL:	749	~100.0 %

As these results show, the disambiguation accuracy for the MDFC was considerably higher than for the UDFC. The accuracy of UDFC increased when the number of contexts was increased, whereas the accuracy declined for MDFC. This probably was due to the fact that MDFC was optimized for TWA contexts whereas UDFC was not, i.e., some of the pruned words might have proved useful in new contexts etc.

Then a very rough estimation was made of the contribution that the feature-sets (Parts, Functions) linked to basic-level information (hypernyms, parts, functions) made towards the overall disambiguation. For this the 193 pruned contexts from TWA were used. First, the parts and functions clusters from the MDFC were removed and the remaining clusters only were used for disambiguation. As the word *palm*'s salience varied within the context, being sometimes in the foreground sometimes in the background, it was decided to conflate the part information between adjacent levels: all tree parts were considered together and all body parts were considered together. Similarly, all tree function words were considered together, and all body function words were considered together.

Table 6. Results for the two major senses (part-of-hand, tree) of the word palm in 749 contexts when disambiguated with the MDFC set. Two MDFC clusters, parts, and functions, are not used in this MDFC

Parts and functions clusters not included					
Wide context			Narrow context		
correct:	121	62.7 %	correct:	102	52.8 %
undecidable:	49	25.4 %	undecidable:	84	43.5 %
equal:	13	6.7 %	equal:	1	0.5 %
wrong:	10	5.2 %	wrong:	6	3.1 %
TOTAL:	193	~100.0 %	TOTAL:	193	~100.0 %

The disambiguation accuracy exceeded the 50/50 (Table 6) with significant results, but a lot of scope was left for improvement, which shows that the inclusion of parts and functions in the clusters used in MDFC is essential for accuracy. This is shown even clearer when we include only the parts and functions clusters and remove all others from MDFC (Table 7).

Table 7. Results for the two major senses (part-of-hand, tree) of the word palm in 749 contexts when disambiguated with the MDFC. Only parts, and functions clusters are used in this MDFC

With parts and functions clusters only					
Wide context			**Narrow context**		
correct:	149	77.2 %	correct:	144	74.6 %
undecidable:	2	15.0 %	undecidable:	40	20.7 %
equal:	9	4.7 %	equal:	6	3.1 %
wrong:	6	3.1 %	wrong:	3	1.6 %
TOTAL:	193	~100.0 %	TOTAL:	193	~100.0 %

7. Discussion

Although, as the very first experiment with the unmodified set returned by InfoMap shows, the disambiguating word set needs to be modified for more accurate functioning, the size of the set (200 words for each sense) seems adequate. Our preliminary experiments with other disambiguous words have shown that an ontology relating the words through structures including the novel categories used here would ideally suit for word sense disambiguation. We have previously successfully used WordNet for disambiguating words based on an artificial taxonomy (animals) (Legrand and Pulido 2004) and expect that by augmenting the relations within WordNet to include categorical relations that appear to have some relation with basic-level categories and idealized cognitive models we could make it more suitable for disambiguation purposes. However, there are many questions to be solved about the basic-level categories, ICMs and their relations to context before a more comprehensive system can be developed. For example, something perceived as basic level varies amongst individuals: for an expert *eucalypt* may appear as a basic-level object, whereas for many ordinary city-dwellers it is *tree* that is seen as the basic-level object. The salience of the word within the context, i.e., whether it is in the background or in the foreground, affects the gestalt experienced also. There may be hundreds of different types of ICMs judging by the variety of examples given by Lakoff and others. Some of this information is already coded in different ontologies, albeit referred to by different terms, such as thematic relations, partonymy etc. It is likely, as Rosch and Lakoff have pointed out that basic-level structures are a mere surface phenomena, and one needs to dig deeper to get to the gist of what happens in the cognition when dealing with categories, in order to allow us to build structures that can be used in disambiguation

Complex as it might seem considering the reservations above, the research is justified on the grounds that a human being can disambiguate linguistic context better than a machine, and unless we are able to come up with a superior algorithm or mimic this disambiguating behavior, we can never be sure whether the results that our machine translation and other applications come up with are correct. We need to communicate globally and rapidly and need to be able to do it without the fear of being misunderstood.

REFERENCES

Archambault, A., Gosselin, F. and P. Schyns (2000). "A natural bias for the basic level?" *Proceedings of the 22nd Annual Conference of the Cognitive Science Society.* NJ: LEA: 585–590.

Brewster, C. (2002). "Techniques for Automated Taxonomy Building: Towards Ontologies for Knowledge Management". *Proceedings CLUK Research Colloquium.* Leeds, UK.

Brown, R. (1958). "How Shall a Thing be Called?" *Psychological Review*, 65: 14–21

Cañas, A. J., Valerio, A., Lalinde-Pulido, J., Carvalho, M. and M. Arguedas (2003). Using WordNet for Word Sense Disambiguation to Support Concept Map Construction Proceedings of SPIRE 2003 – 10th International Symposium on String Processing and Information Retrieval, October 2003, Manaus, Brazil

Digester can be downloaded from: http://jakarta.apache.org/commons/digester/

Fauconnier, G. (1985). *Mental Spaces.* Cambridge, Mass. MIT Press.

Fillmore, Charles J. (1982). "Frame semantics". *Linguistics in the Morning Calm.* Seoul: Hanshin Publishing Co.: 111–137.

Fellbaum, C. (ed.) (1998). *WordNet: An Electronic lexical database.* MIT Press, Cambridge, MA.

Geertz, C. (1973). *The Interpretation of Cultures.* New York. Basic Books.

Gospodnetic, O., Hatcher, E. (2004). *Lucene in Action.* Manning Publications, Geenwich, CT.

InfoMap information mapping project web interface at http:// infomap.stanford.edu/

Koffka, K. (1922). "Perception: An introduction to the Gestalt-theorie". *Psychological Bulleting*, 19: 531–585.

Lakoff, G. (1987). *Women, Fire, and Dangerous Things.* The University of Chicago Press. Chicago and London.

Langacker, R. (1986). *Foundations of Cognitive Grammar.* Vol 1. Stanford. Stanford University Press.

Legrand, S., Pulido JGR. (2004). "A Hybrid Approach to Word Sense Disambiguation: Neural Clustering with Class Labeling". Knowledge Discovery and Ontologies (*KDO-2004*) workshop in 15th European Conference on Machine Learning (ECML) and 8th European Conference on Principles and Practice of Knowledge Discovery in Databases (*PKDD*) Pisa, Italy, September 24, 2004

Li X., Szpakowics, S. and S. Matwin (1995). „A WordNet-based Algorithm for Word Sense Disambiguation". *Proceedings of IJCAI-95.* Montréal, Canada, 1995.

Lucene Java Libraries can be downloaded from: http://lucene.apache.org/java/docs/index.html

Miller, G. A., Beckwith, R., Fellbaum, C. D, Gross, D. and K. Miller (1993). "Five Papers on WordNet". *Technical report.* Princeton University, Princeton, N.J.

Mihalcea, R. and D. Moldovan (2000). "An Iterative Approach to Word Sense Disambiguation". *Proc. of Flairs 2000.* Orlando, FL: 219–223.

Nastase, V. and S. Szpakowics (2001). "Word Sense Disambiguation in Roget's Thesaurus Using WordNet". *Proc. of the NAACL WordNet and Other Lexical Resources Workshop.* Pittsburgh, June 2001.

Rosch, E., Mervis, C. B., Gray, W. D., Johnson, D. M. and P. Boyes-Braem (1976). "Basic objects in natural categories". *Cognitive Psychology,* 23: 457–482.

Rosch, E. (1988). "Principles of Categorization". *Readings in Cognitive Science, a Perspective from Psychology and Artificial Intelligence.* Allan Collins & Edward E. Smith. Morgan Kaufmann Publishers. San Mateo, California: 312–322.

Schütze, H. (1997). "Ambiguity Resolution in Language Learning: Computational and Cognitive Models". *CSLI Lecture Notes 71,* CSLI Publications, based on revised PhD Thesis, Stanford University, Dept. of Linguistics, July 1995.

Stevenson, M. (2002). "Combining Disambiguation Techniques to Enrich an Ontology". *Proceedings of the Fifteenth European Conference on Artificial Intelligence (ECAI-02)* workshop on "Machine Learning and Natural Language Processing for Ontology Engineering", Lyon, France.

Takayma, Y., Flournoy, R. S. and S. Kaufmann (1998). *Information Mapping. Centre for the Study of Language and Information.* Stanford University. Available at: www-csli.stanford.edu/semlab/infomap/Papers/takayama-infomap.ps

Tversky, B. (1989). "Parts, Partonomies, and Taxonomies". *Developmental Psychology,* 25. No. 6: 983–995.

Tversky, B. and K. Hemenway (1984). "Objects, parts, and categories". *Journal of Experimental Psychology: General,* 113: 169–193.

TWA sense tagged context data in http://www.cs.unt.edu/~rada/downloads.html

Widdows, D. (2004). "Geometry and Meaning". *CSLI Lecture Notes 172,* CSLI Publications, Stanford University.

Wittengstein, L. (1953). *Philosophical Investigations.* MacMillan, New York.

John Newman and **Jingxia Lin**

University of Alberta

THE PURPOSEFULNESS OF GOING: A corpus-linguistic study

1. Introduction

There would seem to be an obvious role for corpus linguistics in cognitive linguistics, given the importance generally assigned to actual usage, as opposed to abstract theorizing, as a basis for claims about linguistic structure. Langacker (1987: 62) regards the grammar of a language as "a characterization of established linguistic convention", where convention is understood as something "shared ... by a substantial number of individuals". This kind of goal for grammar suggests a corpus linguistic methodology, at least as one relevant methodology. Despite the availability of large-scale electronic corpora for some years now, reliance on corpora in support of cognitive linguistic claims has not been especially widespread. This would appear to be a contradictory aspect in the practice of cognitive linguistics (cf. Schönefeld 1999: 165), though the collections of papers in Barlow and Kemmer (2000) and Gries and Stefanowitsch (to appear) show the increasing extent to which corpora are being relied upon in cognitive linguistic approaches. In this paper we turn our attention to some lesser-studied properties of GO[1] in English, relying on corpus-based data to make observations about the degree to which the purposefulness associated with GO is conventionally encoded as part of the sentence or utterance.

2. GO in Cognitive Linguistics

Verbs of motion, and particularly GO, have been favoured topics for study in cognitive linguistics. They present an opportunity to investigate aspects of

[1] We use small caps, as in GO, to indicate the lemma and we use italics, as in *go, goes, gone* etc. to indicate particular word forms.

'concrete' motion of a three-dimensional object through space and time as well as 'abstract' or metaphorical kinds of motion (see, for example, Lichtenberk 1991, Radden 1996, and Shen 1996). It is not surprising that GO should be an object of special interest when it comes to studying motion verbs in English. After all, GO is the most frequent motion verb in English, outranking even the other very frequent verb COME, as can be appreciated through examining the tables provided in Biber *et al.* (1999: 373–379), based on the Longman Spoken and Written English corpus (LSWE). GO ranks third overall, in terms of frequency of lexical verbs in the LSWE corpus, after SAY and GET, and it is especially common in conversation and fiction. It is not surprising that the most frequent motion verb of English should have received detailed attention.

A well-known representation of English GO is shown in Figure 1, adapted from a representation in Langacker (1991: 6). The diagram captures a number of the key points to be made about verb semantics in Langacker's approach, e.g., the distinction between trajectory (TR) and landmark (LM), with the trajector showing increasing physical distance from the deictic region of the landmark (represented by the eclipse around LM). Heavy lines in this, as in other such diagrams in Langacker (1991), indicate a profiling, or foregrounding, of entities and relations. In this case, the profile is the evolution of a relation between the trajectory and the landmark, through time. As simple as the diagram might appear, it has proved a useful starting point for discussions of both concrete and abstract motion. Variants of Figure 1, with appropriate profiling choices, are relevant to representing the semantics of the past participle *gone* (requiring a representation similar to Figure 1, but only the end stage is profiled) and the adverb *away* (where only the information visible at the end stage of Figure 1 is present and profiled).

Figure 1, though it captures some key elements of the semantics of GO, does not express everything that could or should be said about this verb. This should not come as a surprise, since there are typically multiple dimensions relevant to the semantics of a morpheme. Langacker's approach makes explicit provision for such multiple dimensions, or domains, as part of the representation of the semantics of a morpheme (cf. Langacker 1987: 147–182). He uses the term "complex matrix" for the collection of relevant information drawn from different domains (Langacker 1991: 4–5). So, for example, the complex matrix for the noun *knife* includes references to the typical shape of a *knife*, a "cutlery frame" consisting of a certain typical arrangement of a knife, a fork, and spoon, and a "cutting" frame conveying the notion of the typical action associated with *knife* when used as an instrument. Just as there is a complex matrix associated with *knife*, so we may also recognize a complex matrix associated with GO. GO is very underspecified semantically and one may think that there is nothing much more to say about the verb in this case.

However, there is one key aspect about GO when used with animate subjects: GO is purposeful motion, not random or robotic, and a fuller semantic representation of its semantics, as in a complex matrix, should acknowledge this dimension. We need to recognize a mental domain in which properties of a mental state of a participant involved in an event may be represented. In this case, we would be indicating that the person encoded as the subject of GO is typically participating in the motion with a purpose to this motion in mind.

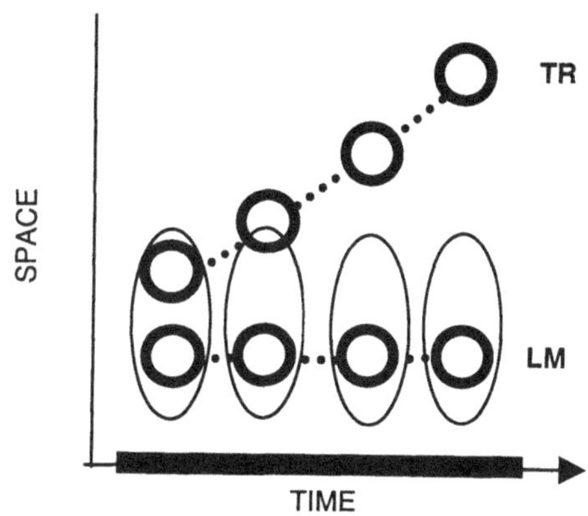

Fig. 1. Representation of GO, adapted from Langacker (19916)

It should be pointed out that there are numerous verbs in English (and other languages) where purposefulness is present. Ordinary, human experiential reality is a reality characterized for the most part by purposeful human behaviour. We do not live our lives as mindless, zombie-like creatures roaming the countryside without having purpose behind our movement through space. It is the human condition to engage in purposeful activities. A linguistic counterpart of this larger aspect of experiential reality is that most verbs of language, when used with human subjects, refer to purposeful human activity. "Agency" is sometimes used to describe a common property of such verbs, though this term subsumes a constellation of properties relating to an "agent", such as the exercise of control, the execution of an act, as well as the property of purposeful behaviour. The focus in this paper is on the purposefulness associated with agency, rather than assorted other properties, but we recognize that purposefulness is one component of this more inclusive concept. Sometimes, of course, we experience events which are unintended, unforeseen, unplanned, beyond our control, etc.

For example, we may trip over something, slip on a wet surface, cough uncontrollably, sneeze, etc. Purposefulness defines the dominant, everyday reality of human existence, even if we also experience events which are not part of our purposes. Or, to express this in linguistic terms, there will be many verbs in a language that typically refer to purposeful events, even if some verbs do not. GO, in English, is not unique in the way in which a human trajector in its clause structure is typically purposeful, but it is worthy of special attention since it is a highly frequent verb in terms of usage. It is also of interest as a verb which is often discussed in the cognitive linguistics literature, though it is usually discussed with a focus on the spatio-temporal domain (as illustrated in Figure 1) rather than the mental domain.[2]

There is another consideration motivating our interest in the purposefulness associated with GO, namely, the extension of a 'go' verb to purposive marking as a possible path of grammaticalization. Heine and Kuteva (2002: 163–165) provide a number of examples from different language families of a change of a 'go to' verb to 'purpose' marking. Their 'purpose' label covers a variety of senses and morpheme types relating to a purpose, e.g., a 'purpose clause marker' in Tepo (Niger-Congo), a 'subordinating conjunction of goal, purpose etc.' in Rama (Amerind), etc. Heine and Kuteva (2002) is a summary of observed, completed historical changes drawn from a sampling of languages and is of great interest to cognitive linguists in terms of understanding the cognitive processes which might have lead to such changes. Heine and Kuteva (2002) should also be of interest to corpus linguists of any language, since a corpus provides a unique and intriguing opportunity to discover supporting data. In the case of a corpus, we might be able to observe collocational tendencies linking words or phrases, which in other languages, are linked through completed grammaticalization paths.[3] Newman and Rice (2004) have demonstrated the effectiveness of this methodology by showing how the collocational data associated with SIT, STAND, and LIE in the British National Corpus mirror, to some extent, the categorical, completed grammaticalizations of these verbs found in other languages. Our interest in the corpus data concerning GO in English is in part motivated by the interest we have in comparing our results with Heine and Kuteva's observations about grammaticalizations and how the former might contribute to a better understanding of the latter.

---

[2] Possibly, the near-ubiquity of purposeful activity in our lives is part of the reason why the purposefulness associated with verbs has not received more attention.

[3] Manning (2003: 316) makes the same point in terms of *hard* and *soft* constraints: "The same categorical phenomena that are attributed to hard grammatical constraints in some languages continue to show up as soft constraints in other languages."

3. A corpus study of GO

We set out to investigate the extent to which the purpose associated with English GO was encoded in the same clause or utterance (a more appropriate unit when it comes to the study of conversation). The underlying idea behind this approach is that the co-occurrence of words/phrases x and y within a clause or utterance establishes an "association" between x and y. Such an association may provide synchronic arguments supporting the feasibility of a diachronic change from x to y or from y to x. Admittedly, a co-occurrence relationship is not the only kind of relationship which might be of interest to linguists, but it is a fairly basic one and underlies the interest in collocational studies in corpus linguistics. A study of simple co-occurrences with respect to English SIT, STAND, and LIE by Newman and Rice (2004) illustrates the kind of insights which can be achieved despite the apparent simplicity of such an approach. In the case of that particular study, the authors paid special attention to the co-occurrence of the three posture verbs with other verbs in conjoined structures of the type *sit down and* V, *sitting and* V-*ing* etc. The co-occurring verbs in these structures display certain semantic properties, or prosodies, which mirror in many ways the categorical grammaticalizations which SIT, STAND, and LIE have undergone in some other languages, e.g., the development of posture verbs to aspect markers. In the present study, we identify co-occurrences of GO and encodings of the purpose of going in order to see whether one can claim any special, close relationship between these concepts. A close relationship of this sort could be seen as a synchronic, syntagmatic tendency reminiscent of the diachronic relationship documented for other languages.

We proceeded by selecting 100 randomly chosen examples of the use of (literal) GO in the conversation sub-corpus of the British National Corpus (BNC) and examining in some detail each example. We decided on the conversation sub-corpus (described as "spoken demographic" in the categorization scheme employed in the BNC) because of the more spontaneous nature of conversation, compared with the written BNC. Furthermore, the conversational genre is more likely to be a genre in which grammaticalizing tendencies first appear and so would appear the genre most relevant if we are to seek commonalities with known grammaticalization trends. While a sample of 100 utterances of conversation is extremely modest in size, there are two good reasons for this. Firstly, the identification of the linguistic form which expresses the purpose of an event can require subtle judgments and therefore a close reading of each example utterance. There is, in our way of approaching the problem, no straightforward, form-based way of identifying the purpose component of an utterance. Secondly, we foresaw the need to make comparisons between GO and other verbs in order to fully appreciate the significance of the GO results, and we therefore wanted a comparable amount of data for each verb to be examined. This consideration made it desirable to work with a modest amount of data for each verb, while accumulating data for a number of verbs. We worked only with examples of GO exhibiting a physical motion sense, excluding abstract motion (*He went crazy*, *The story goes like this* etc.). This meant that we initially chose more than 100 random examples of GO, to ensure that we still had 100 examples of literal GO after the non-literal examples were eliminated. We relied on the in-built randomization option of BNC examples through the BNCWeb interface.

An immediate challenge in this study was to decide on how the expression of purpose was to be identified and quantified. We did not make any *a priori* assumptions as to exactly what form the expression of purpose might take. The sequence *in order to* comes to mind as one of the most explicit ways to signal purpose in English, but we did not wish to assume that any particular form had to be present in an utterance to count as an expression of purpose. In the following discussion, we identify different kinds of purpose expressions in the GO examples, discussing in turn how each constitutes a kind of purpose. The full set of GO examples in which an expression of purpose was identified are listed in KWIC format in Appendix 1, categorized by the various forms that the expression of purpose can take.

The single largest category consists of variations of the GO *and* V construction, where the coordinated clause following GO expresses the purpose, e.g., *Go and get her*, *They want me to go and do my shopping*, *You could go to the bank and ask for a loan.* In this construction, the semantic contribution of GO is variable. While movement away from a deictic centre is present in all the examples listed, the GO sense can be relatively weak, compared with the informational salience of the purpose clause. In the example *So you're gonna have to ... go and make me a cup of tea!*, it is the preparation of the cup of tea which feels weightier, in terms of relative importance. The request to make a cup of tea already implies an initial motion phase, whereas motion away does not imply the making of the cup of tea. A second category consists of variations of the GO *to* V construction, e.g., *I mustn't go to see William, When they first went up there to live.*[4] Again, the infinitival purpose clause often feels the more significant in terms of the communicative value of this construction. The use of the *going to* form as a semi-auxiliary verb of intention or futurity, lacking any requirement that there be physical motion, was excluded from our examples

[4] There were no instances of GO with the *in order to* V construction. *In order to* V may be the most unambiguous expression of purpose in English, but it is by no means the most frequent.

since we restricted ourselves to uses of GO where physical motion was a necessary component of the meaning, even if physical motion was not particularly salient.

We considered certain reason clauses to express purpose. Purpose and reason *can* be differentiated: 'purpose' requires some intentionality whereas the 'reason' for something happening may be completely devoid of any human intentionality. For example, rain constitutes a *reason* why the ground may be wet, but we would not say that the *purpose* of rain is to make the ground wet. However, when there *is* intentionality present, such a distinction is much more difficult to draw. Consider the example *I'm very ... happy that we're going to Sarah's because quite honestly ... I've gotta get out of that ... house.* One could say that my need to get out of the house is either the 'reason' *or* the 'purpose' in my leaving the house. Whether one speaks of 'reason' or 'purpose' here seems more a matter of subtle construal preferences: if one construes the later event of leaving the house as the main focus, then the prior need to leave is a 'reason'; if one construes the existing need to leave the house as the main focus of attention, then the subsequent event of leaving the house is a 'purpose'. We included *because/'cos* clauses where the presence of human intentionality allowed the clauses to be considered as either reason or purpose. Similarly, we included *for* prepositional phrases as in *When she goes out for a meal, she's got a problem.*

Our last category of purpose expressions is the least obvious one. We took the use of some nouns which refer to destinations to involve, as well, conventionalized purposes. The relevant phrases are listed in Table 1.

Table 1. The use of GO expressions with conventionalized purpose

go to (a) school
go to bed
go to nursery
go to work
go to the bank
go to the library
going on a nice train journey
going to the shop
going up the pub
went home
went into hospital
went up the club
going to the reception

The destination words/phrases in Table 1, such as *school*, *bed*, *nursery*, *work*, *bank* etc., do refer to places where the motion leads to and are rightly called 'goals'. Described in this way, we are focusing attention on the spatio-temporal domain. But associated with such places there is a common, shared understanding of the practices and protocols, ('frames') implicit in being at such places. Going to school, for example, is a matter of intended motion to a place which serves a particular purpose (instruction, teaching/learning, routines of sitting, listening, talking etc.). Going to school is done for the purpose of participating in these routines. The place word is associated through a kind of metonymy with conventional purposes. We therefore included such cases as yet another kind of expression of purpose.

Table 2 summarizes the types of purpose expressions appearing with GO in our 100 examples. Just on 50 = 50% of the examples in our database occur with an expression of purpose.

Table 2. Types and frequency (in 100 examples) of expression of purpose with GO

GO *and* V	18
GO (*to*) V	10
GO *because*	5
GO *for*	8
GO for some conventionally understood purpose	15
Sub-total of occurrences of purposes	53
Overlapping purposes (e.g., *go to the bank and* V)	3
Total no. of examples where purpose is expressed	**50**

4. A corpus study of other selected verbs

The fact that 50% of the GO sample has some indication of purpose within the utterance demonstrates an association of some sort between GO and purpose. But to appreciate the significance of this result, we need to compare this result with results for other verbs in English. It may be, for example, that most verbs have this degree of association with indications of purpose, in which case one shouldn't attach special significance to the result for GO. Ideally, one would like to have results for many verbs of English, along the lines of what we have found for GO, so that one may better evaluate the results for GO. Unfortunately, the lack of a purely form-based search technique for this problem makes a comprehensive study of the purposefulnesss of many verbs a daunting task. Nevertheless, we needed to have some comparative data for us to have any real sense of how to evaluate the results in Table 2. To this end, we carried out the same kind of sampling (100 examples of conversation from the BNC) for three other verbs: RUN, WALK, and WAIT. We chose RUN and WALK in order to compare GO with other common motion verbs. We chose WAIT as an example of a verb with a more 'stationary' meaning, though one which seemed intuitively to have an interesting association with purposefulness.

Since the methodology employed to investigate RUN and WALK is identical to that introduced above for GO, it is not necessary to explain each of the categories as we did above. Tables 3 and 4 summarize the results for RUN and WALK respectively. We decided to include the two utterances *Just grabbed her bag and ran off with it* and *He grabs it of you and go run away with it*, since the larger utterance clearly refers to a familiar frame of running off/away with something. In this frame, a thief snatches some object and runs away to avoid capture. The use of the verb GRAB in both cases is also indicative of the thief-stealing-something frame. In the case of RUN, we found that 23 example sentences (= 23% of the sample) contained an indication of the purpose of running; in the case of WALK, we found just 14 example sentences (= 14% of the sample) with such an indication. RUN, therefore, seems somewhat more prone to occur with indications of purpose than does WALK. Intuitively, this makes sense since the additional effort and speed associated with running seems to correlatc with heightened purpose compared with walking. In neither case, though, is purposefulness, as operationalized in our methodology, anywhere as frequent as with GO, where we found that 50% of examples contain some indication of purpose. Compared with these other (also frequent) motion verbs of English, GO appears to be relatively purposeful.

Table 3. Types and frequency (in 100 examples) of expression of purpose with RUN

RUN *and* V	7
RUN *because/'cos/that's why*	5
RUN (*to*) V	4
RUN *for*	2
RUN for some conventionally understood purpose	7
Sub-total of occurrences of purposes	25
Overlapping purposes (e.g., *run home and* V)	2
Total no. of examples where purpose is expressed	**23**

Table 4. Types and frequency (in 100 examples) of expression of purpose with WALK

WALK (*and*) V	7
WALK (*to*) V	2
WALK for some conventionally understood purpose	7
Sub-total of occurrences of purposes	16
Overlapping purposes (e.g., *walk up to the bar and* V)	2
Total no. of examples where purpose is expressed	**14**

We also obtained results for WAIT, using the same methodology. As mentioned above, WAIT contrasts with GO, RUN, and WALK since it refers, typically, to a more stationary kind of event.[5] Might it be the case that verbs referring to more stationary kinds of activities occur with less expression of purpose? Again, we adopted a relatively inclusive approach to the task of identifying the expression of purpose. We found not only the categories that presented themselves for the motion verbs but also a number of additional formal categories. One of these additional categories involved *until/till* clauses. Such clauses are not necessarily purpose clauses, but we believe that the examples we counted are correctly interpreted as indicating purpose. Some examples are: *You'll have to wait until he goes away*, *Wait till I show you this*, *Your dad'll wait until you come back*, *I'll wait till Maggie finishes her danish.* Indeed, *until/till* clauses constituted the single largest category, in formal terms, of the expression of purpose with WAIT (15/100). The next largest category (13/100) involved WAIT with a *for ... to* Infinitive construction: *You put your hand up and wait for me to ask you*, *Just waiting for your boy friend to come in*. There is in fact considerable diversity in the way in which purpose is expressed with WAIT, as summarized in Table 5. Clearly, WAIT has a strong association with the expression of purpose, in spite of it being relatively stationary compared with motion verbs and actually has the strongest association of the verbs considered here.

[5] Clearly, WAIT can involve some motion (one can drive around a parking lot waiting for parking space to become available). It would be more correct to say that motion is not a criterial component of WAIT.

Table 5. Types and frequency (in 100 examples) of expression of purpose with WAIT

WAIT *until/till*	15
WAIT *for* someone/something *to* V	13
WAIT *for/on*	11
WAIT *to* V	10
WAIT *for* someone/something V-*ing*	4
WAIT for some conventionally understood purpose	3
WAIT *and* V	3
WAIT *cos*	1
WAIT miscellaneous	4
Sub-total of occurrences of purposes	64
Overlapping purposes	0
Total no. of examples where purpose is expressed	**64**

5. Discussion

The first main result from our study concerns the relatively high degree of expression of purpose with GO (50%), compared with RUN (23%) and WALK (14%). Of the three motion verbs, as used with animate subjects, GO is the most 'purposeful' (as operationalized in our methodology). This is just the kind of synchronic, corpus-based association that we were interested in discovering. It is a synchronic piece of evidence in support of a special relationship between GO and purposefulness which has been found in grammaticalization studies of other languages (cf. Section 2 above).

Our result about the purposefulness of GO does not, of course, explain *why* there should be greater expression of purpose with GO than with the other motion verbs. A key consideration in attempting to explain this result would appear to be the relative schematicity, or lack of semantic specificity, of GO, compared with the more specific WALK and RUN which encapsulate aspects of the manner of movement lacking with GO. The relative non-specificity or 'lightness' of GO facilitates, we claim, the inclusion of more informational detail within the rest of the utterance. Underlying this mode of argumentation is the idea that there is an optimal amount of new information that is conveyed within an utterance (or clause). The less there is of new information being conveyed about the nature of the motion, the more information can be conveyed about the purpose, motivation, destination etc. Admittedly, this is no more than speculative at this point, though it is consistent with the kind of reasoning which has been offered in connection with some other phenomena. A comparable form of argumentation concerning certain syntactic properties of SAY is appealed to in Radden and Panther (2004: 12–14). The authors argue that it is the lack of semantic specificity of SAY, compared with INSIST, PROCLAIM, ANNOUNCE, INDICATE etc., that helps to motivate a shift of the informational load to a following subordinate clause. The difference in the semantic weight of the verb explains certain syntactic phenomena which depend on how easily the pragmatic focus of the sentence can be associated with the subordinate clause. Our position with respect to the purposefulness of GO is comparable: the relative lack of semantic content with GO invites a greater elaboration of the associated purpose of the motion.

Our second main result concerns the frequency with which purpose is expressed with WAIT (64%). This result demonstrates the need for verb-specific studies of purposefulness. While, in general, motion towards some goal might seem more purposeful than non-motion, there can be specific instances of non-motion verbs, like WAIT, which are relatively purposeful. Indeed WAIT would appear to be an *intrinsically* purposeful kind of activity: one doesn't wait without some purpose to the waiting. Purposefulness is clearly not a property restricted to motion verbs. A further question which arises is why we do not see WAIT grammaticalizing to 'purpose' markers just like GO does. At least in the overview provided by Heine and Kuteva (2002), GO is a source morpheme for 'purpose' whereas WAIT is not. A number of considerations may be relevant to understanding this difference in the behaviour of GO and WAIT. One consideration is that the purposefulness associated with GO is of a different, and more intense, kind than that associated with WAIT. The purposefulness attaching to controlled, human motion to a place seems more obvious and effectual than that associated with the more passive (often stationary) activity of waiting. GO, therefore, may present a more vivid kind of source image than WAIT as a source for purposefulness. Also, GO is highly schematic and for this reason may be more amenable to extension to other meanings.

6. Conclusion

We have shown how the purposefulness of English GO can be identified and quantified through a corpus-based approach and were able to show empirically the relative high degree of purposefulness of GO compared with RUN and WALK. We adopted a relatively inclusive approach to identifying the expression of purpose. One could opt for a more conservative approach to operationalizing the expression of purpose. One could, for example, restrict the expression of purpose just to co-occurring *(in order) to* V clauses (considering these as the most direct expression of purpose). Results would not have been that much different had we adopted such an approach: GO occurs 10% of the time with such clauses, RUN 4%, WALK 2%. GO still occurs with purpose expressions more than twice as frequently as happens with RUN and WALK. Adopting a more inclusive approach to expression of purpose yields larger percentages overall, with more certainty to their significance.

This study has also demonstrated the potential insights that a corpus-linguistic approach can offer cognitive linguists interested in grammaticalization. Grammaticalization paths can sometimes appear puzzling and their original motivation may no longer be transparent to us. The corpus-based methodology proposed here provides one way in which some of the conceptual associations underlying grammaticalizations can be understood. Obviously, studying an English corpus as we have done can not shed light on the actual diachronic details of grammaticalizations in languages such as Tepo or Rama. What a study such as ours can do, though, is to add further evidence for the naturalness of the conceptual relationships which are evident in completed grammaticalizations.

REFERENCES

Barlow, M. and S. Kemmer (eds) (2000). *Usage-Based Models of Language.* Stanford: CSLI Publications.

Biber, D., S. Johansson, G. Leech, S. Conrad and E. Finegan (1999). *Longman Grammar of Spoken and Written English.* Harlow: Pearson Education Limited.

Gries, S. Th. & A. Stefanowitsch (eds) (to appear). *Corpora in Cognitive Linguistics: The Syntax-Lexis Interface.* Berlin/Heidelberg/New York: Mouton de Gruyter.

Heine, B. and T. Kuteva (2002). *World Lexicon of Grammaticalization.* Cambridge: Cambridge University Press.

Langacker, R. W. (1987). *Foundations of Cognitive Grammar.* Vol. 1: *Theoretical Prerequisites.* Stanford: Stanford University Press.

Langacker, R. W. (1991). *Concept, Image, and Symbol: The Cognitive Basis of Grammar.* Berlin/New York: Mouton de Gruyter.

Lichtenberk, F. (1991). "Semantic changes and heterosemy in grammaticalization". *Language*, 67: 475–509.

Manning, C. D. (2003). "Probabilistic syntax". In: Bod, R., J. Hay and S. Jannedy (eds). *Probabilistic Linguistic.* Cambridge, Mass.: The MIT Press: 289–341.

Newman, J. and S. Rice (2004). "Patterns of usage for English SIT, STAND, and LIE: A cognitively-inspired exploration in corpus linguistics". *Cognitive Linguistics*, 15: 351–396.

Radden, G. (1996). "Motion metaphorized: The case of 'coming' and 'going'". In: Casad, E. H. (ed.). *Cognitive Linguistics in the Redwoods: The Expansion of a New Paradigm in Linguistics*. Berlin/New York: Mouton de Gruyter: 423–458.

Radden, G. and K.-U. Panther (2004). "Introduction: Reflections on motivation". In: Radden, G. and K.-U. Panther (eds). *Studies in Linguistic Motivation*. Berlin/New York: Mouton de Gruyter: 1–46.

Schönefeld, D. (1999). "Corpus linguistics and cognitivism". *International Journal of Corpus Linguistics*, 4: 137–171.

Shen, Y.-M. (1996). "The semantics of the Chinese verb 'come'". In: Casad, E. H. (ed.). *Cognitive Linguistics in the Redwoods: The Expansion of a New Paradigm in Linguistics*. Berlin/New York: Mouton de Gruyter: 507–540.

APPENDIX 1. Corpus results for GO

GO *and* V (18/100)

	Go	to nursery and school and work and do different
	Go	and get her.
Thought want me to	**go**	and do my shopping.
You can always	**go**	and get them out, if you want to.
Well	**go**	and hit one .
so you're gonna have to ma ,	**go**	and make me a cup of tea!
I'd	**go**	and see him regularly because he did it really
Oh I better	**go**	and see if there's any erm if my Christmas
one hairdresser there called Paul, whom I'd	**go**	and see regularly .
Now I'll	**go**	and sort out what we want.
oh got out of assembly because I had to	**go**	and speak to this maths teacher who's dead
Yeah you	**go**	and stand in a corner in a minute.
Go on Andrew,	**go**	and wash your hands, you can't possibly eat with
I thought Clare would	**go**	out and play with her new racket, she's not really
You could	**go**	to the bank and ask for a loan.
he can't leave him alone he sits there and he	**goes**	or something like that and jumps on him and
Bloody	**gone**	out and bought one fourteen quid
she said oh I'd like them, but Sue said she	**went**	sort of a bit earlier and see how they got on and

GO *(to)* V (10/100)

I mustn't	**go**	to see William.
Just go in for the day till their parents	**go**	to work I think.
Are you	**going**	to work?
Yeah nanny's	**gone**	look.
cos she had erm, some mice problems so dad	**went**	in there to have a look round, seeing the
The bear	**went**	over the mountain, to see what
so lo and behold those two	**went**	to see Phantom of the Opera.
I once	**went**	to get the buggy out and I'd accidentally left
Well, can I tell you the first one we went to we	**went**	to get food and there was none left!
you know they, when they first	**went**	up there to live, they er, had quite a problem,

GO *because* (5/100)

Well we've got to	**go**	round there if we're out to because erm we've
while it's quieter, the man keeps them for me, I	**go**	straight across the leisure centre to soft clay
I, I am friendly with them you know I, I	**go**	every Wednesday there, for er, well when I can,
They	**go**	because they need to cover some sort of guilt,
I'm very ha happy that we're	**going**	to Sarah's because quite honestly I go I've gotta

GO *for* **(8/100)**

a good jumper to wear in the evenings when we	**go**	for our evening walks by the sea.
Used to	**go**	in for your model paints and coloured marbles
you don't	**go**	on a motorway for driving lessons
I admitted that, but I mean just to	**go**	out for an evening.
let's, or we can	**go**	to brewery for another five grand, we'll do the
when she	**goes**	out for a meal she's got a problem, now if that
I'm	**going**	in there for one,
We're	**going**	for a meal on Friday aren't we?

GO **for some conventionally understood purpose (15/100)**

you know that he had to	**go**	to a **school** in Northumberland,
If you don't, you	**go**	to **bed**.
	Go	to **nursery** and **school** and **work** and do different
You could	**go**	to the **bank** and ask for a loan. (overlap with GO
I wanted to	**go**	, go to the **library** but I thought I'd start in
all these children that like to	**go**	to the **library**.
Oh she's alright, she	**goes**	to **school**.
I love	**going**	on a **nice train journey**!
	Going	to the **shop** please?
You're gonna have to go a long then, cos I'm	**going**	up the **pub**, ha, ha.
And heart to heart, having sat through two, I	**went**	**home** it was heavy.
it was all weighed up and finished a before we	**went**	**home**, all done.
comes round with her sometimes she's er she	**went**	into **hospital** on Tuesday er er Monday that's
after funeral you know my husband we	**went**	to erm, like the **reception** bury, you know
it feels like, I	**went**	up the **club** last week and there, cos er, we

Total = 53- 3 overlaps = 50/100 where some indication of purpose is given.

Agnieszka Kaleta

Świętokrzyska Academy, Piotrków Tryb.

A CORPUS BASED RESEARCH INTO METAPHOR – WHAT DO WE GAIN

1. Introduction

The enormous boom in figurative language studies that we have witnessed over the last two decades has to be traced back to the works of researches subscribing to the so called *cognitive* paradigm. Beginning with the 1980 seminal work of Lakoff and Johnson, a large number of publications devoted to exploring the topic of conceptual metaphors have appeared in the scholarly circles forcefully undermining the traditional reductionist or substitution theory of metaphor. On the cognitive view, metaphors, far from being merely ornamental or rhetorical devices, tend to be described as cross-domain conceptual mappings, experientially grounded and indispensable for our meaningful functioning in the world. More specifically, those patterns, which obtain in our physical experience (labeled as source or donor domain)[1] tend to lend their inferential structure to non-physical, non-tactile and thus less clearly delineated domains (termed target or recipient domain), which is the basic mechanism behind metaphorical mappings of different kinds.[2] These mappings, in turn, give rise to systematic and coherent networks of linguistic expressions. On cognitive account thus metaphor comes primarily as a matter of thought and

---

[1] In cognitive linguistics literature the general patterns of our preconceptual, that is directly embodied, sensorimotor experience are presented in the form of highly schematic gestalt structures typically referred to as image schemata. A number of such basic structures has been identified ad discussed in some detail by cognitively oriented researchers, most notably Johnson in his "The Body in the Mind: The Bodily Basis of Meaning, Imagination, and Reason".

[2] Such a perception, in turn, fits in with a more general cognitive theory of *embodiment* according to which our conceptual systems draw largely upon the nature of our own bodies, our relations with the external environment and a variety of cultural experiences. Consequently, language, being a part of our embodied cognitive apparatus, can be adequately described only in terms of the general experiential and cultural knowledge of the world we live in.

reason, language is of secondary consideration in that it is merely a reflection, a kind of 'by-product' of the underlying cognitive patterns. To give an example, the conceptual mapping UP IS MORE is represented in language by an unimaginably large repertoire of expressions such as 'His income rose', 'The prices skyrocketed', 'Inflation soared, 'Sales jumped'. Thus, the sensorimotor experience of verticality is extended to the abstract concept of quantity, which finds its reflection in numerous conventional metaphorical expressions as illustrated above.

Metaphors, as defined above, appear to constitute a ubiquitous part of human cognition permeating our thought, language, and action. As the relevant literature reveals, an extremely large number of abstract concepts, from the most ordinary ones such as time, states, change, causation, and purpose to the most sophisticated scientific theories can only be comprehended via metaphor. It has to be pointed out that only a portion of this vast and intricate system of cross-domain mappings has been brought to light. Consequently, researches in the field do not give up on their attempts to unveil and account for new facets of our metaphorical thought.

The present article has been aimed as a tiny contribution to the fast growing body of research into the metaphorical structure of abstract concepts. More specifically, in the remainder of the paper we discuss a case study that examines the metaphorical structure of the domain of business and/or economic activity. The author's major interest has been in, what might be termed, *axiological metaphors*, which give structure to evaluative notions inherent in business communication. The research in question has been designed as a cross-linguistic study. Consequently, it contrasts English and Polish-language data to draw some conclusions concerning the degree of cross-linguistic universality or specificity of conceptual metaphors as they structure the target domains in focus. For the purpose of this investigation, we have used the common method of accessing the underlying metaphorical concepts through their surface linguistic representation. The lexical investigations have been conducted with the aid of corpus-based methodology which has been put to test for its usefulness for researching patterns of figurative thought and language.[3] The research finding will be presented in a few sections, each of them focusing on a different facet of the target linguistic material.

In a nutshell, the first section deals with the metaphorical structure of the target axiological domains in the light of language specific data, tracing the

[3] The research has been conducted on a specially compiled bilingual, comparable corpus of English and Polish language articles drawn from selected business daily newspapers – The Wall Street Journal, The Financial Times, Puls Biznesu, and Parkiet.

figurative lexicon back to the underlying cross-domain conceptual mappings (qualitative analysis). The second one concentrates on the frequency patterns of metaphorical items and explores, in some detail, the issue of cognitive entrenchment of the mappings as outlined in the preceding section (quantitative analysis). The third section, in turn, makes some general observations about the collocational patterns of figurative lexicon in the light of cognitive approach to language analysis. It also touches upon selected morphological and syntactic aspects of metaphorical lexis.

Finally, in the concluding section, we comment briefly on the possible merits and limitations associated with applying corpus-based methodology to researching into metaphor in its conceptual and linguistic dimension.

2. The qualitative analysis

The qualitative analysis of the corpus data has shown that axiological metaphors are, to large extent, universal, which is to say that English and Polish language journalistic texts draw on analogous or similar metaphorical models[4] rooted in a variety of experiential structures, among which spatial image-schemas (UP/DOWN; FRONT/BACK, INSIDE/OUTSIDE, MOTION/ STANDSTILL) figure most prominently. Furthermore, the experience of STRENGTH and WEAKNESS as well as human bodily condition of HEALTH and ILLNESS have proved to be rich sources of figurative language in both corpora. However, English-language texts have turned out to be more productive in terms of the number of the relevant metaphorical models, which is to say that they have yielded expressions rooted in two additional source domains, which have been given the mnemonic labels of EMOTIONAL STATES and ACTS OF VIOLENCE. Some of the ontological relationships holding between the source domains as mentioned and different facets of the target domain of business performance along with some corpus examples are as follows (the mappings unique to English-language part of the corpus have been marked with a single asterisk double asterisk indicates the correlations traced only in Polish-language data):

- UP
- FORWARD } → upward market trends, economic growth/progress

[4] The notion of metaphorical model has been used in the sense of the complete repertoire of ontological correspondences between the Source and the Target.

(1) The market has shot up in the last two months.
(2) AMSTERDAM powered ahead, rising 17.15 or 3 percent to 583.66 on the AEX index…
(3) Ropczyce rosną jak na drożdżach [Ropczyce grow as if on yeast]
(4) Zrobiliśmy ogromny krok naprzód: zapoczątkowano proces destrukturyzacji, zmniejszono koszty...
[We have made a giant step forward: we have initiated the process of restructuring, the costs have been reduced …]

- DOWN
- BACKWARDS } → downward trends on stock markets, in business sectors

(5) The US Treasury market tumbled yesterday and dragged the European markets down as the dollar fell to its lowest against the Japanese yen in more than two years.
(6) The market has pulled back 50 points since, but this has been put down to profit-taking and a reaction to falls on Wall Street.
(7) Po ogłoszeniu upadłości Piaseckiego kurs akcji tej spółki nurkuje do dna. [After Piasecki's collapse has been announced, the company's shares dive to the bottom]
(8) Akcje banków zostały w tyle za czołówką GPW. [The banks' shares lagged behind the GPW lead]

- LACK OF MOTION → recession, economic slump

(9) Following the Russian crisis, financial markets in the US seized up.
(10) Gospodarka wciąż nie może wyraźnie ruszyć z miejsca (...) [The economy still cannot move from the spot]

- RACE → business competition

(11) AMD has gained ground recently against Intel in the US retail PC market (…)
(12) Unię dogonimy za prawie 60 lat. Polską gospodarkę czeka długi pościg. [We will catch up with the Union in 60 years. Polish economy is in for a long chase]

- INCREASE IN SPEED
- VIGOR/ ENERGETIC BEHAVIOR } → increase in business activity

(13) The international bond markets maintained their lively pace yesterday with a number of large dollar offerings.
(14) The other FTSE indices also perked up after a rather sluggish start.
(15) Tymczasem w Polsce gospodarka powoli rozpędza się i będzie przyśpieszać w wyniku skumulowanych efektów cięć stóp procentowych. [In the meantime, in Poland the economy is gathering momentum and is likely to accelerate]

- DECREASE IN SPEED → economic slowdown

(16) Tight monetary policy will rein in UK economic growth this year, according to a forecast from the Economist Intelligence Unit.
(17) W raportach widac już było, że gospodarka hamuje [The reports has shown that the economy is braking]

- SETTING INTO MOTION → improvement in business/economic performance

(18) "They wanted to jump-start the market," says Mr Huo, "but a lot depends on psychology and now everyone is discussing the political situation."
(19) ... kiepskie wyniki budownictwa wskazują ze nie nastąpiło jeszcze długo oczekiwane ożywienie w inwestycjach, bez którego gospodarka nie ruszy „pełną parą". [... the poor performance of the building sector indicates that the expected revival, without which the economy will not move at full steam, has not, as yet, taken place]

- STRENGTH → economic prosperity; secure financial position

(20) These figures are still higher than normal for periods of economic strength, mainly because of the rise in personal bankruptcies.
(21) Impexmetal rośnie w siłę [Impexmetal grows in strength]

- WEAKNESS → business depression

(22) Economists blame the drop in factory gate prices on economic weakness in Asia
(23) Gdyby obecnie rząd sprywatyzował najlepsze kopalnie, to słabsze przedsiębiorstwa sektora węglowego musiałyby upaść [if the government privatized now the best mines, the weaker companies in the coal sector would have to collapse]

- PHYSICAL WELL-BEING/HEALTH ➞ successful business performance

(24) While the American economy ended 1998 in much the same condition it started the year – rude good health ...
(25) Na rynku jest niewiele zdrowych, ciekawych spółek, które poprawiają wyniki. [On the market, there are very few healthy interesting companies whose performance is improving]

- PHYSICAL INDISPOSITION/ILLNESS ➞ poor business performance

(26) Analysts say the industry suffers from too many banks, a lack of transparency, the government's failure to privatise unhealthy state-owned banks
(27) Rynek leków w stanie podgorączkowym. [The medicines' market in subfebrile condition]

- MEDICAL TREATMENT ➞ attempts to improve business performance

(28) Prescribing medicine for corporate ills: COMPANY DOCTORS by Emiko Terazono ...
(29) Vistula do reanimacji. [Vistula for resuscitation]

- RETURN TO HEALTH ➞ return to efficient functioning

(30) Some of the biggest internet stocks continued to recover from the sharp falls they suffered last week
(31) Następnie wymienił uzdrowienie finansów publicznych, pokonanie plagi bezrobocia, podniesienie poziomu konsumpcji obywateli [Next, he mentioned healing public finances, defeating the plague of unemployment, and raising the level of the citizens' consumption]

- **DEATH ➞ bankruptcy

(32) Spółka walczyła ponad rok [...] próbowała dokonać restrukturyzacji, by w lutym 2003 r. ostatecznie dokonać żywota. [a company fought for over a year [...] trying to restructure, only to depart this life in February 2003]

- *APATHY/ LETHARGY ➞ economic stagnation

(33) Bond markets were listless on Thursday in the final day's trading of 1998

- *POSITIVE EMOTIONAL STATES → upward market tendencies
- *NEGATIVE EMOTIONAL STATES → trade recession

(34) Exuberant Helped by the strong early tone on Wall Street and a cut for interest rates in Brazil, Latin America was looking its most cheerful for some weeks.
(35) He is expected to outline the government's policy for the country's troubled economy and its financial sector in particular.

- *ACTS OF VIOLENCE → adverse business/economi phenomena
- *THE VICTIMS OF VIOLENT BEHAVIOR → business institutions affected by adverse phenomena.

(36) Brazil's battered currency took another blow on Wednesday as an interest rate increase by the central bank failed to convince nervous currency traders
(37) The chief casualties have, inevitably, been weaker brands which were already losing momentum.[5]

As can be seen from the above examples, the source domains in focus are axiologically bipolar, which is to say that they have either PLUS or MINUS axiological load. Consequently, the former lends its structure to the target domain of *successful business performance* while the latter gives us a conceptual handle on the notions associated with the domain of *negative business/economic phenomena*.[6]

Finally, it has to be observed that that the target axiological concepts tend to be expressed in quantitative terms, that is as an *increase* or *decrease* in stock prices, intensity of business activity, productivity, profitability, just to give a few examples. Consequently, the underlying cognitive mappings typically involve the activation of generic metaphorical pairs of the following kind: UP IS GOOD and UP IS MORE; DOWN IS BAD and DOWN IS LESS; FORWARD IS GOOD and FORWARD IS MORE; BACKWARD IS BAD and BACKWARD IS LESS; STRONG IS GOOD and STRONG IS MORE; WEAK IS BAD and WEAK IS

[5] The above correlations should be treated as indicative rather than exhaustive of the rich network of mappings traced on the basis of corpus data. The limits imposed on the length of the present paper as well as the considerations of clarity have refrained us from a more detailed presentation of the research findings.

[6] The axiological parameter as an inherent property of image schemas has been thoroughly discussed by T. Krzeszowski in his book "Angels and Devils in the Hell".

LESS; SLOW IS BAD and SLOW IS LESS; FAST IS GOOD and FAST IS MORE; HEALTHY IS GOOD and HEALTHY IS MORE; UNHEALTHY IS BAD and UNHEALTHY IS LESS, just to mention the most salient ones.

In sum it can be stated that a host of basic evaluative notions for taking about market phenomena arises as a result of the simultaneous activation of *axiological* and *quantitative* conceptual metaphors as exemplified above.

3. Quantitative analysis

The quantitative analysis of the corpus data allows to draw some conclusions on the cognitive entrenchment of particular metaphorical models. This analysis has been two-dimensional, which is to say that it has been concerned with the differences in the productivity of particular metaphorical models as wholes (the so called macroanalysis), but also with quantitative relationships between items within particular models (microanalysis). The results of the former can be presented in the following diagram (the raw frequency counts of metaphorical expressions associated with particular source domains have been normed to the basis per 10.000 words so that Polish and English-language corpora could be compared accurately):

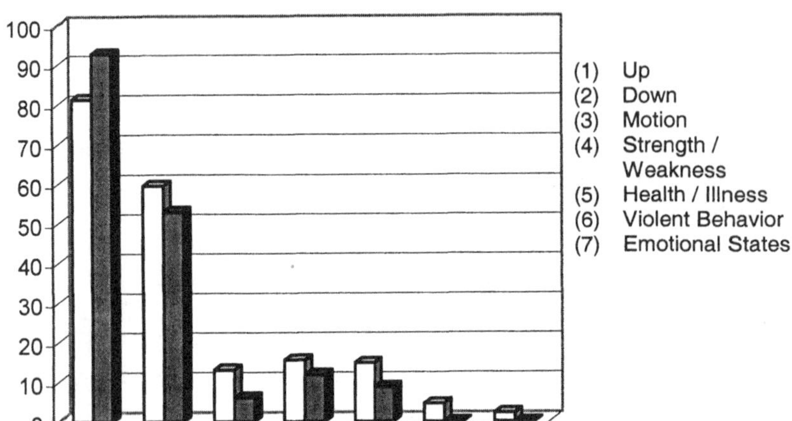

	1	2	3	4	5	6	7
□English	81,28	59,41	12,92	15,39	14,67	4,43	2,17
■Polish	92,7	52,8	5,96	11,71	8,69	0	0

As can be seen, some considerable discrepancies in the productivity of particular metaphorical models have been recorded. UP and DOWN schemas have turned out to be the richest sources of metaphorically extended senses. Next in order there comes the STRENGHT/WEAKNESS source domain followed by HEALTH/ILLNESS scenario with VIOLENT BEHAVIOUR and EMOTIONAL STATES models occupying two last positions in the frequency hierarchy.

As to the comparative conclusions, the normed frequencies point to a slightly higher productivity of UP schema in the Polish-language corpus. However, the other common source domains show higher productivity if evoked by English-language items. Generally speaking, English language texts show much higher density of metaphorical items than the Polish-language ones both in terms of the number of source domains involved in metaphorical projections (seven as opposed to five common ones) as well as the productivity of particular models, with the exception of UP schema as mentioned above.

The study has also revealed some regularities at what we have referred to as the *micro-level* of frequency counts. Thus, the general tendency is that each of the source domains is represented by a few highly productive lemmas and much larger repertoire of items of a very low frequency, often single occurrences. The underlying cognitive mechanism involved here seems to be that the most productive items are more prototypical instantiations of a given source domain than the low frequency ones which typically belong to much more peripheral areas. For instance, the highly frequent lemmas GROW, or RISE (accounting for, respectively, 27% and 23% of the total representation of UP schema) seem to be more central instantiations of UP schema than BALLOON or SKYROCKET, which are represented by single occurrence. By the same token, HEALTHY and SICK which figure very prominently in the corpus data, are more prototypical members of HEALTH/ILLNESS scenario than the more specific symptoms of bad health such as PNEUMONIA, SNIFFLE, HANGOVER, which occur on idiosyncratic basis in corpus texts. It might be thus concluded at this point that there is a direct relationship between the degree of prototypicality of experiential notions and the productivity of their metaphorical extensions.

It should be also noted here that the lemmas belonging to the low frequency pole of the productivity continuum have a greater image potential than those on the other side of the continuum. This is to say that the former, among which we encounter one-shot metaphors, are capable of evoking more vivid mental pictures than the items characterized by a greater conceptual scope (cf. rise vs. balloon). Additionally, it is at this less productive end of the frequency continuum that some discrepancies between the English and Polish-language data tend to emerge. For example, only English texts have yielded items that refer to *objects for rising in the air* (balloon, skyrocket). Conversely, lexical references to various *technical devices for lifting object or people* (DŹWIGNIA [a lever], WINDOWAĆ (cf. Polish 'winda' ['escalator'], LEWAROWAĆ [to jack up]) and sports activities (WYSKOK, WYBICIE [a take off/ spring]) have turned out unique to Polish-language part of the corpus. In the same vein, the source domain of *liquid* activated by a range of English items (e.g. DIVE, PLUNGE, SINK, DIP) has a marginal representation in Polish materials.

4. Metaphorical extensions, collocational frames and syntactic patterns

The notion of lexical metaphors functions as an umbrella term for a great diversity of linguistic meanings and forms. In addition to single lexical items and fully fixed expressions, including idioms, we encounter a large variety of more extended stretches of metaphorical language, which yet do not have the status of idioms. They have been given the label of *metaphorical clusters*. As we have observed, there is an enormous diversity of such clusters and their organization into some general categories is by no means a straightforward task. However, the cognitive approach with its emphasis on the underlying experiential structures seems to provide some tools for dealing with this chaos of linguistic meaning and forms. Thus, we have distinguished two general categories that have been termed *coherent* and *incoherent* metaphorical clusters. The former term refers to expressions consisting of metaphorically extended lemmas rooted in the same or conceptually related experiential domains. Here are some examples drawn from both English and Polish-language corpus:

(38) The shares rose steadily to reach a peak of 550p inn May 1996
(39) The real dropped to the bottom of its new band of R dollars 1.20-RDollars 1.32.
(40) National Savings fell off its perch at the top of the savings ladder last year
(41) ... indeks największych spółek wspiął się do 1258 pkt, czyli w okolice szczytów poprzedniej fali wzrostowej [the index of the biggest companies climbed to 1258, that is somewhere around the peaks of the former rising wave]
(42) ... kurs akcji tej spółki nurkuje do dna [.... the company's shares dive to the bottom]

The phrases underlined are examples of collocational relationships which involve the activation of a single UP schema (cf. rise, reach a peak), DOWN schema (drop, dive, bottom), or both of them simultaneously as in the last example where the related schemata for downward motion (fall off) and upward orientation (top of the ladder) are brought together.

The incoherent clusters on the other hand, bring together cognitively unrelated structures as in the following examples:

(43) (…) the shares hit a high as the market appreciated
(44) The dollar flirted with collapse again yesterday',
(45) … further fuelling the Japanese currency rise'

The above collocations draw on cognitively distant domains of experience e.g. VIOLENT BEHAVIOUR (hit) and UP orientation (high) come together despite their apparent lack of compatibility at the experiential level. In the next two examples the domain of human relationships (flirt with) overlaps that of downward orientation (collapse) and the scenario associated with the functioning of vehicles (fuel) is triggered simultaneously with the motor experience of upward motion (rise).

From all the above examples, it follows that, if approached literally, incoherent clusters are semantically opaque, that is they do not evoke meaningful structures of imagination (e.g. we can fuel a vehicle but not a rise, we flirt with other people and not with collapse and so forth) as opposed to coherent clusters which are more transparent and thus more meaningful on literal interpretation.

A fact worth of note in this section is that incoherent metaphorical clusters are much more common for English-language data, Polish texts being almost devoid of such conceptualizations.

Our corpus-based investigation into metaphor has also enabled us to detect some morphological patterns of figurative language usage. First of all, a mention should be made of certain morphological transformations of source domain components under metaphorization, which have been given the label of *morphological extensions*. In English, these are usually compounds representing morphologically modified correlates of spatial image-schema e.g. UPGRADE, UPSURGE, UPTURN, UPBEAT, DOWNTURN, DOWNGRADE, SHORTFALL, UNDERPERFORM, SETBACK. This category should be supplemented with a range of Polish–language items such as ZNIŻKA, ZWYŻKA, ZAPAŚC, ZASTÓJ (cf. Polish 'zniżać' [to lower], 'wyższy' [higher], 'zapadać się' [to slump], 'stanąć' [to come to a halt).

Secondly, it seems worthwhile to note the regularities involved in the distribution of metaphorical senses depending on the grammatical class a given item belongs to. As we have observed in the course of the research, certain syntactic forms function exclusively or predominantly as metaphorical extensions while their other morphological variants have both figurative and literal uses. For instance, the nominal forms of the lemmas HIGH, LOW, SLUMP and the verbal uses of PEAK and SKYROCKET refer to a range of quantity or intensity related notions. The point is that the connections with the source domain of verticality are not reflected in their semantics, as can be judged on the basis of corpus data as well as the relevant dictionary entries.

5. Concluding remarks

The conclusion to be drawn in this final section is that corpus-based methodology provides a useful tool for researching into metaphor. Given the systematic nature of figurative lexicon, computer resources such as lemmatization, word lists and, first and foremost, concordancing programs turn out to be an invaluable aid in searching for the underlying patterns of conceptual mappings as well as in-depth treatment of the relevant lexicon. Even more importantly, corpus methodology seems to be ideally suited for studying frequency patterns of metaphorical items. This, in turn, seems to pave the way for large-scale comparisons of conceptual metaphors in terms of the degree of their cognitive entrenchment, which is an area hardly touched upon in the relevant research. Furthermore, the methodology under discussion provides effective and reliable means for tracing collocational and syntactic patterns characteristic of figurative lexicon, as it has been indicated in section four.[7] When coupled with cross-linguistic data, corpus methodology seems even more encouraging allowing for efficient extraction of analogies and/or discrepancies that inevitably exist in different linguistic systems.

Finally, a few words of reservation need to be added to the above points. What should be emphasized most is that, in actual fact, the method in question is by no means effort-free. This is to say that computer-based techniques come to our assistance only after substantial amount of effort has been invested on the part of the researcher into deciding on or searching for the items to be subjected to computer processing. For instance, concordancing programs can be employed to assess the rate of recurrence of items selected in the course of browsing through the relevant corpus material or through 'intuitive deciding'. However, even at this later stage, the linguist has to face the laborious task of separating

[7] Section four should be treated as merely suggestive of insights that can be gained through applying corpus methodology to tracing collocational and morphological patterns of figurative lexicon.

the literal and figurative uses of words or expressions as they appear in KWIC format. It seems that computer dictionaries based on semantic fields (or thesaurus) principles are what metaphor researchers would find most encouraging and helpful in their studies. Yet, the other point is that corpus methods, well suited for tracing what is productive and regular in language, seem to be of limited application when it comes to novel or creative extensions of conceptual metaphors. In such cases it is the researcher's informed intuition that inevitably takes precedence over mechanical manipulation of linguistic material. These limitations, in turn, should be traced back to the most fundamental and basic issue, namely that corpus-based inquiries allow us to gain insights only into those aspects of language that the researcher sets out to investigate. To put it differently, corpus studies do not lead to automatic and effortless generation of linguistic patterns and regularities. On the contrary, the role of other sources of information such as introspection or elicitation can by no means be overlooked. Thus, instead of viewing corpus linguistic as an exclusive methodology it seems more rational to view it as complementary to other possible ways of obtaining and analyzing linguistic data.

REFERENCES

Croft, W. and Cruse, D. A. (2004). *Cognitive Linguistics. Cambridge Textbooks In Linguistics*. Cambridge: Cambridge University Press.

Gibbs, Raymond W. and Steen, Gerard J. (eds) (1997). *Metaphor In Cognitive Linguistics. Selected Papers From The Fifth International Cognitive Linguistics Conference*: Amsterdam/ Philadelphia: John Benjamins Publishing Company.

Henderson, W. (1986). "Metaphor in economics". In: Coulthard, M. (ed.). *Talking about Text (Discourse Monograph No 13)*, Birmingham: English Language Research: 109–27.

Kaleta, A. (2002). "Metaphors we do business by". In: Lewandowska-Tomaszczyk, B. (ed.). *PALC 2001 Practical applications in Language corpora*. Peter Lang: 447–464.

Kalisz, R., Kubiński, W and A. Buller (1996). *In Search of a Frame of Mind. An Introduction to Cognitive Linguistics and Artificial Intelligence*. Gdańsk: Gdańsk University Press.

Krzeszowski, T. P. (1990). "The axiological aspect of idealized cognitive models". In: Tomaszczyk, J. and B. Lewandowska-Tomaszczyk (eds). *Meaning and Lexicography*. Amsterdam/Philadelphia: John Benjamins: 135–165.

Krzeszowski, T.P. (1993). "The axiological parameter in preconceptual image-schemata".
In: Geiger, R. and B. Rudzka-Ostyn (eds). *Conceptualizations and Mental Processing in Language*. Berlin, New York: Mounton de Gruyter: 307–329.

Krzeszowski, T. P. (1997). *Angels and Devils In The Hell.* Warszawa: Energia

Kubiński, W., Kalisz, R. and E. Modrzejewska (eds) (1998). *Językoznawstwo Kognitywne. Wybór Tekstów.* Gdańsk: Wydawnictwo Uniwersytetu Gdańskiego.

Lakoff, G. (1980). *Metaphors We Live By.* Chicago and London: The University of Chicago Press.

Lakoff, G. (1987). *Women, Fire, and Dangerous Things. What categories Reveal about the Mind.* Chicago and London: The University of Chicago Press.

Lakoff, G. (1993). "Contemporary theory of metaphor". In: Ortony, A. (ed.). *Metaphor and Thought.* Cambridge: CUP: 202–250.

Lakoff, G. and M. Johnson (1999). *Philosophy in the Flesh. The Embodied Mind And Its Challenge To Western Thought.* New York: Basic Books.

Lakoff, G. and M. Turner (1989). *More than Cool Reason. A Field Guide to Poetic Metaphor.* Chicago and London: The University of Chicago Press.

Ortony, A. (1979). *Metaphor and Thought.* Cambridge: Cambridge University Press.

Ortony, A. (1993). *Metaphor and Thought.* 2nd edn. Cambridge: Cambridge University Press.

Sinclair, J. (1991). *Corpus, Concordance, Collocation.* Oxford: Oxford University Press.

Part III

E-LEARNING

F. G. F. Schulte

Fontys Universities; Open University, the Netherlands

THE EFFECTIVENESS OF MOODLE AS AN INSTRUMENT TO ASSIST E-COACHES AND CAREER SWITCHERS IN MASTERING AND REFINING THEIR PROFESSIONAL COMPETENCIES AS E-COACHES AND AS TEACHERS

Introduction

This is the text version of a presentation given at the Palc Conference Lodz, on April 8, 2005. The parts of the presentation on blended learning, digital learning objects and Moodle can be viewed at: http://members.chello.nl/f.schulte2/palc.htm, choose link 1. In this article version I will outline the backgrounds to the Moodle experiment, the steps taken in using Moodle to assist e-coaches and career switchers in mastering advanced e-coaching competencies and the evaluation (together with conclusions and recommendations) of the experiment.

The threatening shortage of teachers in the Netherlands and the "career switcher law"

In the Netherlands the baby boom generation will be the last to profit from attractive early retirement schemes. The prediction is that the baby boomers among the teaching population will avail themselves of this opportunity on a massive scale. For 2007 a shortage of 10.000 fulltime teachers is predicted (http://members.chello.nl/f.schulte2/palc.htm, choose link 2). This shortage can in no way be met by the number of teachers produced by the teacher training institutes through their regular fulltime and parttime courses. One of the many measures of the Dutch Ministry Education to deal with this threat of a massive shortage of teachers in Dutch education was the so-called "career switcher law"

(2000). A career switcher is a university graduate in a subject, taught in schools, (e.g: English, geography, history etc.) who lacks proper teaching qualifications but has been employed as a subject specialist outside education for a number of years. Schools are now allowed to employ these career switchers as regular teachers, provided the career switchers will acquire their formal teaching qualifications within 1.5 years.

The law enables the career switcher to acquire his teaching qualifications in a dual trajectory:

1) by learning on the job (so while actually teaching) with coaching/intervision/supervision by colleagues from the schools he is teaching at;

2) by obtaining specific pedagogical-methodological competencies with coaching by experts from a neighbouring teacher training institute.

The assessment centre of the teacher training institute determines whether or not the career switcher is already competent enough to start teaching in the subject he graduated in and which specific competencies he will have to master to become a fully qualified teacher in his subject. For the specific pedagogical-methodological competencies the career switcher is then referred to experts of the teacher training institute. A contract is drawn up, listing the competencies which still have to be acquired and outlining a time path which may not exceed 1.5 years. The school pays the career switcher a regular teaching salary and the ministry (indirectly through a special subsidy to the school) pays for the specialist training by experts from the teacher training institute. At the end of the trajectory the career switcher is submitted to a final assessment procedure to determine whether or not he has succeeded in mastering the missing competencies. If he has indeed done so, the teacher training institute will then officially certify the career switcher as a fully qualified teacher.

As career switchers are as a rule employed fulltime,often combining a teaching job and a job outside education, they can't be expected to attend regular, face-to-face courses in the (specialist) competencies they still have to acquire. The teacher training institute then has to facilitate forms of electronic distance teaching and distance coaching (e-learning and e-coaching) to enable the career switcher to acquire the missing competencies "anyplace anytime". In practice this means that both the teacher training coaches and the career switcher have to be trained in handling methods, materials and tools for e-learning and in particular e-coaching, the latter being a relatively new phenomenon in the world of Dutch teacher training.

The role of the Ruud de Moor Centre of the Dutch Open University and the "e-coaching project"/pilots

As part of the implementation of the career switcher law the Ministry of Education commissioned (and financed) the Dutch Open University in 2003 to research, produce and test methods, materials and tools for the electronic distance education of career switchers. The condition was that the results and materials would be made freely available to schools, teacher training institutes, coaches and career switchers. The Open University then set up the Ruud de Moor Centre to explore this new territory of e-learning, digital methodoloy and e-coaching of career switchers. (http://members.chello.nl/f.schulte2/palc.htm, choose link 3, website is in Dutch). The objectives were to carry out research, to test out materials and tools/instruments, to produce samples of "best practice", to generate lists of "do's and don'ts" and to disseminate the results and products of the activities of the Centre. Since 2003 the Ruud de Moor Centre has been running various projects, including the so-called "e-coaching project", which started in 2004. All of the projects can call upon expert ICT-expertise collected in the ICT-taskforce "virtual work- and learning place" of the Ruud the Moor Centre.

In the e-coaching project, 6 pilots were run in which a career switcher worked on the acquisition of his missing competencies with the help of an e-coach. In their collaboration both career switcher and e-coach (almost) exclusively relied on electronic tools and methods for e-coaching. In the process the participants experimented with an e-learning environment and advanced tools such as (video) chat, discussion forums, one-to-one videoconferencing, on-line telephony etc. The pilots were closely monitored, data and experiences were collected and a website was developed for the on-line dissemination of the "work in progress" and of preliminary results and products (see: http://members.chello.nl/f.schulte2/palc.htm, choose link 4, website is in Dutch).

The pilots were based on the following definition of e-coaching:

> E-coaching is personal coaching at a distance of a career switcher in his efforts to find answers to questions of both a subject-related and a professional nature with the help of on-line tools such as chat, e-mail, discussion forum, webphoning, one-on-one videoconferencing, which may or may not be integrated into an electronic learning and coaching environment.

Before actually starting the pilots interviews were held to determine the needs of the three e-coaches and six career switchers involved. The needs analysis led first of all to the drawing up of an overall competency profile of the e-coach.

Competency profile of an e-coach:

1. The competency to combine a broad knowledge of a (school) subject with the ability to find, unlock and make accessible digital (on-line and off-line) subject-related sources and carriers of information; the competency to direct, monitor and manage individual subject-related learning processes with an effective use of available media and methodologies and with referral to colleagues and experts who are available on-line and/or off-line.
2. Knowledge of and insight into digital (subject) methodology and its relationship with traditional, analogous methodology; the competency to facilitate, manage and monitor individual e-learning processes in the field of digital (subject) methodology on the basis of this knowledge and competency with an effective use of availabe (digital) media and methodologies and with referral to colleagues and experts, available on-line and/or off-line.
3. The compentency to engage effectively in oral and written CMC (computer mediated communication) both synchronously and asynchronously and with the tools that are appropriate for each communicative coaching situation and objective.
4. The competency to use ICT in order to build, stock, structure and organise a digital coaching and learning envrionment in such a way that individual learning processes have a maximum effectiveness when (almost) exclusively conducted and monitored at an electronic distance.

One of the main objectives of the e-coaching project and of the pilots was to ensure that the participating e-coaches would master and/or further refine each of the (sub) competencies of the profile. In the remainder of this article I will concentrate on competency 4 (ICT) and the steps taken to ensure that the three e-coaches involved in the pilots would indeed master the subcompetencies included in compentency 4 in the course of bringing the pilots to their conclusion.

Mastering (ICT-)Competency 4: Step One: Advanced ICT-training

The project started in January 2004. As the actual run of the pilots was scheduled for October 2004–May 2005, the period of January–June 2004 was reserved for recruiting the e-coaches and for helping them to acquire the ICT-skills needed to coach career switchers with ICT-instruments and tools only. The training had to be arranged in such a way that the e-coaches in their turn could easily transfer their newly acquired ICT-competencies and insights to the career switchers each of them would be e-coaching from October onwards. This meant that all the instructions, manuals, guides, workshops, on-line courses, frequently asked questions etc. produced in the course of training the e-coaches were stored and made retrievable/reusable with the help of metadata in the "courses, materials and showcase" section of the project website.

The e-coaches selected all commanded the basic ICT skills at the level of the digital European driving licence. All had extensive experience in regular, f2f-coaching of teacher training students in the final, schoolpractice-oriented stages of their training. They were subsequently given f2f as well as on-line training in the use of e-coaching tools such as e-mail, discussion forum, video/audio chat (MSN Messenger, one-on-one video conferencing, webcams, Netmeeting and Click to Meet), producing and editing audio and video files and on-line telephony (Skype). They were also trained in advanced management of files and in using a metadata editing and storage system such as MyBase. Finally they were given a crashcourse in methods and materials for e-coaching and in digital methodology with the help of the on-line courses developed in the course of the Elise/Minerva project (see: http://filolog.uni.lodz.pl/elise/).

Mastering (ICT-)Competency 4: Step Two: Selecting an e-learning environment for e-coaching purposes

When the pilots reached the stage of actually getting started, the project group decided to leave the choice of e-learning environment within which the e-coaching would be conducted to the school of the career switcher. If the school had its own learning environment and the career switcher wanted to work within that environment, then the project and the e-coach would also work within that environment. However, if the school and career switcher had no e-learning environment, then the project would make one available for the school and the career switcher. As it turned out, none of the schools and career switchers either had an e-learning environment or had one which the career switcher wanted to use. So, in all pilots an e-learning environment suggested by the project was used. For all pilots that was the same e-learning environment: Moodle (http://moodle.org) .

The projectgroup had the following reasons for choosing Moodle:

1. Moodle is free, open source software.
2. Moodle can easily be installed on any server on which PHP and MySQL (widely used and free server software) have been installed.
3. Moodle is low threshold and very user friendly.
4. Moodle is an acronym for Modular Object Oriented Dynamic Learning Environment and is constantly being improved on by a worldwide network of experienced and teaching-oriented users and programmers.

5. Moodle has been designed specifically for social-constructivist methodology and for the promotion of collaborative learning and as such seemed a priori well suited for the project and the e-coaching pilots.
6. Moodle has all the functionalities of standard e-learning environments such as Blackboard, WebCT, N@tschool:
   a. chat
   b. discussion forum
   c. test generator (multiple choice, gap filling, drag and drop etc.)
   d. group modus
   e. shared, on line workspace (the wiki)
   f. peer-to-peer assessment
   g. uploading of documents and attachments in almost all current file formats: doc, ppt, html, jpg, gif, xls, wav, avi, wmv, wma, mpeg1-4 etc.
   h. detailed monitoring (and storing) of participants' activities
   i. importing additional and external materials such as Hot Potatoes exercises
   j. exporting an entire module or "room" as an xhtml/SCORM package
7. More and more schools in the Netherlands are using Moodle and consequently teacher training institutes and their (e-)coaches have to familiarise themselves with Moodle.

Mastering (ICT-)Competency 4: Step Three: Working with Moodle as an e-coaching instrument and environment (actual experiences and conclusions)

Digital Portfolio/Discussion forum

Moodle was subsequently installed on the server of the project (www.school-ict.nl/moodle). Two weeks before the start of the pilots a f2f- meeting for each pilot group was scheduled in which an ICT expert from the Ruud de Moor Centre (acting as the Moodle account manager and administrator) guided the e-coaches and career switchers through the log-in procedures and familiarised them with the basic functionalities of Moodle. He also referred them to on-line manuals and discussion groups pertaining to Moodle. For the duration of the pilots the ICT /Moodle expert was available for on-line consultation on Moodle matters. By the start of the pilots the e-learning environment was "technically" in place and participants in the pilots were sufficiently equipped to conduct their e-coaching experiment in the e-learning environment. It now remained to be seen how well suited Moodle actually was for the specific objective of e-coaching career switchers towards the acquisition of professional competencies.

In four of the pilots Moodle was first of all used by the e-coaches to implement a digital portfolio approach. Each of the competencies the career switcher still had to work on was uploaded by the e-coach as a separate "subject" in the Moodle room, prepared for the e-coach and career switcher by the project's ICT-coach (acting as the Moodle "administrator"). The career switcher could then use the discussion forum, attached to each subject/competency, for specific guidance on how to master the particular competency, for clarification of what was meant by a particular competency and of the kind of "proof" expected by the e-coach of his having mastered a particular competency. The career switcher would then upload his "proof(s)", study and reflect on the comments by the e-coach and make revisions, if necessary.

Example:
Competency 2 in the Moodle room:

Competency 2: I can stimulate, motivate and coach my pupils in their autonomous learning activities and in doing so I can take the way they experience life both inside and outside the school environment into account.

2.1 I can direct pupils towards meta-cognitive reflection on their own learning processes.
2.2 I can stimulate pupils' thinking processes by asking appropriate questions and by continuing to question them if the answers are unsatisfactory.
2.3 In choosing and preparing assignments I can take the pupils' background and expectations into account.
2.4 I can talk with pupils about their motivation.
2.5 I can leave certain matters to the pupils'own initiative, I am not afraid of delegating tasks to them.
2.6 In coaching pupils I can give pupils feedback without actually feeding them the answers.
2.7 I can interact with pupils in a way that makes them feel understood and appreciated.
2.8 I can coach pupils in their own mini-research and project activities.

Proof:

Uploading in Moodle of a questionnaire on items 2.1–2.7 completed by 23 pupils (with additional comments) with these scores:

insufficient	**barely adequate**	**sufficient**	**good**	**very good**

2.1. The teacher stimulates me, helps me to think about how I learn and how I can best tackle my learning tasks.

	2	**1**	**16**	**4**

2.2. By asking questions the teacher makes me think about the subject he is teaching but also about other matters.

		9	10	4

2.4. I can talk to my teacher about my motivation.

		2	12	9

2.5. The teacher is not afraid of leaving things to me.

		6	15	2

2.6. When I ask a question, the teacher helps me without immediately giving the correct answer.

	1	3	15	4

2.7. When I ask a question, I have the feeling the teacher understands me: my question but also my reason for asking the question.

	2	1	9	11

Example of a comment by an e-coach in the discussion forum:

Dear xxxx,

Here's my feedback on the materials you've uploaded so far.

In general:

The Moodle room is filling up nicely. I could now open the "green bits" portfolio document and could see that you've made quite some progress, that document too is filling up nicely.

All the other materials are fine and relevant to completing the overall picture of your professional progress as a grade2/grade 1 teacher. I am curious about your supervisor's evaluation of your schoolpractice. Can that be included in the Moodle room as well?

Apart from the evaluation(s) by pupils (see my e-mail) what I miss (important for me as an e-coach) is a "reflection document" in which you comment on what you've learned so far from your various and manifold activities. This too can be a "growth" document, which you can expand and add to as you work your way towards the end of the various assignments.

I am thinking of things like "tips and tricks", "looking back ....", "I'd never guessed....", "what I found most useful, enlightening, disappointing etc ....", "what I will focus on next .....", "what I would like to explore in more detail ....", "what I found truly surprising ....", especially because you are now in a position to compare yourself at the start of this year

> and halfway through the year. Your reflections could then culminate in some kind of "SWOT" analysis document/chapter/part, in which you analyse your:
>
> Strengths (as a teacher of English)
>
> Weaknesses (as a teacher of English)
>
> Opportunities (as a teacher of English)
>
> Threats (as a teacher of English)
>
> You could then finish with a kind of professional development plan (things to work on) for the (near) future when you've finished your courses and are a fully qualified teacher of English.

Proofs could, for instance, consist of scanned copies of documents (lesson plans, lesson evaluations by colleagues/supervisors, reports of meetings and inservice sessions etc.), of the results of questionnaires on classroom performance or performance as a coach/mentor/tutor, of (digital) lesson materials (on-line or off-line) prepared or selected/adapted by the career switcher. It was also possible to prove competencies by uploading video fragments of recorded classroom performance. The project administrator set the maximum upload size at 16 MB. As Moodle can handle compressed video files in the wmv format, the career switcher could upload files containing 10–15 minutes of recorded classroom performance. (for a sample see: http://members.chello.nl/f.schulte2/palc.htm, choose link 5 .)

Video files larger than 16 MB could be made available for review by the e-coach as follows. For all participants in RdMC projects the ICT-expert group of the Ruud de Moor Centre had created accounts with with they could access and upload large video files in all current compression formats (Windows Media, Real, Quicktime etc.) to the video streaming server of the RdMC. The server, running on Helix video streaming software, was installed in accordance with the expressed needs of all the various projects and after extensive field research by the ICT expertise group. So career switchers could upload their large video files to the special and secure "e-coaching" directory on the streaming video server, generate the url and then include the url in their Moodle digital portfolio and/or answers in the discussion forum. With the help of the project's virtual "cutting machine" (http://members.chello.nl/f.schulte2/palc.htm, choose link 6) additional urls could be generated by e-coach or career switcher to highlight particular fragments in large (and long) video files, without actually editing the video files themselves. For a demonstration of highlighting a short fragment out of a much longer video with the help of the cutting machine, follow this link (http://members.chello.

nl/f.schulte2/palc.htm, choose link 7), which will lead you to a fragment of 16 seconds of the longer video referred to in the previous paragraph.

The e-coach commented on each of these "proofs", came up with suggestions for improvement and (sometimes after revisions) accepted them as attesting to the career switcher having mastered certain (sub)competencies. Occasionally when typing out the comments would be far too time-consuming, the e-coach would audiorecord his comments and upload the sound files. Everything could be stored in Moodle and easily be retrieved with the help of Moodle's metadata system and statistical survey of activities, arranged by date and time of day.

The digital portfolio annex discussion forum approach in Moodle worked to everybody's satisfaction. When interviewed about his portfolio experiences in the Moodle environment, one career switcher commented:

> The digital portfolio in the Moodle environment has many advantages. The main advantage is the fact that I have been able to do all the work on putting the portfolio together from my own home. With a fulltime job and a family this was very convenient. In addition, everything I collected was stored in one, coherent package. Whenever I wanted I couild easily go back to my proofs and review and revise them. My e-coach always gave me useful feedback. For him too it must have been an advantage that he could react 'anytime anyplace' to my questions. The discussion forum gave my e-coach and myself a discussion platform through which we could interact in a nuanced and carefully considered manner. The approach gave me the opportunity to work in a streamlined and all-comprehensive way, tailored to my own needs and preferences. For me this was very efficient. Distance, space and time no longer formed the obstacles they were when I did my original degree course in the traditional manner in the early 1990s.

In their evaluations each of the three career switchers who had worked with a digital portfolio in Moodle gave the experiment a score of 9 out of a possible 10.

Once the time comsuming process of putting a personalised portfolio into Moodle has been completed, the Moodle environment facilitates quick exchanges, sharing of all kinds of files and documents and easy retrieval of materials, discussion threads, comments etc. together with records of actual amounts of time spent in Moodle and/or activities undertaken in Moodle. Moreover, if a career switcher gave his permisison, others (colleagues, other career switchers, experts) could be given guest accounts and be invited to join the discussions. All career switchers gave their permission for this opening up of their "private" workspace to interested outsiders. In their evaluations they all highly appreciated these comments from colleagues and experts from which they said they learned a lot.

Wiki

"Wiki wiki" means "quick" in Hawaiian and is now used to refer to a website that can be quickly edited by its visitors with simple formatting rules. Developed by Ward Cunningham in the mid 1990s to provide collaborative discussions, there are several "Wiki" tools on the market for creating such sites, including www.editme.com, www.seedwiki.com, www.socialtext.com and www.swiki.net. Moodle too offers the wiki functionality, thus enabling career switcher and e-coach to collaborate (also simultaneously at a distance!) on producing on-line documents and websites. This proved very convenient in coaching a career switcher in producing on-line/html/website materials for classroom use. The career switcher could produce a first version of his website materials in the wiki of the Moodle room, the e-coach could insert his comments and revisions (in a Moodle wiki previous versions can always be retrieved), which the career switcher could then incorporate in the next version of the wiki. This saved laborious sending back and forth of separate html files through e-mail and archiving first, second, third etc. versions of materials.

Here is a sample of part of a wiki for a webquest on World War One with comments inserted (in red) by the e-coach:

Version One:
[on the screen pupils see five World War One paintings]
Assignments: Give your interpretation of each war painting:
Comment e-coach: Hi XX, I think this assignment is far too abstract for 16–18 year olds. You have to make it more concrete and take them step by step towards an interpretation and appreciation of these paintings (nice selection by the way) and to integrate this assignment with what they have been finding out about cubism and realism in the previous assignment. So, ask them about which aspect of the war each painting deals with, which style the artist works in: cubism and realism and which appeals most to them and why.

Version Two:
[on the screen the pupils see five World War One paintings]
Assignments:

Give your interpretation of each painting:

- What style did the artist use? Cubism or Realism?
- What aspect of the war is shown by the paintings?
- Which of these paintings appeals to you most? Explain why.
- Use the next link to find out more about war- paintings. Choose two more paintings which appeal to you and explain why.

Art of the first World War

Follow this link to see the definitive version of the webquest: http://members.chello.nl/f.schulte2/palc.htm , choose link 8.

Five of the career switchers in the pilots used the wiki to produce on-line digital learning objects, varying from reading assigments to complete webquests. They all managed to finish their object well ahead of schedule, mainly because of the speed and ease with which comments and suggestions by the e-coach (and on occasion experts) could be incorporated into the revised versions. In their evaluations they gave this feature of Moodle likewise a score of 9 out of a possible 10.

Log

In most cases, a (web)log is a web page containing a series of entries listed chronologically with the most recent entries at the top of the page. Moodle offers the functionality of the log in a privatised manner, in contrast to the much more open and public nature of (web)logging on the Internet. The e-coach can prepare a general log for all Moodle activities or a separate log for each "subject", activity or competency. Logs in Moodle are private and personalised and "read only". They can only be visited and viewed by the e-coach and the career switcher writing the log prepared for him. They cannot be opened up to visitors or fellow students/career switchers in the same Moodle room. This makes (b)logging in Moodle a private activity, very well suited for intimate and personal reflections on the career switcher's professional development and experiences, provided he is willing to share them with his e-coach. As it turned out, only two of the six career switchers were willing to use the log in this private manner as a sort of personal diary of their professional life and "ups and downs". The others preferred the more impersonal medium of the (open) discussion forum and/or contacting the e-coach on more personal matters by such tools as video and audio chat/digital telephony. The argument was on the whole that for them with their busy schedules logging was an activity that was far too time-consuming to be kept up at a regular basis with a frequency of at least twice a week. The career switchers who volunteered to use the log function quickly abandoned the logs after they had served their initial purpose of informing the e-coach of their experiences in a particular area for a brief period of time e.g. the experiences of actually trying out some of their materials with pupils. The overall score for this functionality was a 5 out of a possible 10. This was not so much because of the awkwardness of the Moodle log as because of the reluctance in general to engage in (b)logging. Career switchers said it was good the log functionality was there, but that it should only be used for a specific and brief occasion.

Here is a sample from a log entry:

> "The *On the Beach* assignment (my Moodle debut) has been a success. Pupils all reacted and they really did work hard on their assignment. Occasionally I had to help pupils in using the forum, but on the whole everything went well. Nice feeling to leave the work to pupils and check afterwards what they submitted. If someone does not pull his weight, it is actually documented in 'black and white' – good to show to parents who won't believe me when I tell them their kid is underachieving! The kids take to Moodle like a duck to water: bits of text, icons, pictures, uploading, reacting, being on-line et. Today (April 4) also introduced h4 to Moodle. Striking to see how the kids enjoyed recognizing pupils who had already been registered. 'He, I know that bloke ....' Sense of community."

Chat

Moodle offers a chat function, but it works in text mode only and does not support audio and/or video communication. On top of that it is relatively slow and, with multiple users, not very reliable. This is a matter of serious concern for Moodle developers all over the world and in the next "stable" Moodle versions the chat function will be vastly improved, although as yet not supporting audio and video chat. Moodle experts are also figuring out ways to integrate Moodle and MSN Messenger and such like services, but have as yet not been successful. So the chat function in Moodle was not really used. However, in the pilots there were enough alternatives outside Moodle (MSN Messenger, Netmeeting, Click to Meet), which could be used by the e-coaches to finetune their synchronous e-coaching skills.

Mastering (ICT-) Competency 4: Conclusions about Moodle as an instrument to help e-coaches in mastering this e-coaching competency

In their evaluations the three e-coaches expressed their satisfaction with Moodle, which all of them worked with for the first time. Unanimously they praised Moodle's ease of use and in particular its suitability as an instrument for asynchronous e-coaching. They had used tools tools for synchronous e-coaching but found that career switchers on the whole preferred asynchronous communication within Moodle to, for instance, synchronous communication through chat (MSN Messenger). Both e-coaches and career switchers said that asynchronous commnication perfectly suited their needs because they could use it "anytime anyplace" (provided the other party would reply within a reasonable time limit, let's say 24 hours), could thoroughly prepare their materials and questions and reflect on comments and suggestions in a relaxed and nuanced manner. The career switchers and e-coaches liked the opportunity to use chat but said they used it mainly for emergencies and/or questions which would requite only short answers. Most of them tired quickly of chat simply because of the effort to try and keep up a normal tempo of spoken conversation in typing.

The Moodle wiki had finetuned the skills of e-coaches in offering guidance in the design and production of digital learning objects and had heightened their insight into digital methodology, in particular the methodology of collaborative learning. What the e-coaches liked above all was the ease and speed with which Moodle handled all kinds of files and documents, including advanced audio and video files. For them this opened up hitherto unexplored ways of exploiting the advantages of a digital portfolio. The e-coaches concluded that they had all grown considerably in their competency to use a wide array of ICT-tools and hence in their ability to select an instrument that was the perfect match for their particular e-coaching objective. Their experiences are borne out by Moodle users all over the world:

> Moodle was designed from the beginning by an unsatisfied WebCT admin, who has a degree in Computer Science and a Master in Education and wanted to make a much better system than WebCT (the best commercial one, in my opinion). So, its design involves both TECHNOLOGICAL AND PEDAGOGICAL thinking. I think that right now, Moodle is the best option as a Learning Management System. I like very much its design and simplicity and I think that anyone can create good e-learning systems with it.
> (David Delgado, e-learning systems developer, University of Las Palmas de Gran Canaria, http://moodle.org/mod/forum)

On the basis of the experiences in the pilots, the conclusion is warranted that Moodle is also a very good option as an e-coaching management system.

Recommendations

1. Use Moodle in particular for e-coaching activities which will lean heavily on asynchronous communication.
2. Exploit the possibilities Moodle offers for working with a digital portfolio and for collaboration on webpages (wiki).

3. Use applications such as MSN Messenger, Netmeeting, Click to Meet rather than Moodle for synchronous communication.

4. Prior to an e-coaching trajectory a f2f-session should be organised about working with and in Moodle. Use that session also to take care of log-in procedures.

5. Set up a Moodle helpdesk which is available for the entire duration of the e-coaching activities.

6. Create a separate Moodle room for archiving and "reusing" experiences, materials, instructions, urls which may be relevant for all participants in the e-coaching activities. Enrol all participants as members/students/teachers of that "generic" Moodle room. Use the possibilities Moodle offers for metadating and searching documents.

7. Regularly visit the worldwide Moodle discussion forum (http://moodle.org) for experiences and "tips & tricks" with reference to Moodle.

BIBLIOGRAPHY

Books/Articles:

Abbott, C. (ed.) (2002). *Special Educational Needs and the Internet: Issues in Inclusive Education*. London (Routledge Falmer).

Terry Anderson (2004). Theory and Practice of On-Line Learning (Athabasca).

Bates, A.W. (1995). *Technology, open learning and distance education*. New York (Routledge), x + 266 pp..

Baylor, A. L. and D. Ritchie (2002). "What factors facilitate teacher skill, teacher morale, and perceived student learning in technology-using classrooms?". *Computers & Education* 39(4): 395–414.

Bess, James L. e.a. (2000). *Teaching alone, teaching together. Transforming the structure of teams for teaching*. San Francisco (Jossey-Bass), xi + 258pp.

Boxtel, C. e.a. (2000). "Collaborative learning tasks and the elaboration of conceptual knowledge". *Learning and instruction* 10: 311–330.

Bransford, J. D., A. L. Brown and R. Cocking (1999). *How people learn*. Washington D.C. (National Academy Press).

Brooks, Jacqueline & Martin (1995). The case for constructivist classrooms. URL: http://129.7.160.115/INST5931/Constructivist.html

Bruce, Betsy e.a. (2000). *Getting started with online learning*. San Francisco (Macromedia Inc.), 130 pp.

Bvenet (2000). Learning Space en perception. URL: www.bvenet.nl/bvenetnieuws/161299/LLS.htm

Conlon, T. and M. Simpson (2003). "Silicon Valley versus Silicon Glen: the impact of computers upon teaching and learning: a comparative study". *British Journal of Educational Technology* 34(2): 137–150.

Cox, M. J. and M. Webb (eds.) (2004). *An investigation of the research evidence relating to ICT pedagogy*. Coventry, Becta / London, DfES

Curran, K. (2002). "An online collaboration environment". *Education and Information Technologies* 7(1): 41–53.

Danaher, P. A. e.a. (1994). *Teachers' professional development through open learning technologies*. (paper op 24e Annual Meeting of the Australian Teacher Education Association, Brisbane).

Jochems, W., van Merriënboer, J. and R. Koper (eds.) (2003). *Integrated e-learning.: Implications for pedagogy, technology & organization*. London (RoutledgeFalmer).

Ko, Susan and Rossen, Steve (2001). *Teaching online. A practical guide*. Boston / New York (Houghton Mifflin Company), xvii + 348 pp.

Lin, B. S. and C. T. Hsieh (2001). "Web-based teaching and learner control: a research review". *Computers & Education* 37(3–4): 377–386.

McDuffie, A. R. and D. Slavit (2003). "Utilising online discussion to support reflection and challenge beliefs in elementary mathematics methods classrooms". *Contemporary Issues in Technology and Teacher Education* 2(4).

Papert, S. (2003). Why are schools afraid of digital technology? http://www.elearningeuropa.info/doc.php?lng=1&id=1424&doclng=1 (2003-06-02).

Powell, J. V., Aeby, V. G. J. and T. Carpenter-Aeby (2003). "A comparison of student outcomes with and without teacher facilitated computer-based instruction".. *Computers & Education* 40(2): 183–191.

Rosas, R., Nussbaum, M., Cumsille, P., Marianov, V., Correa, M., Flores, P., Grau, V., Lagos, F., Lopez, X. and V. Lopez (2003). "Beyond Nintendo: design and assessment of educational video games for first and second grade students". *Computers & Education* 40(1): 71–94.

Schrum, L. and S. Hong (2002). "From the field: characteristics of successful tertiary online students and strategies of experienced online educators". *Education and Information Technologies* 7(1): 5–16.

Stacey, E. (2002). "Social presence online: networking learners at a distance". *Education and Information Technologies* 7(4): 287–294.

Websites:

http://www.ta.doc.gov/reports/TechPolicy/2020Visions.pdf

Visions 2020: transforming education and training through advanced technologies; een reeks van 14 toekomstgerichte essays in pdf, 85 pp.

http://www.uidaho.edu/evo/distglan.html

Site van de University of Idaho about distance learning; 12 "guides" for the whole domain:

#1 Distance Education: An Overview #2 Strategies for Teaching at a Distance #3 Instructional Development for Distance Education #4 Evaluation for Distance Educators #5 Instructional Television #6 Computers in Distance Education

#7 Print in Distance Education #8 Strategies for Learning at a Distance #9 Distance Education: Research #10 Interactive Videoconferencing in Distance Education #11 Distance Education and the WWW #12 Copyright and Distance Education #13 Glossary of Distance Education Terminology

http://www.macromedia.com/learning/

Portal of Macromedia; instructtions and manuals for instructional design withiun e-learning.Recommended: click through to Getting Started with Online Learning (PDF file, 1.34MB).

http://www.e-learningcentre.co.uk/eclipse/Resources/index.html

Rich portal for all aspects of e-learning.

http://www.links4learning.com/

Portal for e-learning.

John Osborne

University of Savoy

WHY DO THEY KEEP MAKING THE SAME MISTAKES? EVIDENCE FOR ERROR MOTIVATION IN A LEARNER CORPUS

1. Persistent errors: from stabilization to fossilization

Persistent L2 errors answer to a variety of names. Among those listed in recent publications (most notably, Han 2004: 13–14; 25–26) are the following terms: *backsliding; stabilized errors; persistent non-target-like performance; learning plateau; de-acceleration of the learning process; ingrained errors; systematic use of erroneous forms; variable outcomes; cessation of learning; structural persistence; errors that are impervious to negative evidence; random use of grammatical and ungrammatical structures; long-lasting free variation; persistent difficulty; non-nativelikeness; fossilization; the f-word; rigor mortis; stopping short; permanent optionality; nomadic grammars; siesta*... But whatever label they carry, these errors are an annoying reality for most language learners, whose grammars evolve up to a certain point and then stabilize, in such a way that continued exposure and practice does not appear to result in any perceptible further progress towards systematic production of correct target forms. Such grammars are often characterized by optionality – the correct forms are used in most cases, but "backsliding" errors appear from time to time. If this situation becomes permanent, then the grammar will appear to have fossilized, although the idea of fossilization needs to be treated with caution, if only because it is difficult to determine what criteria might be used to determine whether any individual's L2 grammar has permanently ceased to evolve. Just because it doesn't seem to be moving doesn't necessarily mean that it is in *rigor mortis*.

Among the reasons which have been offered to account for fossilization, Han (2004) distinguishes four main groups of factors: environmental (lack of input, etc.), cognitive (L1 influence, lack of attention, transfer of training, etc.), neuro-biological (age, neural entrenchment, etc.) and socio-affective (satisfaction of communicative needs, etc.) – in total, more than fifty possible causes of fossilization. In view of this impressive inventory, it might be wondered whether we really need any more reasons, but Long (2003: 514) considers that a satisfactory explanation is still lacking: "What almost all explanations on offer have in common is that they do not work – at least not for fossilization, even when they may for stabilization". The problem is to explain why certain structures stabilize or fossilize while others do not, and why this affects certain learners but not others. Long suggests (517) that the most promising line of investigation might be to look at the interaction between perceptual saliency (a feature of individual structures) and input sensitivity (a feature of individual learners). Potentially fossilizable structures are likely to belong to certain high-risk categories: cases where there is no simple form-function relationship (e.g. articles), semi-productive rules (dative alternation, stress shifts, etc.), and arbitrary units such as grammatical gender, prepositions and collocations (see Todeva 1992; Long 2002).

However, it does not appear to be necessary for a linguistic feature to be particularly complex for it to be a candidate for stabilization (cf. Han 2004: 139). Each of the following features of English, although they can be formulated in a fairly straightforward way, are nevertheless known to cause learning difficulties, even at quite advanced levels:

– adjectives are invariable for number

– nouns such as *information*, *advice*, etc. do not pluralize or take an indefinite article

– present-tense verbs take -s in the 3rd person singular

– adverbs are not placed between a verb and its direct object.

The purpose of this study is to track the persistence of such errors in the productions of post-intermediate learners of English. Learner corpora have profitably been used to study various kinds of diffuse errors: questions of under- or over-use of certain items, inappropriate collocations, and so on. We are concerned here with another type of diffuse error – those which, thanks to a relatively long period of language-learning, have become infrequent but have not disappeared altogether (and which are perhaps destined never to disappear). Analysis of corpus data should provide information not only on which errors persist, but also about the contexts in which they appear. Two corpora are used for the study. The first is a 1-million word corpus of essays collected at the University of Savoy. The learners are 2nd and 3rd undergraduates specializing in languages and are all native speakers of French; the essays are untimed, with an average length of 3000 words, mostly on "contemporary society" topics such as *Smoking in America, Native Americans, ICT in education, Juvenile boot camps,*

Aboriginal Health and Social Problems, Sexually transmitted diseases, Birth control, Illiteracy in America, The Britons' attitude towards foreign languages. The second is a 26,000-word "mini-corpus" collected from pupils in year 6 (*Première*) of a French secondary school. Their productions are short essays and final web-quest writing tasks with an average length of approximately 200 words. The two corpora will be referred to as the "university corpus" and the "school corpus", respectively. The extract below, taken from the school corpus, illustrates the kind of unstable grammar that we are interested in:

(1) Approximatively in 1998, the chanel four (chanel 4) created a show on the T.V. which give you a chance to win an house in France. You choose an house between four differents houses which have the same budget and you can win it.
It's really the new trend in England and a lot of families want to take part in the show to win their dream "to own an house in France."
Some of French think that English have a wrong vision of France. It's true in very small villages but in Paris there is criminality, it rains often and daily-living is more expensive than in a village. The only thing which is really true is the fact that the real estate business is cheaper than England and French food is famous to be very good.
So, English compare France to a Paradise and it's probably because they don't really know it. Do you think that Paradise exist on dry land?

Why is it that in the same short text an obligatory feature (3rd person -s) is correctly provided in one context (*it rains often*), but not in others (*which give you a chance / that Paradise exist*)? Conversely, why does a superfluous feature (noun-adjective agreement) appear incorrectly in one context (*differents houses*) but not in another (*very small villages*)? Are these errors random, or is there some pattern to the contexts in which they appear? By looking at their occurrence in the productions of learners at different stages, it may be possible to gain a better understanding of how developing grammars stabilize and what degree of optionality remains at more advanced levels. If the optionality is durable, then the feature in question may be a candidate for fossilization. Following Sorace's definition of terminal optionality, the question is whether it is possible to pin down the circumstances in which non-target choices appear:

> In the typical L2 end state characterized by optionality, optional variants are not in free variation: a steady state is reached in which the target option is strongly but not categorically preferred and the non-target option surfaces in some circumstances. (2003: 139–140, emphasis added)

We shall therefore look at two areas where "simple" errors persist – noun-phrase errors (adjective-noun agreement and pluralized mass nouns) and verb-phrase errors (3rd person subject-verb agreement and verb-raising) – to see whether there are specific circumstances that favour their appearance.

2. Teenagers look for extremes sensations

Superfluous adjective-noun agreement is a well-known transfer error among French-speaking learners of English (French adjectives agree with the noun for gender and number). As is to be expected, the frequency of this type of error is much higher in the small school corpus than in the productions of the more advanced university-level learners (Table 1).

Table 1. Pluralized adjectives

	occurrences	/100,000 words
school	27	102
university	72	6.8

What may seem surprising is that this error should appear at all in the carefully monitored written productions of learners who have 9–10 years of English study behind them, so it is worth looking more closely at the contexts in which they do appear, to see if there is any plausible explanation – other than random error – for their persistence. The 99 occurrences of pluralized adjectives occurring in the two corpora can be grouped into the following categories:

- recategorized units, mostly adjectivized nouns (*adults smokers*), noun+noun combinations (*bathrooms fittings, diets ads*) and nominalizable adjectives (*heterosexuals couples*)
- derived adjectives (*financials problems, historics monuments*)
- French cognates (*extremes sports, recents attempts*)
- double-marked demonstratives (*theses ideas*)
- differentiating adjectives (*others people, differents alphabets*)
- other monosyllabic adjectives (*bigs cities, blacks students*)

The distribution of these types is shown in Table 2. It will be noticed that while French cognates account for a third of all the erroneously pluralized adjectives produced by the lower-level learners, they have almost disappeared from the university corpus, where just one type – adjectivized nouns and other re-categorized units – accounts for more than half of the errors, with the single adjective *other* accounting for another third.

Table 2. Types of pluralized adjective

pluralized adjectives	school corpus	university corpus
adjectivized nouns etc.	15%	51.5%
derived adjectives	18.5%	1.5%
French cognates	33%	1.5%
demonstratives	–	5.5%
different	11%	3%
other	19%	30%
monosyllabic	3.5%	7% (*Black*)

There appear therefore to be specifiable error-inducing contexts which facilitate the appearance of residual errors of this kind. Other possible contexts are formulaic expressions such as *in others words* or *in theses cases*, and phonetic environment in cases such as *bigs cities, adults smokers, others solutions,* where the following /s/ at the beginning of the noun may encourage adjective agreement, even in written production. But at the more advanced level, two main categories account for nearly all errors: differentiating adjectives such as *other* and *different*, and recategorized units such as adjectivized nouns. It is arguable that this category of grammatically ambiguous units should also include the only frequently pluralized monosyllabic adjective in the university corpus – *black* – which, in four out of the five occurrences, is also capitalized (*Blacks students*, etc.) Interestingly, the only other monosyllabic adjective to be pluralized in this corpus appears, as if by contamination, in association with *Black*:

(2) ...because all the news Blacks voters would certainly tend to give their votes to a Black candidate

3. In which you can find every sorts of informations

Another persistent noun-phrase error is the use of non-count nouns like *information* as count nouns, materialized by the presence of plural -s and/or a plural verb. This too can be easily explained as a transfer error, since the nouns in question typically correspond to items (cognate or not) which function as count nouns in French. But it is also a clear case of conflict between learners' explicit knowledge and their usage. As table 3 shows (adapted from Osborne 2003), explicit awareness of (non)countability is high among the more advanced learners, but this is not necessarily reflected in spontaneous usage. In the case of *advice*, for example, 93% of French undergraduate informants (n = 97) judged that it could not be used as a count noun, yet more than a third of the occurrences of *advice* in the university corpus do just that. Not surprisingly, in comparable essays by L1 English students, neither *advice* nor *information* ever appears as a count noun.

Table 3. Pluralized mass nouns – explicit knowledge and use

	judged non-count: Fr university	% used as count: school	% used as count: university	% used as count: NS students
freedom	100%	18	3.5	1.8
information	95%	36	14.5	0
advice	93%	n/a	35.3	0
understanding	87%	n/a	40.5	58.3
behaviour	66%	0	22.6	0
training	64%	100	17.6	0
research	46%	11	15.8	0

Are these learners' count-like uses of non-count nouns just haphazard, or are the errors motivated? Analysis of occurrences extracted from the corpus suggests that particular contexts may favour non native-like usage. Among these are qualification and quantification of the noun, particularly (examples 4–5) where there is incrementation, and contexts where there is an effect of contamination from conjunction with a neighbouring count noun (6–7).

(3) It is used to give moral or friendly advices or predictions
(4) seems to be important a priori, since very little information are available.
(5) it needs further evidences and informations to be fully understood...
(6) its image, its sales and can also have more informations of the market....
(7) The numerous photos or evidences gathered after the wreck or provided...
(8) The holistic sequences could be evidences of that same knowledge...

4. It's alcohol that kill

One of the very first facts that students learn about English morphology is that verbs with a 3rd person singular subject take -s in the present tense. As morphological rules go, this one is particularly easy to formulate, and yet failure to supply obligatory -s is a remarkably tenacious learner error.

Table 4. Absence of 3rd person subject-verb agreement

	occurrences	/100,000 words
school corpus	65 *(50)**	242 *(189)*
university corpus	71	6.9

Table 5 shows the occurrences of verbs with 3rd person singular subjects which carry no mark of agreement. In the results from the school corpus (line 2), the second figure in parentheses gives the number of unmarked 3rd person verbs after excluding those which appear to have past time reference. In the university corpus, past tense morphology is applied more systematically, and all the cases of zero-ended 3rd person verbs are clearly intended to have present or atemporal reference. Like the superfluous adjectival -s, the missing 3rd person -s becomes much less frequent but continues to appear (or rather not appear) in the university corpus. But also like the adjectival -s, this error tends to favour certain contexts, listed below:

- complementizers : *...due to the fact the player stay very static*
- relatives and cleft constructions: *children whose illness prevent them from going to school*
- compound/complex subject NPs (N's N / N of N / NN): *The progression of the white-collar sector permit a growing number...*
- collective subject nouns: *TV news prepare them to the consequences of extreme behaviour*
- quantified mass nouns: *Many evidence have proved*
- each/every N: *Every reporter from each side agree*
- indefinite subjects: *... and so when something happen*
- categorizers: *all kind of education have their advantages ...*
- past time reference: *I wasn't <scared>, until a bomb get near to our shelter*

Table 5. Contexts for non-agreement

	school corpus	university corpus
complementizers	4	6
relatives / clefts	16	29
complex subject NPs	4	6
collective subject Ns	8	6
quantified mass nouns	0	6
each/every N	0	5
indefinite subjects	4	3
categorizers	0	2
past time reference	15	0
others	14	8

The distribution of these contexts is shown in Table 5. Although all contexts continue to cause a certain number of errors even at the more advanced level, there is a clear evolution towards one dominant error type, triggered by the use of relative or cleft constructions, as in (9) and (10):

(9) Moreover British universities as well as public schools have a special status that allow them to ask for money coming from private persons or organisations.

(10) It is obvious that it is the budget that deter parents to send their kids to Muslim schools.

There could be several possible reasons for this. One is that the immediate subject is the relative pronoun *that* (or *who/which*), which is itself invariable, and this may render the singular-plural contrast less salient. In some cases, relative clauses appear inside sentences containing one or more plural noun phrases, thus perhaps distracting attention from the singular nature of the real antecedent. Finally, it is possible that the processing effort required to produce syntactically complex structures may also distract attention from the morphological details inside the structure, even in careful production. When several factors combine, producing a cumulative error frame, the risk of distraction appears to increase, as in the examples below:

- every + relative: *and say thank you to every person who pass*
- complementizer + quantifier + relative: *It can be noted first that in Oxbridge "barely 52% of the students are drawn from the maintained sector which educate 93% of the school population"*
- categorizer + collective N + relative: *because it is not the form of government which correspond the best to a democratic country*
- complex NP + relative: *rapidly increase the concentration of oxygen which circulate in the body*

5. Do you enjoy killing progressively your love?

The English 3rd person -s is anomalous in a language which is otherwise characterized by weak agreement. A corollary of the weak agreement feature is that verbs in Present-Day English do not raise past the negative or past adverbs, as they do in French. This is the source of another type of error, giving non native-like adverb placement in learner productions. Examples (11)–(15), all taken from the university corpus, illustrate how the same adverb can appear in various positions in L2 English:

(11) Sampson clearly that the Britons are aware of this difference ...
(12) It clearly defines the two words from their origins to their uses in contemporary English.
(13) The fact that the characters are animals allows Orwell to underline the issue more clearly
(14) Smith et al explain clearly the effects of too much time spent watching television.
(15) It is quite hard to define very clearly this word.

Examples 11–13 would no doubt be judged acceptable by native speakers of English; 14 is more questionable, but does in fact correspond to a type of structure sometimes used in NS English (see below), whereas 15 is almost certainly not possible in NS English. In the university corpus, this V Adv O order continues to represent a proportion of adverb usage, even though other more native-like positions are preferred (see Table 6). For this particular item, it is not meaningful to make comparisons with the school corpus, in which adverbs are relatively infrequent and where it is not always clear whether surface errors stem from incorrect adverb placement or from confusion about the form of adverbs and adjectives; example (16) below seems to result from this confusion, while (17) is ambiguous.

(16) ...the French Air Force decide to going in help to the English army for fight this terribly thing together...
(17) ... The Indian soldiers undergo constantly attacks...

Table 6. V Adv O order in the University corpus

	-ly adverbs	all adverbs
V Adv O: This declaration is frightening and illustrates completely the perils that the reproductive cloning can entail.	92	270
Adv V O: They completely disregard the other animals' welfare and run the farm for their own convenience.	561	1457
Adv final: It was a sort of ethnic balance, but it failed completely.	329	1150

Could it be the case that residual V Adv O order in the university corpus is not in fact an "error" (a divergence from native usage) but something that native speakers and writers do too? In (18) below, taken from a text by Michael Hoey, there are two factors that might account for the atypical placement of the adverb: heavy NP shift (*the claim that +S*) and a strong collocational tie between verb and adverb (*treat-seriously*), to the extent that it is difficult to see what other position the adverb could occupy.

(18) We are treating seriously the claim that each sentence is a separate package of information.

Heavy NP shift certainly could account for some of the occurrences of V Adv O order in the university corpus, but as can be seen in Table 7, nearly half of the adverbs used in this position are followed by relatively "light" object NPs. By comparison, V Adv O sequences extracted from the LOB, Brown and Wellington corpora show a clear preference for heavy NPs.

Table 7. "Heavy" object NPs

	uiversity corpus	LOB etc.
light (1-3 word) NPs (N, Det+N, Det+Adj+N)	43%	8%
medium (4-6 word) NPs (mostly N of N constructions)	35%	37%
heavy (6+ word) NPs (relatives, *that* complements, coordinate NPs)	22%	55%

Collocational effects, on the other hand, do play a significant role, particularly in the case of associations between a verb and reinforcing or "improving" adverb, as in the examples below:

illustrate
...This illustrates well that stereotypes are not ...
...This quote illustrates well that it is a choice...
... Louis Pojman illustrates well what the white students me ...
... is frightening and illustrates completely the perils that the reprod ....
understand
...The reader, himself, understands very quickly the subterfuge ...
...for Mr Lockwood to understand entirely what she evokes
...necessary in order to understand correctly the symptoms of a
... that to know and understand fully a country, one should..
know
... managers who know very well the Japanese language...
... is then necessary to know perfectly Japanese traditions.
...because they knew exactly one's phobia and they...
explain
...second part of this study explains more clearly the utterer's mental
...Smith et al explain clearly the effects of too much ...
... through new examples to explain fully the use of here and there .
affect
...Undeniably, the language affects badly the learning process of the...
...abolition of slavery would affect more injuriously the condition of...

There are thus conditions which favour non native-like adverb placement just as for the other, more elementary errors discussed here. Both L1 and L2 writers of English show optionality in adverb placement, but the zone of optionality is greater for L2; the factors triggering non target-like placement (heavy NP-shift, strong collocational ties) are also present in L1 usage, but with weaker effects. Collocational V-Adv-O sequences may also result from compensating for lexical deficiencies, as in examples (19)–(20), where the need to use an adverb at all could have been avoided by using a different verb (for example, *...hinders the learning process* and *...reorganised my ideas*, respectively):

(19) Undeniably, the language affects badly the learning process
(20) Consequently I classified again my ideas and I imagined a new outline.

6. Backsliding into sloth?

The four error types briefly discussed here are all cases of apparent backsliding; lapses which contravene rules that are familiar to the learners and which run counter to innumerable exemplars of target-language usage that they have encountered during their learning career. The term backsliding has clearly negative connotations, as do most of the other terms cited at the beginning of this paper (the BNC, for example, yields examples such as *...sinful behaviour and backsliding* and *...backsliding into sloth*). This should not lead us to conclude that such persistent errors are the result of random slovenliness. The evidence, at least from the learner corpus examined here, suggests that they tend to appear in specifiable frames. Typically, these frames enable non-target patterns (carried over from L1 or triggered by contextual conflicts) to over-ride explicitly-learnt rules. Such errors are not necessarily evidence of fossilized grammars, but possibly of interference between different types of processing – between the demands of larger syntactic units at the expense of lower-level morphology, or between conflicting categorisations. Understanding that such errors may be motivated will not necessarily make them go away, but at least it offers the hope that if a cause is there, it may eventually be resolved.

REFERENCES

Birdsong, D. (2004). "Second language acquisition and ultimate attainment". In: Davies, A. and C. Elder (eds). *Handbook of Applied Linguistics*. Oxford: Blackwell: 82–105.

Birdsong. D. (2005). "Why not fossilization?" In: Han, Z. and T. Odlin (eds). *Studies of Fossilization in Second Language Acquisition*. Clevedon: Multilingual Matters: 173–188.

Gibson, E. (1971). "Perceptual learning and the theory of word perception". *Cognitive Psychology* 2: 351–368.

Han, Z. (2004). *Fossilization in Adult Second Language Acquisition*. Clevedon: Multilingual Matters.

Han, Z. (2003) "Fossilisation: from simplicity to complexity". *International Journal of Bilingual Education and Bilingualism* 6/2: 95–128.

Long, M. 2002. "Stabilization and fossilization in interlanguage development". In: Doughty, C. and M. Long (eds). *The Handbook of Second Language Acquisition*. Oxford: Blackwell: 487–535.

Osborne, J. (2004). “Articles and non-count nouns in learner English: perception and production”. In: Lewandowska-Tomaszczyk, B. (ed.). *PALC 2003*: 359–369.

Sorace, A. (2003). “Near-Nativeness”. In: Doughty, C. and M. Long (eds). *The Handbook of Second Language Acquisition*. Oxford: Blackwell: 130–151.

Todeva, E. (1992) “On fossilization in (S)LA theory”. In: Staub, D. and C. Delk (eds). *Proceedings of the Twelfth Second Language Research Forum*. Michigan State University: 216–254.

Agnieszka Leńko-Szymańska
Warsaw University

THE ROLE OF L1 INFLUENCE AND L2 INSTRUCTION IN THE CHOICE OF RHETORICAL STRATEGIES BY EFL LEARNERS

1. Background and rationale

The research reported in the paper is a by-product of a large scale project, whose aim is to compile and explore a Polish learner corpus of written English. The focus of the project is the description of the lexical command of advanced learners of English and the investigation into the process of second language vocabulary acquisition. In order to ensure a close comparability of the data, a section of the corpus contains student essays written in almost identical conditions and on the same topic. For comparative purposes the corpus also contains a batch of essays written on the same topic and in similar conditions by American native speakers of English.

However, during the process of coding the corpus data it was noticed that despite the fact that Polish and American essays were written on the same topic and in similar conditions, they differed greatly on the textual level. The differences concerned both the content of the compositions as well as the ways of expressing the content. Thus, the decision was made to pursue this observation in a more rigorous way.

The differences in the content of the Polish and American essays were examined in a different study (Leńko-Szymańska 2006). The research reported in this paper focuses on how native and non-native students differ in the ways of delivering the content, that is in the use of rhetorical strategies. Specifically, this study concentrates on the use of self-mention by the two groups of writers.

Before reporting on the study and discussing its results, the concept of metadiscourse is reviewed with a particular emphasis on the functions of I-reference in formal writing. Next, two possible factors influencing EFL performance – L1 transfer and L2 instruction – are briefly presented.

2. Propositional content and metadiscourse

Every discourse is about something, that is to say, it expresses propositions about some kind of reality. However, in addition to its propositional content every discourse contains the elements which do not refer to the reality outside the text, but concern the text itself, its author and its audience. This non-propositional content of discourse has been termed metadiscourse and can be broadly defined as 'the range of devices writers use to explicitly organise their texts, engage readers, and signal their attitudes to both their material and their audience' (Hyland and Tse 2004: 156). Thus, it can be said that metadiscourse is a set of linguistic resources which enable writers to manifest their existence and project their identity into the discourse.

Several detailed classifications of metadiscoursal resources have been advanced in the literature (e.g. Vande Kopple 1985, Crismore *et al.* 1993).The model adopted in this paper was proposed by Hyland (2000: 109–113) and it is summarised in Table 1 below.

Table 1. Categories of metadiscourse (Hyland 2000: 110)

textual metadiscourse	
logical connectives	express semantic relation between main clauses
frame markers	explicitly refer to discourse acts or text stages
endophoric markers	refer to information in other parts of the text
evidentials	refer to source of information from other texts
code glosses	help readers grasp meanings of ideational material
interpersonal metadiscourse	
hedges	withhold writer's full commitment to statements
boosters	emphasise force or writer's certainty in message
attitude markers	express the writer's attitude to propositional content
relational markers	explicitly refer to or build relationship with reader
person markers	explicit reference to the author(s)

3. I-reference as a rhetorical strategy

The study reported in this paper focuses on the class of person markers. This category includes first person singular and plural personal pronouns, possessive pronouns, reflexive pronouns and possessive adjectives (*I, we, me, us, mine, ours, myself, ourselves, my our*). It allows for the most visible manifestation of the writer's presence in a text (Petch-Tyson 1998, Tang and John 1999) since by choosing person markers writers make their existence explicit in discourse. However, while using first person reference the writer may also try to achieve other goals (2002, Ädel forthcoming). Tang and John (1999) claim that I-reference helps the writer construct his/her own identity as an author in a text and self-mention can signal one of several different identities the writer can assume. They list six possible identities the writer can take in academic writing:

- 'I' as the representative – the person who belongs to and identifies with a larger group of people. (This category in fact only covers the generic inclusive use of *we*.)
- 'I' as the guide through the essay – the person showing the reader through the text by locating the reader in time and place, drawing his/her attention to important points, or pointing to a conclusion.
- 'I' as the architect of the essay – the person who organises, structures, and outlines ideas and writes the text
- 'I' as the recounter of the research process – the person who conducted the research reported in the text
- 'I' as the opinion holder – the person who expresses opinions, views or attitudes towards the facts and ideas presented in the text
- 'I' as the originator – the person who forms new ideas or claims

The different identities of the author recognised by Tang and John can be associated with different levels of discourse. The identities of the guide and the architect clearly perform the metadiscoursal textual function helping the reader to see the purpose and the route through the text. The identities of the opinion holder and the originator belong to the interpersonal metadiscourse allowing the writer to express his/her stance. 'I' as the representative and particularly 'I' as the recounter contribute to the propositional content of the text by expressing the facts which belong to the external reality. Obviously, the decision of the author to emphasise his/her role in the description of the external reality has the metadiscoursal function, but, as it was observed by Hyland and Tse (2004), there usually is some overlap between the propositional and non-propositional components of discourse.

Ädel (forthcoming) also acknowledges that I-reference does not necessarily have to perform the metadiscoursal function. In argumentative essays authors can write about themselves as experiencers of the world or recount episodes from their own lives.

4. The model of writing in the EFL instruction

Most of the research on writers' use of self-mention is based on the analyses of academic writing. Studies compare the use of I-reference across different disciplines (Hyland 2001), or between professionals and non-native student writers (e.g. Tang and John 1999, Hyland 2002). Fewer studies focus on the use of I-reference in argumentative essays written by native and foreign language students (e.g. Petch-Tyson 1998, Ädel forthcoming)

Unlike in academic prose, students writing argumentative essays have little opportunity to use external sources and they have rarely conducted their own research to refer to. Thus, they have to rely on their world knowledge and personal experience and have more opportunities to express their stance. Such limitations of the genre should invite a more visible presence of the author in his/her work. On the other hand, the model of writing students are exposed to and taught explicitly, especially at the tertiary level of education, is academic writing, which has 'traditionally been thought as a convention-bound monolithic entity that involves distant, convolute and impersonal prose' (Tang and John 1999: S23). Therefore, it should be interesting to see how students manage to reconcile the influence of instruction with the demands and limitations of the writing task.

5. Writing as a culture-bound activity

A very important issue for the study reported in this paper is the influence of native culture on the writer's use of self-mention in argumentative writing. Such an assumption may be based on the fundamental claim underlying all research in the field of contrastive discourse analysis which says

> that language and writing are cultural phenomena. As a direct consequence, each language has rhetorical conventions unique to it. (Connor 1996: 5)

The differences in rhetorical conventions followed in different cultures can involve the use of metadiscourse. As Markkanen *et al.* (1993) state,

> [i]t can be assumed that the ways of using metadiscourse in writing may vary from one language to another, that the conventions followed in its use may be different in different cultures. (p. 138)

When writing in a foreign language learners may show a tendency to transfer not only the linguistic features of their native tongue but also its rhetorical conventions. These conventions can also pertain to the ways self-mention is used in the learners' first-language writing tradition.

The discrepancy between native and EFL writers in the use of I-reference has already been demonstrated by Petch-Tyson (1998), Hyland (2002) and Ädel (forthcoming). However, none of these studies involved a comparison of foreign language texts with the production of learners in their first language. Thus, so far it has not been proven beyond doubt that such a discrepancy is the result of transfer of rhetorical conventions from writers' native tradition to the production in a foreign language.

6. The aims of the study

The research reported in this paper aims to explore how Polish advanced learners of English use self-mention in argumentative writing. Specifically, the study is to investigate if there are any differences in the frequency and patterns of use of I-reference between Polish learners writing in L2 English and American students and experts writing in their first language. The study also attempts to trace possible sources of influence on the use of self-mention by Polish learners. L1 transfer and L2 instruction are considered as possible sources. This will be done by comparing the frequency and the patterns of self-mention by Polish and American writers writing in their native languages and by groups of learners at different stages of language proficiency and instruction in writing.

Due to space imitations, the analysis of the distribution of first person plural pronouns and adjectives has to be omitted and this paper will focus solely on the patterns of use of singular I-reference.

7. Data

The data used in the study was drawn from the PELCRA corpus, which is a collection of written data produced by Polish advanced learners of English. The corpus size approximates 800 thousand running words. It contains argumentative, descriptive, narrative and quasi-academic essays as well as formal letters written by students of English at the University of Łódź and its affiliated teacher training colleges as end-of-the-year exams or in-class assignments.

One section of the corpus contains 281 closely comparable essays written by university students of English in their first, second, third and fourth year of studies. The essays were written in almost identical conditions (as an in-class timed assignment) and on the same topic: "The mobile phone – the curse or the blessing of the end of the 20th century". The choice of the topic was fairly arbitrary, as the project aims are not related in any way to the study of attitudes or lexis pertaining to this particular area. The learner data from this section was selected for the purpose of this study. The essays were further divided into four subcorpora based on the students' year of studies. It was assumed that the four years correspond to four levels of proficiency.

It is worth mentioning that in addition to the instruction in British and American culture, literature and linguistics, students of English in Poland undergo a very intensive training in EFL. A very important part of this training is the development of learner's writing skills. Students are familiarised with different genres, exposed to model texts and offered style guides.

Two other corpora employed in the study comprise essays written by Polish and American students in their mother tongues. The American collection was already part of the PELCRA resources. It contains 81 essays written in similar conditions (in-class timed writing) and on the same topic as the learner compositions. The compositions were produced by freshman (first-year) and sophomore (second-year) non-English majors at South West University in Marshall, Minnesota. The Polish collection was compiled especially for the purpose of this study. It includes 90 essay written in Polish by secondary school students in their final two years. The essays were also written on the same topic as the learner and American compositions and in similar conditions.

Additionally, a corpus of 15 signed editorials taken from the special edition on mobile phones from the on-line version of the Guardian published on 11 November 2002 was used as a control of the native professional norm. The data were assumed to be the best match for the Polish, American and EFL essays in terms of genre comparability.

Thus, the total of seven small corpora were used in the study. The sizes of the corpora are presented in Table 2 below.

Table 2. Corpora used in the study

	Tokens	Texts
Learner1	29527	79
Learner2	28769	81
Learner3	21017	54
Learner4	29196	67
American	34875	81
Professional	17196	15
Polish	30141	90

8. Procedure

Corpus-based methodology was chosen in order to analyse the data. The analysis consisted of two steps: the quantitative and the qualitative one. First the frequencies of first person pronouns in the seven corpora were calculated and compared. This was followed by the scrutiny of concordance lines in search of characteristic patterns of use. These patterns were also correlated across the corpora.

The concordance package *Wordsmith Tools* (Scott 1999) was used to process the data. The search items for the English and Polish corpora were:

- I/I'*/me/my/mine/myself

and for Polish

- ja/mnie/mną/mój/moj*/moi* *ę/*am/*em/*bym

Polish abounds in inflections and at the same time it is a null-subject language, which means that self-mention can be marked not only through the use of pronouns, but also through verbal suffixes. That is why the list of Polish search items includes first person singular conjugational suffixes in addition to first person pronouns and their inflected forms. The concordance lines were examined manually in order to delete the hits which were not first-person pronouns or verbs.

9. Results and discussion

Table 3 presents the observed frequencies of self-mention in the seven corpora. Since the data collections were not equal in size, the frequencies were normalised per 10 thousand words.

The analysis of the frequencies in Table 3 already reveals a lot of interesting facts about the use of self-mention by Polish advanced learners of English. First of all, Polish learners of English use I-reference less frequently than their American counterparts and British professional writers. However, such underuse cannot be explained by transfer from the first language since Polish students writing in their mother tongue use self-reference even more frequently than the Anglo-Saxon writers.

Table 3. Frequencies of self-mention in the seven corpora

	Tokens	Absolute Freq	per 10,000
Learner1	29527	419	142
Learner2	28769	391	136
Learner3	21017	216	103
Learner4	29196	142	49
American	34875	706	202
Professional	17196	288	167
Polish	30141	731	243

It should be borne in mind that the frequencies of I-reference are not directly comparable. Each of the two languages allows for some degree of redundancy in person marking. In Polish the pronominal subject is frequently dropped but it can also be retained for stylistic reasons. Also in English one occurrence of self-mention can be marked twice, like in example 2 below:

(1) *I* was on *my* own, which was a mistake.

Thus, the frequencies in Table 3 cannot be interpreted as the numbers of discrete instances of self-reference in each corpus. Yet, it can be assumed that large disparities between the corpora are evidence of the differences in the use of self-mention by the groups of writers under study.

What can also be noticed in the analysis of data in Table 3 is that the frequency of self-mention in the EFL writing decreases with years of learning. This observation is quite surprising because it suggests that more advanced students in fact move away from the Anglo-Saxon norm. There are two possible explanations of this phenomenon. The first one suggests that the instruction which Polish EFL students receive promotes the standard of writing other than the one represented by the two native corpora. As it was already noted above, students at the tertiary level are predominantly exposed to the academic model of writing traditionally described as distant and impersonal. Another explanation is that the native corpora used in this study are not big enough to provide a full account of the Anglo-Saxon rhetorical conventions. This can be particularly true about the professional corpus since it is small (17 thousand words) and contains only 15 different texts, so the writers' personal style can have an enormous influence on the final results. More research is needed to find a satisfactory justification of the observed phenomenon. Yet, it should be noted that EFL writing clearly demonstrates the effects of instruction.

The frequencies presented in Table 3 can be compared with an earlier study conducted by Petch-Tyson (1998). She analysed several features of writer/reader visibility across four corpora of essays written by EFL students of different L1 backgrounds and a corpus of texts written by American students in their first language. The data were drawn for the International Corpus of Learner English (ICLE) and the comparable Louvain Corpus of Native English Essays (LOCNESS). The EFL texts forming the ICLE were written by students at approximately the same level of proficiency (third-year university students of English), and they are equivalent to the Learner3 and Learner4 corpora used in the present study. Table 4 below presents the frequencies of I-reference reported by Petch-Tyson and Table 5 contains these figures from the present study which are comparable with Petch-Tyson's results. For a more meaningful comparison, the frequencies for the Learner3 and Learner4 corpora were coalesced.

Table 4. Frequencies of 1st person singular pronouns in the ICLE and the LOCNESS (adapted from Petch-Tyson 1998:112)

	Tokens	Absolute Freq	per 10,000
Finnish	56910	599	105
Swedish	50872	448	88
Dutch	55314	391	71
French	58068	364	63
US	53990	167	31

Table 5. Frequencies of 1st person singular pronouns in the PELCRA corpus

	Tokens	Absolute Freq	per 10,000
Polish EFL	50213	358	71
American	34875	706	202

The comparisons of the data reveal that although there is some variation between the different EFL corpora, the frequencies of self-mention stay within the same range – from 63 per 10,000 words in the French collection to 105in the Finnish one. The Polish EFL frequency stays within this range and is identical with the Dutch results. This can be a further indication that the frequency of EFL learners' I-reference use is not influenced by L1 rhetorical conventions. However, such a conclusion needs further confirmation by an examination of equivalent native texts in each of the languages.

What is striking is the great disparity between the results of the American students in the two studies. Such a discrepancy can be explained by two factors: either by the incomparability of the text types in the two collections or by the effects of instruction. The American compositions analysed in the present study are typical argumentative essays written by novice writers right at the beginning of their university writing instruction. The texts were produced in class without prior preparation and with no access to secondary sources. Unfortunately, Petch-Tyson does not give detailed information about the makeup of her sample. Other sources (Ädel forthcoming) indicate that the LOCNESS is a much more heterogeneous collection containing compositions written in timed and untimed conditions and with or without access to secondary sources. Some texts are examples of academic writing whereas some others are argumentative essays. No information is available on the students who contributed their essays to the LOCNESS and about their exposure to writing instruction. Thus, the exact reason for a large difference in use of first person singular pronouns in the two collections of American essays cannot be established.

The next stage in the analysis was a scrutiny of concordance lines generated for each of the seven corpora. What could be immediately observed in the Polish L1 and EFL essays was the recurrence of a few fixed phrases containing first person singular pronouns. The repeated English chunks were: *I think, I believe, in my opinion and my (point of) view* and the Polish ones included: *uważam, myślę, sądzę* (all equivalent to *I think* and *I believe*) and *moim zdaniem* (equivalent to *in my opinion*). What is particularly interesting is that the recurrent phrases in English and Polish are direct translation equivalents. All of them are examples of interpersonal metadiscourse signalling the author's stance on the discussed issue. Therefore, the frequencies of these chunks were computed for each corpus and they are presented in Tables 6 and 7.

The data in Tables 6 and 7 clearly demonstrate that all the groups of apprentice writers (American, Polish and Polish EFL) use the fixed phrases including first person markers much more frequently than the professionals. This can indicate that apprentice texts contain more occurrences of interpersonal metadiscourse, but it can also be the case that expert writers use a wider and more subtle array of resources to mark their attitude to the discussed problem. The two hypothesis will be further explored below.

Table 6. Frequencies of the Polish recurring chunks

	(English equivalent)	**Polish**
uważam	(I believe)	77
moim zdaniem	(in my opinion)	28
myślę	(I think)	21
sądzę	(I think)	17
TOTAL % of all		143 19,56%

Table 7. Frequencies of the English recurring chunks

	Learner1	Learner2	Learner3	Learner4	Amer	Profess
I think	36	18	8	2	43	1
I believe	4	12	1	6	35	1
in my opinion	22	10	4	4	5	0
my (point of) view	9	4	0	2	1	0
TOTAL % of all	71 16,95%	44 11,25%	13 6,02%	14 9,86%	84 11,90%	2 0,69%

Another observation that can be made based on the analysis of the data in Tables 6 and 7 is that Polish texts show a higher recurrence of the stance phrases than the American apprentice texts. The frequently repeated chunks constitute almost 20% of all the instances of self-mention in the Polish corpus, compared to 12% in the American one. The frequencies of the repeated expressions in the EFL essays are also higher but only at the beginning of the university instruction. Then they diminish with years of learning and even drop below the American level moving towards the professional standard. However, it should be noted that even more advanced EFL students overuse the fixed stance expressions in comparison with the native norm. A similar observation was made by Ringbom (1998) who noticed a conspicuous overuse of the phrase *I think* by advanced EFL learners with seven different L1 backgrounds.

The frequencies of the recurrent phrases in the seven corpora may indicate that at the beginning of the tertiary education Polish EFL essays show strong evidence of L1 transfer in the patterns of use of self-mention. When writing in their first and foreign language Polish students tend to rely on a small set of fixed phrases to express their views. However, with years of learning, the instruction seems to counterbalance the effects of transfer. Yet, the instruction does not seem sufficient to teach students how to take advantage of metadiscourse resources used by professional writers to communicate their stance.

The concordance lines were further analysed qualitatively to validate one of the two hypotheses put forward above concerning possible causes of differences in the frequencies of fixed chunks in the seven corpora. It was suggested that either apprentice texts are richer in metadiscourse, or the professional writers use a wider range of metadiscoursal devices. Figures 1–5 below show samples of 10 concordance lines drawn randomly form five corpora used in the study: Learner 1, Learner 4, Polish and American and Professional. The lines containing metadiscoursal functions of I-reference are marked in italics.

1 l and I got used to the fact, that any time I want **I** can call my mom or my friends or even for an
2 *ether this addiction is something bad, but what **I** can say for sure is that any addiction is not ve*
3 on us by the devil. I, myself have got the cell so **I** know something about it from the horse's mou
4 *lf am not really found of mobile phones and thus **I** regard it a curse of the end of the 20th century*
5 *and that it can be harmful for human health but **I** think it is only a matter of keeping some balan*
6 *ot to mention their importance in our daily life. **I'm** of the opinion that it is difficult to imagine de*
7 tions. Once my mobile phone somehow helped me **my** car broke down and I didn't have the slig
8 *ll a blessing or a thing, I couldn't do without. For **me**, a mobile phone is an extremely useful thin*
9 *ry. Certainly teachers and lecturers can confirm **my** assumption since pupils using such device*
10 judged by having a mobile phone. If I ask **my** friends at classes whether they have a mob

Fig. 1. A sample of concordance lines from the Learner1 corpus

1 d write love confessions in an SMS form. I suppose **I** am old-fashioned but I would much more apprecia
2 *t in this case it is rather running faster than fashion **I** guess. Human beings have always sought for m*
3 nema. Sometimes it drives me crazy unless I really **I** have my own. On the one hand the mobile phone
4 ho simply wanted to show off. Today whenever **I** go I hear the rings. In the bus, at the tram stop, in the
5 ations and not limiting them to; "yes, I am fine and **I** love you. Bye ! Certainly, some would claim that
6 *wo people possess cellular phones. On the whole, **I** would like to say that mobile phones are a fantast*
7 *ing at a cell-phone as an intruder into a private life, **I** would recommend to read instructions carefully.*
8 *nding without a mobile in our pocket. What strikes **me** is to what extent we really need to know 'what*
9 some people choose as their 'somebody-is-calling-**me**' melodies. The others may not like the showing
10 n my friends wanted to contact me they had to call **my** aunt and ask about my schedule, or leave a m

Fig. 2. A sample of concordance lines from the Learner4 corpus

1 ne or someone could call you. Many people as did **I** ask why do you need a phone that would do anyt
2 *both upsides and downsides to mobile phones, but **I** feel the good out ways the bad. The level of con*
3 n the road you can call for help on your cell phone. **I** have heard of many stories, especially in our area
4 I found out on my phone I have over 100 numbers, **I** have voice mail I can have 30 different rings, I hav
5 *ates of America face an unspeakable evil or should **I** say "speakable evil". No, I am not talking about te*
6 *, classes, and they shouldn't even have them on. **I** think cell phones for the most part are good if the*
7 use of it by someone buying or ordering something. **I** waitress for one of my jobs and it gets to be quite
8 d them, they get them just to have one, just to say **I'm** fashionable because I have a cell phone. Cell
9 he other hand, I don't know what I would do without **mine**. It has come in so handy this year at college.
10 looking into getting one soon. For me, I purchased **my** first cell phone and plan when I was sixteen y

Fig. 3. A sample of concordance lines from the American corpus

1 , and nurses staring at me. But there wasn't a lot **I** could do about it. Someone took some photos
2 hich turned out to be the Kosovo Liberation Army. **I** decided to investigate with another cameraman,
3 be able to swim to shore because of the currents. **I** got my mobile out and called the coastguards.
4 from and heading to, and that I would phone when **I** made it safely across. But I never got that far.
5 *t which are now packaged together in one device. **I** am told it can also be used to speak to other hum*
6 I got my mobile out and called the coastguards. **I** was in a sea kayak, which has watertight comp
7 y, when some freak waves turned the canoe over. **I** was on my own, which was a mistake, but I wo
8 e wide world. "Soon after my arrival in the camp, **I** was told by neighbours of a man who had called
9 Jul: @club? [At the club?] Rom: OK [Thinks. **I'm** on, "gr8 6 2nite" - great sex tonight!!] The d
10 to be puzzled by my decision to put the phone in **my** inside jacket pocket, but I wasn't to know ho

Fig. 4. A sample of concordance lines from the Professional corpus

1 *czy 3, które uważają, że nie jest im potrzebna. A **ja** się cieszę, że ktoś wynalazł "komórkę" i nie prz*
2 porozumiewać się nawet na dużych odległościach. **Jestem** chyba jedną z niewielu osób na świecie, kt
3 *. Dla mnie telefon kom. jest błogosławieństwem, ale **mam** do tego wynalazku dystans. Dla kogoś, kto st*
4 względu na cenę), a reszta funkcji w moim telefonie **mnie** nie interesuje (a czasami też nie potrafię z nic
5 *to męczące. Jednak ja nie wyobrażam sobie teraz **mojego** życia bez telefonu komórkowego. Zawsze*
6 pacer do parku nie mam zagwarantowanego, że nie **napotkam** na swojej drodze posiadacza słynnej "ko
7 *ie niepotrzebne i wręcz utrudniające życie. A ja się **pytam**: dlaczego? Czy z powodu zbyt głośnych dz*
8 komórkowy i wielu wypadkach bardzo mi pomógł. **Staram** się używać go wtedy, kiedy jest na to miej
9 *nych jest w wibracje. Jest to bardzo pomocne. Nie **umiem** jednoznacznie powiedzieć, czy telefon kom*
10 zainstalować sobie stałe łącze z Internetem. Teraz **wysyłam** sms-y "za darmo" nie tracąc pieniędzy z

Fig. 5. A sample of concordance lines from the Polish corpus

As it can be seen from the samples above, professional texts contain practically no instances of metadiscoursal I-reference. Expert writers use self-mention almost exclusively in its ideational function in order to refer to and recount their personal experience. All the collections of apprentice essays, on the other hand, contain examples of both metadiscoursal and ideational uses of first person singular pronouns, even if in varying proportions. Following this observation it can be concluded that the explicit reference to the author as such in a text is characteristic of untrained style. Thus, the abundance of recurring expressions signalling stance in Polish, American and EFL texts is a manifestation of a more general tendency of apprentice writers to explicitly mark their identity as authors.

It should also be noted that, as in the case of stance expressions, there is a difference in the frequency of metadiscoursal I-reference in the Polish and American L1 essays which can point to the discrepancy in the rhetorical conventions between the two cultures concerning the amount of metadiscourse expected in a text. Furthermore, the EFL production demonstrates a complex relationship between L1 transfer and instruction effects in the patterns of self-mention use. While first-year students use I-reference in its metadiscoursal function as frequently as the Polish native writers, four-year students are close to the American patterns of distribution.

Yet, it has to be borne in mind, that the conclusions above are based on the qualitative examination of concordance lines. A quantitative analysis of the data was not performed in this study, so the explanations remain speculation requiring further investigation. However, the results of similar studies involving EFL learners of other L1 backgrounds can bring a wider perspective on the investigated issue. Ädel (forthcoming) demonstrated that Swedish EFL writers use a much higher proportion of personal metadiscourse than both American and British apprentice writers. Similarly, Petch-Tyson (1998) observed that Swedish, French, Dutch and (to a lesser extent) Finnish advanced EFL learners use fewer first person singular pronouns in their ideation function in comparison with American apprentice writers, who exploit I-reference mainly to recount their personal experience. Moreover, in French, Dutch and Swedish data the main function of self-mention is to refer to the author as such. The results of these two studies can indicate that either Anglo-Saxon rhetorical conventions differ substantially from those of other European writing traditions in the economical use of personal discourse (and EFL writers tend to transfer their L1 strategies when writing in English), or a frequent reference to the author as such is a general strategy used by all learners when writing in L2. The comparison of Polish and American L1 essays can be interpreted as evidence in support of the former explanation, yet more research is necessary to resolve this question beyond doubt.

10. Conclusions

Self-reference is an important pragmatic feature. It allows writers to organise their texts, to signal their stance and to gain credibility for expressed propositions by referring to their personal experience. Yet, different genres and different disciplines have their own convention of the author's visibility in a text. What is more, "disciplinary conventions are enabling rather than deterministic, and typical patterns of self-mention only provide broad parameters of choice" (Hyland 2001: 224). By making a conscious decision about the degree of their presence in a text writers construct their own identity as authors. For that reason, the patterns of use of I-reference vary not only across genres but also among writers.

In that context, the examination of EFL learners' performance becomes a difficult task. The results of the analysis depend to a large extent on a sample of L1 texts chosen as a benchmark for comparison. This can explain why the study reported in this paper has yielded many tentative conclusions and speculations requiring further investigation. However, while the interpretation of the frequency of personal pronouns in EFL texts remains an open question, a few facts concerning the preferred functions of I-reference by EFL and L1 writers have been demonstrated. First, Polish EFL learners tend to transfer the patterns of self-mention use from their mother tongue. Specifically, they tend to employ metadiscoursal I-reference more frequently than their native-speaking counterparts and they show a heavier reliance on a small set of fixed phrases to mark their stance. Second, instruction in writing exerts its influence on EFL learners' self-mention use, and with years of learning they come closer to the patterns demonstrated by American apprentice writers. Third, instruction does not seem to be sufficient to teach EFL students expert practices concerning the conventions of self-reference use.

The study offers important implications for teaching. It proves that style guides presented to EFL learners are often inaccurate and misleading. They encourage students to use impersonal language in their writing, failing to account for the functions and the effects of I-reference, and for a possible scope for variation. They also ignore cultural differences in self-mention usage which can be a source of transfer. It is only with a deeper understanding of these intricacies that EFL learners' written production can become more native-like, more expert and, above all, more effective.

REFERENCES

Ädel, A. (forthcoming). "Metadiscourse across three varieties of English: American, British and advanced learner English." In: Connor, U., E. Nagelhout and W. Rozycki (eds). *From Contrastive to Intercultural Rhetoric*. Amsterdam: John Benjamins.

Connor, U. (1996). *Contrastive Rhetoric: Cross-cultural Aspects of Second Language Writing*. Cambridge: Cambridge University Press.

Crismore, A., R. Markkanen and M. S. Steffensen (1993). "Metadiscourse in persuasive writing: A study of texts written by American and Finnish university students." *Written Communication*, 10: 39–71.

Hyland, K. (2000). *Disciplinary Discourses: Social Interactions in Academic Writing*. London: Longman.

Hyland, K. (2001). "Humble servants of the discipline? Self-mention in research articles." *English for Specific Purposes*, 20: 207–226.

Hyland, K. (2002). "Authority and invisibility: Authorial identity in academic writing." *Journal of Pragmatics*, 39: 1091–1112.

Hyland, K. and P. Tse (2004). "Metadiscourse in academic discourse: a reappraisal." *Applied Linguistics*, 25: 156–177.

Leńko-Szymańska, A. (forthcoming). "The curse and the blessing of mobile phones – a corpus-based study into American and Polish rhetorical conventions". In: Wilson, A., D. Archer and P. Rayson (eds). *Corpus Linguistics Around the World*. Amsterdam–New York, NY: Rodopi.

Markkanen, R., M. Steffensen and A. Crismore (1993). "Quantitative contrastive study of metadiscourse: Problems in design and analysis of data." *Papers and Studies in Contrastive Linguistics*, 28: 137–152.

Petch-Tyson, S. (1998). "Writer/reader visibility in EFL written discourse." In: Granger, S. (ed.). *Learner English on Computer*. London and New York: Longman: 107–118.

Ringbon, H. (1998). "Vocabulary frequencies in advanced learner English: a cross-linguistic approach." In: Granger, S. (ed.). *Learner English on Computer*. London and New York: Longman: 41–52.

Scott, M. (1999). *Wordsmith Tools. Version 3.0.* Oxford: Oxford University Press.

Tang, R. and S. John (1998). "The 'I' in identity: Exploring writer identity in student academic writing through the first person pronoun." *English for Specific Purposes*, 18: S23–S39.

Vande Kopple, W. J. (1985). "Some exploratory discourse on metadiscourse." *College Composition and Communication*, 26: 82–93.

Kanyarat Getkham

National Institute of Development Administration, Bangkok

THE EFFECTS OF USING THE MULTIMEDIA COMPUTER PROGRAM ON VOCABULARY ACQUISITION AND RETENTION

1. Introduction

Vocabulary knowledge is a key for successful second or foreign language (L2 or FL) learning. Several studies have proved that it is basic to the development of second or foreign language proficiency (Ellis 2001; Groot 2000). It is also basic to communication and often seen as the greatest source of problems by second or foreign language students (Krashen 1989).

For many years, foreign language teachers have used CALL applications to provide supplemental exercises. Advances in computer technology have motivated teachers to use computers in their instruction and many of these teachers consider it a valuable part of daily foreign language learning. Innovative software programs, authoring capabilities, compact disk technology, and elaborate computer networks are providing teachers with new tools to encourage students to improve their vocabulary knowledge and vocabulary retention (Farmer 2001). Moreover, the students' role in learning has dramatically changed and they have become more active learners. They tend to form their own knowledge instead of just receiving information from teachers (McDonough 2001; Tapscott 1998). In addition, Foreman (2004) reports that game-based learning increases motivation and engagement and thereby improves learning opportunities.

The researcher believes that the findings in this current study will shed light on the issue of using multimedia computer programs, including game-based learning exercises, and how these programs can enhance students' vocabulary acquisition and retention. The findings also can contribute to our understanding how the use of technology affects the L2 learning process and may help teachers decide whether or not to include CALL applications in the L2 learning process, especially at the graduate level.

2. Historical perspective

Second Language (L2) Vocabulary Acquisition and Retention

Second language vocabulary acquisition can be defined as the way in which people learn target vocabularies other than their mother tongue vocabularies inside or outside of a classroom Ellis 2001; Hulstijn *et al.* 1996 (cited in Reongmanee 2001) approached two concepts of vocabulary learning: intentional and incidental. Intentional vocabulary learning occurs when students wish to learn new words for a specific purpose and make a conscious effort to do so. In this type of learning, the students use mental effort to memorize the words until comprehension occurs. Thus, it is claimed that intentional vocabulary learning is more effective for retention than incidental vocabulary learning (Koren 1999).

Conversely, incidental vocabulary learning occurs without conscious effort. Students learn without a plan nor a specific intention to learn new words (Hulstijn *et al.* 1996; cited in Reongmanee 2001). According to Laufer and Hill (2000), incidental vocabulary is learned as a by-product of other activities, such as reading or communication. For example, during the reading activity, unknown words are looked up in a dictionary in order to understand the text and to perform comprehension assignments. Consequently, some new words are remembered even though the main task was not vocabulary related, nor was it the reader's intention to learn new words in the text. Learning was thus incidental or unintentional.

Channell (1998; cited in Nikolova 2002) presents a theory about the active role of learners in the process of vocabulary acquisition. It is stated that the associations between form and meaning of unknown lexical items, either during guessing or checking of meaning in reference sources (marginal glosses or dictionary), lead to successful L2 vocabulary acquisition. Therefore, students should be encouraged to make their own lexicological associations when they are actively learning new vocabulary. The deliberate act of checking a guessed meaning in the dictionary brings positive reinforcement. It also allows for a longer manipulation of the form and the correct word meaning, which most likely leads to the associations.

In addition, several L2 vocabulary instruction studies conclude that when word meanings are provided (either by bilingual dictionary use or by marginal glosses), recall is enhanced (Davis 1989; Knight 1994; cited in Grace 1998).

The Effect of CALL on Vocabulary Acquisition and Retention

CALL has been integrated in the language curriculum for decades. It is claimed that students who gain expertise in task-based computer environments can experience an increase in self-confidence and status amongst their peers. According to Brown (1994) and Ellis (2001), confidence is an essential element of L2 acquisition. Moreover, Lockhart and Craik (1990) asserted that using a multimedia computer program in language learning can lead to better encoding and better information retention. In addition, Hill (1998) stated that the advantage of CALL on vocabulary learning is that students can set their own learning pace. They can also hear the words repeatedly and test themselves as often as they wish. Provided that the exercises and texts are presented in a clear and interesting manner, students are generally more motivated toward autonomous learning. Furthermore, computers can provide excellent support and reinforcement of the learning process.

Several studies were conducted to investigate the effect of CALL on vocabulary learning. Some investigated the effects of dictionary use and look-up behavior of readers on vocabulary learning or reading comprehension by using computerized dictionaries in their studies (e.g., Chun and Plass 1996; Hulstijn 1993; Knight 1994). Several studies using computer-mediated texts with glossaries demonstrated the positive effects of electronic glossaries on vocabulary learning or reading comprehension (Al-Seghayer 2001; Aust *et al.* 1993; Grace 1998; Groot 2000; Koren 1999; Leffa 1992; Nikolova 2002; Reongmanee 2001; Svenconis and Kerst 1995; cited in Hill 1998). These studies reported the positive effect of multimedia computer programs on vocabulary knowledge. With regard to the recall of vocabulary information, numerous studies revealed that a combination of several media (picture, text, and sound) enhances retention and recall(Chun and Plass 1996; Fendrich *et al.* 1995; Grace 1998; Groot 2000; Koren 1999; Laufer and Hill 2000; Leffa 1992; Lockhart and Craik 1990; Nikolova 2002; Reongmanee 2001; Svenconis and Kerst 1995). Moreover, students learning vocabulary through a multimedia computer program are more motivated since the program includes several types of games. According to Foreman (2004), game-based learning increases motivation and engagement and thereby improves learning opportunities.

Errors in Writing

L2 students sometimes make errors or mistakes. According to Corder (1981), mistakes are the result of some failure of performance. These may contain what are often called slips of the tongue, false starts, and changes of mind. The noticeable thing about mistakes is that they are normally readily self-corrected or correctable by the writer.

In addition, Ellis (1994) proposed that a mistake is what the student knows but is still unable to perform correctly. On the contrary, an error is a gap in a student's knowledge. It occurs because the student does not know what is correct in the target language.

Errors are considered as things that occur with L2 students who do not have full command of a system yet. It is systematic, and reveals the student's underlying knowledge of language. A mistake, on the other hand, refers to failure to use a known system correctly. It can be self-corrected. An error may occur from memory lapses, physical states and psychological conditions (Ellis, 1994), mother tongue interference, overgeneralization of the rules, or inadequate mastery of grammar (Burt and Kiparsky 1972).

According to Ellis (1994), an error can be classified into two categories: global and local errors. He states that global errors violate an overall structure of a sentence and may make it difficult to process. On the other hand, local errors affect only minor constituents in the sentence and are less likely to create any processing problems.

Burt and Kiparsky (1972) used the distinction between global and local errors as a theoretical base for developing taxonomy of student writing errors. A global error causes native speakers to misinterpret meaning or consider the meaning incomprehensible within the total context of the error. On the other hand, a local error makes a sentence appear ungrammatical but causes little or no difficulty in understanding the underlying intended meaning of a sentence, given its contextual framework. Moreover, Burt and Kiparsky divided global and local errors into subcategories. They are the misuse or omission of English lexicon, morphology, syntax, and orthography. The subcategory of lexicon includes misuse or omission of nouns, verbs, adjectives or adverbs. The subcategory of morphology includes such items as the misuse or omission of required bound morphemes such as *ed (in played, used), un_* (in incomprehensible etc.). The syntactic subcategory consists of misuse or omission of determiners, modals, qualifiers, prepositions, conjunctions, subordinates, connectors, or question words. The last subcategory of orthography consists of addition, omission or rearrangement of letter(s) in any lexical, morphological or syntactic form of structure.

As stated, errors committed by students in their writing indicates a stage in the learning process. It provides English teachers with guidelines for improving remedial teaching programs. These errors occur from different sources.

According to Ancker (2000), one obvious cause is interference from the native language. Students may make errors because they assume that the target language and their native language are similar, whereas in fact they are different.

Another obvious cause is incomplete knowledge of the target language during the learning process. Moreover, the complexity of the target language is a common cause of errors. Several studies supported this notion (Duskava (1995, cited in Abdulsata 2000; Khamput 2004; Kubota (2002); Rujikiatgumjorn and Chiewkul 1987; Wang and Wen (2002); Woodall 2002).

In addition, Myles (2002) points out that errors in L2 writing derive from social and cognitive factors. One social factor is student attitude toward the target language. In classroom observation, she found that there is a direct relationship between students' attitude and motivation. If learners show an overall interest in the target language (integrative motivation) and have a desire to achieve their professional goals (instrumental motivation), they can become more proficient in their ability to write in English. Another social factor is the lack of progress in L2. Much interaction is needed if learners are to progress. If they lack interaction with native speakers, little progress will be achieved. A third social factor is a wide social and psychological distance between students and the target culture. Finally, a lack of integrative and instrumental motivation for learning is one of the causes of committing errors.

3. Research Methodology

Subjects

At the beginning, 75 part-time graduate students from the MA in Language and Communication program voluntarily participated in the study. These students were enrolled in the first semester of academic year 2004. Forty students were enrolled in the Multimedia for Language and Communication course while the other thirty-five students were not. The researcher randomly assigned twenty-five students from the multimedia class to the experimental group and twenty-five from the other class to the control group.

The significant difference between the two group in terms of average pretest scores was not found ($t = 1.53$, $P = 1.34$). Thus, it was assumed that their prior knowledge of the selected vocabulary is similar.

Instrumentation

The six instruments used in this study were the pretest, the immediate posttest, the delayed posttest, the Triple Play Plus Program, the printed text, and the questionnaire.

Pretest, Immediate Posttest, and Delayed Posttest

These tests were developed to test the subjects' vocabulary knowledge and recall of the vocabulary information. The vocabulary test had 20 pictures. All of these pictures were selected based on the difficulty index. The test required subjects to fill in the blanks with the word corresponding to each picture. The total score for this test was 20 points. The immediate posttest and the delayed posttest had identical items but were rearranged in different orders.

Triple Play Plus Program

The Triple Play Plus English comes on a CD-ROM. This software package is a multimedia language tool designed for EFL or ESL students. It has been used successfully by students who enrolled in the Multimedia for Language and Communication course. The program offers game-based exercises in six subject areas (food, numbers, home and office, places and transportation, people and clothing, and daily activities). In this study, the researcher asked the subjects to practice vocabulary in three subject areas: food and drink, home and office, and people and clothing. The software allows students to practice aural comprehension, reading, and speech recognition. There are drill-and-practice vocabulary exercises, more complex games relating to verbs, tenses, prepositions, and other subjects; and comic-strip conversations built around everyday activities. After choosing a mode (aural comprehension, reading, or speech recognition) and a subject, students choose a game and begin to play. Several games such as Concentration, Memory Mania, Bingo and Square Off were provided. The goal of many of the games is to teach and reinforce vocabulary. Within some games, the software also offers students different levels of difficulty at which to play the game. So this software encourages students to work at their own pace.

Traditional Printed Text

The traditional printed text was developed from the Triple Play Plus software package. It consisted of 75 pictures in three subject areas, identical to those presented in the multimedia computer program except that there were no games to play with. In the text, a word corresponding to each picture was provided for students to practice.

The Questionnaire

The questionnaire was developed to collect subject's demographic data including name, age, GPA, major field of study, and type of university from which they graduated.

Data Collection

The data collection took place from August 19th to October 20th, 2004. One week before the experiment, subjects in both groups were given the pretest which lasted 20 minutes. Their pretest scores were recorded. They were also asked to complete the questionnaire. The experimental group was asked to practice vocabulary exercises using a multimedia computer program for two months while the control group was asked to learn the same words using the printed text for the same duration. Both groups were advised that they would be tested after two months. At the end of the experiment, they were given the immediate posttest. The scores from this administration of the immediate posttest were used to obtain data on vocabulary knowledge. One month after that, they were given the delayed posttest to obtain data on the recall of vocabulary information. The scores from the two tests and the mistakes made by the subjects were analyzed.

Data Analysis

Data were analyzed using paired-sample t-tests, independent sample t-tests, Pearson Correlation, and Multiple regression analysis.

Results

The results can be summarized as follow:

1. The comparison between the vocabulary knowledge and the recall of vocabulary information for each group revealed that students using the printed text could not recall vocabulary very well.
2. Students in both groups improved their vocabulary knowledge after practicing vocabulary exercises for two months. However, the students using the printed text outperformed those using the multimedia computer program in short-term retention.
3. When tested for recall of vocabulary information, students using the multimedia computer program outperformed those using the printed text.

Apparently, the multimedia computer program enhanced long-term retention.

4. Students in both groups had three sources of errors: misspelling, lack of plural markers, and use of wrong words. However, a difference between the students using the printed text and the students using the multimedia computer program occurred in the immediate posttest. Those using the printed text made many more errors relating to the use of wrong words.
5. Of the four predictors (age, GPA, major field of study, and type of university), none was a good predictor of vocabulary knowledge or recall of vocabulary information. However, correlations indicated that subjects who were more proficient in English could gain and retain more vocabulary information than those who were less proficient.
6. Subjects whose majors were language or communication tended to be younger than those whose majors were not language or communication.

Discussion

This discussion relates to improvement of vocabulary knowledge and recall of vocabulary information, errors in vocabulary writing, predictors of vocabulary knowledge and vocabulary information, and relationships among variables under investigation.

Improvement in vocabulary knowledge and the recall of vocabulary information

Both groups of students improved their vocabulary knowledge after they practiced vocabulary for two months; however, students using the printed text outperformed the students using the multimedia computer program in vocabulary knowledge. These findings revealed that printed text accompanied by pictures could better enhance short-term retention. Students using the printed text may have concentrated more on the target words because they they did not have as much time to practice as the students using the multimedia computer program and who were enrolled in the Multimedia for Language and Communication course. This finding was consistent with the studies of Knight (1994) and Koren (1999) which found that students studying vocabulary intentionally outperformed those studying vocabulary incidentally.

With regard to the recall of vocabulary information, students using the multimedia computer program could recall better than those using the printed text. The finding was consistent with several studies (Chun and Plass 1996; Fendrich *et al.* 1995; Grabe and Stoller 1997; Grace 1998; Koren 1999; Laufer and Hill 2000; Leffa 1992; Lockhart and Craik 1990; Nikolova 2002; Reongmanee 2001; Svenconis and Kerst 1995). These studies revealed that a combination of several media (picture, text, and sound) enhances retention and recall. Moreover, students learning vocabulary through a multimedia computer program are more motivated since the program includes several types of games. According to Foreman (2004), game-based learning increases motivation and engagement and thereby improves learning opportunities. The computer program provided excellent support and reinforcement of the learning process.

Errors in Vocabulary Writing

Three sources of errors: misspelling, lack of plural markers, and using wrong words were found in this study. Students in both groups made similar errors in the two posttests. However, the students using the printed text used wrong words more than those using the multimedia computer program. In general, the students in this study were confused by the substitution of raincoat by a coat, sneakers by shoes, and interchangeably used beans and peas.

With regard to using a coat for a raincoat, it is common in Thai to refer to any clothes worn to cover a regular outfit as a coat. The use of shoes for sneakers is similar in that in Thai the word "rong tao" is used as a general term to refer to anything worn on the feet (shoes). Modifiers can be used to identify different types of shoes; for example, "rong tao gee la" refers to sport shoes (gee la = sport); "rong tao taa" refers to casual shoes with rubber soles (sneakers). This explains why the students used shoes (rong tao) when they did not know the word for sneakers. It is obvious that culture plays an important role in language.

There are no plural forms in Thai language. Plurality is expressed by adding "nouns of multitude" or classifiers in the form of noun-number-classifier. For example, when a Thai wants to refer to seven singers, she will use "singers seven persons". In English, such classifiers are usually absent (five boxes) or optional (two glasses of milk or two milks). In Thai, a classifier is almost always used (milk two glasses). Lack of plural markers in this study was certainly influenced by mother tongue interference. The finding confirmed that L1 interference is the cause of errors (Abdulsata 2000; Ancker 2000; Carl 1998; Duskava 1995, Ellis 2001; Khamput 2004; and Widdowson 1996).

Predictors of Vocabulary Knowledge and Recall of Vocabulary Information

Age, GPA, background knowledge, and type of university from which the subject graduated were not good predictors of vocabulary knowledge and recall of vocabulary information. This might be due to the design of the study. The researcher did not consider these variables when assigning the subjects to each treatment.

Relationships among Pretest, Immediate Posttest, Delayed Posttest, Age, GPA, Student's Major, Type of University Graduated, Vocabulary Knowledge, and Recall of Vocabulary Information

In this study, the pretest scores significantly correlated with the delayed posttest scores and the immediate posttest scores highly correlated with the delayed posttest scores. It was obvious that students who were more proficient in English could gain more vocabulary knowledge and could recall more vocabulary information than those who were less proficient. This finding was consistent to Kubota's study (2002) in that English proficiency played an important role in the target language performance of L2 students.

Conclusions

Theorists and practitioners propose that multimedia computer programs can enhance vocabulary acquisition and retention. Empirical studies report the effects on vocabulary learning and recall from the use of multimedia computer programs. This study was conducted to broaden the research base beyond examination of empirical research and to see whether findings can be generalized to other groups. In this study, a comparison is made between two groups; one group using a multimedia computer program and the other one using a traditional printed text.

Results from the comparison of three tests indicated that those subjects using printed text achieved significantly different scores on the immediate posttest and the delayed posttest. In contrast, in the group using the multimedia computer program, significant differences were not found among the three tests. Furthermore, a comparison of the scores for the three tests between the two groups indicated that the group using the printed text outperformed the group using the multimedia computer program in short-term retention.

However, with regard to the recall of vocabulary information, both groups were the same. Both groups forgot vocabulary information but a comparison of the decreases in the immediate posttest scores with those of the delayed posttest scores revealed that the scores of students using the multimedia computer program decreased less than the scores of students using the printed text. Thus, it appears that the use of a multimedia computer program can enhance long-term retention.

Sources of errors included misspelling, lack of plural markers, and use of wrong words. However, in the immediate posttest, the printed text group made more errors than those in the multimedia computer group.

In terms of predictors of vocabulary knowledge and recall of vocabulary information, it appears that student's age, GPA, background knowledge, and type of university from which they graduated were not good predictors. However, there are relationships among the scores on the pretest, the immediate posttest, and the delayed posttest as well as between age and background knowledge. Students who were more proficient in English were able to learn more vocabulary and could recall more vocabulary information. Younger students tended to major in language or communication.

Implications

Given the findings from this study, the following implications can be drawn for classroom practice and for further research.

Implications for Instruction

The findings of this study support the assertion that a multimedia computer program can enhance long-term memory. It was obvious that students using the multimedia computer program can recall better than those using traditional printed text. Thus, teachers should integrate a multimedia computer program into language learning to enhance long-term retention as this is the ultimate goal of the language learning process. If a computer program is not available for some reason, traditional printed text including pictures can also be used to facilitate vocabulary learning because visual input plays an important role in vocabulary learning. However, this method does not appear to enhance long term retention of vocabulary information. Moreover, emphasis needs to be given to spelling, plural markers, and confused words in vocabulary writing.

Implications for Future Research

More studies should be conducted to allow for greater generalization of results and to provide better understanding of how software can be developed and used best in CALL environments. Also, to identify more clearly what students learn from computer assisted vocabulary activities. Those studies should include:

1. Subjects from different educational levels, different language backgrounds, and different geographic areas
2. The use of other subject areas in the Triple Play Plus program or other multimedia computer programs
3. The grouping of subjects according to factors used in this study
4. Academic vocabulary instead of daily life vocabulary
5. Different language tasks such as writing, reading, listening, speaking, or translation
6. A comparison of incidental and intentional vocabulary learning.

REFERENCES

Abdulsata, P. (2000). *An error analysis of second year English major students' compositions*. An independent study report for the Master of Arts in English, Graduate School, Srinakharinwirot University.

Al-Seghayer, K. (2001). "The effects of multimedia annotation modes on L2 vocabulary acquisition: A comparative study". *Language Learning and Technology*, 5: 202–232.

Ancker, W. (2000). *Errors and corrective feedback: Updated theory and classroom practice*. Retrieved August 7, 2004, from http://exchanges.stste.gov/forum/vols/vol38/no.4/p.20htm.

Aust, R., Kelly, M. J. and W. Roby (1993). "The use of hyper-reference and conventional dictionaries". *Educational Technology Research and Development*, 41(4): 63–73.

Brown, D. (1994). *Principles of language learning and teaching* (2nd ed.). Englewood Cliffs, NJ: Prentice-Hall.

Burt, M. and C. Kiparsky (1972). "Global and local mistakes". In: Shumann, J. H. and N. Stenson (eds). *New frontiers in second language learning*. Rowley, MA: Newbury House: 67–85.

Chun, D. M. and J. L. Plass (1996). "Effects of multimedia annotations on vocabulary acquisition". *Modern Language Journal*, 80: 183–198.

Corder, S. (1981). *Error analysis and interlanguage*. Oxford: Oxford University Press.

Ellis, R. (1994). *Second language acquisition*. Oxford: Oxford University Press.

Ellis, R. (2001). *Learning vocabulary in another language*. Cambridge: Cambridge University Press.

Farmer, A. (2001). "Human factors in computing: The influence of multimodal design upon long-term L2 vocabulary retention". *Traffic*, 1: 82–102.

Fendrich, D. W., Gesi, A. T., Healy, A. F. and L. E. Bourne (1995). "The Contribution of procedural reinstatement to implicit and explicit memory effects in a motor task". In: Healy, A. F. and L. E. Bourne (eds). *Learning and memory of knowledge and skills: durability and specificity*. Thousands Oaks, CA: Sage Publications: 30–65.

Foreman, J.(2004). "Game-based learning: How to delight and instruct in the 21st century". *EDUCAUSE Review*, 39 (5): 50–66.

Grace, C. (1998). "Retention of word meanings inferred from context and sentence – level translations: implications of the design of beginning-level CALL software". *The Modern Language Journal*, 82(4): 533–544.

Groot, P. (2000). "Computer assisted second language vocabulary acquisition". *Language Learning & Technology*, 4(1): 60–81. Retrieved September 10, 2004 from http://llt.msu.edu/vol4num1/groot/

Hill, M. M. (1998). "A Word in your Ear: vocabulary acquisition by Chinese tertiary students". In: Bird, N., Falvey, P., Tsui, A. B. M., Alison, D. M. and A. McNeill (eds). *Language and Learning*. Hong Kong: Government Printer.

Hulstijn, J. H. (1993). "When do foreign-language readers look up the meaning of unfamiliar words? The influence of task and learner variables". *Modern Language Annals*, 14: 415–422.

Khamput, P. (2004). First language interference on second language writing of Mattayomsuksa 5 students. An independent study report for the Master of Arts in English, Graduate School, Khon Kaen University.

Krashen, S. (1989). "We acquire vocabulary and spelling by reading: Additional evidence for the input hypothesis". *The Modern Language Journal*, 73: 440–464.

Koren, S. (1999). "Vocabulary instruction through hypertext: Are there advantages over conventional methods of teaching?". *TESL-EJ*, 4 (1): 25–42.

Kubota, R. (2002). "An investigation of L1-L2 transfer in writing among Japanese university students: Implications for contrastive rhetoric". *Journal of Second Language Writing*, 7(1): 69–100. Retrieved June 30, 2005 from http://www.sciencedirect.com

Laufer, B., and M. Hill (2000). "What lexical information do L2 learners select in a CALL dictionary and how does it affect word retention?". *Language Learning and Technology*, 3(2). Retrieved December 6, 2003, from http://llt.msu.edu/vol3num2/laufer-hill/index.html

Leffa, V. J.(1992). "Making foreign language texts comprehensible of beginners: An experiment with an electronic glossary". *System*, 20: 63–73.

Lockhart, R. S. and F. Craik (1990). "Levels of processing: A retrospective commentary on a framework for memory research". *Canadian Journal of Psychology*, 44: 87–111.

McDonald, S. (2001). "Way beyond drill and practice: foreign language lab activities in support of constructivist learning". *International Journal of Instructional Media*, 28(1): 75–81.

Myles, J. (2002). "Second language writing and research: The writing process and error analysis in student texts". *TESL-EJ*, 6: 1–20.
Nikolova, R. (2002). "Effects of student' participation in authoring of multimedia materials on student acquisition of vocabulary". *Language Learning and Technology*, 6(1). Retrieved December 30, 2003, from http://llt.msu.edu/vol6num1/nikolova/index.html
Reongmanee, R. (2001). *The effects of computer-assisted language learning on vocabulary acquisition and reading comprehension of Thai employees at a multinational company: a case study of Allegiance Healthcare (Thailand) Limited, Rayong, Thailand.* An independent study report for the Master of Art in Language and Communication, the National Institute of Development Administration, Bangkok, Thailand.
Rujikiatgumjorn, S. and S. Chiewkul (1987). *An error analysis of English language performance of 1987 KKU freshmen students.* An independent study report for the Master of Arts in English, Graduate School, Khon Kaen University, Khon Kaen, Thailand.
Tapscott, D. (1998). *Growing up digital: The rise of the net generation.* New York: McGraw-Hill.
Wang, L. and Q. Wen (2002). "L1 use in the L2 composing process: An exploratory study of 16 Chinese EFL writers". *Journal of Second Language Writing*, 11(3): 225–246. Retrieved June 30, 2005 from http://www.science direct.com.
Widdowson, H. G. (1996). *Linguistics.* Oxford: Oxford University Press.
Woodall, R. B. (2002). "Language-switching: Using the first language while writing in a second language". *Journal of Second Language Writing*, 11: 7–28. Retrieved June 30, 2005 from http://www.sciencedirect.com.

Somsak Boonsathorn[1]

National Institute of Development Administration, Bangkok

C-TESTS REVISITED: A VALIDATION OF SEMANTIC/SYNTACTIC TESTS (S-TESTS) FOR ADVANCED STUDENTS[2]

Abstract

The C-Test is a format of the cloze procedure proposed by Raatz and Klein-Braley (1981) to resolve the problems facing the systematic deletion cloze test. Each C-Test usually employs four to six short passages (50–100 words each) in order to avoid content bias. In each passage the second half of every second word is deleted except for words in the first and last sentence. These two sentences are left without deletions. The total number of deletions will be at least 100. The test taker's task is to read and complete the missing part of each word.

Since many English words (specifically, content words – nouns, verbs, adjectives and adverbs) are in the form of BASE + SUFFIX (ES), the first half and the second half of the word must be essentially different. While there is normally more semantic information in the first half, there will be more syntactic/structural information in the second half. A modified C-Test, the MC-Test, in which the first half of the word is deleted, was then developed by the author (Boonsathorn 1987) and the results compared with those obtained from the original C-Test. The results indicate that the MC-Test is superior to the C-Test with respect to discrimination power, reliability, and "structural" validity.

---

[1] E-mail: somsakb@nida.nida.ac.th or bsomsak89@yahoo.com

[2] The author is grateful to the NIDA Research Promotion Endowment Fund for granting a research fellowship (April 1999 to March 2000) in support of the original research project entitled "A Validation of S-Tests: Rational C-Tests," on which the data in this paper are based. He would also like to thank Ms. Patchara Wonghiransombat, Ms. Thitirat Thongsa-nga, and Ms. Sudarat Patarathaworn, his research assistants; Mr. Jeff Durand and Mr. David Rogers, who made valuable suggestions; and all the students who participated and gave him their honest reactions. His appreciation is also extended to NIDA for supporting him to participate in this international conference.

Although both the C-Test and the MC-Test appear to be efficient, reliable and valid tests, there is still a considerable difference between function word items and content word items. Most function word items are usually far too easy, resulting in low discrimination power. The author therefore proposes to concentrate on only content words by deleting half of every second content word. The term S-Test, Semantic/Syntactic Test, is used because content words contain both semantic and syntactic information.

An S1-Test, with the first half of the word deleted, and an S2-Test, with the second half of the word deleted, were trialed with graduate students in the Language and Communication program at NIDA. Statistical analyses reveal that the S1-Test is superior to the S2-Test with reference to reliability, concurrent validity, and difficulty suitability. Surprisingly, the questionnaire data indicate that S-Tests have high face validity. The author therefore recommends use of the S1-Test as a section in proficiency tests.

1. Introduction and background

The need for general proficiency tests that are reliable and valid, as well as easy to make and score is a crucial issue in the field of language testing and evaluation. The use of the cloze test to estimate foreign language proficiency or global language ability by Carroll, Caron and Wilds (1959), was an important step forward. The cloze test, which is very easy to construct and score, and which was reasonably reliable and valid, was very popular among language teachers and test practitioners for at least two decades. It was used for a variety of purposes – as general proficiency tests, placement tests, and classroom tests. At present, it is still commonly found as part of many placement, proficiency, and entrance examinations in Thailand.

1.1. The development of the C-Test

As an integrative skills test, the cloze test, specifically the systematic deletion of every n^{th} word, is simple to construct and score. Favorable results from earlier studies led to assumptions that the cloze test was automatically more reliable and valid. After about two decades, however, a few researchers (e.g., Alderson 1979, 1983; Raatz and Klein-Braley 1981; Klein-Braley and Raatz 1984; and Brown 1983, 1984) have challenged the reliability and validity of the cloze test. The major problems are as follows:

1. The systematic n^{th} word deletion does not necessarily produce a random sample of the elements of the text.

2. Different deletion rates and different starting points applied to the same text produce tests which vary considerably in difficulty, reliability and validity.

3. Acceptable-word scoring procedures cause problems with criteria for acceptability; the use of exact-word scoring often makes the test too difficult.

4. Since educated native speakers themselves rarely obtain a perfect score, how can they be expected to make accurate judgements of acceptability when they act as scorers?

5. The use of only one or two texts easily creates a source of bias in the test scores due to text content.

To resolve these questions with the systematic deletion cloze test, a list of criteria for a new test was prepared by Raatz and Klein-Braley (1981).

1. The new test should use several different texts.
2. It should have at least 100 deletions.
3. Educated native speakers should obtain virtually perfect scores.
4. The deletions should affect a representative sample of the text.
5. Only exact-word scoring should be possible.
6. The test should have high reliability and validity.

A new test, the C-Test, was therefore proposed by Raatz and Klein-Braley to meet the above requirements. In the C-Test, four or more short passages (50–100 words) are recommended to avoid content bias. Deletions in each passage begin in the second sentence; the second half[3] of every second word is deleted. The test-taker's task is to read and supply the missing parts of the words. Following, is an example of a C-Test.

C-TEST (30 items)

Many foreigners find that Thailand is a very pleasant place to have a holiday. They ***disc*** _ _ _ _[4] *that* ***th*** _ _ _ *are* ***ma*** _ _ *interesting* ***thi*** _ _ _ *to* ***d*** _ *and* ***t*** _ *see.* ***Th*** _ _ *say* ***th*** _ _ *the* ***bea*** _ _ _ _ *are* ***cl*** _ _ _ *and* ***t*** _ _ *scenery* ***i*** _ *beautiful.* ***Ma*** _ _ *say* ***th*** _ _ *the* ***hot*** _ _ _ *are* ***exce*** _ _ _ _ _ _ *and* ***n*** _ _ *too* ***expe*** _ _ _ _ _ _. *They* ***exper*** _ _ _ _ _ _ *with* ***diff*** _ _ _ _ _ _ *kinds* ***o*** _ *Thai* ***fo*** _ _ *and* ***fi*** _ _ *that* ***i*** _ *tastes* ***deli*** _ _ _ _ _ _. *They* ***a*** _ _ *delighted* ***wi*** _ _ *Thai*

---

[3] For a word having an odd number of letters, half of the number + 1 shall be deleted (i.e., 2 out of 3, 3 out of 5). For a single-letter word (I or a), the whole word may be deleted or (depending on the purpose) ignored so that the following word is deleted.

[4] A gap of equal length for each mutilation is possible and will make the test more difficult.

mu *_ _ _ and* ***fasci*** *_ _ _ _ _ by* ***Th*** *_ _ dancing. Visitors from all countries often say that Thai people are warm and friendly.*

In addition to English, the C-Test has been developed in several different languages. A variety of language learner samples have been tested, and a number of different questions have been investigated. According to Klein-Braley and Raatz (1984), the C-Tests have been used for English, French, German, Spanish, as well as for Hebrew and Turkish. It was claimed that the results were promising.

1.2. The development of the MC-Test

Although the C-Test seems to resolve many of the problems facing the systematic cloze test, it is often too easy for students at the intermediate or advanced level. Taking word formation of content words in English into consideration, it is evident that the first half and the second half of the word must be significantly different. Because most English content words (i.e., nouns, verbs, adjectives, and adverbs) are in the form of BASE + SUFFIX (ES), the first half will normally carry semantic information while the second half contains syntactic information. A modified C-Test, the MC-Test, was therefore developed by the author (Boonsathorn 1987) and the results compared with those from a C-Test. In the MC-Test, the first half, instead of the second half, of every second word is deleted.

The following example of an MC-Test was constructed from the same text used for the sample C-Test.

MC-TEST (30 items)

Many foreigners find that Thailand is a very pleasant place to have a holiday. They _ _ _ _ ***over*** *that _ _ _* ***re*** *are _ _* ***ny*** *interesting _ _ _* ***ngs*** *to _* ***o*** *and _* ***o*** *see _ _* ***ey*** *say _ _* ***at*** *the _ _ _ _* ***hes*** *are _ _ _* ***an*** *and _ _* ***e*** *scenery _* ***s*** *beautiful. _ _* ***ny*** *say _ _* ***at*** *the _ _ _* ***els*** *are _ _ _ _ _* ***lent*** *and _ _* ***t*** *too _ _ _ _ _* ***sive.*** *They _ _ _ _ _* ***iment*** *with _ _ _ _ _* ***rent*** *kinds _* ***f*** *Thai _ _* ***od*** *and _ _* ***nd*** *that _* ***t*** *tastes _ _ _ _ _* ***ious***. *They _ _* ***e*** *delighted _ _* ***th*** *Thai _ _ _* ***ic*** *and _ _ _ _ _* ***nated*** *by _ _* ***ai*** *dancing. Visitors from all countries often say that Thai people are warm and friendly.*

The results of an investigation (by the author in 1987) of the C-Test and the MC-Test with 389 high school students (L1) and 104 adult students (L2) in Alberta, Canada, can be summarized as follows.

1. The C-Test and the MC-Test are essentially different types of tests. They are functionally and structurally different.

2. The MC-Test is more difficult and discriminates better than the C-Test in both L1 and L2 data.

3. Different starting points of deletion do not affect the difficulty, reliability and validity of the tests.

4. Results of factor analyses suggest that the C-Test and the MC-Test have different factor structures. The MC-Test seems to require more of the normal reading processes than the C-Test does.

5. The Michigan Test correlates moderately high with the C-Test / MC-Test. The C-Test, however, appears to predict performance on the Michigan Test a little better than the MC-Test does.

6. While the restoration of the C-Test passages appears to rely primarily on the orthographic cues available in the items, interview results show that the processing of the MC-Test items necessitates the use of all the strategies required by readers in the process of normal reading.

In general, the newly-developed MC-Test appears to be empirically superior to the original C-Test in several respects. The MC-Test discriminates better, has greater reliability, and is more valid with reference to factor structures.

1.3. Why Semantic/Syntactic Tests (S-Tests)?

The literature review reveals that many researchers (e.g. Raatz and Klein-Braley 1981; Connelly 1997; and Klein-Braley 1997) find the C-Test to be a reliable, and valid test. On the other hand, those who find the C-Test too easy (e.g. Boonsathorn 1987; Cleary 1988; Sigott and Köberl 1993; Prapphal 1994, 1996; and Wonghiransombat 1998) experimented with the MC-Test (or X-Test) and found that the MC-Test is more difficult, discriminates better, and therefore is more appropriate for advanced students.

Although most studies on the C-Test and the MC-Test appear to support that both tests are efficient, reliable, and valid, some weaknesses have been noted. Cleary (1988) and Dörnyei and Kotona (1992) show that the "grammatically unmarked items" or the "function word items" are far too easy. Jafapur (1995) suggests that the difference in difficulty levels between content word items and function word items is considerable.

Since most function words are short, consisting of only one or two syllables, they are usually too easy in both the C-Test and the MC-Test, resulting in low discrimination power. The author, therefore, proposes to concentrate on only content words by deleting half of every second content word. And because most content words contain both semantic and syntactic information in themselves, the term Semantic/Syntactic Test (S-Test) will be used. The S-Test in which the first half of the word is deleted will be called the S1-Test, while the one in which the second half is deleted will be called the S2-Test. The S-Tests are considered a rational C-Test because the author has a rationale in deleting only content words instead of systematically deleting every second word.

2. Purpose of the study

The purpose of this study is to examine S-Tests, rational C-Tests, in which half of every second content word is deleted, focusing on:

A. The reliability of the S-Tests,
B. The difficulty level of the S-Tests,
C. The concurrent validity of the S-Tests, and
D. The face validity of the S-Tests.

3. Methodology

3.1. Subjects

The sample in this study was 97 graduate students in the Language and Communication part-time program, Class 1, in the second semester, 1998, at NIDA.

3.2. Instruments

1. The S-Tests

Two parallel forms of S-Tests, the S1-Test with the first half of every second content word deleted and the S2-Test with the second half of every second content word deleted, were developed. Each form consisted of the same six short texts (110–172 words; readability, Flesch-Kincaid Grades 10.2 to 16.8), totaling 150 items. After piloting the tests, only four texts (Grades 12 to 16.8) or 100 items were selected to be included in the final form of the tests. Following, are examples of an S1-Test and S2-Test constructed from the same text.

S1-Test (12 items)

Tom was a student who wasn't interested in studying. He preferred to _ _ ***ve*** *a good _ _* ***me****. Naturally, when he _ _* ***ok*** *his examinations, he didn't _ _* ***t*** *good _ _ _* ***ks****. Since he knew his _ _ _* ***her*** *would be _ _ _* ***ry*** *with him, he sent a _ _ _ _* ***gram*** *to his brother's _ _ _* ***se****.In the telegram he _ _ _* ***ed*** *his brother to _ _ _ _* ***are*** *his father for the _ _* ***d*** *news. The next morning, he received the following answer: "Father is prepared. You'd better prepare yourself."*

S2-Test (12 items)

Tom was a student who wasn't interested in studying. He preferred to ***ha****_ _ a good* ***ti****_ _ . Naturally, when he* ***to****_ _ his examinations, he didn't* ***g****_ _ good* ***ma****_ _ _ . Since he knew his* ***fat****_ _ _ would be* ***an****_ _ _ with him, he sent a* ***tele****_ _ _ _ to his brother's* ***ho****_ _ _. In the telegram he* ***as****_ _ _ his brother to* ***pre*** *_ _ _ _ his father for the* ***b*** *_ _ news. The next morning, he received the following answer: "Father is prepared. You'd better prepare yourself."*

---

2. Proficiency Test

A non-secure form of TOEFL was used to measure students' general proficiency. There were three sections – Listening Comprehension, Structure and Written Expression, and Reading Comprehension.

3. NIDA Entrance Examination for the Language and Communication Program

This test includes four sections – Listening Comprehension, Error Identification, Cloze Test, and Reading Comprehension. In this study, the author used the students' Entrance Examination scores, which were readily available.

4. Questionnaire

A nine-item questionnaire was developed by adapting Jafarpur's (1995) questionnaire and the author's (Boonsathorn 1987) interview schedule. The purpose of the questionnaire was to establish the face validity of the S-Tests.

3.3. Procedure

All students who participated in the study took the non-secure form of TOEFL in the second semester of 1998. Their TOEFL scores were then used as a basis for dividing them into two groups in terms of proficiency level. Both groups had the same number of students.

Two weeks later, Group 1 took the S1-Test while Group 2 took the S2-Test.

3.4. Analyses

The results of the S1-Test and the S2-Test and their corresponding TOEFL scores and Entrance Examination scores were separately analyzed by form using the Statistical Package for Social Science (SPSS / PC + 6.1.4). The statistics obtained from these analyses were:

1. Cronbach's alpha,
2. Means and standard deviations,
3. Pearson's product-moment correlation coefficients, and
4. Percentage points and mean scores of questionnaire data.

4. Results

The results are based on the purpose of the study and displayed in both tabular and descriptive forms.

A. The Reliability of the S-Tests

Table 1. The Reliability of the S1-Test and the S2-Test

Test form	N	Alpha
S1-Test	50	.8740
S2-Test	47	.8043

In Table 1, the alpha of the S1-Test is 0.8740 while the alpha of the S2-Test is 0.8043. The S1-Test appears to be more reliable than the S2-Test; however, both can be considered reliable.

B. The Difficulty Level of the S-Tests

Table 2. Means and t-test Statistics

Form	N	*M*	SD	<u>t</u>	<u>p</u>
S1-Test	50	59.60	10.52	–9.755	.000 (p<.001)
S2-Test	47	76.47	8.95		

Table 2 shows that the S1-Test is more difficult (M = 59.60, S.D. = 10.52) than the S2-Test (M = 76.47, S.D. = 8.95). Obviously, the difference in terms of difficulty is significant ($p < .001$).

Table 3. Item Discrimination

Discrimination Interval	S1-Test (No. of items)	S2-Test (No. of items)
> .75	1	5
.51 to .75	8	9
.26 to .50	26	17
< .26	65	69
Total	100	100

In relation to the discrimination power of the tests, Table 3 indicates that the number of items whose discrimination indices are low (< 0.26) is somewhat smaller in the S1-Test (65) than in the S2-Test (69). However, the number of items with very high discrimination indices (> 0.75) is greater in the S2-Test (5) than in the S1-Test (1).

C. The Concurrent Validity of the S-Tests

Table 4. Correlation Coefficients between S1-Test Scores, TOEFL Scores and the NIDA Entrance Examination (ENTR) Scores

	S1-Test	TOEFL	ENTR
	(n = 50)		
S1-Test	--	.6211*	.5762*
TOEFL		--	.6894*
ENTR			--

*p = .000 (p < .001).

Table 5. Correlation Coefficients between S2-Test Scores, TOEFL Scores and the NIDA Entrance Examination (ENTR) Scores

	S2-Test	TOEFL	ENTR
		(n = 47)	
S2-Test	--	.6057*	.5619*
TOEFL		--	.6462*
ENTR			--

*p = .000 (p < .001)

The information from Tables 4 and 5 reveals that the scores of the S1-Test and the S2-Test both correlate with the TOEFL scores (0.6211 and 0.6057) and the NIDA Entrance Examination scores (0.5762 and 0.5619). The S1-Test scores appear to correlate better with both the TOEFL scores and the NIDA Entrance Examination scores than the S2-Test scores do.

The correlation coefficients between the TOEFL scores and the NIDA Entrance Examination scores are moderately high in both the S1-Test subjects (0.6894) and the S2-Test subjects (0.6462).

D. Face Validity of the S-Tests

Table 6. Questionnaire Data of the S1-Test in Percentage Points and Mean Scores (1 = strongly disagree; 5 = strongly agree)

	1	2	3	4	5	M
1. The S1-Test is a language test.	2.00	4.00	18.00	28.00	48.00	4.16
2. It is an interesting test.	2.04	6.12	8.17	53.06	30.61	4.04
3. It is a challenging test.	0	6.12	2.04	42.86	48.98	4.35
4. The S1-Test measures:						
4.1. Vocabulary	2.04	0	2.04	30.61	65.31	4.57
4.2. Grammar	6.12	12.24	38.78	22.45	20.41	3.39
4.3. Reading	4.08	6.12	12.25	40.82	36.73	3.77
4.4. General English Proficiency	2.04	0	14.29	53.06	30.61	4.10
4.5. Background knowledge	0	4.08	2.04	30.61	63.27	4.53
4.6. Intelligence	4.17	6.25	14.58	43.75	31.25	3.92
4.7. Other (specify):__________						
5. It is a fair test of English.	6.12	16.33	40.82	26.53	10.20	3.18
6. It is a good test of English.	4.08	12.24	36.75	36.73	10.20	3.37
7. It is fun to do this type of test.	8.16	2.04	10.21	42.86	36.73	3.98
8. It causes a lot of anxiety.	14.29	16.33	16.31	38.78	14.29	3.22
9. The S1-Test can be used as:						
9.1. A general English proficiency test.	10.20	10.20	30.61	32.65	16.33	3.35
9.2. Part of the entrance examination for the Language and Communication program.	12.24	12.24	32.65	30.61	12.24	3.18

The S1-Test

The questionnaire data in Table 6 suggest that most respondents either agree or strongly agree that the S1-Test is a language test (M = 4.16), is interesting (M = 4.04), and is challenging (M = 4.35). They believe that the S1-Test mainly measures vocabulary (M = 4.57), background knowledge (M = 4.53), and general English proficiency (M = 4.10). They somewhat agree that it is fun to do the S1-Test (M = 3.98), while they are not quite certain whether it is a good test of English (M = 3.37), a fair test of English (M = 3.18), or causes a lot of anxiety (M = 3.22). The respondents, however, do not quite agree that the S1-Test can be used as a general English proficiency test (M = 3.35) or part of the entrance examination for the Language and Communication program (M = 3.18).

Table 7. Questionnaire Data of the S2-Test in Percentage Points and Mean Scores (1 = strongly disagree; 5 = strongly agree)

	1	2	3	4	5	M
1. The S2-Test is a language test.	4.26	8.15	12.76	14.89	59.57	4.17
2. It is an interesting test.	6.25	6.25	25.00	25.00	37.50	3.81
3. It is a challenging test.	6.38	8.51	17.03	23.40	44.68	3.91
4. The S2-Test measures:						
4.1. Vocabulary	4.26	2.13	10.63	12.77	70.21	4.43
4.2. Grammar	4.17	4.17	20.83	19.17	41.67	4.00
4.3. Reading	4.17	2.08	20.83	22.92	50.00	4.13
4.4. General English Proficiency	2.17	4.35	23.91	19.57	50.00	4.11
4.5. Background knowledge	4.26	4.26	21.27	27.66	42.55	4.00
4.6. Intelligence	6.52	6.52	28.27	23.91	34.78	3.74
4.7. Other (specify):_______						
5. It is a fair test of English.	8.33	12.50	35.42	35.42	8.33	3.23
6. It is a good test of English.	8.33	18.75	31.25	18.75	22.92	3.29
7. It is fun to do this type of test.	6.25	8.33	12.51	33.33	39.58	3.92
8. It causes a lot of anxiety.	19.57	26.09	34.78	6.52	13.04	2.67
9. The S2-Test can be used as:						
9.1. A general English proficiency test.	6.25	14.83	16.66	41.67	20.83	3.56
9.2. Part of the entrance examination for the Language and Communication program.	10.42	20.83	20.84	27.08	20.83	3.27

The S2-Test

Table 7 shows that in general the respondents agree that the S2-Test is a language test (M = 4.17), is rather interesting (M = 3.81), and is challenging (M = 3.91). They consider that the S2-Test mainly measures vocabulary (M = 4.43), reading (M = 4.13), and general English proficiency (M = 4.11). They agree that it is fun to do the S2-Test (M = 3.92), but they are not sure whether it is a good test (M = 3.29) or a fair test (M = 3.23) of English. The S2-Test does not seem to cause as much anxiety (M = 2.67) as the S1-Test. The respondents tend to agree that the S2-Test can be used as a general proficiency test (M = 3.56) rather than as part of the entrance examination for the Language and Communication program (M = 3.27).

5. Discussion and Conclusion

Statistical analyses reveal that both the S1-Test and the S2-Test have high reliability, one of the most important qualities of tests. The S1-Test is more reliable than the S2-Test. This finding supports those of previous studies (e.g., Boonsathorn, 1987; Cleary, 1988) which show the MC-Test to be more reliable than the C-Test.

The S1-Test is more difficult than the S2-Test as expected. The S1-Test, with a mean of 59.60, seems to be more appropriate for these graduate students than the S2-Test, because the mean of 76.47 shows that it is probably too easy. Thus, the texts with Flesch-Kincaid Grades of 12 to 17 are probably appropriate for Thai graduate students. Item discrimination indices also support that the S1-Test has generally higher discrimination power than the S2-Test.

Correlational analyses indicate that both the S1-Test scores and the S2-Test scores can predict the performance on the TOEFL and the NIDA Entrance Examination to a certain extent, in spite of the different natures of the tests. The S1-Test scores correlate better than the S2-Test scores. This is contradictory to the author's 1987 study. The correlation coefficients between the TOEFL scores and the NIDA Entrance Examination scores are rather high, probably because they have a similar format.

The questionnaire responses show that respondents generally agree that both the S1-Test and the S2-Test are language tests and that they are interesting and challenging. The S1-Test is considered more challenging than the S2-Test. The respondents agree that the S1-Test mainly measures vocabulary, background knowledge and general English proficiency while the S2-Test mainly measures vocabulary, reading, and general English proficiency. They somewhat agree that it is fun to do this type of test but are not quite sure whether it is a good and fair test of English or not. The S1-Test causes more anxiety than the S2-Test. The respondents are not sure whether the S1-Test and the S2-Test should be used as a general English proficiency test or part of the entrance examination or not. In general, the S1-Test and the S2-Test appear to have high face validity. The findings are completely contradictory to Jafarpur's (1995) results which show that the C-Test has no face validity.

In conclusion, both the S1-Test and the S2-Test have been shown to be reliable and valid tests. The S1-Test, however, appears to be superior to the S2-Test in all respects – reliability, concurrent validity, face validity, and difficulty suitability. The author therefore recommends use of the S1-Test as a section in NIDA Test of English Competence (N-TEC), which will be developed in the near future.

REFERENCES

Alderson, J. C. (1979). "The cloze procedure and proficiency in English as a foreign language". *TESOL Quarterly*, 13(2): 219–227.

Alderson, J. C. (1983). "The cloze procedure and proficiency in English as a foreign language". In: Oller, J. W. Jr. (ed.). *Issues in Language, Testing Research*. Rowley, Massachusetts Newbury House: 205–217.

Boonsathorn, S. (1987). "C-Tests, proficiency, and reading strategies in ESL". *Unpublished doctoral dissertation*. University of Alberta, Alberta, Canada.

Brown, J. D. (1983). "A closer look at cloze: validity and reliability". In: Oller, J. W. Jr. (ed.). *Issues in Language Testing Research*. Rowley, Massachusetts: Newbury House: 237–250.

Brown, J. D. (1984). "A cloze is a cloze is a cloze?" In: Handscombe, J., Orem, R. A. and B. P. Taylor (eds.). On *Tesol' 83*. The Question of Control. Washington, D.C.: TESOL: 109–119.

Carroll, J. B., Caron, A. S. and C. P. Wilds (1959). "An investigation of cloze items in the measurement of achievement in foreign languages". *Report on research conducted under a grant from the College of Education Entrance Examination Board*. Cambridge, Massachusettes: Graduate School of Education.

Cleary, C. (1988). "The C-Test in English: Left-hand deletion". *RELC Journal*, 19(2): 26–38.

Connelly, M. (1997). "Using C-Test in English with post-graduate students". *English for Specific Purposes*, 16(2): 139–150.

Dörnyei, Z. and L. Katona (1992). "Validation of the C-Test amongst Hungarian EFL learners". *Language Testing*, 9(2): 187–206.

Jafarpur, A. (1995). "Is C-testing superior to cloze?" *Language Testing*, 10(1): 195–216.

Klein-Braley, C. (1997). "C-Tests in the context of reduced redundancy testing: An appraisal". *Language Testing*, 14(1): 47–84.

Klein-Braley, C. and U. Rattz (1984). *A survey of research on the C-Test. Language Testing*, 1(2): 134–146.

Prapphal, K. (1994). "A study of the C-Test and the X-Test performed by first-year science-oriented university students". *PASAA*, 24: 16–23.

Prapphal, K. (1996). "An investigation of the general and academic English X-Tests in measuring grammatical competence of Thai science students". *PASAA*, 26: 73–79.

Raatz, U. and C. Klein-Braley (1981). "The C-Test – a modification of the cloze procedure". In: Culhane, T., Klein-Braley, C. and D. K. Stevenson (eds.). *Practice and problems in language testing*. Department of Language and Linguistics Occasional Papers No. 26. Colchester: University of Essex: 113–138.

Sigott, G. and J. Köberl (1993). "Validating the X-Test". *Language Testing Update*, 14: 53–58.

Wonghiransombat, P. (1998). "A validation of the MC-Test as a test of English proficiency". *Unpublished master's research paper*. The National Institute of Development Administration, Bangkok, Thailand.

Mousa A. Btoosh

University of Texas at Arlington

LEXICAL COMPLEXITY AND FREQUENCY IN L1 AND L2 STUDENTS' WRITING: A Computer Corpus Linguistics Approach*

1. Introduction

On the basis of the modern themes of linguistics research, it is probably fair to say that the path of linguistics has shifted dramatically since the arrival of machine-readable corpora onto the scene in the second half of the previous century. This factor explains the recent evident concern with some subfields (e.g. lexicology and lexicography) largely ignored in the literature of previous approaches. However, the shift from the most studied targets in linguistics (syntax and phonology) to lexicology and lexicography should not be solely ascribed to the ever growing supply of software products and machine-readable corpora but also to the recent growing awareness of the centrality of lexicon in language and language acquisition.

Gass and Selinker (2001) argue that lexicon, the most neglected part in research, "may be the most important language component for learners" (p. 372). Perhaps the awareness of the importance of lexicology is no more clearly stated in the contemporary research than in Laufer (1997: 147):

> Vocabulary is no longer a victim of discrimination in second language learning research, nor in language teaching. After decades of neglect, lexicon is now recognized as central to language acquisition process, native or non-native.

Research on corpora (Kennedy 1990; Biber *et al.* 1998, to name just two) has shown that a well-compiled and representative corpus can provide researchers and learners with numerous lexical features that would be otherwise hard to obtain. These features include:

---

* An earlier version of much of this work appeared in Btoosh, M. A. 2004 (Unpublished Ph.D. dissertation).

(i) the different contextual meanings associated with a particular word;
(ii) the commonly found words that co-occur with a particular word (collocations);
(iii) the frequently used vocabulary in a language or a domain, and
(iv) the non-linguistic association patterns that a particular word has to a register or dialect

From an empirical perspective, the naturally occurring data that a corpus provides are believed to be superior to any hypothetical and non-natural (elicited) data. It should be born in mind that evidence within corpus linguistics framework is based on experience and observance rather than prediction or guessing. Kennedy (1998: 7–8) states that corpus linguistics is not a theory in competition with other linguistic theories but rather a source of evidence that comprises the core of any linguistic study. For Aijmer and Altenberg (1992: 2), corpora have become excellent resources for a wide range of tasks. This, they claim, is due to two main reasons:

1. Language corpora have provided a more realistic foundation for the study of language than earlier types of material, a fact which has given new impetus to descriptive studies of English lexis, syntax, discourse and prosody.

2. Language corpora have become a particularly fruitful basis for comparing different varieties of English, and for exploring the quantitative and probabilistic aspects of the language.

However, the divergent themes of linguistics, along with the incapability of general corpora to meet all of linguistics' subfields' demands, have pushed the idea of specialized corpora to the fore. Hence the existence of what are called *learner corpora*, a collection of texts or essays produced by learners of a language.

This study presents the lexical analysis of a 70,307 token corpus of the writing of Arab students of English as a second language. 429 undergraduate students enrolled in their second to fourth year at five public and private Jordanian universities volunteered to participate in this study. For contrastive purposes, the lexical investigation of the learner corpus (L.C., hence after) required the existence of a similar-sized authentic or reference corpus (R.C., hence after), which was, in turn, methodically selected from *Louvain Corpus of Native English Essays* (LOCNESS). Consider Table (1) for further details.

For illustrative and analytical purposes, there are four main considerations in this study, viz.:
(i) Learners' lexical complexity and richness;
(ii) The most salient lexical and stereotyped features of the learner corpus;
(iii) How far the learner corpus is influenced by learners' L1 (Arabic); &
(iv) How far the learner corpus is deviant from the reference corpus in terms of the features and percentages of the 100 most frequent tokens.

As for the software programs, this study has made use of the following tools:

1. Platform: *Windows*
2. Part-of-Speech Tagger: *C7 Tagset* (in CLAWS)
3. Concordancer and Wordlist: *WordSmith*

Table 1. Learner and reference corpora

	L.C.	R.C.
Number of tokens	70,307	70,309
Number of essays	429	79
Mean of fluency	163.89	889.99
Native language	Arabic*	– (51.49%) American English – (48.51%) British English
Learner and task variables	– 269 timed essays (exam conditions) – 160 untimed essays (homework assignments) – University students	– Timed essays – Untimed essays – University students

* Only students who never lived in an English speaking country were eligible to participate in this study.

2. Lexical Complexity

Lexical complexity is used in this study as an umbrella term for both lexical diversity and lexical density. While lexical sophistication, the ratio of sophisticated word types to the total number of word types, is often included under lexical complexity, this study, for convenience, is limited to exploring the first two measures.

2.1. Lexical Diversity

Corpus size or length is a critical factor that inversely affects lexical diversity (a measure of the richness of the vocabulary in a text calculated by the number of types (different words) X 100 by the number of all tokens). So, in order to avoid its inverse role when the analysis is carried out on individual essays, which vary in their length, this measure was carried out on a full corpus basis (equal basis). Figures 1 and 2 present the findings of lexical diversity in both the learner and reference corpora, respectively.

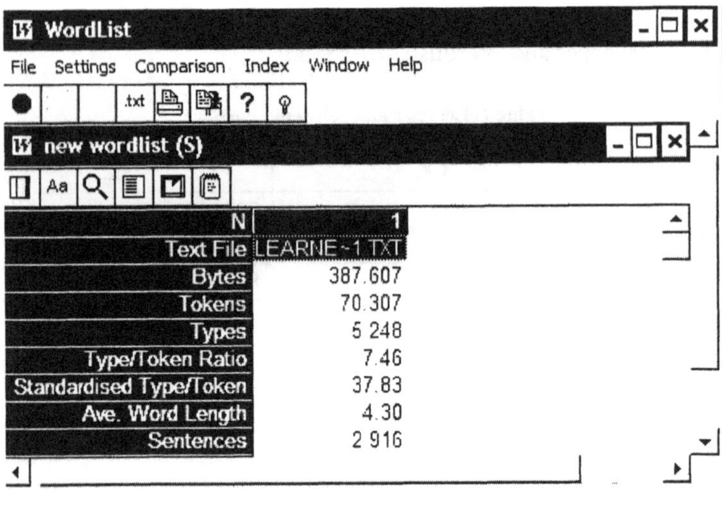

Fig. 1. Type-token ratio in the learner corpus

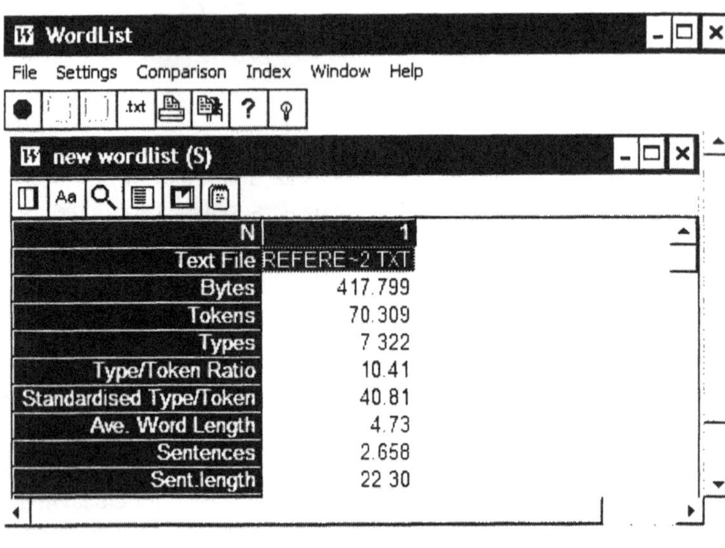

Fig. 2. Type-token ratio in the reference corpus

As shown in Figures 1 and 2, the results, in regard to lexical diversity in the learner corpus compared with the reference corpus (7.46 vs. 10.41), are highly suggestive. The substantial disparity in the number of the types (unique words) shown above (5,248 vs. 7,322) properly indicates that the lexical diversity in the reference corpus exceeded considerably the learner counterpart. While it was not unexpected for the type-token ratio in the reference corpus to outnumber the learner counterpart, the marked percentage of diversity (28.3%), which favored the reference corpus, goes far beyond expectations. By taking into account the approximately five times higher diversity of the learner corpus over the reference corpus in regard to the number of subjects, and the three times higher diversity in regard to topics and themes, the findings become potentially striking. However, a look at all of these results, together with the findings of previous research, reveals the learners' limited word stock and their excessive reliance on repetitive lexemes and patterns to convey messages in the target language.

Are we to ascribe the disparity in type-token ratio only to the learners' developmental stages? Such a conclusion would be unwarranted if we proceed to consider three crucial aspects: (1) the oversimplification of L2 input, (2) the high tolerance of learners' lexical errors (particularly those resulting from near-synonyms, word match, and incorrect collocations), and (3) the rhetoric of learners' L1, where repetition or the *beating around the bush strategy* is a prevalent rhetorical device. While the first two points deal with the prevailing L2 teaching strategies, the third one reflects the unconscious transfer of the linguistic and cultural rhetorical patterns and strategies to L2.

Oversimplification of the L2 lexicon, which is harshly criticized by Fox (1979: 68), often leads learners to rely on a limited number of lexical items that could be incorrectly used to stand for other presumably difficult lexical items which share a common meaning. However, oversimplification is not limited to the lexicon. Rather, it is extended to other aspects of L2 (e.g., syntax). Building on previous research (e.g., Blau 1982: 525, Yano *et al.* 1994), Oh (2001) argues that input simplification has serious problems. First, the use of limited vocabulary and short and simple sentences is likely to result in "choppy, unnatural" discourse that may deviate significantly from authentic texts. Second, the elimination of unfamiliar linguistic items shields learners from exposure to items that they should learn. Consequently, learners who experience an oversimplified lexicon would graduate with a minimal word stock and an apparent inability to deal with authentic texts or discourses. The high tolerance of L2 lexical errors is no less destructive than oversimplification. Given these aspects in addition to the universal learners' dominant repetitive tendency, the gap between the two corpora in terms of type-token ratio may be more understandable.

Although the sizable gap between the two corpora in terms of lexical diversity is evident, in favor of the reference corpus, this ratio might be affected if such an analysis was carried out on different sized corpora. To be more precise, lexical diversity is strongly influenced by size; the more tokens a corpus has, the lower its diversity. For this reason, the best analysis is one carried out where the corpus size criterion has been neutralized. By displaying the type-token ratios carried out on individual essays, which vary in their length, Table 2 provides powerful evidence for the sensitivity of lexical diversity to size. The means of the type-token ratios shown below have been computed with the *Wordlist*.

Table 2. Mean values of lexical diversity

	L.C.	R.C.	Difference
Mean	56.43	42.70	13.73*
SD	7.0098	7.886	

* The difference between the two corpora is significant at the $\alpha = 0:05$ *level* ($t = 14:3907$; $p<0001$) using two-sided parametric t-test assuming equal variance.

However paradoxical it might appear at first glance, the learners' lexical diversity ratio significantly outnumbers that of the native speakers. Yet, this would be an ungrounded conclusion and should be immediately questioned since it ignores the size of the essays, which plays a significant role here. Knowing that the mean of learners' fluency/essay length is 163.89 tokens and the mean of the native speakers' fluency is 889.99 tokens, then, it becomes obvious that lexical diversity and size almost always stand in an inverse relation and this is why we see the reverse ratios shown in Table 1. As a precaution against overgeneralizing, it should be noted that evidence from the literature indicates that there are some cases where lexical size and lexical diversity correlate. This occurs when much of the text in question includes a list of items, such as names of persons, machines, items on restaurant menus, etc.

2.2. Lexical Density

Lexical density is calculated by dividing the total number of content words X 100 by the total number of all tokens in the given corpus. Findings of lexical density in the learner as well as the reference corpora are reported in Table 3 below. Unlike lexical diversity, which is extremely sensitive to the size or length notion, lexical density is completely independent of size (McCarthy 1990). This entails that an individual-by-individual analysis is needed to get reliable results.

Table 3. Mean of lexical density and standard deviation

	L.C.	R.C.	Difference
Mean	44.75	47.51	2.76*
SD	4.85	5.00	

* The difference between the two corpora is significant at the $\alpha = 0{:}05$ *level* (t = 14:3907; p<0001) using two-sided parametric t-test assuming equal variance.

Owing to its insignificance in much of the previous literature as a discriminating measurement between the interlanguage of the NNSs and the language of the NSs, and also between different stages of learners' development, the debate over the reliability of lexical density has not yet been settled. However, this measurement has been typically and successfully used as a discriminating factor between spoken and written texts.

Lexical density percentages, according to Ure (1971), generally tends to be over 40% in written texts and less than 40% in spoken ones. By contrasting written and spoken versions of one and the same text, Eggins (1994: 61) furnished reliable support for Ure's argument. Lexical density, according to the findings of her study, was 9% higher in favor of the written texts (33% vs. 42%). Knowing that the percentages of lexical density in the learner corpus and the reference corpus were 44.75% and 47.51% respectively, it becomes manifest that both corpora support Ure's findings in this respect.

3. Over- and Underproduced Lexical Categories and Items

The previous findings concerned with the number of content words arouse one's curiosity to ask whether the lexical density percentage in the reference corpus consistently outnumbers the lexical density percentage in the learner corpus in the four major word classes. To this end, annotated versions of both corpora were run on *WordSmith's* concordancer. Consider Figure 3 for illustration.

Figure 3 reveals that lexical density in the reference corpus outpaces its learner counterpart in the number of nouns, adjectives and adverbs while it is less in the number of verbs. In the following subsections, an attempt is made to examine whether or not such percentages match the findings of previous literature.

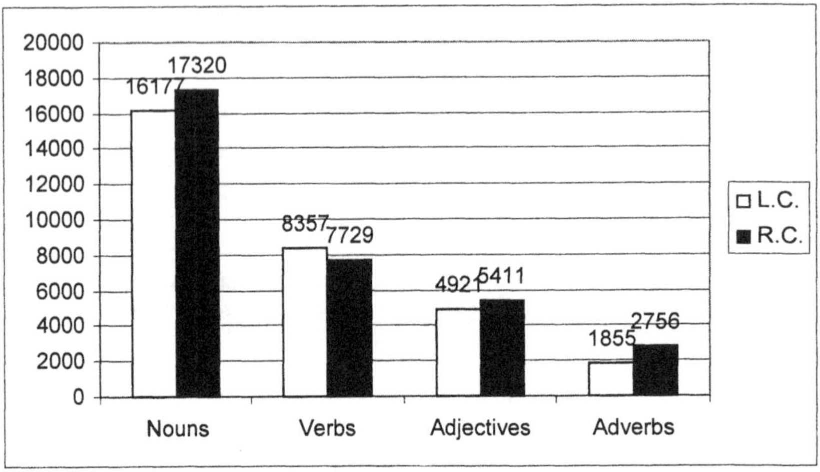

Fig. 3. Overall frequency of content words in leaner and reference corpora

3.1. Verbs & Nouns

With reference to the findings of previous research, it is obvious that the high percentage of nouns in comparison with the other three major word classes is quite normal. At least three reasons can be given in support of this initial conclusion. First, a high percentage of nouns vis-à-vis other parts of speech has been attested in the literature (Biber *et al.* 1998, 1999, Halliday 1989, among others). Despite the wide gap between the number of content words, Biber *et al.* (1999) found that in overall frequency nouns are the most frequent category among all the word classes though nouns are the least frequent in conversation (Guo 2003: 1). Second, by examining excerpts from Bertrand Russell's writings to check the use of nominalization in modern English, Halliday (1989) concludes that modern English is really "highly nominalised" and that "lexical meaning is largely carried out in the nouns" (p. 72). Third, in the context of academic writing, it is relevant to mention that the more proficient writers use more nominalizations than do the less proficient writers (Grant and Ginther 2000). Thus, the learners' underuse of nouns in comparison with the NSs might be attributed to their low level of proficiency in L2. It is relevant to mention that the percentage of nouns (in the total number of all word categories) in the reference and learner corpora (24.53%) and (23.01%) respectively supports most of the previous research findings. For example, the percentages of noun categories in the *Brown* and *LOB* corpora (1,000,000 tokens in each) are 26.80% and 25.2% respectively.

The learners' overuse of content verbs in comparison with the NSs is also attested in the previous literature. In a comparison between a sampled LOB corpus (S-LOB) and the corpus of the Chinese EFL learners' written production (ILC), Dafu (1994) found that "native speakers use more nouns, adjectives, wh-determiners, articles and prepositions while the Chinese EFL learners prefer verbs, adverbs, pronouns, general determiners and conjunctions..."

Recent research on learners' use of word classes has also attested learners' underuse of nouns and overuse of verbs. Guo (2003) examines the use of 25 verbs and their noun equivalents in COLEC (a corpus of learner English mainly composed of Chinese university students' essays in national exams) and LOCNESS (native) corpora. Findings show that NNSs mainly use verbs where NSs prefer nouns. By examining the frequency of the same 25 verbs and their noun equivalents used in Guo (2003), this study, as shown in Table 4, furnishes clear-cut support for learners' preference of using verbs over nouns.

Table 4. The frequency of 25 verbs and their equivalent nouns

Word	Verbs (L.C.)	Verbs (R.C.)	Nouns (L.C.)	Nouns (R.C.)
Number	192	248	63	187
Percentage	75.29	57.01	24.71	42.99

The ratio of nouns to verbs in the reference corpus (42.99% vs. 57.01%) seems to be normal, and it is much closer than the ratio between nouns and verbs in the learner corpus (24.71% vs. 75.29%). The percentage of difference between the two corpora in terms of the use of nouns (18.28%), which favored the reference corpus, indicates that learners prefer to use verbs where NSs use nouns.

3.2. Adjectives

The percentage of adjectives to other content word classes in the learner and reference corpora is almost identical (≈16%) while the proportions of adjectives to all other word classes in both learner and reference corpora are 7.7% and 7%, respectively. These proportions appear to be normal when compared with other corpora. For example, the percentage of adjectives in the 1,000,000 token corpora of *Brown* and *LOB* were 7.07% and 7.3%, respectively.

3.3. Adverbs

A striking diversity between the two corpora is clearly seen in the number of adverbs (1,855 vs. 2,756), which favored the reference corpus. By comparing compositions written by Swedish learners of English and NSs' writing, Linnarud (1986) attests that the largest differences between the groups lie in the adjectives and adverbs. While there is surprisingly little research on this particular aspect, it is possible to attribute the divergence in the number of adverbs between the two corpora to the following causes:

(i) L1 Influence: there is no real class of adverbs in Arabic that corresponds to the English category of adverbs. Rather Arabic has a number of adverbial particles (e.g., faqaṯ 'only/no more'), which follow the verb (Bateson: 2003). Also, adverbs in Arabic are used less commonly than in English (Smith 1987). As a result, it is possible to partially attribute the diversity between the two corpora in the number of adverbs to learners' L1 influence.

(ii) Use: learners' use of adverbs is somewhat different from that of the NSs; for learners, the use of adverbs is largely restricted to intensification and (quasi-nominal adverbs of) time. However, for NSs adverbs are multifunctional (e.g., adjuncts, conjuncts, cohesive and referential devices, hedges, evidentials, amplifiers) (Hinkel 2002: 121–22). This means that NSs use more adverbs than NNSs.

3.4. Personal Pronouns

The overuse of pronouns in the learner corpus is primarily attributed to learners' preference for visibility in the text. Support for this argument comes from the excessive use of the first person pronoun *I* in the learner corpus (1,433 times) compared to only 184 times in the reference corpus. The huge gap between the two corpora in the use of the first person pronoun *I* reflects the extension of the subjectivity of Arabic discourse to the target language, where objectivity rather than subjectivity is almost always the optimal candidate.

In coming to understand the discourse subjectivity and learners' preference for visibility in the text, an attempt is made here to compare the use of the conjugations of the first person pronouns in both corpora.

Table 5. Writer visibility in learner and reference corpora

Feature	L.C.	R.C.
First person singular pronouns (I, I'x, me, my, mine)	2,441	250
First person plural pronouns (we, we'x, us, our, ours)	1,023	370
Total first person pronouns	3,464	620

From this brief comparison, it becomes manifest that learners' subjectivity vastly outweighs that of the NSs. It might be argued that the overuse of the first person pronouns is a general developmental tendency rather than a language specific feature. While this is unquestionably true, the extreme overuse of such pronouns in the present learner corpus compared with other learner corpora makes these pronouns attributable to the L1 rhetoric, too. Support for this conclusion comes from Petch-Tyson (1998). In an analysis of the features of writer/reader visibility, Petch-Tyson (1998: 112) found that Dutch, Finnish, French and Swedish learners of English markedly overused more first and second person pronouns in comparison to NSs, as shown in Table 6.

Table 6. Writer/reader visibility

Feature	Dutch (55, 314)	Finnish (56, 910)	French (58, 068)	Swedish (50, 872)	US (53, 990)
First person singular pronouns (I, I'x, me, my, mine)	391	599	364	448	167
First person plural pronouns (we, we'x, us, our, ours)	484	763	775	1, 358	242
Second person pronouns (you, you'x, your, yours)	447	381	257	227	76
Total first/second person pronouns	1,322	1,743	1, 396	2,033	485
Total first/second person pronouns per 50,000 words	1,195	1,531	1,202	1, 998	449

By taking the number of token in each corpus into consideration, none of the learner corpora shown in Table 6 above outnumbers the present learner corpus in terms of the frequency of the first person pronouns. This appears to indicate that ascribing the overuse of the first person pronouns solely to the general tendency or developmental stages is ungrounded.

3.5. Emphatics, Intensifiers & Hedges

In the context of comparison between the writings of NSs and NNSs, there usually seems to be no escaping the frequency of overstatement in the NNSs corpora. While it is feasible to attribute adjectival intensifiers and emphatics used in the learner corpus to a universal learner tendency, it is even more appropriate (due to the excessive overuse) to ascribe them to the influence of the L1, where such items are prevalent.

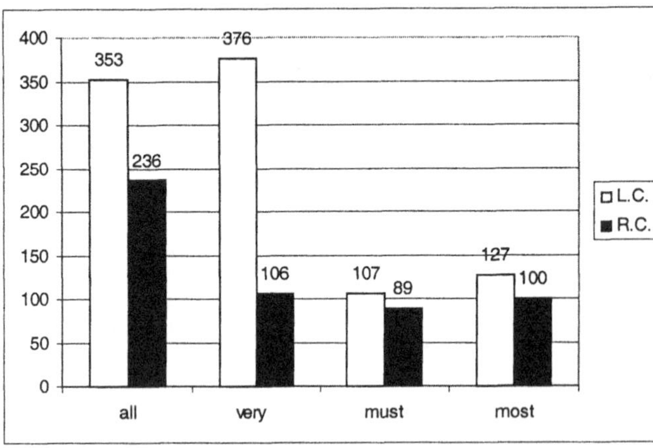

Fig. 4. Intensifiers and emphatics

The primary reason that learners use emphatics and intensifiers is to strengthen the force of their propositions, a feature highly favored in Arabic discourse. Again, these findings are well-grounded in the previous literature. By examining the non-native/native differences in the actual inventories of adjective intensification in two native corpora and two non-native ones (around 100,000 words each), Lorenz (1998) found that a prominent difference between German learners of English and NSs' usage lies in the learners' overuse and misuse of intensifiers.

Another key result that might also be cited here to shed light on the differences between the learner and reference corpora is the learners' underuse of some lexical items compared with the NSs. Since divergence in terms of frequency is expected among homogeneous groups (between two groups of NSs) or heterogeneous groups (between NSs and NNSs), it is important to keep in mind that the examples cited in this subsection (3.5) represent only those items markedly divergent in the two corpora. In a corpus characterized by an excessive overuse of emphatics and intensifiers, it is reasonable to examine the use of hedges, as a polar opposite (see Figure 5).

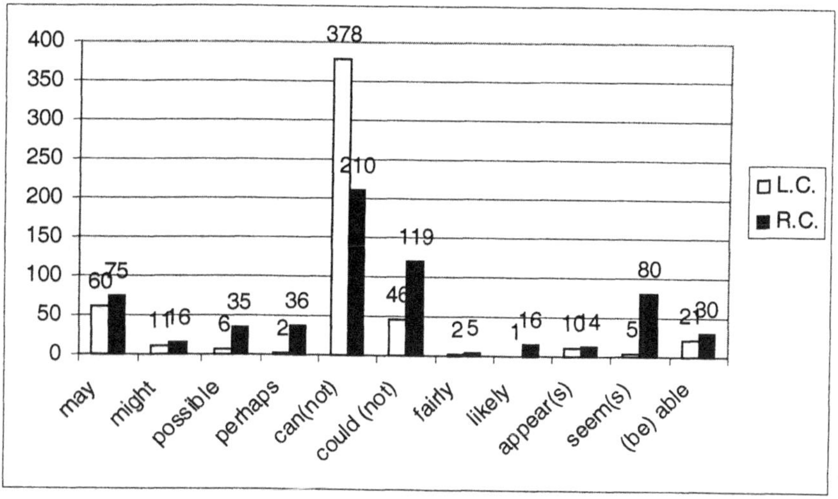

Fig. 5. Hedges in learner and reference corpora

The examples given above (in Figures 4 and 5) reveal that learners' lexicology lies between two extremes (overuse or underuse). While Figure 4 presents the markedly overproduced lexemes in the interlanguage corpus, Figure 5, on the other hand, shows some markedly less frequent lexemes. Again, the explanation for the underused lexemes shown above might feasibly be understood with reference to the learners' L1 rhetoric.

4. Top 100 Frequent Tokens

There is a strong consensus among corpus linguists on the importance of word frequency lists in corpus analysis (McEnery and Wilson 1996, Kennedy 1998, among others). Drawing on its multifunctional uses, creating a word frequency list is a fruitful and productive technique, in the sense that it might be used for various purposes ranging from designing syllabi to text analysis. This technique has also shown great reliability in revealing the nature of the subject matter of a text or corpus and several other lexical aspects such as active or inactive vocabulary, the differences between spoken and written discourses, hapax legomena (words used one time in the corpus) and the influence of L1. Moreover, frequency lists provide unique insights into the repetitive mechanism and other rhetorical aspects including the overuse or underuse of lexemes in learner corpora compared to the authentic (native) ones.

Beyond the previous uses, recent research on SLA has shown the centrality of frequency lists in measuring learners' vocabulary. The Lexical Frequency Profile (LFP), proposed in Laufer and Nation (1995), is now considered the most reliable and powerful measure of learners' vocabulary proficiency or knowledge. Likewise, frequency lists help determine the number of vocabulary items learners need to become proficient or fluent in L2. Laufer and Nation (1999) argue that 79.9% of written English uses only the top 2000 most frequent words in the language. This indicates that mastering such words guarantees a good command of the target language. Figures 6 and 7 present the top 100 frequent tokens in the learner and reference corpora respectively.

Along with the tokens, six notable points immediately emerge from Figures 6 and 7. First, function words occupy the top positions in terms of frequency in both corpora. Out of the 200 tokens used in the above extracts, only 51 tokens were content words. Second, due to the excessive use of some vague nouns and generic adjectives (e.g., people, way, life, important, great, old), which are attributable to lexical developmental stages and the influence of the L1, the learner corpus leads the reference corpus by 9% in terms of the content words in the top 100 frequent tokens. Third, learners' L1 rhetorical devices (e.g., overstatement, writer visibility *I*) have a noticeable effect on word frequency. Fourth, the two corpora share approximately two-thirds of the used tokens. Fifth, as one scrolls down, frequency, together with the percentage of tokens, consistently but sharply declines in both extracts (from 4,524 to 86). Sixth, though it is much higher in the learner corpus than in the reference corpus, the top 100 tokens in both corpora take up more than 50% of the total number of the tokens in the entire corpora.

While approximately (65%) of the lexical items in the top 100 frequent tokens are shared between the two corpora, it appears to be unsound to rely on this ratio as an indicator of similarity or difference between them. There are, at least, two reasons that may justify this statement. First, the high percentage of the shared types between the two corpora is misleading since more than 70% of these tokens or types are grammatical words, which always occupy the top positions in any corpus, whether native or learner. This is what led Halliday (1989: 65) to categorize lexical items into three categories rather than two: (i) grammatical words, (ii) high frequency lexical items and (iii) low frequency lexical items. By so doing, Halliday (1989) assumes that grammatical words are always high in terms of frequency. Second, in most cases, the top unshared frequent types reflect the divergent themes of the texts providing the database of the corpora.

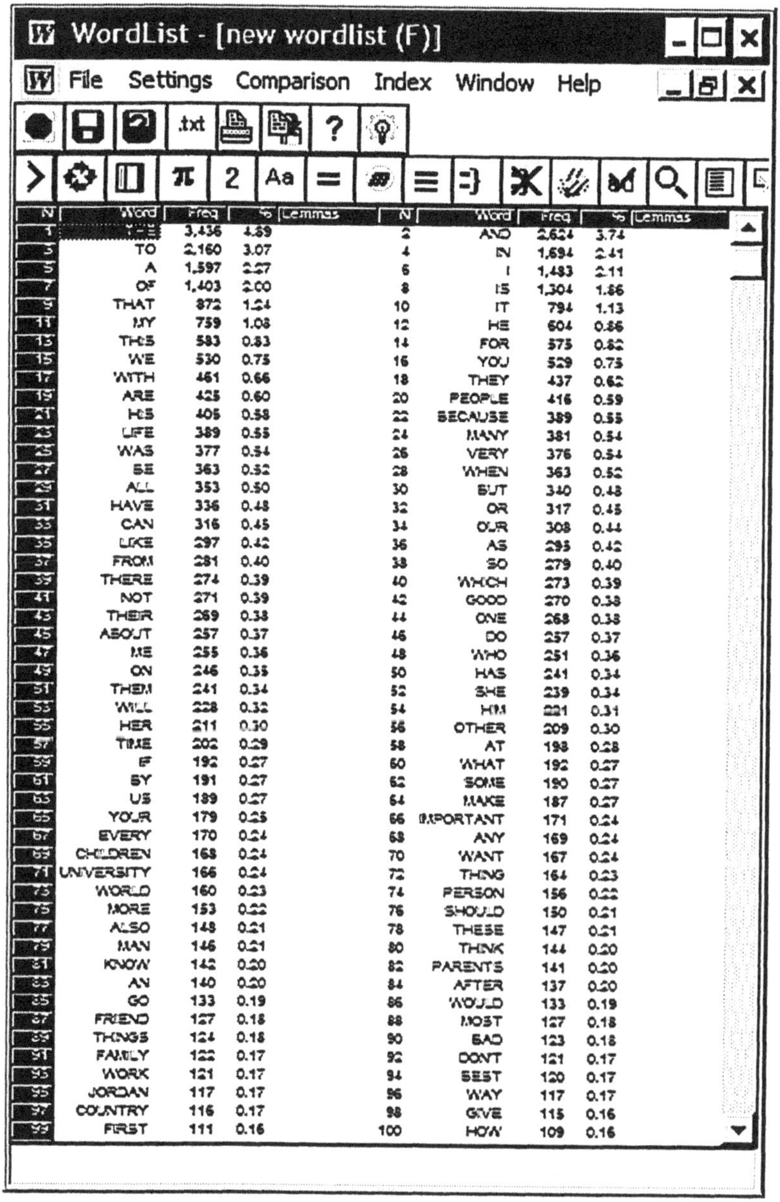

N	Word	Freq	%	Lemmas	N	Word	Freq	%	Lemmas
1	THE	3,436	4.89		2	AND	2,624	3.74	
3	TO	2,160	3.07		4	IN	1,694	2.41	
5	A	1,597	2.27		6	I	1,483	2.11	
7	OF	1,403	2.00		8	IS	1,304	1.86	
9	THAT	872	1.24		10	IT	794	1.13	
11	MY	759	1.08		12	HE	604	0.86	
13	THIS	583	0.83		14	FOR	575	0.82	
15	WE	530	0.75		16	YOU	529	0.75	
17	WITH	461	0.66		18	THEY	437	0.62	
19	ARE	425	0.60		20	PEOPLE	416	0.59	
21	HIS	405	0.58		22	BECAUSE	389	0.55	
23	LIFE	389	0.55		24	MANY	381	0.54	
25	WAS	377	0.54		26	VERY	376	0.54	
27	BE	363	0.52		28	WHEN	363	0.52	
29	ALL	353	0.50		30	BUT	340	0.48	
31	HAVE	336	0.48		32	OR	317	0.45	
33	CAN	316	0.45		34	OUR	308	0.44	
35	LIKE	297	0.42		36	AS	295	0.42	
37	FROM	281	0.40		38	SO	279	0.40	
39	THERE	274	0.39		40	WHICH	273	0.39	
41	NOT	271	0.39		42	GOOD	270	0.38	
43	THEIR	269	0.38		44	ONE	268	0.38	
45	ABOUT	257	0.37		46	DO	257	0.37	
47	ME	255	0.36		48	WHO	251	0.36	
49	ON	246	0.35		50	HAS	241	0.34	
51	THEM	241	0.34		52	SHE	239	0.34	
53	WILL	228	0.32		54	HIM	221	0.31	
55	HER	211	0.30		56	OTHER	209	0.30	
57	TIME	202	0.29		58	AT	198	0.28	
59	IF	192	0.27		60	WHAT	192	0.27	
61	BY	191	0.27		62	SOME	190	0.27	
63	US	189	0.27		64	MAKE	187	0.27	
65	YOUR	179	0.25		66	IMPORTANT	171	0.24	
67	EVERY	170	0.24		68	ANY	169	0.24	
69	CHILDREN	168	0.24		70	WANT	167	0.24	
71	UNIVERSITY	166	0.24		72	THING	164	0.23	
73	WORLD	160	0.23		74	PERSON	156	0.22	
75	MORE	153	0.22		76	SHOULD	150	0.21	
77	ALSO	148	0.21		78	THESE	147	0.21	
79	MAN	146	0.21		80	THINK	144	0.20	
81	KNOW	142	0.20		82	PARENTS	141	0.20	
83	AN	140	0.20		84	AFTER	137	0.20	
85	GO	133	0.19		86	WOULD	133	0.19	
87	FRIEND	127	0.18		88	MOST	127	0.18	
89	THINGS	124	0.18		90	BAD	123	0.18	
91	FAMILY	122	0.17		92	DONT	121	0.17	
93	WORK	121	0.17		94	BEST	120	0.17	
95	JORDAN	117	0.17		96	WAY	117	0.17	
97	COUNTRY	116	0.17		98	GIVE	115	0.16	
99	FIRST	111	0.16		100	HOW	109	0.16	

Fig. 6. Top 100 frequent words in the learner corpus

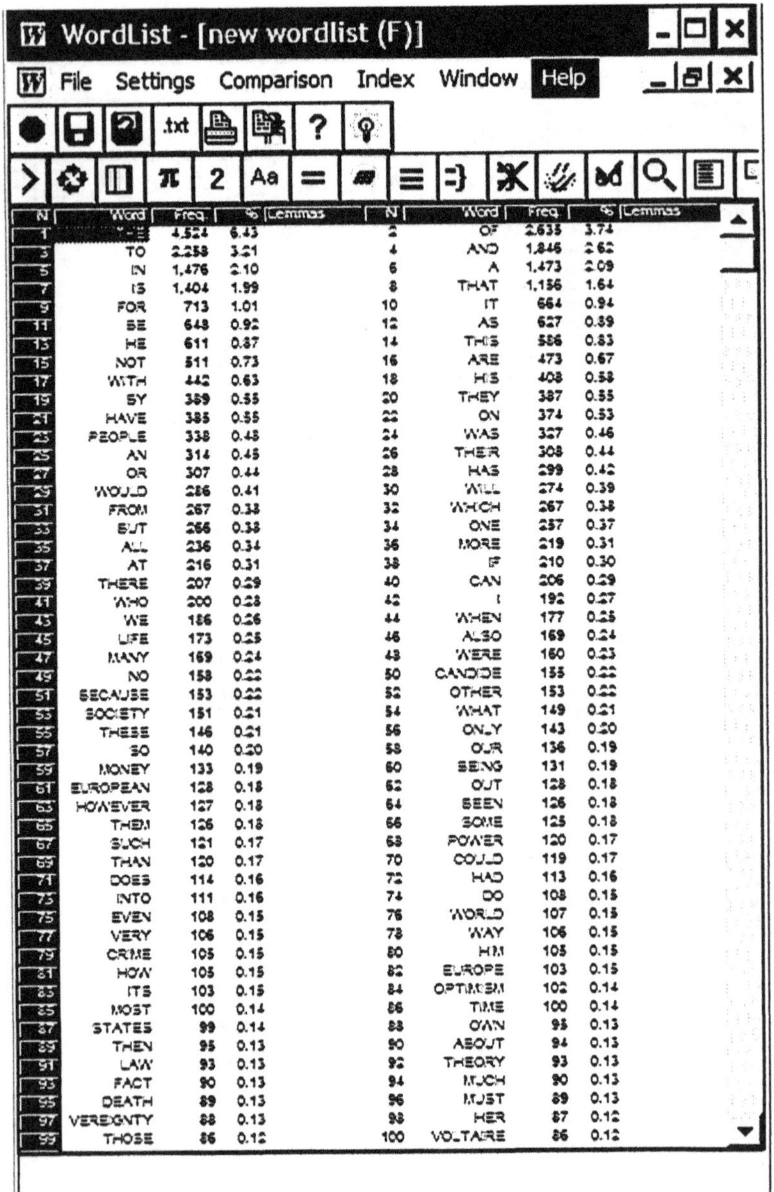

N	Word	Freq.	%	Lemmas	N	Word	Freq.	%	Lemmas
1	THE	4,524	6.43		2	OF	2,635	3.74	
3	TO	2,258	3.21		4	AND	1,846	2.62	
5	IN	1,476	2.10		6	A	1,473	2.09	
7	IS	1,404	1.99		8	THAT	1,156	1.64	
9	FOR	713	1.01		10	IT	664	0.94	
11	BE	648	0.92		12	AS	627	0.89	
13	HE	611	0.87		14	THIS	586	0.83	
15	NOT	511	0.73		16	ARE	473	0.67	
17	WITH	442	0.63		18	HIS	408	0.58	
19	BY	389	0.55		20	THEY	387	0.55	
21	HAVE	385	0.55		22	ON	374	0.53	
23	PEOPLE	338	0.48		24	WAS	327	0.46	
25	AN	314	0.45		26	THEIR	308	0.44	
27	OR	307	0.44		28	HAS	299	0.42	
29	WOULD	286	0.41		30	WILL	274	0.39	
31	FROM	267	0.38		32	WHICH	267	0.38	
33	BUT	266	0.38		34	ONE	257	0.37	
35	ALL	236	0.34		36	MORE	219	0.31	
37	AT	216	0.31		38	IF	210	0.30	
39	THERE	207	0.29		40	CAN	206	0.29	
41	WHO	200	0.28		42	I	192	0.27	
43	WE	186	0.26		44	WHEN	177	0.25	
45	LIFE	173	0.25		46	ALSO	169	0.24	
47	MANY	169	0.24		48	WERE	160	0.23	
49	NO	158	0.22		50	CANDIDE	155	0.22	
51	BECAUSE	153	0.22		52	OTHER	153	0.22	
53	SOCIETY	151	0.21		54	WHAT	149	0.21	
55	THESE	146	0.21		56	ONLY	143	0.20	
57	SO	140	0.20		58	OUR	136	0.19	
59	MONEY	133	0.19		60	BEING	131	0.19	
61	EUROPEAN	128	0.18		62	OUT	128	0.18	
63	HOWEVER	127	0.18		64	BEEN	126	0.18	
65	THEM	126	0.18		66	SOME	125	0.18	
67	SUCH	121	0.17		68	POWER	120	0.17	
69	THAN	120	0.17		70	COULD	119	0.17	
71	DOES	114	0.16		72	HAD	113	0.16	
73	INTO	111	0.16		74	DO	108	0.15	
75	EVEN	108	0.15		76	WORLD	107	0.15	
77	VERY	106	0.15		78	WAY	106	0.15	
79	CRIME	105	0.15		80	HIM	105	0.15	
81	HOW	105	0.15		82	EUROPE	103	0.15	
83	ITS	103	0.15		84	OPTIMISM	102	0.14	
85	MOST	100	0.14		86	TIME	100	0.14	
87	STATES	99	0.14		88	OWN	95	0.13	
89	THEN	95	0.13		90	ABOUT	94	0.13	
91	LAW	93	0.13		92	THEORY	93	0.13	
93	FACT	90	0.13		94	MUCH	90	0.13	
95	DEATH	89	0.13		96	MUST	89	0.13	
97	VEREIGNTY	88	0.13		98	HER	87	0.12	
99	THOSE	86	0.12		100	VOLTAIRE	86	0.12	

Fig. 7. Top 100 frequent words in the reference corpus

5. Conclusion

Overall, this paper has explored numerous aspects of lexical complexity and text-profiling in the learner corpus in comparison with the reference corpus. Comparative corpus evidence has shown numerous areas of convergence and divergence between the two corpora. By addressing the results with reference to the previous literature, it was possible to delineate the features attributed to the influence of the L1 and the features that are likely to be classified under general tendencies.

REFERENCES

Aijmer, K. and B. Altenberg (eds.) (1991). *English Corpus Linguistics*. London: Longman.

Bateson, M. C. (2003). *Arabic Language Handbook*. Washington, DC: Georgetown University Press.

Biber, D., Conrad, S. and R. Reppen (1998). *Corpus Linguistics: Investigating Language Structure and Use*. Cambridge: New York: CUP.

Biber, D., Johansson, S., Leech, G., Conrad, S. and E. Finegan (1999). *Longman grammar of spoken and written English*. London: Longman.

Btoosh, M. A. (2004). *Interlanguage Lexicology of Arab Students of English: A Computer Learner Corpus-Based Approach*. Unpublished Ph.D. Dissertation, University of Texas at Arlington.

Dafu, Y. (1994). *Interlanguage Errors and Cross-linguistic Influence: A Corpus-based Approach to the Chinese EFL Learners' Written Production*. Unpublished Ph.D. Dissertation.

Eggins, S. (1994). *An Introduction to Systemic Functional Linguistics*. London: Pinter Publishers.

Fox, L. (1979). *On Acquiring an Adequate Second Language*. Journal of Writing 2: 68–79.

Grant, L. and A. Ginther (2000). *Using Computer-Tagged Linguistic Features to Describe L2 Writing Differences*. Journal of Second Language Acquisition 9: 123–145.

Guo, X. (2003). *Between Verbs And Nouns And Between The Base Form and the Other Forms of Verbs-A Contrastive Study into COLEC and LOCNESS*. English Language Postgraduate Seminars Autumn Term, University of Birmingham.

Gass, S. M. and L. Selinker (2001). *Second Language Acquisition. An Introductory Course* (second edition). Mahwah, NJ: Lawrence Erlbaum Associates.

Haliday, M. A. K. (1989). *Spoken and written language*. OUP.

Hinkel, E. (2002). *Second Language Writers' Text: Linguistic and Rhetorical Features*. London: Lawrence Erlbaum Associates, Publishers.

Kennedy, G. (1990). *Collocations: Where grammar and vocabulary teaching meet.* In: Anivan, S. (ed). *Language teaching methodology for the nineties*: 215–229. Singapore: RELC Anthology Series 24 [LOB].

Kennedy, G. (1998). *An Introduction to Corpus Linguistics.* London: New York: Longman.

Laufer, B. (1997). "What's in a word that makes it hard or easy: some intralexical factors that affect the learning of words". In: Schmitt, N. and M. McCarthy (eds). *Vocabulary: Description, Acquisition and Pedagogy*. Cambridge: CUP.

Laufer, B. and P. Nation (1999). *A vocabulary size test of controlled productive ability.* Language Testing 16: 33–51.

Laufer, B. and P. Nation (1995). *Vocabulary size and use: lexical richness in L2 written production.* Applied Linguistics 16: 307–322.

Linnarud, M. (1986). *Lexis in composition. Lund Studies in English.* Malmo: Sweden: Liber Forlag.

Lorenz, G. (1998). "Overstatement in advanced learners' writing: stylistic aspects of adjectives intensification". In: Granger, S. (ed). *Learner English on Computer*: 53–66. London; New York: Longman.

McCarthy, M. (1990). *Vocabulary*. Oxford: OUP.

McEnery, T. and A. Wilson (1996). *Corpus Linguistics*. Edinburgh: EUP.

Oh, S. (2001). *Two Types of Input Modification and EFL Reading Comprehension: Simplification and Versus Elaboration.* TESOL Quarterly 1: 69–96.

Petch-Tyson, S. (1998). "Writer/reader visibility in EFL written discourse". In: Granger, S. (ed). *Learner English on Computer*: 119–131. London; New York: Longman.

Smith, B. (1987). *Learner English: A teacher's guide to interference and other problems.* Cambridge: CUP.

Ure, J. (1971). "Lexical density and register differentiation". In: Perren, G. E. and J. L. M. Trim (eds.). *Applications of linguistics: Selected papers of the Second International Congress of Applied Linguistics.* Cambridge, 1969 (pp. 443–452). Cambridge: CUP.

Richard Profozich

University of Łódź

Tomasz Pludowski

Akademia Świętokrzyska and Collegium Civitas

TOWARDS E-LEARNING? STRATEGIES FOR SUCCESSFUL ONLINE EDUCATION AT UNIVERSITY OF MARYLAND UNIVERSITY COLLEGE

1. Significance of on Online Distance Education in the U.S.

A growing number of students in the U.S., both in higher education and in secondary education, enroll in online distance education courses. University of Maryland University College (UMUC), the adult education component of the University of Maryland, has an enrollment of over 100,000 online students a year ("Best Online" 2004: 3). The Florida Virtual High School has over 18,000 students (Nitkin 2005: 30). Virtually every college and university in America provides a distance education option to regular face-to-face classes. Courses are offered either with an online component to enhance regular classroom sessions or entirely online. And 41% of American school districts planned to offer online courses in 2004–05 (Ibid.: 32). Zhang reports that "distance education programs have been rapidly increasing as alternative course delivery systems in the United States" (2005: 45), with an accompanied advancement in educational technologies and delivery systems.

The two most popular online course platforms in the U.S. are Blackboard and WebCT. These are commercially available, relatively low cost platforms that schools can use to place courses on the Web. The University of Maryland has developed its own delivery platform, WebTycho.

Most advocates of distance learning say that online courses are not a replacement for traditional classrooms. Many educational institutions limit the number of online courses that students may take, especially young students. The Massachusetts school system limits students to two online courses per semester, for instance. Yet an increasing number of college degree programs, both undergraduate and graduate, are being offered entirely online.

2. Reasons For Taking Online Courses

Online distance education courses are becoming more and more popular as is shown by the increase in enrollment every year. The most common reasons that students cite for choosing online courses are flexibility, the self-paced nature of classes, and the convenience of working from home or work and not having to attend classes. Many students like to work independently and manage their time. Online courses appeal to young students who want to take special or advanced courses that are not available at their school. Distance courses also help them to fit courses into already packed schedules of classes, work, sports, and other extracurricular activities. Adult students like them for basically the same reasons, balancing work and family responsibilities with earning a college degree, and saving time and money by taking classes outside of traditional classroom settings.

3. Effectiveness of Online Courses Compared to Traditional Classroom Courses

With the proliferation of online courses, there is a growing interest in assessing the quality and effectiveness of online instruction. Most research concludes that there is no significant difference between instructional effectiveness of online and traditional courses. In reporting a summary of current research, Zhang (2005) shows that gender, for instance, is not an important factor associated with distance learning receptivity. However, prior computer experience and technology familiarity are positively related to distance learning receptivity. Learning style also seems to be important. While learning style generally is found to be a significant factor in contributing to students' overall academic success in all courses, studies show that varied support mechanisms in distance education courses accommodate different learning styles as well as in traditional courses. Therefore, learning style is not found as a significant factor in contributing to students' academic success when comparing the two teaching modes. While many researchers conclude that more studies need to be conducted to determine the relationship between learning styles and students' attitudes toward distance learning, some studies have shown interesting relationships.

Online students seem to be more independent and less collaborative. On-campus students tend to be more collaborative, more competitive, and participatory in the classroom. They also expect rewards from the instructor and work to meet the instructor's expectations, while online students seem to be more motivated by intrinsic motives.

In her own research study conducted at McNeese State University in Louisiana, Zhang (2005) found that gender, age, computer experience, and learning style were not significant factors on the receptivity of distance learning, saying that this finding is consistent with most distance learning research in this area. Still, online instruction is different than face-to-face instruction, and Zhang's study did conclude that students who took an educational technology course showed a higher distance learning receptivity than students who did not take the course, showing that helping students become familiar with the formalities of distance learning is important. Again, this is consistent with the body of research on this issue.

The bottom line is that online distance education is shown to be just as effective as traditional education, but that online education, because of its high level of technical apparatus and its asynchronous nature, requires special considerations in applying effective instructional practices. Teaching and learning online are different experiences. DuCharme-Hanson and Dupin-Bryant point out that "while the idea of taking a standard course curriculum and using a different vehicle to facilitate learning seems like a logical and somewhat uncomplicated initiative, teaching and learning online takes more than a mere shift in modalities" (2005: 31). They recommend creating distance education plans to develop systematic distance education activities, methods and strategies to optimize the online learning experience. Their emphasis on the learning process rather than on the technical aspects of distance learning is part of a current trend. As Knowlton has commented, "The emphasis should be on managing the learning experience, not on managing the technology" (2000: 11). Notar, Wilson and Montgomery (2005) agree with this assessment, saying that online education requires a "learner friendly" approach where "the designer's focus is more on the instruction than on using the tool to create instruction." Delivery methods need to adapt to the changing educational environment of online instruction, but curriculum content has remained constant, and basic instructional techniques also remain constant. "All types of instruction require dialog. Learning is sharing. Most learning occurs in communication between students and instructors and among students themselves. The teaching model requires person-to-person interaction" (Ibid.: 21). Asynchronous instruction requires adaptation of these principles, not entirely new ones.

4. The UMUC Research Project

Being one of the leading American institutions engaged in adult education and in distance learning, the University of Maryland University College (UMUC) is much involved in research concerning the effectiveness of online distance education. In 2003 it launched the Best Online Instructional Practices (BOIP) Study. The purposes of the study are to develop effective teaching strategies that have the potential to improve the quality of education in general, and to improve the instructional quality and effective teaching practices of online education specifically, "in order to highlight how quality teaching and learning in online education can be achieved' ("Best Online" 2004: 3).

The study is based on the hypothesis that the most highly endorsed principles of online teaching are ones that focus on the process of learning. Faculty who use these principles focus on creating a learning environment that is conducive to interaction and the exchange of information, in other words, on collaborative learning.

From one author's participation in the study and from both authors' long-time experience with online distance education instruction, we see four basic principles of distance learning which are drawn from basic process and collaborative teaching approaches that were developed for the traditional face-to-face teaching mode. To our thinking, these principles form the basis upon which the study is built, and which it uses to guide its design.

Principle One is that distance learning is student-centered rather than teacher centered. Students bring prior knowledge and experiences with them to a class, and have their own interests and goals in studying the subject matter, providing a wealth of information to the class setting.

Principle Two is that learning is best achieved by interaction between learners and instructors, learners and learners, and learners and external experts. This principle is based on the belief that learning is better achieved when the learner is actively engaged in the creation of knowledge, rather than the passive recipient of information.

Principle Three is that the distance-learning teacher needs to be a facilitator rather than the traditional expert source of knowledge.

Principle Four is that collaboration is a key component to distance learning. Students and instructors collaborate in achieving course goals, and students actively participate in what and how knowledge is imparted.

5. Research Design

As noted earlier, most research into distance learning has concluded that the principles of teaching in an online environment are not significantly different from those proven effective in the traditional classroom. The four principles outlined above are generally recognized as important to any setting that focuses on the learning process. Yet, the differences in communicating online versus face-to-face mandate a need to identify strategies that implement these principles in the online environment.

The goal of the study was to "highlight which teaching strategies are perceived by online faculty and students to be linked to increased learning outcomes, student and faculty satisfaction, and student retention" ("Best Online" 2004: 14). The UMUC study identified eight teaching strategies that were associated with effective online education. The eight strategies are as follows:

1. Make learning goals and one or more paths to them clear.
2. Use deliberate practice, including opportunities to continue the effort until skill or content is mastered.
3. Provide prompt constructive feedback.
4. Provide an optimal balance of challenge and support that is tailored to the individual student's readiness and potential.
5. Broaden the learners' experience of the subject matter.
6. Elicit active, critical reflection on student's growing experience base.
7. Link inquiries to genuine problems or issues of high interest to the learners.
8. Create an institutional environment that supports and encourages inquiry.

The study, therefore, addressed the following two research questions: "What are the teaching practices that are associated with faculty and student satisfaction and student learning outcomes? How do faculty members implement these practices?" (Ibid.: 14). The aim was to identify particular teaching practices that support the eight strategies.

A survey, administered online, was used to gather both faculty and student perceptions of the best teaching practices. Of faculty who taught during the Spring 2003 semester, 114 agreed to participate in the study. They and students in their classes answered the online survey. A smaller number of faculty, those whose feedback to the survey was highly confirmed by their students, then participated in phone interviews focused on uncovering the processes by which they achieved the best teaching practices.

6. Findings

Of the eight strategies presented in the study, four were identified in the survey as the most significant. These four then became the focus of the main part of the study: clarifying course goals, providing feedback and guidance, building on student experience, and fostering reflection and interaction.

7. Clarifying Course Goals

An overwhelming number of faculty make course objectives clear in their syllabus, making this one of the strongest teaching strategies of online faculty. Ninety-six percent said that they consistently explain course objectives to their students, and over ninety percent said that they are proficient at this task. However, there was greater variation in the practices that faculty use to accomplish this strategy. Figure 1 shows the proportion of faculty who use eight teaching practices associated with clarifying learning goals.

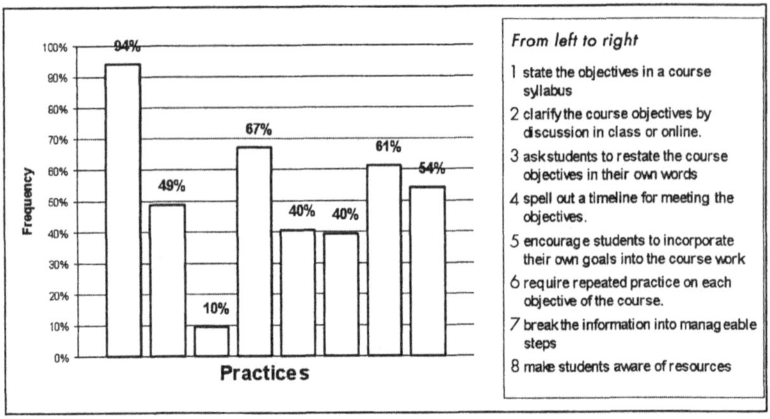

Fig. 1. Making Learning Goals Clear: Frequency of "often or always" Faculty Implementation (Source: Institute for Research and Assessment, UMUC)

The vast majority of faculty reported that they put course objectives in their syllabus, making this the most common teaching practice in support of clarifying course goals. More than half of the faculty also specify a time frame for completing the goals, break the goals down into steps, and make students aware of resources helpful to achieve the goals. But less than half clarify the objectives by discussion, encourage students to incorporate their own objectives into the course, or require repeated practice on each objective. And only ten percent ask students to restate course objectives in their own words.

8. Providing Feedback and Guidance

Feedback from instructors consistently appears in the literature as one of the main issues of online distance education. The fear is that because students and instructors do not meet face-to-face, and because most course work is done in an asynchronous mode, feedback will be minimized. However, many students, often a large majority in an online class, report that feedback is equal to or greater than that received in traditional classroom settings. Figure 2 displays the practices used by UMUC faculty to provide feedback to students.

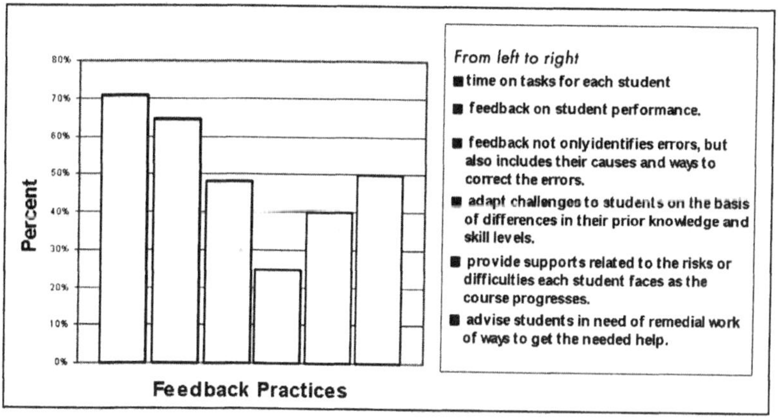

Fig. 2. Top Faculty Feedback Practices
(Source: Institute for Research and Assessment UMUC)

Most faculty, just over seventy percent, reported that they allow sufficient time on tasks for each student as a foundation for their feedback practices, and sixty-four percent say that they always or often provide timely feedback to students. Feedback relates not just to comments and grades on formal assignments or tests, but also to responding to students' questions and concerns, responding to conference postings, and responding to individual topics or tasks within a course segment or textbook chapter. About half the faculty provide feedback that not only identifies errors but also includes ways to correct them, and half advise students who need remedial work of ways to get help. Smaller percentages of faculty adapt course work to individual student prior knowledge and skill levels, or provide support related to individual difficulties each student faces as the course progresses. This may be due to the increased difficulty of employing these practices in an online environment.

9. Building on Student Experience

As noted earlier, students bring a wealth of experience and prior knowledge to a class. Using this knowledge and experience adds significant information and contributes to the student-centered focus of process oriented education. Sharing information, engaging in discussions, conducting research, and challenging one's own ideas and the ideas of others all help to develop a collaborative learning environment which is one of the main principles of online distance education. As well, UMUC is an adult education institution. Its clientele are mainly non-traditional, returning students, including a large number of military personnel. In a university where entering students have a wide range of prior knowledge and skills, using techniques which help students to build on their experiences is important. UMUC online faculty seem to recognize this need, as a majority of them employ a variety of teaching practices toward this goal. Figure 3 shows that faculty use nine different teaching practices that focus on encouraging students to use and expand upon the experiences they bring to the class.

The findings show that the vast majority of faculty use at least some of the practices focused on building on student prior knowledge and experience, as all nine practices indicate at least a fifty percent usage rate. Faculty seem to incorporate a wide variety of learning activities using a number of learning styles and introducing students to a variety of academic cultures and subcultures, as indicated by the nine teaching practices in Figure 3. Faculty seem to inform students of a variety of ways to apply course subject matter.

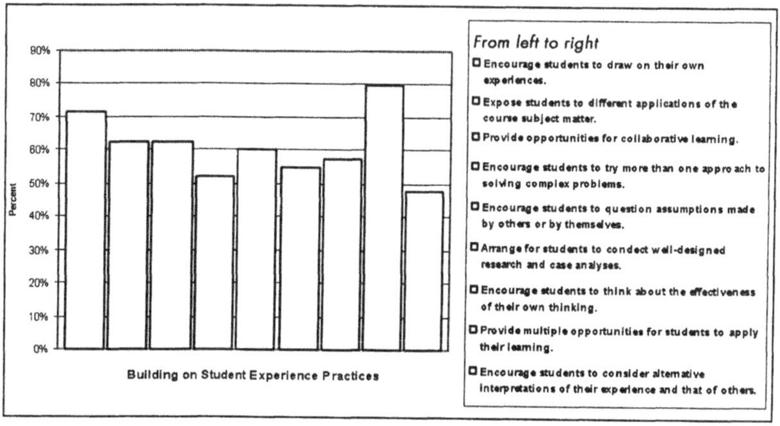

Fig. 3. Top Faculty Practices for Building on Student Experience (Source: Institute for Research and Assessment UMUC)

10. Foster Reflection and Interaction

Developing the student's ability to be a reflective thinker is an important function of higher education. Findings show that the vast majority of faculty use a variety of means to achieve this goal, such as questioning the assumptions made by one's self and others, questioning the validity of personal reasoning as well as that of others, and questioning the credentials of alleged authorities. Many teaching practices displayed in Figure 3 also support student reflective learning. Faculty indicated that they use another important way to develop students' capacity as reflective thinkers by requiring students to keep reflective journals as part of course requirements.

Instructor-student, student-student, and student-expert interactions are encouraged widely by faculty, as data shown in Figure 3 also support this online distance learning principle. Over sixty percent of faculty provide opportunities for collaborative learning in their classes, and fifty-five percent have students conduct research projects and case studies which encourages students to consult outside experts.

Forty-one percent of faculty indicated the importance of encouraging interaction and involvement in the virtual classroom. An important element of this goal is to create an open, inclusive environment that promotes discussion and sharing of information. The vast majority of instructors include participation in class discussions and activities as a significant element in the final grade for the course. Another strategy is to provide opportunities for students to ask each other questions and to comment on other students' assignment postings. Interaction is fostered through email exchanges, chat rooms, review of drafts of a project by another student, collaborative group projects, case studies, and discussion groups.

11. Student Perceptions of Best Teaching Practices

Faculty teaching practices were linked to student course evaluations in corresponding courses as well as to course completion rates and grade performance, so that student confirmation of effective practices was an important part of the research project. Course evaluation forms are structured to measure student satisfaction with instructor performance and ability, course design and content, and level of interaction between students and faculty.

Students show a high level of satisfaction when faculty appear knowledgeable of the subject matter, are informative, have organizational skills, use a logical format for class materials, and show enthusiasm for the course. Students also like faculty who are accessible, provide timely reminders, encourage students to do well, and demonstrate a sense of caring, flexibility, and a willingness to be helpful. Constructive feedback by instructors and feedback that has relevant comments on assignments and suggestions for improvement are also important to students.

Students value courses that have applications to their individual goals and needs, courses that respected students' perspectives, and that have subject matter that is relevant to their interests and careers. Courses that stimulate critical thinking in real world application of the material learned also are rated highly by students. Overall, students place high importance on instructors' teaching style and knowledge of course content. They wish to receive frequent constructive feedback, desire interaction with faculty and other students, and want to apply course content to their individual needs.

Classes in which faculty reported a high level of use of the best teaching practices had lower student withdrawal rates and higher percentage of passing grades. Students are retained at higher numbers in classes that reflect the frequent and proficient use of many effective practices. In addition, class performance as measured by student success rate is also correlated to many of the teaching practices. Some of the most important ones are listed below.

- Provide continuous feedback on student performance

- Encourage students to question assumptions made by themselves and others
- Incorporate student goals into course work
- Draw on experiences gained on the job or in non-course activities
- Implementation of collaborative learning opportunities
- Introduce a variety of cultures and sub-cultures into class materials

12. Conclusion

The study indicates that the four process-focused, collaborative education principles and eight suggested strategies that were initially recommended for the traditional face-to-face environment can be adapted to the online environment. The adaptation requires providing an interactive and lively educational environment to replace face-to-face contact. Faculty must be knowledgeable about course content and about important teaching principles and practices, be well organized, and be willing to pay attention to student needs. Faculty must provide continuous constructive feedback, be creative in involving students with course materials, and incorporate student experiences and goals into the class, making course work relevant to real world applications.

REFERENCES

"Best Online Instructional Practices Study." (May 2004). Unpublished Draft Report. Institute for Research and Assessment, University of Maryland University College, College Park.

DuCharme-Hansen, B. A. and P. A. Duppin-Bryant (February 2005). "Distance education plans: course planning for online adult learners." *TechTrends*, 49.2: 31–39.

Knowlton, D.S. (Winter 2000). "A theoretical framework for the online classroom: a defense and delineation of a student-centered pedagogy." *New Directions for Teaching and Learning*, 84: 5–14.

Nitkin, K. (May 2005). "Online courses are becoming a growing option for students, but experts caution moderation." *NEA Today*, 23.8: 30–32.

Notar, C E., Willson, J. D. and M. K. Montgomery. (March 2005). "A distance learning model for teaching higher order thinking." *College Student Journal*, 39.1: 17–25.

Zhang, Y. (2005). "Distance learning receptivity: are they ready yet?" *The Quarterly Review of Distance Education*, 6.1: 45–53.

Jacek Waliński
University of Łódź

MONITORING E-LEARNERS' FEEDBACK WITH BLOGS

1. Introduction

In the modern world education is seen as a factor stimulating the standard of living and personal development providing individuals with the opportunity to improve their social and economic status. For this reason access to education is perceived as an important issue of our times. Technology plays an increasingly important role in this access. Since the beginning of the current decade the phenomenon of 'electronic learning' (or simply e-learning) has been gaining an increasing interest. A large number of institutions have made investments in e-learning programs seeking the capability to provide effective, flexible, and personalized e-learning platforms.

The prospect of a 'virtual learning environment' enabling students to learn, collaborate, and communicate with each other and teachers from dispersed locations is considered as one of the most crucial challenges for education institutions. Recognizing the importance of this trend for the future of education the European Union is currently one of the most active promoters of e-learning. The "*eLearning initiative*" has become an important part of a broader strategy whose aim is "to become the most competitive and dynamic knowledge-driven economy in the world, capable of sustainable economic growth with more and better jobs and greater social cohesion". (Communication from the Commission, 2000)

Among numerous activities following this strategy is the ELISE (E-Learning in In-Service teacher training in Europe) project which focuses on developing methodology of designing courses delivered remotely and improving practical skills of teachers preparing such courses. The development of methodology is implemented by preparation of subject based e-learning modules, which are subsequently tested and fine-tuned in cooperation with teachers in five different European countries. (For more information see the project's website at: www.elise-edu.org).

From the very beginning the project put strong emphasis on testing and then fine-tuning e-learning modules. Among the tools used to collect feedback from project participants is an elaborate and detailed evaluation questionnaire prepared specially for the project implementation. However, it was noticed that information collected in such a manner is limited and formulaic in certain aspects. Therefore, apart from standard methods some participating institutions employed additional measures to assess the effectiveness of e-learning methodology.

One such initiative involved an attempt to create a collaborative community of teachers using blogs to share among one another their reflections on the use of e-learning in teaching ELT. The following paper presents the experience collected during implementation of this approach to feedback collection at the English Institute of the University of Lodz.

1.1. Blogs in perspective

The term *blog* is a blend of the terms [*world wide*] *web* and *log*. Blogs are personal web sites containing posts reflecting the thoughts, comments, and observations of the blog's creator. A concise definition of a blog taken from the "Glossary of Internet Terms" (Enzer 2005) says that "A blog is basically a journal that is available on the web. The activity of updating a blog is "blogging" and someone who keeps a blog is a "blogger." Blogs are typically updated daily using software that allows people with little or no technical background to update and maintain the blog."

A more descriptive definition comes from Gilmore's book "Generally speaking, [blog] is an online journal comprised of links and postings in reverse chronological order, meaning the most recent posting appears at the top of the page.. […] Weblogs typically link to other websites and blog postings, and many allow readers to comment on the original post, thereby allowing audience discussions." (Gilmore 2005)

It is difficult to pinpoint the exact moment when "blogs" came into existence because they emerged as a phenomenon after a series of events brought about by many people. According to Brady's article (Brady 2005) the first person to use the term 'web log' in 1997 was a writer, Jorn Barger. But the breaking point in blog popularity was 1999 when a number of companies introduced online services that allowed blogs to be created and updated with a user friendly interface. As noticed by Rebecca Blood in her essay "Weblogs: A History and Perspective" it was particularly accelerated by the introduction of "Blogger" – a free, automated online publishing system, which allowed people with little or even no knowledge of HTML to create their own blogs. (Blood 2000)

It is estimated (Smith 2005) that now a new blog is created every second. There are hundreds thousands of blogs written more or less regularly by people all over the world They are very diversified. It was observed (Brady 2005) that: "The type of information contained within a blog varies greatly from individual to individual. Authors of blogs can describe day-to-day observations in their lives, or more specific topics of interest to them, such as web design or cycling. Some frequently visited blogs are topic related [...], other mix this in with personal events in the author's life [...], such as going on holiday or meeting new people." It seems that the opportunity of being one's own publisher motivates an increasing number of people to share their own thoughts and reflections with other.

1.2. Blogs in e-learning

The sudden emergence and growing popularity attracted educators to the idea of using blogs as a potentially powerful instructional technology tool. Blogs are seen as a convenient platform for dissemination of student and faculty-related content. They can be used to share information and reflections about classes, current course events, etc. Taking into consideration their nature they are seen as especially useful for teaching and learning in the areas of literacy and foreign language teaching.

Offering a high level of autonomy in their form, blogs provide a forum for discussion that goes beyond classroom to incorporate various areas of personal exploration and a new opportunity for interaction with other interested individuals. Since learners can learn as much from each other as from instructors or textbooks, blogs can provide an effective mechanism for peer-to-peer knowledge sharing and acquisition.

The aclearn.net (Community Language Resource 2005) lists the following modes for using blogs in education:

- **Tutor to Tutor**
  Tutors can use weblogs to share ideas for teaching activities, resources, games, etc. to use in the classroom, posting descriptions of specific teaching units, providing teaching tips for other tutors.

- **Tutor to Learner**
  Tutors can use blogs to post assignments based on readings or websites and encourage learner reactions and discussions. Blogs can be useful to facilitate collaborative projects such as building a class newsletter using learners articles and photographs.

- **Learning development**
  Blogs have been used to improve learner motivation by allowing students to publish examples of their work such as art, poetry, and creative stories.

- **Learner to learner**
  Blogs have the potential to be entirely learner directed, allowing learners to provide peer support, comment on each other's work, provide stimulus for the learning process or work between geographically separate groups.

A common criticism towards content management systems (CMS) like *Blackboard* or *WebCT* is that they are too strict and hierarchical, leaving no room for student ownership and collaboration. Thus, another approach to the use of blogs in education is to combine them with such instructional technology tools to construct additional medium supplementing the learning environment.

Some educators even perceive blogs as an alternative form of platform for e-learning. Taking into consideration the variety of functions and features blogs have Ashley concludes that: "it might seem natural to look at them as likely candidates for a more flexible kind of CMS. Weblog software doesn't have the complete sets of tools one might expect of a typical CMS, such as a grade book, chat, and confidential file upload, but there are at least three lines of thought regarding the potential of weblogs." (Ashely 2002)

It is obvious that blogging has an enormous potential for bringing together communities of users with similar interests who, by having at their disposal an efficient publishing environment, can easily share their reflection and experiences on common topics. Currently, there is a growing number of educators who use blogs to discuss ways of incorporating e-learning into teaching.

A particular example of such a community is James Farmer's Online Education Weblog (Farmer 2004) which embraces discussion on how blogging can have a qualitative impact on education. Following this example we came up with the proposal to encourage the ELISE participants to use blogging to share and discuss questions and ideas about teaching, technology, and education in the context of e-learning. We hoped to create a Polish virtual community of EFL teachers using blogs to reflect on the e-learning methodology developed in the project, which would be used as an additional way of gathering feedback for evaluation of ELISE.

2. Blogs in ELISE evaluation

2.1. Aim of the project

As described above we decided to encourage ELISE participants to create blogs extending discussions on e-learning methodology beyond class meetings. We intended to create a virtual community of educators who share their experiences and reflect on the effectiveness of e-learning methodology. The aim was to explore important teaching and learning issues to gather additional, more personalized feedback from the project participants and to pilot the use of blogs for such a purpose.

Behind this idea there were three specific objectives:

1. To introduce the participating teachers to the idea of using blogs in e-learning.
2. To provide participants with hands-on experience in blog authoring by giving them opportunity to create and maintain blogs as a part of their e-learning training.
3. To follow participating teachers' reflections on the usability of e-learning for foreign language teaching and to collect this material as additional feedback.

2.2. Participants

The total number of teachers who participated actively in the Polish third run of ELISE methodology testing was 19. All participants belonged to the group of full time teachers from secondary schools. They took part in the vocational training in Pedagogy of Teaching English to develop their skills in different areas of FLT methodology.

Apart form proficiency in English the prerequisite for participation in the program was computer literacy. Among the courses the teachers were offered was the use of ICT in TEFL. A substantial part of the course was devoted to e-learning. The ELISE methodology was used as the main part of the course input.

2.3. Blogging software

The platform selected as the blogging platform was the "Blogger" service (www.blogger.com), which is one of the most popular blogging tools available nowadays. Advertised as "Push-Button Publishing" it enables the user to create a blog in 3 easy steps by creating an account naming the blog, and choosing a visual template. The service is not only free-of-charge and user friendly, but additionally offers an ample collection of how-to documents that help the user get the most out of it.

However, the selection of software for blogging is really extensive. The British "e-Learning Centre" (www.e-learningcentre.co.uk) currently lists over 50 such tools in its directory. It includes both complete online services like Powerblogs (www.powerblogs.com), Typepad (www.typepad.com) and software for hosting blogs on a separate server like excellent WordPress software (wordpress.org). Another comprehensive list of available blogging tools is available on Wikipedia (wikipedia.org) under the entry of 'blog'.

2.4. Implementation and initial results

In the first step the ELISE participants were given a theoretical introduction to the concept of blogging and the range of available tools. At the end of this session they seemed to be very enthusiastic about the idea of creating blogs for sharing their experiences and eager to start blogging. Their practical assignment for the next meeting was to set up their own personal blog using the above mentioned Blogger service. They were also requested to write a short entry on how they felt about participating in the e-learning course.

As the next meeting was planned for the following day, they had one evening to complete this task. The initial results were quite encouraging. The majority of participants (17) set up their own blogs successfully. The remaining two asked for assistance, since "they did not feel quite comfortable about going through this procedure on their own". Nobody wrote a real blog entry, but the participants explained that they had returned home late on the previous day and had too little time to think abut their reaction to the course.

Therefore, the completion of this task was extended until the next meeting, which was planned 5 days later. The participants were supposed to use this time to create at least one entry in their own blogs on the above mentioned topic. They were also encouraged to visit each other's blogs, possibly commenting on the posts.

Unfortunately, even five days later the intended 'virtual community of educators' did not materialize as expected. Although some participants wrote posts in their blogs, none of them was really satisfied with the result. The entries were rather concise and resembled short summaries of what had been covered in the course rather than personal reflections on e-learning methodology.

Almost half of the group failed to create even a single post. They said that they actually had prepared some material, but they were too embarrassed to share it with other people. In that situation the participants were asked to prepare for a discussion on "What is problematic in writing a blog?", which was held in a meeting on the following day.

2.5. Discussion

From the perspective of a week's experience the teachers were asked to explain what the difficulty in creating their blogs was. The following reasons emerged in the discussion why it was difficult for the Polish ELISE participants to write blogs devoted to e-learning issues.

"writing a blog is too time consuming for me" / "I am too busy with my daily chores to find time for writing"

It seems that for a large number of people (especially those who are not accustomed to it) keeping an online diary is something that requires a substantial amount of time. The participant complained that they could not find time to write posts during the day and in the evening they were too tired to focus on writing something that they would like to share with others. Some teachers complained that they had limited access to a computer at work. On the other hand, at home they did not have proper conditions to write a blog because their family members wanted to use the computer all of the time.

"I do not feel comfortable about (I am not used to) sharing my thoughts with other people"

For some participants the idea of sharing their reflections openly with other teachers seemed awkward. They explained that in their daily routine they were used to prepare reports on their activities, learners' progress, etc., but it occurs in a formal setting and involves reporting facts and drawing conclusions rather that sharing subjective personal reflections. Thus, the general conclusion is that some people feel simply uncomfortable about sharing their personal reflections with strangers who do not belong to the their circle of friends and relatives.

Several teachers admitted that they felt a sort of fear about publishing their opinions for public reading. This may be a personal characteristics but another possibility is that it may difficult for educators who belong to the older generation and are not used to this kind of publishing. It seems that they find the idea of publishing personal thoughts for strangers on the Internet rather peculiar.

"I do not find it interesting to write about e-learning" / "it feels artificial to write about things I learn"

Some participants complained that they did not find it particularly interesting to reflect on the material that had been covered in the course. They felt forced to reflect on the course in their blogs. Some teachers claimed that they would prefer to write a blog about something else, like traveling or football, instead of e-learning. This leads to a conclusion that for some educators professional development is a form of duty, which does not make a part of their real interests.

"it feels unnatural to write a personal blog in a foreign language" / "I find it difficult to express my thoughts precisely in English"

A few participants admitted openly that they found it rather difficult to express their thoughts in a foreign language. They said that it would be much more natural for them to express thoughts in their native tongue. A common complaint was about frequently finding themselves at a loss for words. It turned out that even the use of dictionary was often not very helpful in finding the right way of expressing what they had in mind. They felt limited by their writing skills in a foreign language and felt reluctant to share their imperfect output with others, especially as teachers of English.

"my experience with e-learning is too limited to reflect on it" / "I feel embarrassed to share my thoughts with others, because they may be naïve, silly, etc."

Some participants said that they were not confident enough about their competency with e-learning methodology to share their reflections with others. The teachers did not feel comfortable with the perspective that their posts would be read and reviewed by other teachers for the fear that they might be perceived as naïve or silly. They claimed that maybe if their expertise in e-learning had been higher, they would have been more daring to share their reflections with the public. When asked if they would be willing to share their reflections with their learners, the vast majority of participants gave a very strong and definitive answer: never.

The next stage of the discussion was devoted to the question how the participants felt about involving their students in writing blogs in the courses they teach to collect input on how their reactions as well as the material to adjust it according to their students' needs.

Although the majority of participants did not reject the idea completely, judging from their opinions we can conclude that they did not find this idea particularly appealing. The teachers explained that that might be difficult to use blogs with their students due to a number of reasons.

The first argument was that the level proficiency in English required to write a blog is higher than the average level of groups they teach at their schools. This form of activity requires advanced writing skills and some students could find writing a blog in a foreign language too difficult. Another argument was that many young people are not particularly interested in writing in general, so they might find this task not really rewarding.

Some comments pointed out that blogs may be difficult to implement because of the limited number of hours in the curriculum that can be devoted to it in practice. The participants added that using blogs for writing exceeds the practical needs of their learners, so using this methodology may not be very advantageous.

The participant expressed concerns about the role of instructor who introduces such activities to their learners. Some doubts concerned the responsibility for correcting errors made by their students in blogs written in a foreign language. Another observation was that in some cases the teacher would also be responsible teaching computing skills apart from EFL

3. Conclusions

Since this article is only a summary of experience with a small, very specific group of users from a particular country it cannot be used to generalize obtained result for potential blog uses in e-learning. In fact, there are numerous reports showing that learners involved in similar projects can really enjoy and appreciate the opportunity to use blogs in a creative way (Loane 2004). There is also a very interesting observation (Betts 2004) that blogs are especially appreciated by students who generally do not find class discussions particularly interesting and involving.

Therefore, this particular experience does not contradict that maintaining a blog can be a successful and enjoyable means of encouraging learners to develop language skill by writing blogs. It shows, however, that there is no simple and easy way to adopt e-learning with all groups and conditions. It show how complex, and to a large extent still unpredictable, the e-learning methodology is.

Everyday practice within many organizations shows that some individuals do not embrace this new medium of instruction to the extent that it was initially hoped. According to the summary of the findings from the "European survey on quality and e-learning" published in 2002 by Bizmedia "61% of all respondents participating in e-learning courses rated the overall quality of the courses negatively – as 'fair' or 'poor'. Only 1% rated it 'excellent' and only 5% rated it 'very good'." (Massy 2002)

3.1. Usability of e-learning programs

E-learning has become one of the most popular solutions for finding more effective ways to manage growing requirements for learning solutions. Undoubtedly, e-learning has the potential of offering lower costs, broader accessibility, and content personalization. But in reality online learning programs often exhibit higher dropout rates when compared with traditional instructor-led courses leaving many students frustrated or unenthusiastic. (Miller 2005)

There are various factors that contribute to this situation including: quality of courses, relevancy of content, comfort level with the technology, ability to interact with peers, etc. The principles of what works well in online learning, based on research findings or best practices, are still in the making. But another major factor that contributes to this situation may be the poor usability of many e-learning applications.

It seems that even though many institutions have made a great effort to develop e-learning programs for their students, the usability of these e-learning applications is often lacking or entirely overlooked. As summarized by Michael Miller (Ibid.) "While a large number of organizations have adopted e-learning programs, far fewer have addressed the usability of their learning applications. More attention should be devoted to assuring the usability of e-learning applications if organizations are to fully benefit from their investments."

Usability testing offers a way to ensure that most people can use with ease a particular product or service. On the grounds of e-learning the usability can be defined "as the extent to which an application is learnable and allows users to accomplish specified goals efficiently, effectively, and with a high degree of satisfaction. An additional component that should be added to this definition is usefulness; that is, a highly usable application will not be embraced by users if it fails to contain content that is relevant and meaningful to them." (Ibid. 2005)

The usability tests have already proven their worthiness for e-commerce and other applications but they are still something new to e-learning. Usability testing could address some of the problems in the learner experience, as well as provide designers with a set of principles and methods that can be used to create courses that will capture and hold users' interest from start to finish. The e-learning course design in general should be more focused on the principle of learner-centered design, which reflects different backgrounds and characteristics of online learners.

While the usability and effectiveness of e-learning courses are not the same, they have much in common. With a certain amount of tweaking usability tests could be applied successfully to e-learning. (Quigley 2002) Accomplishing this goal should help to ensure that users can actually access the necessary material and have optimal levels of satisfaction with the learning experience. It is also possible that usability testing data will offer insights on the high dropout rates from online education courses.

3.2. Summary of experience

It may be difficult to come up with a universal methodology performing equally well with all learner groups and conditions. The observations presented in the above paper lead to the conclusion that in certain contexts blogs may be not an ideal tool for fostering online collaboration in e-learning programs due to various reasons.

First of all, for some learners the fact that with blogs "they are able to have their own writing 'published' on the web (rather than just written by pen in an exercise book or course file) adds a certain prestige to their work" (Brady 2005). But as shown in the above results exactly the same factor can be as much discouraging for other people.

Additionally, although blogging is very popular nowadays some people feel reluctant towards the idea of sharing their personal thoughts with others in general. Not everybody wants to write a blog. Therefore, for people who do not possess this particular kind of 'blogging personality', the process of keeping an online diary may be unnatural and artificial.

The same reaction was observed in other learning communities. One of the very positive reports noticed that "A small number of students were negative on the value of blogging as a good way to learn or to participate in class. One voiced an opinion that it was intrusive to her privacy." (Betts 2004)

Another crucial factor is the motivation that drives people to invest personal time into sharing their thoughts with others. Blogs are written by people with genuine human passion. “Although bloggers do research in order to write a post, that research is not considered a chore, but rather a pleasure.” (Brady 2005) Therefore, if the topic of a blog does not go in line with personal interests of the author, the driving force behind a blog is missing.

It seems that the concept of blogs is more accessible for younger generation. It was observed at the University of Arizona that “students who have grown up in the information look to the Internet for information can use blogs successfully in their course activities, e.g. for literacy inventories, observation notes, and linguistic analysis”. (Betts 2004) But people belonging to other social and cultural groups may not feel as comfortable with the idea of blogging.

It should also be taken into consideration that the use of blogs in a foreign language teaching / learning is to a large extent restricted by the proficiency level of the language users. Even those who have an advanced level of proficiency in a foreign language may not feel very comfortable about using it for blog publication, because it still is difficult for them to express thoughts in a foreign language.

It seems that some members of the older generation find it difficult to reconcile with the idea of having free publishing tools to publish information online. Moreover, it is possible that there are also some cultural differences between different countries. For people who spent many years of their lives deprived of the free-speech opportunity behind the iron curtain blogging may be too abstract and not really convincing.

Finally, it should be remembered that educators who are not comfortable with blogging themselves are unlikely to use it as a tool in their teaching practice. In the experiment described above the final reluctance was far away from the initial enthusiasm. It shows that new tools and technologies should be given some usability testing before they are employed for the teaching curriculum since they can have substantially different effectiveness in different conditions.

BIBLIOGRAPHY

Ashley, C. *Weblogs, part II: A Swiss Army website?* IST–Interactive University URL: http://istpub.berkeley.edu:4201/bcc/Winter2002/feat.weblogging2.html

Betts, J. D. (2004). *Instructional Models for Using Weblogs In eLearning: A Case Study from a Virtual and Hybrid Course.* School of Information Resources and Library Science, University of Arizona.

Blood, R. (200). *Weblogs: A History and Perspective*, Rebecca's Pocket, 07 Sep 2000 URL: http://www.rebeccablood.net/essays/weblog_history.html

Brady, M. (2005). *Blogging, personal participation in public knowledge-building on the web*, Chimera Working Paper 2005-02. Colchester: University of Essex.

Clark, R. C. and R. E. Mayer (2003). *e-Learning and the Science of Instruction: Proven Guidelines for Consumers and Designers of Multimedia Learning.* San Francisco: Jossey-Bass/Pfeiffer.

Communication from the (2000). Commission *e-Learning – Designing tomorrow's education.* /* COM/2000/0318 final */ URL: http://europa.eu.int/eur-lex/lex/LexUriServ/LexUriServ.do?uri=CELEX:52000DC0318:EN:HTML

Enzer, M. (2005). *Matisse Enzer's Glossary of Internet Terms.* URL: http://www.matisse.net/files/glossary.html

Farmer, J. *Incorporated Subversion: James Farmer's Online Education Weblog*, Monday, April 05, 2004, URL: http://radio.weblogs.com/0120501/2004/04/05.html#a625

Horton, W. (2001). *Evaluating E-Learning.* ASTD.

Loane, T. (2004). *Blogging for Learning – Using Weblogs with Adult Learners.* TrEACL Report 2004 from Hounslow Adult and Community Education. URL: http://www.aclearn.net/content_files/acl/pages/content/focus/treacl/round1/summaries/band-b/hounslow/final-report-ms-word-327kb.doc

Massy, J. (2002). *Quality and eLearning in Europe Survey report 2002.* BizMedia URL: http://www.elearningage.co.uk/docs/qualitysummary.pdf

Miller, M. J. (2005). *Usability in E-Learning.* Learning Circuits, Published: January 2005. URL: http://www.learningcircuits.org/2005/jan2005/miller.htm

Quigley, A. (2002). *Usability-Tested E-learning? Not Until the Market Requires It.* eLearn Magazine (2/04/02) URL: http://www.elearnmag.org/subpage.cfm?section=articles&article=19-1

Rosenberg, M. J. (2005). *Beyond E-Learning: Approaches and Technologies to Enhance Organizational Knowledge, Learning and Performance.* Pfeiffer.

Smith, D. (2005). *Spinning a Better Web*, Macworld Magazine, October 2005. URL: http://www.macworld.com/2005/10/features/betterblog/index.php

INDEX OF TERMS

ŁÓDŹ
Studies in Language

Edited by
Barbara Lewandowska-Tomaszczyk

Vol. 1 Barbara Lewandowska-Tomaszczyk / Patrick James Melia (eds.): PALC'99: Practical Applications in Language Corpora. Papers from the International Conference at the Universtiy of Łódź, 15-18 April 1999. 2000.

Vol. 2 Lou Burnard / Tony McEnery (eds.): Rethinking Language Pedagogy from a Corpus Perspective. Papers from the third international conference on Teaching and Language Corpora. 2000.

Vol. 3 Barbara Lewandowska-Tomaszczyk / John Osborne / Frits Schulte: Foreign Language Teaching and Information and Communication Technology. 2001.

Vol. 4 Piotr Cap: Explorations in Political Discourse. Methodological and Critical Perspectives. 2002.

Vol. 5 Ewa Waniek-Klimczak / Patrick James Melia (eds.): Accents and Speech in Teaching English Phonetics and Phonology. EFL perspective. 2002.

Vol. 6 Barbara Lewandowska-Tomaszczyk / Kamila Turewicz (eds.): Cognitive Linguistics Today. 2002.

Vol. 7 Barbara Lewandowska-Tomaszczyk (ed.): PALC 2001: Practical Applications in Language Corpora. 2003.

Vol. 8 Corpus Linguistics by the Lune. A Festschrift for Geoffrey Leech. Edited by Andrew Wilson, Paul Rayson and Tony McEnery. 2003.

Vol. 9 Barbara Lewandowska-Tomaszczyk (ed.): Practical Applications in Language and Computers. PALC 2003. 2004.

Vol. 10 Imagery in Language. Festschrift in Honour of Professor Ronald W. Langacker. Edited by Barbara Lewandowska-Tomaszczyk and Alina Kwiatkowska. 2004.

Vol. 11 Seana Coulson / Barbara Lewandowska-Tomaszczyk (eds.): The Literal and Nonliteral in Language and Thought. 2005.

Vol. 12 Piotr Cap (ed.): Pragmatics Today. 2005.

Vol. 13 Jacek Waliński / Krzysztof Kredens / Stanisław Goźdź-Roszkowski (eds.): Corpora and ICT in Language Studies. PALC 2005. 2007.

www.peterlang.de

FSC
www.fsc.org
MIX
Papier | Fördert gute Waldnutzung
FSC® C083411

Kolibri 360 GmbH
Ferdinand-Jühlke-Straße 7
99095 Erfurt, Deutschland
produktsicherheit@kolibri360.de

Druck:
CPI Druckdienstleistungen GmbH
im Auftrag der
Kolibri 360 GmbH
Ferdinand-Jühlke-Str. 7
99095 Erfurt